SANG BRANCH SETTLERS

Publications of the American Folklore Society

MEMOIR SERIES

Wm. Hugh Jansen, General Editor

Volume 61   1974

Sang Branch Settlers

Folksongs and Tales of a Kentucky Mountain Family

LEONARD ROBERTS

Music transcribed by C. Buell Agey

PUBLISHED FOR THE *American Folklore Society*
BY THE UNIVERSITY OF TEXAS PRESS, AUSTIN AND LONDON

Library of Congress Cataloging in Publication Data
Roberts, Leonard W
  Sang Branch settlers.

  (Publications of the American Folklore Society.
Memoir series, v. 61)
  Bibliography: p.
  1. Folk-songs, American—Kentucky. 2. Folk-lore—
Kentucky. 3. Tales, American—Kentucky. 4. Kentucky
—Social life and customs. 5. Couch family.
6. Mountain whites (Southern States) I. Agey, Calvin
Buell, 1907–   II. Title. III. Series: American
Folklore Society. Memoirs, v. 61.
ML3551.R62   398'.09769'152   74-3357
ISBN 0-292-77510-5

Composition by G&S Typesetters, Austin
Printing by The University of Texas Printing Division, Austin
Binding by Universal Bookbindery, San Antonio

TO

Dave and Jim Couch, who learned well
the magic of the mountains,

AND TO

Wm. Hugh Jansen, who has long partaken
of the spell with me

CONTENTS

FOREWORD

The folktales and folksongs in this volume were collected from 1951 through 1955 from one family living in Harlan and Leslie counties, Kentucky. This family, the Couches, had lived in the small area of the Kentucky mountains for about one hundred years. After I had "discovered" two or three Couches and had sampled their rich and still living store of tales and songs, I felt that an in-depth study of the family was the obligation of the serious folklorist. The quest was long and, after four years of interviewing and taping, I left the lore of the family still unexhausted.

Since I transcribe in the Introduction the interviews of individual Couches relating their lives and folkways in their own words, I shall briefly summarize here the nature of the lore, its transmission from Europe to America, and my role in arranging and editing it from the beginning to the present.

The Kentucky mountain people, though they delight in tracing their family trees, can only rarely go back more than four or five generations. And when they can follow the limbs and branches (usually by oral transmission) they are vague about nationality, dates, places, kin, and other data. Written records that trace Scotch-Irish immigrants, for instance, from North Ireland to the Piedmont frontiers of Pennsylvania, Virginia, or North Carolina are somewhat scarce. We know that they came by shiploads in the eighteenth century and had to push on toward free space and land into the Appalachian ranges. One of the great migrations in world history occurred in our country when the continent was free for settlement after the Revolutionary War. But what nurture and culture these settlers brought in their heads and habits are beginning to be well known. In the twentieth century we have begun to study these sturdy but poetic peoples, whom Cecil Sharp felt to be predominantly Anglo-Celtic in nature and culture. Only in the twentieth century have we begun to collect vast quantities of oral literature from their descendants. This literature is of course still evolving true to form and content from the muses of old. The fundamental conclusion is that, although a geo-political history of Appalachia has not yet been written, perhaps never can be or need not be written, the region's oral literature and folkways reveal it to be a rich repository of British and European culture.

The present collection may be used to illustrate this repository, although it represents only a fraction of the tales and songs I have partaken of in the mountains and a mere fragment of the scores of folklore collections harvested from the region by others.

The hundred folksongs and hymns are here arranged in the old-fashioned (and somewhat outmoded) order of "Child and Others." Modern folksong students are urging the abandonment of the Francis James Child system of numbered order toward one of textual themes and tune families. Further comments on arrangement of songs and tales are given later. One departure from the order here is the locating of the "headnotes" in sequence in the back.

I begin with eight "Child" ballads (Nos. 1–8), not a very high proportion of the total. This dearth is discussed in the Introduction. It appears that old Tom Couch knew many of the old-time ballads, but in his long life of entertaining he allowed the old to recede from his repertory as he kept up with the new. Jim and Dave Couch went back to him in our last sessions and relearned most of these eight. The next eight pieces (Nos. 9–16) are British imports, mostly from broadsides. These have been classified by G. Malcolm Laws in his *American Balladry from British Broadsides*. Laws also classifies the next sixteen (Nos. 17–32) in his *Native American Balladry*.

Moving out of the ballad classification (folksongs that tell a story), we are short of indexes. The next fifteen (Nos. 34–48) are homiletic and religious songs. In my notes I have been unable to find parallels to many of the hymns in the collections of George Pullen Jackson and others. The largest category here (Nos. 53–91) are the lively folksongs, jigs, and dance numbers in the active repertory of Tom, who performed them for entertainment and in contests and who passed them on to his son Dave for square dancing. The final nine (92–100) are mostly about animals and birds, suitable for entertainment and for singing along with children.

The arrangement of the folktales also departs from the stereotyped numbering order (indexed by Aarne and Thompson in *The Types of the Folktale*) by their being entered in the order collected. I do, however, provide a list of type numbers present in the tales following the Notes.

A glance at the List of Type Numbers reveals a variety of tales, legends, and anecdotes that I gathered from a dozen Couches, men and boys, in almost every session. The animal tales, thought to be fading in modern times as vehicles for allegory and fable, are well represented here. Of the nine in the volume, six are in the animal section (Types 1–299) and three are in the Formula Tale section (Types 2000–2399). Such tales as No. 131, "Cat and Rat," and No. 132, "The Fox and the Cat," are rare old types seldom found today. In the Ordinary Tales section (Types 300–1199) the number of versions in whole or in part total twenty-three. Rare tales represented here but not yet found elsewhere in North America are Numbers 107 and 161, "The One-Eyed Giant"; Number 113, "Nip, Kink, and Curly" (only a few appearances in world collections); and Number 157, "The Magic White Deer." From the Jokes and Anecdotes section (Types 1200–1999) are some thirty-five tales, alone or combined with other tales. The seven types marked in my List with asterisks are marked as rare in the Aarne-Thompson *Types* index.

The present rich one-family treasure of lore came into my hands slowly over five years in the 1950's. A brief résumé of my adventures and the somewhat accidental discovery of the Couches need to be recorded as background for the present publication.

Having studied a year beyond the master's degree during World War II and having spent five years in the Berea Foundation School, I determined to finish the doctorate. Accordingly, in 1950 I left Berea, secured an assistantship at the University of Kentucky, and began course work. While at Berea I had collected a mass of lore from my students in Harlan, Perry, and Leslie counties. This material I was to study and classify under Dr. William Hugh Jansen, chairman of my graduate committee. With funds quite short and prices rising after the war, we arranged for my wife, Edith, to teach in Pine Mountain Settlement School, which eventually became a Harlan County consolidated school.

I finished my committee's assigned course work in a year and the following summer. As I prepared to return to Pine Mountain to study for final examinations, Dr. Jansen secured for me a research grant through the Graduate Dean Dr. Herman E. Spivey to record in depth the folkways of the Pine Mountain community. This I soon began among the local students and friendly workers at the school, and I interviewed all families on Issacs Run and down Greasy, including one Lewis Couch (eldest son of Tom Couch), his children, and his grandchildren. The project of seven reels of tape and a hundred pages of manuscript was duly deposited with Dr. Jansen.

But the project proved to be valuable in many other ways. It helped me to learn about the people of the region, enured me to the rigors of field work, and set me on the quest of the Couch family lore.

The accidental discovery of the Couches occurred in the fall of 1951. I went exploring with the Pine Mountain nurse Miss Grace Rood— down Greasy in a jeep and across the steep mountains and down Cutshin to the home of Amanda Couch Hendricks (detailed in the opening of chapter 3 of the Introduction). She related the experiences of her family with folktales and told me that her younger brother Jim Couch "follered" telling the family tales. If I needed any more evidence it was supplied by an orphan who lived with Mandy, Bobby McDaniel, who told without missing a line two long tales heard from Jim on his visits there. Mandy, since she had become a Christian, did not tell the old tales any more, but she told me where Jim lived and outlined some tales he knew. The quest for the golden apples of Appalachia had begun! Since the Introduction is given over to folkways sessions and the Notes only refer to sessions and dates, I shall label the song and tale recordings here more fully to guide the reader.

First Session: I found Jim, in the fall of 1951, in a plank house on the hill above a string of houses and a lumber mill (detailed at the opening of chapter 1 of the Introduction), and he acknowledged knowing the tales Bobby had told and sketched two or three more.

That was all—for five weeks. He was elusive. We finally met on a Sunday and used the back room, the floor now filling up with glass jars of beans, beets, apples, and the like. Jim recorded six stories and drifted off into his family tree.

Second Session: Three weeks later in October 1951 Jim told some shorter tales and one of his longest strings of Irishman jokes. He liked to take the center of the stage and have his way, and said, "I never did like to set around and just tell one short joke."

Third Session: In the meantime I had helped Dave to a new set of banjo strings, and he promised to sing when he got in practice and over his sore throat. In September 1951 I heard him tell his first tale and play some banjo tunes without singing.

Fourth Session: With my wife out of school with our fourth child, I drove across Pine Mountain every day and taught in Wallins (Harlan County) High School from January to June 1952. In the summer of 1952 I managed a meeting with Dave, Jim, about four of their sons, and others for a long night (until about one o'clock) of tales and riddles in the same back room at Jim's.

Fifth Session: I had dual singing and interviewing with Jim and Dave in September 1952. This event took the form of the old-time swapping of songs and variants of the same song, the two men passing the banjo back and forth.

Sixth Session: We had just got started recording and interviewing in earnest when a shortage of one teacher occurred in the Pine Mountain School staff and I was requested to take the seventh-eighth grade room until December 1952. In the spring of 1953 I was able to arrange only one session with Dave for more songs and his more interesting legends (chapter 2 of Introduction).

Seventh Session: With some written examinations cleared and the dissertation typed in the summer of 1953, I secured a position in a small college in the mountains of Georgia. But we returned in the fall of 1954 to Union College in Knox County, Kentucky. Now we were seventy miles from Pine Mountain and Putney. On my first trip up to Putney I learned that Jim had quit the mines again and had moved to Craft Colley Creek in Letcher County to farm. While at Putney I had an interview with Dave (chapter 4), and later, in August 1954, I visited Jim in Letcher County. He and his eldest son, Frank, living close-by, recorded about twenty folksongs.

Eighth Session: Jim soon moved back to Putney and, acting on his old promise to go with me in search of more Couches, we were on the road a week (chapter 3) and got a lead to visit some of the family in Appalachia, Virginia. There, from Joe Couch, we secured several stories, including another version of "The One-Eyed Giant."

Ninth Session: In September 1955, on a Sunday, we had a fine public session at Jim's house, with Dave, Jim, and Frank passing the guitar and the banjo around. Aside from the requested numbers from the many relatives present, I taped twenty-six folksongs.

Tenth Session: When I returned to Union College after the Ninth Session I began to transcribe and assess the Couch material, thinking that my collecting was about over. But no, the end was not in sight. Jim wrote me saying that they had thought up some more songs and had hovered around their father, Tom, getting all their half-forgotten songs together. Apparently Tom had gone into his deep well of memory and had given them the oldest ones yet—Child Nos. 3, 54, 81, and 274. In November and December 1955 we recorded some twenty songs, presumably leaving their deep wells still unfathomed.

My dissertation had been successfully defended and the degree awarded by June 1954. The principal versions of 105 of the tales were excerpted and published by the University of Kentucky Press, in a volume titled *South from Hell-fer-Sartin*. By 1957 I had transcribed the thirty reels of Couch tapes and ordered the 100 hymns, 61 tales, and 40 riddles in the sequence collected. The manuscript ran to some 700 pages. Commercial publishers returned it with regularity as being too much and too specialized for them. The University of Kentucky Press was interested again, but it, too, backed away for a time. Unable to budget so much, the editors resolved the dilemma by offering to bring it out in two volumes. The folkways, local legends, and experiences should constitute a letterpress volume—and this became *Up Cutshin and Down Greasy*. The mass of songs and tales should be the other, and this became a microcard volume, *Tales and Songs of the Couch Family*, both brought out in 1959.

This divorce of the one-family lore has made me uncomfortable these fourteen years. Lately, when *Up Cutshin* went out of print, I began to conceive of a reunion of the editions. When all obstacles were resolved, I began the re-editing. The songs (already ordered in the microcard edition according to the Child and Other mode) have been placed first to simplify numbering; the bibliographies have been updated and integrated into one; likewise the notes and indexes. Five of the *Up Cutshin* chapters have been reduced and somewhat rearranged. I trust that the whole will carry more folkloric significance than the sum of its two parts. Here now follows an example of the rich oral literature brought by westering settlers from the Old World to the Kentucky mountains.

I should like to thank, however belatedly, the University of Kentucky for the research grant that set me on the long journey and its farsighted officers Drs. Spivey and Jansen for their trust and support. Thanks to Bruce Denbo and his editors of the University Press of Kentucky for constant kindness and expert editing and for permission to make this reprint. While I was at West Virginia Wesleyan College I received a research grant to have my amateur music transcriptions redone. Thanks to Wesleyan and to Dr. C. Buell Agey, chairman of Wesleyan's Music Department, who transcribed the present tunes. And more recently I owe an obligation to Pikeville College and its Appalachian Studies Center for typists and photocopying services to facilitate this major undertaking.

Pikeville College
Pikeville, Kentucky

I. Introduction

1. Jim Couch, His Family Story

Putney, a stringtown along the winding Cumberland River, grew around the old seat of one of the largest sawmills in eastern Kentucky. I can remember well the day, in the fall of 1951, I came over from Pine Mountain School to find Jim Couch, a storyteller from back on the headwaters of the Kentucky River, who was said to know all the stories of the clan of tellers and ballad singers. The houses became thicker along the blacktop, and soon I could see the chimneys of the Intermountain Lumber and Coal Company pouring out acrid smoke on the wind. The level bottoms along the Poor Fork of the Cumberland were covered with acres of lumber stacks. After some inquiry I found where Jim lived and stopped by the road. His home was propped on the hillside in a small drain. I saw three working men on the lower porch and heard the cry of playing children in the lower yard behind a paling fence. I hallooed from the slat gate. A friendly response came from one of the men sitting in a low chair. He was as black as a minstrel from his hard-toed shoes to his mining cap.

I entered the yard and clambered up the steps to the end of the porch. Two of the men (I later learned they were Jim's brothers Alex and Harrison) rose and, after speaking to me, they went to their homes below the road. The seated man waved a black hand to a split-bottom chair, where I sat facing him. "Been over to Cutshin Creek," I began, "saw your sister Mandy. She tells me you know a lot of stories—know all the stories of the family."

"Yeaw," he said. "I used to tell all the old stories that our mother handed down while she was a-raising us. But I've not told them, some of 'em in years. About forgot 'em."

As I enlarged upon my interest in the old handed-down folkstories, Jim removed his hard mining helmet and his heavy electric battery, belt and all, and hung them aside. And then he began to undress in earnest. Off came the hard shoe and sock from one leg, and then the caked overall pants. He unfastened a smooth leather belt from his middle and unlaced a leather casing from his upper leg. Finally he took off a whole leg, shoe and all, and set it against the wall. My line of talk died away. He took up the conversation by explaining, "Lost my leg a few years ago in the mines. Got it caught between two cars. The doc had to take it off. I've been following mining for nine year now."

"What did you do before entering the mines?"

He hung his wet, faded chambray shirt on the back of a chair. "Why, I used to be a lumberman. Worked for this lumber company for nineteen year—from here to lower Greasy Creek. I learnt to measure lumber at the stacks—I was a lumber scaler for my last ten years with 'em." Before I could lead him on much further he said, "Wait till I get my bath. I have to get this black offen me before I can do a thing when I come in."

I waited while he hopped from chair to doorfacing and into the living room, where he squatted in an old oblong tub on the floor. While I looked across the way to the peaks of Big Black Mountain, I could hear his wife pouring water and tempering it to Jim's notion. On first impression Jim was a slight man, as mountain men go, but he was actually of average build. What I had seen of his face was ruddy, and his eyes had a keen and mischievous look about them. His voice was low and rich, with a good flexible vocabulary and mountain idiom. I knew he was fifty, but his crop of still black hair did not show his age, except for the slight receding and parting line across the top. The face was slightly long, as was his head, and I had been aware of prominent high cheekbones. When he hopped back out in clean colored clothes, he did not offer to replace his leg, but, sitting down, he threw the stump across an empty chair and grunted refreshingly.

In the next twenty or thirty minutes Jim ran over about four of the Old World folktales, enough to convince me that he and his family had kept in tradition a heritage of old tales. At this time and for many more sessions I asked him about his family and about his experiences in a mountain home. The following pages set forth what he related to me in his own words.

"Why, yeaw," he began, "I can trace our people back a good piece. My mother allas claimed that her people was Irish, and my daddy said the name of Couch was French. I don't know for sure when they come to this country, but that's what they allas claimed. I guess I know more about our generations than anybody else in the family. I've kept up with 'em and asked 'em questions all my life.

"My great-grandfather on my mother's side went by the name of old Pressley Harris, and he is said to have come from Ireland and settled in North Caroliny. That was back in the 1830's or 40's. And he settled in the mountains of North Caroliny. I don't know who he married, but my mother said her grandmother on the Turner side was a fullblooded Cherokee Indian. He never come to this part of the country till he was old and his chillern was growed and married and his wife dead. But some of his chillern come in here. My grandfather was Lewis, and he settled over here on Greasy Creek in Harlan County. He owned most of the land on what is known as Sang Branch. [*Sang* is from *ginseng*, a valuable medicinal root.] One of his girls, my mother, was named Mary Ann Harris. My father found her there and married her, and they inherited most of the Sang Branch.

"I was a purty good size chap when my great-grandfather died. He didn't know much of our language and never could read and write. He talked with a funny turn of speech, and he was a funny and a rowdy kind of a feller. Knowed more pranks and tricks than anybody nearly. Yeaw, he stayed around with us some and I've talked to him a lot.

"Now the Couches was French, my daddy allas said. My great-grandfather was Anse Couch, and he lived in Virginia, in the county

of Scott. My grandfather was named John, and he married a Dutch-
man by the name of Sally Shepherd. Her mother was said to be a
Wells. Grandfather John came in here and settled on Big Leatherwood
'way before the Civil War. When them troubles broke out, he went
back to Virginia and fought through the Civil War on the Union side.
Grandfather John came back and raised a big fambly, and one of his
boys was named Tom—he is my father. He is living yet, up here in a
cabin above my house. Getting up in years—he is ninety-two now.
Married my mother on the Sang Branch, and they lived there for
about ten years on that branch that had been deeded to my mother as
her part of their inheritance. All you had to do back then was survey
you out a piece of land and write up what was called a bond, take that
and file it at the county seat, and get a patent and send it off to be
recorded in Frankfort.

"Well, they was a land company here in Harlan town claimed all
the land they could get a claim on and tried to go over patents and
get a clearer title to it. That's what they done with my mother's hold-
ings there on Sang Branch. They lawed for that piece of land. My
father got holt of old Jedge Hall, and they beat them fellers and held
the land. And then he turned right around and sold it out to one of
them fellers. He went back to Leatherwood where he come from and
raised us awhile on Clover Fork. We stayed there for several year, and
then we moved here to Harlan County, to Nolansburg, where they
was a big bandmill. By 1918 dad was a big logging contractor, and I
worked on his crew. I went into the World War then and left my
father to shift for hisself. My mother died in 1921. And now since
we have been living here at Putney, dad has come here to live. He
married again fifteen year ago when he was seventy-seven, and he has
two chillern by his last wife; the youngest one, a boy, was born when
he was eighty.

"Now sir, I'll tell you about my mother. She was just as good to
people and treated 'em just as clever [hospitable] as anybody on the
creek. Course she was proud of her fambly, and just like any woman
in the hills she wouldn't have nothing to do with no men strangers.
Always sunt 'em to dad. One time a man come to the house when she
was there with just the least uns, and he wanted to set around till dad

come in. And she told him she didn't want him to. He said something to her made her mad, and she run him off. Got the gun and told him she'd shoot him if he didn't take off for there.

"We was all kindy skittish about strangers that way. We got the idea they wanted to know our fambly affairs, or make fun of us. One time when the Pine Mountain Settlement School was just starting up, the school built a community house down there at the mouth of Big Laurel, and they would have us folks come in there and learn how to can stuff and how to take care of babies and such like. And some of them extension workers would come from Berea and lecture there. A bunch of women stayed there about two weeks oncet. And they got to asking the people to sing songs for 'em and tell stories. I was up there oncet, and they wanted me to tell some of my stories. I told 'em one, I told 'em Jack and the Bull Strap [No. 106], and they took on about it and wanted more. I thought they was making fun, making us out as heathern or something, and I never went back up there and never told 'em another story.

"I guess I learnt to act that a-way from my mother. She was the storyteller in the fambly and would tell one about any time of a day or night. She would tell a story at the ends of corn rows while we was cooling and getting water, and of an evening around a gnat smoke in the yard and of a night before bedtime. But the strange thing I noticed about her—she wouldn't hardly tell stories when they was people at the house. She'd just say, 'No, I'm not going to tell no stories.' And we got so we wouldn't ask her before other people.

"We just lived as famblies, made all we got, and what we couldn't get we done without. We would go out the darkest, rainiest night ever was and help a man in need, and we'd give our last bite of grub—flour, sugar, medicine—to somebody needing it. But let a man come around where he had no business and never state his business, let him say something about us or any of our people, and his hide would pay for it shore as cat tracks.

"The people in the hills was not mean and didn't come around to do anybody any dirt. They was all goodhearted people that I ever knowed. And they didn't want to hide a thing. We knowed the revenues and learnt how to spot 'em as far as we could see 'em. We just didn't see strangers very often—people we didn't know nary thing about—and we was allas curious about 'em, and when one went through we would ask up and down who he was and what he was going through here for. Maybe some house or store would be robbed, somebody murdered on the road. Robbers, outlaws, foreigners come in and get a place for the night and be gone. We'd talk about them fellers for years.

"Now you want to hear about my brothers and sisters, and I may as well start at the top and come down. The oldest one, Lewis, he never got out of Harlan and Perry County in his life, I don't guess. Lives over there on Laurel Fork o' Greasy and has farmed all his life. He's got about eight chillern, or nine, I don't just remember how many, a great gang of 'em he's raised. My next brother, he took these here kindly epilepsy fits and died when he was twenty-four year old, in the hospital at Lexington, and was buried in Lexington graveyard. The next one, Henry L., he got killed. He was a fine boy of fifteen when we lived over there in Perry County, and he was out with a man who dropped a pistol, and it went off and killed him. The next one was a girl—that is Mandy, who lived with us in Harlan till she married a Hendrix, and they settled over there where you saw her in Leslie County and has been there all her life. They raised I think it was eight chillern and has taken in one or two to raise. I stayed with her for years.

"The next one was a girl, too, but she died when she was four year old. And the next was Dave. He growed up about as I did, till he got married and settled in Leslie County, up till about ten year ago. He moved here to Harlan County and has been here ever since. They had twelve chillern and have done purty well, mining mostly since he come here, till a few years ago his eyes got to bothering him. He is purt nearly blind now and can't do no heavy work no more. Well, the next one is I. I married Stella Turner over there on Greasy Creek and we have six chillern. And the next one is Alex, who has lived here in Harlan County ever since he got up any size. Married and has got four chillern. Then comes another sister, Sally, and she married a Stewart and has lived around here most of her married life. She lives in a cabin 'way up over yander on the slope of Black Mountain, and they have now got fifteen chillern altogether. My baby brother lives right down here below the road, Harrison, and he's got four chillern—no, they've got five now. That makes three girls and seven boys old Tom the banjer picker had by my mother and two by his present wife. And altogether, when you count them all up, he has got fifty-nine grand-chillern. Will probably have seventy-five.

"Ah, Lord, I'm such a mixture of French and Dutch, English and Irish and Indian, I've never been able to figure out just what I done and why I done it. I's so mean when I's growing up, I—I, it'd be a shame for a man to tell it, I guess. We was raised on a hillside farm, and it was just get up and work all day, and get out and play all night, about it. We raised everything we had, and if we hadn't a-raised it we wouldn't a-got it. We allas had a big crap of corn for ourselves and our hogs and stock, and we raised beans and 'taters, cabbage, beets— everything that'd grow. Made our molasses into long sweetening and tapped the sugartrees for short sweetening. Ma made our soap out of hogs' guts and potash, and we raised broomcorn for our brooms. We allas had a big gang o' geese for our pillers and feather ticks, and we had guineas and ducks and chickens.

"What clothes we got, about all of 'em, was offen the sheeps' wool. We allas had a big flock o' sheep and we'd drive 'em in of a spring and shear 'em. We little fellers would take the wool to the creek water and tromp it till it was clean, dry it, and help the girls pick the cuckle-burs outten it. My mother, she'd card and spin her wool and weave it on a loom into purty good cloth. Then she'd set down and make us clothes. We'd take some wool off to the store and swap it to some eat-ables. But later, for several years, mother shipped some of her wool off and had it spun into skeins on the shears [shares], about half to come back to us and they kept the rest. The nearest railroad up till 1911 was at Pineville, about forty, fifty mile away. And they was another railhead at Hagan, Virginia, and to get there we went acrost Stone Mountain, Big and Little Black and Brush Mountains and up Catron's Creek, fifty, sixty mile, I guess.

"If my dad went to the railroad in the late summer, he would bring us back our only pair of shoes for the year. They was old brogans, went by the name of Tennessee Ties. Wear 'em from the first frost till barefoot time in the spring. Never needed half-soling; about the only thing to keep handy was some mutton or beef taller to keep 'em greased—till you could get 'em on—and off. Well, sometimes they would need a new pair of strings, and we would go out and ketch a groundhog, bring him in and tan his hide, make strings and harness leather outten it.

"In crap time dad would ketch the old mule and take a highfoot bull-tongue plow and start plowing in the balks of the corn. We'd hit that field about daylight and work till twelve. We didn't have no watches in them days—had an old striking clock but we couldn't pack it around. They was a poplar tree left in the field, and we had a marker on that tree. When the shadder of the sun got up to that marker, we would know that it was noontime. Come out to the house and eat dinner, rest awhile, and hit the field again. My mother would work with us evenings till about four o'clock and come out to do up the work and get supper. We would come out to the house, our clothes salty with sweat, and by suppertime the sun would be down behind the hills and cool air would be stirring in the valley. After supper at about dusky dark we would build up a gnat smoke out in the yard and set around in that smoke till ten o'clock and tell stories, sing songs. My mother would see that the milking was done and the dishes washed. She would come out in the yard in a chear, and we would start bagging her to tell us about old Jack in the Bean Tree [No. 101] or about the Little Black Hunchety Hunch [No. 104]. My dad would have one of us to bring out his old banjer—had a good un all his life. My grandfather made one that lasted for years. The box of it was made outten an old gourd. The strings was connected up some way on the neck, and that thing played right good, I thought. Pa would play Old Groundhog, Cold Frosty Morning, Shoo Fly, Arkansas Traveler [Nos. 86, 89, 80, 87].

"Now we everyone, that is all seven of us at home, learnt to play that old banjer, even all the girls. It wouldn't take me long to learn a piece. I'd just watch him—watch my daddy note the strings and his fingers strike the chords, and then I'd grab the old banjer. I first learnt to play tunes by picking the strings while he noted 'em for me. My arms wouldn't be long enough to reach the neck. And I had an old plug banjer in my house all the time, up till just a few months ago. Swapped it off. Not long ago my daddy was down to the house, and I handed it to him. He was so old and nervous I didn't know what he could do with it. He took it in his arms and tried to play, but he couldn't even hit the strings. Brother Dave down here has one of our old banjers and he can play very well on it.

"Well, there's not nothing much to tell about me in the World War. I never did tell about it much. I went in when I was seventeen, volunteered, back in 1918, and was shipped to France right away. I fought through some of the hardest battles that won the war. I was wounded four times. And instead of coming back when it was over, I reenlisted. Stayed around over in France for some time and then got put into a casual detachment—digging up the dead soldiers and shipping them back to their states. I spent most of this time in Luxemburg, and then stayed in France some more and went to England. It was after the war, you see, and, while handling the dead, they paid me extra for that. Put 'em in their caskets and sealed 'em up and shipped 'em back for burial here. Come back to the States in 1921. My second enlistment wa'n't over, so they stationed me in a number of places: Fort Dix, Plattsburg, Fort Jay, Camp Travlis, Camp Jackson, Fort Perry, Camp Zachary Taylor, Fort Oglethorpe.

"When I finally did get my discharge, I hit it back here to the hills. And what I've done since coming back is a cue to the world. I've logged and lumbered in about ever' holler in these hills, and I have made whiskey, enough to float all them sawlogs out of here. I've been acquainted with three men who was witches and witchdoctors—can do a little witch healing myself. I've been constable two or three times and arrested ever'thing going, about it, from moonshiners to killers. Oh, they hain't nothing going but what I've had some hand in it around here.

"Why, I've worked at ever' job going around a lumber mill. I've worked in the hills cutting trees, have cut logs and run 'em out to the haul road. I've hauled logs out of the hills to the mill, by oxens and mules and by tramroad. I have allas been give up to be the best teamster in the mines or in the woods that ever skinned a mule. I could allas make 'em lay down till their bellies rubbed the ground a-pulling big logs or mining cars."

While I was interviewing Jim Couch at Putney, he was laid off from his mining job at nearby Brookside. He then resolved to quit the mines for good. He traded for a farm in a long branch called Craft Colley in Letcher County. When I made my way up a long graveled road to his door to renew our talks, in the summer of 1954, I found a happy and contented man, with his livestock, corn patches, and vegetable garden. His wife was canning vegetables and drying shuck beans on long strings and pickling corn and cucumbers. A bit later, however, as soon as the corn and truck were taken care of, Jim set out for another job, this time at a sawmill set in Wolfe County. He later went with the mill back to Harlan County—he was keeping his word about quitting the mines. On this visit to Craft Colley I asked him to go into his lumbering experiences in detail.

"Well, it begin when I worked so long for the Intermountain Coal and Lumber Company over there at Putney. Worked for them for nineteen year. Started as a hand stacking lumber. Got to watching the boss measure and grade lumber and worked up to that job. They's a lot to learn about it, more than just building a foundation and throwing up boards. For instance, at this set we're now working out I have twenty-four grades of lumber to sort and stack in the right places. There is three grades for ever' kind of tree they saw, and they cut about all kinds—oak, ash, hickory, sugartree, linn, buckeye, beech. And any other kinds they cut I have to take care of it. But most of the softwood has been cut out of this country. The big companies took it first.

"They're several jobs around a mill set. The timber cutters they usually take contract putting the logs to the bottom of the hill. Somebody else takes contract getting 'em to the skidway of the mill. A skidway man rolls 'em up, washes 'em off and trims the big knots and things offen them, and helps roll 'em on the carriage. The sawyer has the skidway man and the blocksetter level the log up for him so he can make the best cuts and the thinnest slabs and get to the good grain. The blocksetter rides the carriage and watches the sawyer to know how far over to set the log for the inch and two-inch cuts, and the sawyer jams her through the circle saw. They turn the log when she comes back and keep on with it till she is sliced up by the saw. The offbear ketches the slabs and throws 'em in a pile to be carried to the boiler to burn, or to the slabpile, and the good boards he drags over to the roller carriage and shoves 'em down the line. On the line is the cutoff man, and he swings a big whizzing saw over and tips the ends square and cuts out the rotten places and leaves all the boards a certain length—eight, ten, twelve, fourteen foot. One of my men takes 'em from the roller carriage and stacks the prime in a pile on our tram truck and the number one, two, as best he can, after I have trained him a little. And when they change logs—anybody working around a mill soon knows what kind o' wood a board is—he has to keep that separate so we can dump the right kind and grade to the right stack. When he has the tramcar loaded, another of my men goes up and helps push it down along the lumberyard, and they drap off the stuff at the right stacks. I move up and down the yard with my men, stacking it on the stacks. We have to open-stack it so it can dry even, and I lay my strips even in the stacks so they will look like something when we are done.

"Other little old jobs around a mill are the dustboy who wheels the sawdust out of the pit under the circle saw—if the mill don't have a dust blower. And a big important job is the fireman. He has to drag them slabs up in front of the boiler and chop 'em up to about six-foot lengths and stoke 'em in, mixing a little coal to burn the green stuff. He has to keep her full of water and keep the engine oiled, and if he don't have no shed over him nor no hood on the smokestack, he has to fight the firecoals outten his shirt collar. 'Cause when that saw hits a big three-foot hickory log and starts to tonky-tonking and the belts flop up and down, it just about draws the bowels outten that boiler.

"That's about all they are to my job, I guess. But when the boss goes to selling dry lumber and if he don't know where the right grade is, I have to go out and spot it for him, and most of the time that is part of my job—measuring and loading trucks when they come to buy or haul off to ship it in boxcars. I usually take contract stacking by the thousand, taking care of the men and making my own foundations.

But it comes down to a salary most of the time. Now I'm earning ten dollars a day, and that's about as much as I could make on a contract.

"I don't know whether I'd ruther work at a mill or in the mines—have been about the same number of years in both. The mines are hard to stay away from, once you get started, but they are uncertain now and they are dangerous. I was making $18.75 a day—when I worked—last time I was in 'em, before I got laid off and moved over here. But I'm satisfied with my money in timber 'cause it's all above ground. They's danger under the hills. They're what come this leg off.

"The first coal I ever dug was in a little old wagon mines on Bull Creek in Perry County. I was just fourteen year old and got out hunting me a job. I run up on an old feller, and he asked me if I could load coal. I told him I didn't know what loading coal was. He said if I wanted to work, he would learn me. I told him I wanted to work, and he took me on. He run about seven or eight men, and took me in there and give me a shovel. Man alive, that was the hardest work in the world till I got used to it. I had to crawl back in there, and, by the time you get to the face of the coal, you are on your hands and knees or you are duck-walking around in there. The shovel was actually a big scoop, and you start on first one knee and then the other, and then you try it on both knees till it's just about a-killing you. And then you come to the only way they are to load a lot o' coal, and that is to set right flat down and stick your legs out as straight as you can, scooping it up and throwing it up in the car with the small of your back. That'll make a man outten you in about a week—or kill you one. You're hunkered down with a heavy carbide lamp on your cap, you're almost shoveling dust and powder smoke right in your own face, and you're breathing that stale foul air and a-straining ever' muscle on your frame. Sweat pops out all over you in a minute, and that bugdust works up into a compound and ever'where you move you are grinding it into your hide. You talk about white-eying on the job—I come in a pea a-doing it on my first job in the mines.

"They hauled the coal out of this mines with mules and took it to the railroad in wagons. That mule job looked good to me. I loaded coal there a week or two, and finally my boss named mule skinning to me. Boy, I grabbed that job before you could stomp your old hat. I thought I was the biggest thing in the world. I'd get hooked up to a car or two of coal, get my whip ready, and crawl on the end of a car and ride out of there and ride back in with empties. That old mule had a heap more sense than I did about the mines. They are rises and downgrades all under the hills. That old mule would run hisself to death on a down grade in order to get 'em over the next rise. He was working in pitch dark, but he knowed the turns and rises better than I did. I worked there for four or five months, I guess, at two dollars a day. That was what he paid his men for working the mines.

"I quit that job because the same man was running some timber, and I worked in the hills for him about nearly a year. Then I got another job in another mines in east Kentucky, a mule mine, too, but they had a tipple built off the hill to the railroad, where the coal was loaded into gons. I went there and hired as a teamster to drive their mules, and they give me a string of three mules, one behind the other, to bring the cars out from under the hill to the dump. I worked at that job nearly a year, quit, and left.

"I went back to Harlan country and went to work at the Kellioka Mines. This time I was loading coal again. In mines they work in groups or crews. They invented a cutting machine—had a big long nose with revolving teeth on it—and that thing could be drug right up to the face of the coal and right again' the floor. Start her out and cut under the seam of coal six or eight feet or more. Another crew come in of a night and bored holes in the face, put in charges of powder or dynamite, and shot that room down. Went on to the others all night. Smoke settled or was drawed out by the ventilation drift by next morning, and the loaders come in, usually working two to a room, laid their track up to the face where the coal was shot down, and loaded it in one, two, five ton cars. Always loaded it as so much a ton.

"Well, I had a buddy in this mines to help me in my room. One morning we was in there working, cleaning up a rockfall where the top had fell in. I went out looking for a bar to prize with, and, when I come back, he was lying there—killed. Slate fall. Big rock on him that had come down from the top. That cured me of going under the hill. I tore out of there and never went back in the mines again for a long time.

"But a man can't stay outten them, seems like. The next mines I worked in was at Evarts on Bailey's Creek. Another old mule mines. I worked there a right smart bit and quit to work for my brother-in-law at Draper. We was going in one morning with a load of steel tracking loaded behind us. We was riding in front with two more fellers, both setting right beside us. The driver run into some timbers with that big load of steel. I hit the bottom of the car just as flat as I could get, and one of them steel rails rammed right into the feller setting next to me and killed him. He was setting right next to me. I got scared of the mines again and quit and left there.

"I never worked in the mines again for several more years, but I went back in the mines in 1943. I quit logging and took a job at Brookside, loading coal with a big new long-wall, a place where you can get all the way from five to ten cars at a shooting. Me and my brother was working a room, and I cleaned up my side of the wall, but he liked [lacked] about a car or car and a half for a cut when we had to come out. Next morning we went in, and I got down on his side of the wall and was helping him. The top last night was just as sound as it could be. I had got three or four shovelfuls of coal shoveled in the car and stooped back to get me another un, raised up, and here she come. A big rock out of the top about thirteen inches thick come down and covered me up. Got me down. My brother started to run off to get help and leave me, thought I was killed. I hollered at him, told him not to leave me. I was covered with that rock. I knowed my foot was cut off, but besides that, I didn't think I was hurt anywheres else. He come back to me, trying to get me out, and couldn't do much with that big rock. And I told him to get outten there and get enough men in there and get that rock offen me. They come in and finally got me out.

"A little motorman there he hauled me out. My leg had to be taken off. I was out of the mines then for nearly a year. I went back in the same one and found the same man that hauled me out was still there. He come in and pulled my first cars of coal, and then went on to pull another feller's cars right above me. All at once the top fell in on him and killed him. We had to beat the rock offen him and haul him out on top of his own motor.

"Now they are several jobs in the mines that I've not mentioned yet. The track crew keeps up the main line and lays track in the rooms as they are mined out and pull it outten them already worked out. The motorman has a brakesman and coupler who works around the tail end of the load, hooking on, sidetracking cars, pulling the load out of there. Safety crews install fans and test the air gas, and lay down rock dust to keep the bugdust from exploding, and crews on the outside on the tipple screen the coal, wash it, picking out bone and gob. And lots of others in big mines around the machine shop, powerhouse, running the commissary, and all like that.

"I was working down in Jay-main later. Cleaned up my room, me and my buddy name o' Bill Youngblood. We got it clean and then timbered her up the way we allas done to have a safe room. The machine come in and cut it and went on to the other 'n. My buddy started to knock out them timbers. And I told him not to do that. He hammered the top, and it hammered sound. So he knocked that timber out, and down come a piece from the top, rock about twenty-five feet long, and killed him.

"I've worked a many a day under the hill when I wa'n't figuring on getting out alive at night. The top was allas so bad. When we took out a cut o' coal from our room, we would have to set up our timbers to hold the top. Set me four cross collars and timbers under 'em. In a lot of mines they are seams of coal about six feet above the one you are working, and, when you take out the cut underneath, that six-foot layer of rock between the seams would come loose—where it was cracked and faulty—and set right down on your timbers. You would be working in a death trap all the time, sorter like a deadfall you ketch animals in. But after that rock had all settled down, it wouldn't do no more till you took out another cut. As fast as you took her out, that rock would fall without a sound—if you didn't have your timbers set. They was holding up all that rock and the rest of the mountains.

"The weight of the whole ridge above you was wanting to come down. Why, man, you can hear all kinds of popping and groaning back in the mines. I've seen my timbers break and kick out and fly fifteen feet sometimes, so much weight on 'em. They are all kind of noises in the mines to scare you. You could hear cracking and grinding all the time. Some of it got to be imagination. But you get a man in a death trap in under these old hills, and I reckon he orght to be scared after seeing so much death and killing."

Jim told of his experiences casually, as if they happened to men every day. And they do. Lumbering and mining are the region's chief industries, employing perhaps a hundred thousand men in rough, hard labor. Jim will report on other folkways of his family in later chapters.

2. Dave Couch, His Family Story

At times Jim Couch was very elusive on his day (sometimes two days) off in the week. "He don't stay here much on Saturday when he don't work," his teen-age son Elmer would say; "generally takes off sommers and lays out a corn patch or half the garden for me to hoe. I've not got into that corn up yander yit—don't expect to."

And again, "We don't know when he's going to come back in the door when he takes off. He goes down there in that town [Harlan] and stands around joking with ever'body, and he shoots pool all over the place, and then he might wind up in the picture show and not come in till the bus runs at sebem o'clock, or somebody brings him in."

One Saturday, later in the fall of 1951, I was determined to catch Jim, and left Pine Mountain School an hour earlier than I ever had. But they told me he had left "sommers" just a few minutes before and that he might still be down at Harrison's. I did find him on the road at his brother's place, but the two were hustling to go somewhere in a waiting car. I called before they could get moving, "Hello there, Jim; where are you off to today?"

He came up to the car with a wicked smile and his lips pouched out. "What do you say, ole pal? We just can't get together a-tall, seems like. Can't talk any today, have to go on some business with my brother." I don't know how helpless I looked, but I felt let down. He continued, "Get out and talk with my brother Dave. He's here. That's him standing over yander. Dave, come over here—man wants to see you."

A lean man came our way, dressed in baggy pants and some kind of wool coat, pipe in one side of his mouth, heavy-lensed glasses in round metal frames nearly dropping off his nose. A bit taller than Jim, he walked with wide, cautious strides. He came inquiringly in our direction.

Jim continued, "Here's the feller I's telling you about, collecting them old stories and songs. He wants to know can you sing any songs with that banjer. He puts 'em on record."

Dave said, "Howdy," took his pipe out, and leaned against the car door. "Why, I used to could sing some of 'em. What ones have you already ree-corded?"

Jim and I named a few. Dave said, "I used to play on the banjer some, but I hain't been able in a few years. Eyes got bad and had to retire from work. I'll study some up and get that old banjer in order. Hain't no strings on it now. You let me know when you're coming again—come back in two weeks, a month, and I'll see what I can do for you."

With this uncertain state of affairs I could not arrange a definite time to see him again—he was sure he could not sing any songs for recording until his sore throat got better. But to do all I could to speed the time, I bought a set of banjo strings in town and left them with him on my return that day. He received them with some surprise and, though he didn't say it, perhaps with some obligation to record for me.

Dave lived a mile or so below the mill town of Putney, below the highway and across the railroad tracks, in an average-sized yellow frame house. A few steps from the front porch a rustic bridge spanned a small ravine. The Cumberland River made a long clear sweep on the lower side and had in time cut away a portion of Dave's precious garden. He had built up a high stone wall in front to control the ravine and on the river side to keep the river away. There were fruit trees all about the place, and all around the house were rank cabbages, beets, onions, and other truck. If Dave and the boys wanted to catch any fish from the river, all they had to do was to stand in the garden and cast their hooks over into the rippling water. He had only one neighbor in the long bend of the river.

There was a chill in the air on the riverbank the first part of September when I drove down to Dave's house for our first talk. Two or three dogs greeted me, but there were no people in sight. Some smoke oozed up from the living-room chimney. The noise of my car and the barking of the dogs brought two of the boys, Bige and Birchel, healthy, bright fellows of about sixteen and twelve, to the door. Yes, their father was in the house by the fire, one said, as they left the door open and retired from the threshold. I could now see Dave inside, opposite the warm heating stove in the middle of the small, square room. He was in his lounging chair, taking even puffs on his bent-briar pipe. He asked me to come in, motioning to a couch facing the front of the stove. The evening shadows in the deep valley, aided by the close apple trees in the yard, darkened the room.

We talked for several minutes on current news, Dave becoming talkative, pleasant, and hospitable. Of his eleven children, about half were grown and married, or off working somewhere. Two small ones, younger than the twelve-year-old boy, ventured into the room on short errands and returned to the dining room, where the mother and two older girls worked with the pots and pans. As my eyes got accustomed to the shadowy interior, I noticed that the house was well kept and had the usual pictures on the walls and a few sentimental posters on religious themes. Several potted plants had been brought indoors and rowed along the wall opposite the couch. To my surprise, I caught sight of a good-looking guitar in another corner of the room. Birchel played around on it, they told me, but he let it sit there unplucked for the time. Bige spoke of a banjo in the bedroom, went for it, and handed it to its rightful picker—the father. Dave complained of his voice and played a few pieces without singing the words.

By this time I was at home. The mother came in with a lighted oil lamp and set it on a ledge and then retired again. She was strikingly short, with a round face and black hair swept back to a knot at the nape. She was well preserved after mothering eleven. The murmuring stove and simple light cast the right spell for tales. I asked Dave if he was ready to tell a few. His silence heightened the spell of magic in the room; the smaller two children left their play on the floor and went to his chair.

"Oh, I'll tell one so's these little fellers 'll go to bed."

The older children grew quiet and respectful, while the smaller two mulled over the ones they would like to hear. The youngest boy named one that just suited him. It was for children, the cumulative type, with its simple formula and constant repetition. The other voices became silent when the father began testing his vocal cords. He slid his pipe down his coat and into the pocket and told the story of the Cat and Rat [No. 131]. The children went off to bed.

For the remainder of that session and in many more that followed, I asked Dave questions about his home life and listened to his stories and songs. He liked to tell of his early days, lingering over some with pleasure and others with something like tears in his voice.

"I lived a life on a farm," Dave began, "up till I was grown, till I was about seventeen. My father had to farm purty heavy to make a living for us ten children, and he had to make everything except what we had to buy, such as coffee, sugar, salt, hardware, and things like that. We had five cows to milk, eighteen or twenty head of hogs to feed, chickens, geese, ducks. But still I think we had a easier time of it than what people have now. Now most of the time people go to the store and buy what they can get. They have to get out and work it out, and then get out and pack it in. I'd take old times now again.

"We lived in a big log house, had two sixteen-foot rooms, with two porches, one on each end. The dogtrot between these two rooms was covered over and made a good place to store up things like plowstocks, feed, and wood for the fires. As for gyarden truck, we didn't have cans to can things back then. We would hole up nearly everything we raised, such as turnips, 'taters, cabbage, apples—even hole up our beets. Take our beets up when we needed 'em on the table and pickle 'em fresh. We would have enough fresh cabbage and stuff in them holes to last us till growing season the next spring, and I think that was a purty good living. I'll tell ye what all we would put up other ways. We would pickle up a sixty-two-gallon barrel full of beans, my mother would. And she had a fifty-five-gallon barrel she would put up full of roas'in' years, and kraut a fifty-gallon barrel full of kraut.

When the heavy frosts come, we would get out and kill about eight hogs, put up sausage and meat and lard. Milk them five cows and have plenty of meat, milk, and butter. We lived a purty good life back in them days.

"Now we would do more with beans than just pickle 'em. We would dry a sight of beans by stringing them and threading them up on strings to dry. I've knowed my mother to dry as many as eighteen bushel thrashed out for soup beans. We boys would get them right real dry, and take and put them in sacks, get us some big sticks, and go to work. I've beat 'em out a many a time that way, going atter 'em just like killing snakes, bust them hulls up, take them out on a sheet or something, and sort the beans out of the hulls. We called these shelly beans.

"I remember one summer we had in a big crop and my father got down with the sore-eye. He had taken it and went nearly blind till he couldn't see and left everything to do, with just me and my mother and the other littler uns. We pitched into that work and got the crop laid by, and then we needed money, so we sanged in the woods and got money to buy our shoes and things we had to have in the winter we couldn't get no other way. I was just nine year old, and that was the first time I recollect going out sanging. I learnt to sang because my mother didn't have nobody to go with her. I went along to keep her company and to carry the sang. But in a couple or three days I learnt what sang was, and I went to digging it. I dug about half what she would, and I felt proud because I was helping out a little. I've been a-sanging ever since. I guess I've dug and sold $10,000.00 worth, if not more. It sold about five dollars a pound back when we first begin to dig it, and it has raised to about fifteen dollars now. I made $798.00 summer before last sanging and digging ginger. Last summer I was sick all the time and didn't get to sang none, and I hain't getting to sang any this summer. Maybe I'll get all right and sang some this fall. I'd ruther sang in the fall. You'll find as much sang in the spring before all the weeds come as you will in the fall, but it'll dry away half in the spring, but it won't dry away any to amount to nothing in the fall. You can see it all right in the spring, in the summer you've got to get in under the weeds, but in the fall you can see its big pod of red berries sticking up and it commences getting yaller and you can see about all of it.

"My mother would start her spinning on her wheel early enough in the fall to have yarn for us a pair of socks around before it got cold. Then later she would get time and spin all of her yarn and knit the other need-cessities. We got two pair of socks a year. My younger sisters didn't learn how to run the wheel, but they hope [helped] Mother with the wool and they could knit, help her run off socks, gloves—a pair a year—and they'd knit 'boggans or toques to wear on our heads, and sweaters, and my mother used to knit shawls for the women to put around 'em when it was cold. She would color that yarn. Mother had about three colors she would generally prepare. She'd take warnut roots, skin the bark off, boil it, and make yaller color. Take chestnut-oak roots and make a dye out of it, but it was about the same color warnut was. She would take mulberry roots and make another color, on a yaller color but more darker. Other dyes she got from her neighbors or the store, or ordered it from a company.

"The first salt I remember seeing I was about eight year old. My father he went to Goose Creek on a sebem-day journey going and coming to get our salt. And I want to tell you while I'm into it what he hauled it on. I guess it'll sus-prise you. He had a big cart, and he made it hisself. He made the axles out of hickory, well seasoned, and he made his wheels out of blackgum, the toughest wood in the world, wood that wouldn't split. You could split it one way as good as you could the other. He sawed off big solid cuts offen that blackgum, about twenty inches in diameter, with big auger holes in the center for his axles, and pagged on. Never had a nail then and weren't a nail in the whole wagon. Made a bed for it and a tongue and doubletrees for his oxen. Oxen had double yokes on 'em, and the leaders would have a big chain hooked to a swivel in the yoke of the ones behind.

"His wagon was pulled by two yoke of oxens and he would be gone from sebem to nine days. He would go out and get a load and divide it out with his neighbors, and then they would go for one when that run low. He would bring back about two thousand, three thousand pounds of it, bring back a big load in about one-bushel sacks. It didn't cost more'n about fifty cents a hundred, but that trip cost more than the price again' they got it back home. That was the only way to get salt, go to the works over there where they 'vaporated it in kittles. No railroads in this country back then.

"Coffee that we'd have was bought at the clostest place, and we would generally buy it in fifty-pound sacks of green grains. We had to parch it and then grind it; my mother had that to do every morning for breakfast. Them fifty pounds would last us about six months, and sacks of sugar would be brought in at the same time, fall, so we wouldn't have it to do in the winter.

"Now they had watermills to grind their meal, after we quit grinding or gritting it at home. My father had a big watermill over in the Sang Branch where we lived. When it would start into raining in the fall, we would get busy and grind up our corn to make our bread through the winter and up till summer. And we had to have a certain way of putting it up to keep it from sp'iling. We'd have coaloil barrels made out of staves that helt about fifty-five gallons. Most of them barrels never had coaloil in 'em, but we just called all barrels that, I reckon. We'd put our meal in 'em this way. Put in about two bushel and then put in a layer of salt to hold the meal from sp'iling, and then put in another two bushel and another layer of salt. Several barrel was supposed to last us till up in the summer, when our corn come in and we had water to grind more. We had to put up everything that way to do us.

"We didn't raise no wheat. We didn't have no biscuits in the house till after I was grown, and then we had so fer to go to get groceries like that we didn't have no biscuits except on Sunday for breakfast. The railroad finally come through to Pineville and later up the river to the Pore Fork. Still it was about twenty-sebem mile from where we lived. We would start out from home on mules on a Sunday morning, over the Pine Mountain, and get to the store there at night. Stay all night, and early Monday morning we would load up with flour and stuff and head back acrost the mountain for home. We didn't eat flour like people do now sebem days a week. We had cornbread three times a day. But it was good. It was baked this way. We had a big farplace where my mother cooked, and she had a big baker and led [lid]. They was ten of us chillern, and she had to bake a lot. She would fill that thing full of dough, draw out the farcoals and make a place to set it, put it in the hot ashes, and put that led on and then cover it plumb over with hot coals. It come out of there brown all over, and it was the best bread you ever eat, and if you hain't eat none of it, you've missed something. Put it in that far and let it bake, and pull her out of there and eat. Man, oh, man, you don't know how good that is. Take butter and good ham meat—awful good. I wish times would come back just like they was back then.

"We would hunt all the spare time we had. Didn't have much hunting time in the summer, but in the winter we would hunt possums, groundhogs, coons, things like that. No big game in that country. Of a winter we'd catch, oh, eighty, hundred hides and ship 'em off or sell to some buyer. We done a lot o' squirrel hunting, and we could get a mess ever' time we went out. Used an old hog rifle most of the time. The first squirrel I ever kilt was with one of them. Me and my brother—I was only thirteen and he was elebem—we started out one morning with our squirrel dog, and I took along the old shotgun because I had two shells fer it. Got two squirrels and come back. Looked over the old hog rifle and saw I had just fourteen caps and some powder. So I took my bullet molds and molded me fourteen bullets. Me and him started out again that evening, about a mile above where we lived, up a holler. The dog treed one, and I kilt it. He went on and treed again, and I shot that un out. Jim was coming along carrying 'em. First thing I knowed, we had thirteen squirrels and started out to the house. The dog treed another un up a small tree. Hit was setting up there looking at me, and I raised up to aim with the last load I had. I went to far on that squirrel, and the cap dropped off. I couldn't find it. Back then we had old redheaded matches. You could lay one on a rock and bust it, and it would go like a dynamite cap. I cut me off a head from one of them matches and put it on the tube of my gun and let her go and killed that un. Made me sixteen squirrels I kilt that day.

"Well, we got to school part of the time. Our school was four mile from where we lived. While I was small, I didn't get to go because it was too fer, but time I's thirteen, I went every day I could, three, four days a week if it wa'n't bad. We'd go most of the time to get to play, had games at school, play and throw rocks going and coming. Be tard playing and running all day and wouldn't get home till near dark, and we would have to get in wood and kindling, do up the work, feed the stock.

"I'd study my lessons of a night so I'd know 'em the next day and get to play all I could. We had some old books, called readers then, from the primer to sebemth, eighth readers. I went through the fourth reader, was as fer as I got. When I was eighteen, going on nineteen, my mother died, and I never got to go to school any more. My father, then he broke up housekeeping, and we went to live with the neighbors and kinfolks. I went to stay with my brother on Gabe's Branch on Greasy. Stayed there and worked for him and got to making whiskey. While my mother was living, I never made no moonshine, for she wouldn't let me. She made us go to church on Sunday, and she wanted us around close through the week where she could keep in touch with us, afeared we might get into something another. After she died and left us, then our father he didn't take too good a care of us. He just about turned us out, or else we just left. I had a living to make for myself. Got into whiskey making and bootlagging. Thought I's having a good time, but I wa'n't. I just wa'n't satisfied the reason I done that. I didn't have no mother to go to, and I had to have some place to stay. And I got so I'd just as soon be in the hills at a still as at somebody's house.

"The lastenest thing I can remember at school was the teacher's thrashing and whupping us. The last year I went to school I was a big man—thought myself a man. And this last year I taken a whuppin' offen a teacher, but the teacher took one, too. I fit the old feller. When he'd hit me, I'd hit him. It was over fighting. Me and some boys got into a fight. He wanted to whup me and leave them out. I told him if he didn't whup them, I wa'n't aiming to take my whuppin'. It made him mad, and he said he's going to whup me anyhow. He got a-holt of me and went to thrashing me, and I went to fighting him back, and me and him just fit it out. He whupped me all right, cut the blood outten me, but I kicked his shins and skinned 'em all over. He told my dad and said if I didn't come back to school, he's aiming to have me sunt off. Dad sunt him back word that if he'd treat us all alike, they wouldn't 'a' been no fight of it. Whup me and the other boys and give it to all the chillern when they needed it. And the old man was right. The teacher wanted to whup me, and I didn't think it was right.

"Well, we would play ball and base and other games. The ball game was about like baseball. We would get thirty minutes for morning recess, an hour at dinner, and a half an hour for evening recess. And we'd play after school till we had to go home. I took many a whuppin' for coming in late, but I liked to play. On Sunday we'd go to church and take all day for it. We'd play with our friend boys till dark, just about it. Get in home to do the work so that on Monday we could hit the fields. Spring we went to grubbing and getting the ground in shape, plant the corn and go to hoeing it, and work every day till it was laid by.

"When the crops come in, we'd have to start gathering 'em and putting 'em up. When our beans come in, we'd have bean stringings. Many of a time I've gone to the field with my mother to pick sacks of beans. You understand, beans then hain't like they are now; we could pick three, four times as many offen a row then. No bugs then, and we had big rich fields. I've picked many a three-bushel meal sack offen a row. Pick till dinnertime, and our father would come and help carry them beans in. Pick twenty bushel in the day. Then they would let us all tell our neighbors to come in for a bean stringing. Father and Mother would tell us if we got them beans strung and not waste any, we could play the rest of the night. Sometimes it would be two o'clock in the morning when we got 'em worked up and threaded on strings and broke up for pickling, but we worked patiently till we'd git 'em finished on account o' getting to play all we could. We would have six or sebem bean stringings a season.

"Then we would start playing. I allas played the banjer for the sets and never did get to run any sets, but I've played for many a set to be run. Some would have to wait—couldn't get in the set—and they'd stand back and clap their hands to keep up the movement. When they would get tired, they'd play quiet games like Pleased or Displeased. They danced a lot, and they would get me to pick. I played for sets from the time I was twelve year old. If I didn't get to run many with 'em, I got a big kick outten playing the banjer for 'em.

"They would play in the house all the time. Back then people was kindly curious about letting a big gang bunch up outside. If they got to running in and out and carrying on, they would have to go home. I've been to places where they had jugs of whisky out in the weeds to run to, but, at home and while my mother was alive, she wouldn't have no jugs of whiskey at our parties. She was a Christian—from the time I can recollect till she died, she was a Christian. She would get down on her knees and pray by her bedside of a night. I've heared her pray for her sick chillern many of a time. The sweetest prayers I ever heared pray was from the lips of my mother.

"We had other parties when there was other things going on in the neighborhood. We'd raise cane and have molasses all the time. Everybody raised cane. We would have a stir-off every night when we got to making 'lasses. Get the cane in to the mill and grind it into juice of a day, and then it would take us till sometimes two o'clock in the night to get it stirred off. Then we would carry the molasses in and get everything cleaned up for the next night. We would have some of the same games we had at the other get-togethers. Run sets, play Pleased or Displeased, or Old Dock Jones, London Bridge. I don't know how many different games they would play, but a lot of them. The sets was about like them they have here today. I didn't call any and didn't learn 'em. I played the banjer all the time, 'cause they wa'n't just anybody who could play one. Had to play fast for the dances. When they would start, somebody would call it, and all could get in went round with 'em while others stood out and clapped. They would be making so much noise with their hands and feet you couldn't hear nothing. Had to play the banjer loud.

"Old Dock Jones was just a circle game:

> Old Dock Jones was a fine old man,
> He told a thousand lies,
> Gentlemen and ladies sail away.

They would go round and round, you see, getting faster and faster all the time. They would be one in the middle, and the others would say, 'Kiss whoever you please.' The one in the middle would kiss one that was in the ring, and the one kissed would have to go in the middle and let that one take his place in the set.

"In London Bridge two would hold their hands up, you know, like a bridge, and they would go around atwixt them under their arms and say,

The London Bridge is a-fallin' down,
Fallin' down, fallin' down——

and finally it would fall down and catch one. That's the way they played it.

"Now in Pleased or Displeased they would all set down in a line, and they took it in rotation. Commence with the first one and say, 'Pleased or displeased?' 'Displeased.' 'What would it take to please you better?' You could make any wish you wanted to to the crowd, you see. Maybe it would be for one to go bark up the chimbly, or kneel down and pray, or whatever you put on him to do he had to do it. Make 'em go wade the water, bring in a load o' wood for the far, bring you a drink, stand on their head. But most of the time it was hugging and kissing. Say it would please you to see some boy hug a purty girl, or some girl kiss a purty boy, you know, getting all the fun outten it you could. Sometimes some smart boy would want you to go pick up a rock and pack it a piece and lay it down, or go rub farcoals on your face and make your face black. Anything to get a good un on somebody.

"We went to church every Sunday. Didn't have any meetings of a night like they do now. We had church about all day Sunday. Commence about ten o'clock, have four, five preachers going on till late dinnertime. Sometimes we had dinner on the ground. And when we didn't, we would go home with somebody who wanted to set a big dinner at the house. That day then and this day now is different. That day then you could get a meal anywhere just by going home with a crowd of the meeting folks. Fifty people eating at the table of their neighbor was a small thing then. I've seen fifty eat at our house a many of a time, and up in fifty. When they took dinner to church, they would make up fruit cake and sweetbread, and fill baskets with pies and chicken and take to the meeting, and when they finally called a recess, hour maybe, we would all eat and go back to preaching. Maybe it would be a baptising or decorating the graves. The evening meeting would break up about three o'clock, and all would go home. They would be five or six preachers and would all preach, give 'em all a chance, and sometimes one would preach an hour, maybe two hour. Get them old Baptists started, Hardshell Baptists, into it, and they wouldn't know when to quit. They was a few other denominations, but most of the old people were Hardshell Baptist. We would sing them old songs by lining 'em out. I learnt many of them, and I've heared my father and mother sing 'em all day.

"One of the best times for my mother to tell us them old stories was when dad would be out and couldn't get back in till late. My mother would have the grub ready, but we would have to wait till he come, even if it was 'way in the night. And to keep us pacified, she would tell tales. Dad would not get to work often, and, when he did, it would be eight, ten mile from home. He would work till dark and then come in home so we could all set to the table and eat together and go to bed. Mother would tell us a tale, and, if he hadn't come in, we would want another un, and she would be willing to go on telling. When he come, mother would set down and let one of the girls wait the table. She would turn thanks, and then she retch the food and broke bread for the chillern and got us all started eating. My father wa'n't a Christian till my mother died, he never went to church much till after she died, but my mother made it a Christian home.

"We all had a good time, got along good; they wa'n't no quarreling in the family like they is today. We all hung together, and when one started to the field, we knowed what to do. We all knowed where to hang our hoes and where they was next morning. When one hollered for us in the morning, we knowed to get up and go to the field. When our father told us it was quit time, we would all quit. We'd never bag him to quit like chillern do now.

"My father used all the signs in his planting. He planted corn and beans when the sign's in the arms; 'taters when the sign was in the feet; sowed his cabbage and things like that growed heads when the sign was in the head; planted all his vines when the sign was in the secrets. We allas raised plenty of stuff and never did fail. They's three days of the year, called barren days, when he wouldn't plant anything. We allas tended fifteen to twenty acres of corn every year, sowed hay and mowed it. We had stock and had to raise food for it. We would kill our hogs all the time on the old of the moon. Never would kill 'em on the new of the moon on account of the meat being tough and we wouldn't get as much lard out of it on the new of the moon as we would on the old of the moon. The old people could tell about when it was going to rain by the wind or clouds. My father could look at the clouds or watch the wind of an evening, and, when he would say it would rain by morning, it generally rained. People went by the signs then more than they do by the almanac now. They didn't have almanacs then, and it was mostly their signs that they went by. We could tell what time it was by the sunset, you see. We had a sun mark to tell when twelve o'clock come. When we was in the field and our shadders slipped right up under us, we knowed it was about dinnertime. About quit time we would watch the sun on the other side of the mountain, and when it got to what looked like about six inches from the top, we went out. It was about dark.

"Another thing that we done with food back then I don't hear mentioned anymore was the way we handled our berries. We would dry our berries just the way we dried apples and then put 'em away in something tight. Get them out in the wintertime when you get ready to cook 'em. Put them in water, and they would be just like fresh from the vines. We picked a lot of huckleberries along the tops of the ridges and dried them. Man, they was good in pies along about Christmastime. Some people dried their blackberries that way.

"I begun making moonshine back before my mother died, but she bagged me not to make. I quit and went to Pine Mountain School to work and stayed with my oldest brother who lived on Gabe's Branch about five mile from the school. I worked for the school for about thirteen months for seventy-five cents a day, and I paid my brother twenty-five cents for board. After working there for about a year, year and a half, why, my mother died. She had cancer in her left breast. She passed away at the age of sixty-four years old. My father sold about all we had, except what my mother give the chillern before she died."

The next years of his life, Dave's main occupation was making moonshine, although he worked for a time on the railroad near Hazard and again at a mine on Bailey's Creek. "But they's not much more for me to tell. After that I got a job at Lynch working on the railroad.

Worked some more at Bailey's Creek. And then for eighteen year I worked for the Intermountain Coal and Lumber Company. That was on Pore Fork at Putney. There's where I live now. I'm fifty-five year old, going on fifty-six. I hain't worked nowheres in two year. I've been under medical treatment and in the hospital. Had a operation two year ago and haven't worked any since. That's brought you up to right now, and I guess that's about all that I can recall at this time."

3. Other Couches, Their Stories

Mandy Hendrix, older sister of Dave and Jim Couch, still lived in an isolated valley on the northeast slope of the Pine Mountain. She was the first member of the family that I met, and, although she never told me any folktales, it was she who directed me to Jim at Putney. My experiences on the trip that discovered her are among the highlights of my life as a folklore collector.

Miss Grace Rood, the field nurse for the hospital of the Pine Mountain School, invited me to go with her to the Cutshin valley. We went down Greasy, up Big Laurel, and over a very rugged ridge, and came out on the gap between Big Leatherwood and Cutshin. Miss Rood was driving her tried and trusted four-wheel-drive jeep—and we needed it. We dropped down the lane of a small mining camp in the gap, passing cabins on stilts along the woods on either side.

At the end of the row the muddy road became an unimproved trail in the rocks and branch water of Cutshin. We bounced along in the bed of the small ravine, here taking a rutted highroad over a ledge and there plunging into the water again. The little streams were swollen with recent rains and continued to add their volume to the main creek. Soon we were fording Cutshin endways, with not a single foot of highroad left. Rocks and driftwood became the main hazard as we navigated the rushing, rolling stream. The water was soon lapping the bottom of the vehicle and seeping through the holes in the floor. Unexpected boulders about the size of number-seven washtubs tossed the tires up into view and let them fall again into the fresh mountain water. I could only grip the iron bars of my seat and trust to the instinct of the driver. She could see no more road than I could. As the water became deeper, I was afraid for our safety. The hills were higher because we were lower in the trough of two steep mountain slopes. The thickets of rhododendron and mountain laurel came down to the rocks that lined the canyon. Although I had been in the hills of Kentucky most of my life, I believed this to be the wildest and most untouched section I had seen.

At last a house appeared. It was not much, but it was a house, the kind people live in through the hills. It was a log building with a porch, a paling fence around it and the garden patch, a shed for the old bony cow, and washtubs beside the little ravine that gurgled down to join the main creek. It was a sight to lift sagging spirits. Just below the house the road rose to a notch in the hill and wound along above the rolling waters.

Still farther on we came to the mouth of an apparently rather long creek, judging from the volume of water issuing across the road. Right in the mouth of the valley was a vast oblong rock fifty feet long, almost blocking the valley. Our jeep chugged around the base of the rock and under one long ledge into a pretty mountain dale. There, as if hidden from the world, was a large white store, and to the left beside the stream was a white dwelling house. Horses were hitched to the rail beside the store, where a knot of men talked until they had to step aside to let us pull into the level yard and stop. The storekeeper, a youngish man with ruddy face and pleasant manners, came out and called Miss Rood by name. I spoke of stories and tellers. He said, "Come right on in and make yourselves at home. My mother lives here with us, and she knows about everybody in here and maybe some stories. If she don't know any, she knows who does."

A little old lady sat in a rocker before the open grate and clicked a pair of knitting needles in her small delicate fingers. Her gray hair was pulled back and tied in a ball. She had a bit of fire to take the chill and dampness out of the house. We were received with the most warmhearted welcome that one can experience.

I asked about Jack stories, fairy tales, and witch legends. Her face lighted up, and she chuckled in spite of herself. "I know just the kind you are looking fer. It's them old-fashioned fireside stories. Many's the time I set and listened to them when I was growing up. But I'm no hand to tell stories—the way they are likely to be told. No," she said regretfully. "I never was any hand to tell them old-fashioned tales, but used to I'd druther hear somebody come in and tell stories of a night than to eat. I've set and listened to 'em, and ghost tales, they allas come last and would make us little uns so scared we would be afraid to go in the back room to bed.

"Now let me sorter study." She clicked her needles for a minute and mumbled a few names under her breath. And then she told us of a person who could tell them the best in the long ago, but she was not sure the woman followed storytelling any more. I pursued her for the name. "She is Mandy Hendrix, down here on Cutshin. She used to tell them stories while her chillern were growing, but I hain't heared much about her and her stories for years now. She used to be the best un I know of in here now."

Mandy's house lay farther down the Cutshin road and up the first hollow to the right. We stayed with the notch above the stream for three miles, passed through a beech grove whose old worn roots tossed the jeep to and fro, and finally came again to the creek, now a fairly raging flood. On the other side was a steep incline, almost running with mud because a new road was being graded up the valley. Above the fill of mud was a very steep ascent into Guthers Branch, where Mandy lived.

The water rose up under the seat and rolled away from us in muddy waves. The tires spun and threw sand behind as we cut our way up the hill and finally leveled off in a sandy trail untouched by recent travel. Below the first house we ran into a child's sand castle with battlements and stickweed flagpoles. The valley as usual widened out and stretched onward into the towering hills. We took the left branch, along the slick rocks in the roadbed, until the trail twisted up another incline and wound around to the very yard of a house. A model mountain cabin, it was made of small unhewn logs, daubed with yellow clay, and covered with rived boards from a clear water oak. Vines ran up at the corners and almost covered the small-paned windows. Flowers were everywhere—in little rows along the graveled walk leading to the plank door, beside the house, and in old automobile tires about the front yard. A pole shed-and-barn stood above the humble dwelling. The hills rose steep and rugged on all sides. Out in the ravine was the family spring, with the customary washkettle and tubs beside it.

A tall lean man of about sixty-five years appeared in the doorway and walked with a game leg out toward the jeep. His faded chambray shirt sagged, and his brown jeans pants hung low on his hipless frame and dropped from broad suspenders. His blond arms and face were mottled with spots of pink and tan.

"Well, if it hain't Miss Rood, 'way up here in this lost holler. Get out, you fellers, and come on in to the house. Who's that with you, Miss Rood? Bring him and come on in where you can set a spell."

This kind and unreserved hospitality, known in my early years, came back to me again and hit me with a sharp delight. It is surely the choice virtue of the Appalachian people. Needless to say, we went in the direction of the house as if drawn by enchantment. Two little boys met us on the way, one about six and the other perhaps twelve, the small one still a chubby child, the other, wearing threadbare overalls and a flop-bill cap, bashful and lean and sad looking. Inside the door sat the woman of the house, close to the fire, her knees almost touching the jambrock. She had an old cloth under her chin and tied at the top of her head over sandy silvery hair brushed back and caught with hairpins. With some effort she rose and made way for us to enter, setting out her chair and drawing another from the back part of the room. "Take this chear, Miss Rood. Set down. I'm ailing," she was saying, "and hain't been able to do a lick o' work for several days," and she pulled her hair back and smoothed down her long, sacklike dress. "I've got a risin' in my year, and hit's about to kill me. Maybe you can doctor me a little."

Upon entering, I saw that the small cozy sitting room was carefully swept, the wrinkles had been patted out of the feather ticks on the three small beds in the corners, and the garments were hung around the walls. The inside of the room was a typical mountain interior. The walls, ceiling, and even the door facings had been spring-papered with catalog and magazine leaves; the fireboard [mantel] was covered with precious objects, such as bottles of medicine and boxes of salve, a kerosene lamp, and the Bible; the beds were covered with handmade crazy quilts; and an old table in the center of the room had its crocheted centerpiece, as did the ledge of the fireboard.

The smaller boy was Mandy's grandson by a daughter who lived farther up the ravine; the older boy, Bobby, was an orphan she had taken to raise when he was three years old. "Hit's a good child and hain't nary bit of trouble to me," Mandy said. "My seven chillern growed up and married off, and I found this un over on Leatherwood. I was glad to give it a home"—then regretfully—"but hit hain't had no schoolin'. Hit's so fer out of here I hain't been able to send it nary day. I wush it could go to school."

After a few more words about the distance from school—five miles down on Cutshin—Mandy continued, "Hit could 'a' gone back to Leatherwood when it was six and maybe 'a' went some, but it didn't want to go, did you, Bobby? I tried to get some of his people to keep him just for the schoolin'. Hit's a McDaniel, and its family broke up and scattered when it was just a sit-alone baby. Hits mother had to be sunt off, and its daddy never tried to keep house anymore. I took hit to raise, and it's been satisfied with me ever since. Don't want to go to its own people to live. I counsel and teach him all I know, just as I tried to counsel and teach my own houseful of young uns. He minds me and does all the little jobs fer me. I am good to him, maybe better to him than I was to some of my own chillern."

The boy sat with his hands pressed between his knees, his head down, and his eyes hid by the long cap bill, not talking while he was being talked about. But a few minutes later when I had mentioned collecting stories, his head came up, his eyes lighted, and he was speaking about stories he knew, telling lines of the boy up the bean tree [No. 101]. I recognized the authentic oral pattern and turned to Mandy for comment. She said, "We used to tell stories when I was growing up, but I guess my brother Jim is 'bout the only one that tells 'em any more.''

"Where did you hear that one, Bobby?" I asked.

"I guess I heared it from Jim, when he used to come over here."

"Brother Jim used to come over and stay with me," Mandy continued, "and ever' night he'd set here and tell stories. He'd have this house full of chillern. They'd be all around him and on both knees. Hit'd pleasure the chillern to death everwhen he come over here. We heared all kinds of stories from our mother, and Jim learnt most of them. After I's married, he stayed with me till he was grown and went off to the World War."

"Mandy, will you tell some of the stories to me?" I asked her. "Your mother seems to have handed down a lot of fine old stories to you children."

"She did hand down a heap o' stories, but I never was no hand to tell 'em. You'll have to look up brother Jim. He lives over there on the river at Putney. He knows more stories than I do and has follered telling 'em. I hain't never told them old fireside tales since my chillern was little."

Not wishing to be put off if it could be avoided, I continued reviewing stories they knew and learned that they had heard their parents tell a great store of tales. Finally I asked her again, only to hear her say, "I've quit telling stories. I've been a Christian for nineteen year and don't tell any more of them big tales. Any more I allas tell the truth."

If this did put a stop to my requests, it was not a new excuse to me. I had heard it from many women and a few men. In the hills the women had begun to equate stories with lies and with obscene yarns not told in mixed company. Mandy's mother years before would not tell stories in the presence of visitors. The ballads had been fading out of tradition for a generation or two. They had come to be called "love ballets" or "devil's ditties," and had begun to die on the lips of the folk, even before the phonograph and the radio inundated them.

The trip was not in vain, of course. Mandy had set me on a trail that I was to follow for the next four years, trying to collect all of those stories handed down by the mother. Even Mandy wanted to help, for at the end of my sessions with all of the family, she promised Jim she would go over all the stories with us to see if she knew of any still uncollected. We did just that, but she was unable by that time to contribute. Also, the boy Bobby told interesting versions of two long tales. But above all, I was now on the quest for Jim, the man who could "pleasure chillern to death" with his stories.

For most of these next four years I was a frequent visitor at Jim's house. Since Dave didn't have electricity, it was necessary for me to drive him and others to Jim's home for many sessions of family reminiscences, songs, and tales on the tape recorder.

Early in my quest I wanted to see the father of these folk, the champion banjo picker of the country a generation ago, Tom Couch, who lived on the hill above Jim's house. "And after you get him to talking," Jim warned, "he'll tell you a-plenty. I can't get up and down that hill very good, but you take Elmer to show you the way and go on."

We went up a zig-zag path until we struck a notch carved in the hillside (an old tramroad across Pine Mountain), and around it, passing through groves of shrubbery and by a coalbank in the hill. The water was dammed up—where the old man got his water, Elmer said. After a few more turns under strips of trees, we came to an open flat, in the middle of which stood an ancient cabin. It was a rude plank box with rougher planks over the cracks, surrounded by a broken hedge of shrubs, wild bushes, flowers, old rose stools; the roof was of tarpaper, almost flat, with a stovepipe jutting out the back side—this was the homeseat of the old man after the spacious home life described and idolized by Jim and Dave! The inmates of the cabin, warned of our approach by the barking of an old shaggy dog, poured out—a boy perhaps twelve, a girl about fourteen, and a long-haired, black-eyed woman of about forty years. Elmer, telling them we had come to hear Grandpa Tom tell big tales, set the boy off in a run up the path calling wildly, "Dad, Dad. Some men want to see you." Old Grandpa Tom was up in the forest cutting wood and rolling down chunks for the fires. He came dragging poles in each hand, and at the edge of the notch he dropped them and worked his way out to the ten-foot drop.

To my warning him away from the high bank, he replied with a fuss full of fiery pride, and, taking sprouts in hand, he worked over the edge and landed like a cat at my feet. He was the spriest man of ninety-two I had seen in the hills. Except for the constant and disconcerting tremble of his hands and a red lawless growth on his high cheekbone, he was well preserved.

He had me sit with him in the doorway, although the interior of the cabin was sizzling hot. Within were two beds, a round heater, and a cast-iron cookstove. The boy sat on the doorsill at his father's feet, constantly interrupting the old man. Tom tried to make him mind his manners—"Hush, hush! I want you to hush so I can talk with this man"—batting the wind with his hand.

His people had always lived in the hills of Kentucky, Tom insisted, ignoring or suppressing his probable French origin. One of his forebears started the tradition of picking and singing by making himself a banjo from an old gourd. Sometime in his young manhood Tom took an interest in the banjo and became a contender for prizes at Fourth of July celebrations and in other contests. He related some of his early experiences as if they had happened only yesterday.

"I was down in Hyten [Hyden, seat of Leslie County] when they 'rested me for packin' moonshine, but, the Lord, I never had more 'n that much in a lettle old half-pint bottle," he protested, measuring a few inches with his trembling fingers. "Was in there a week or two— a stranger, ye see, and didn't have nobody to go my bail. Le's see, I believe I had my banjer with me, leastways I could whup on one purty good at that time. I heared they was going to have a banjer contest in town and bagged awful hard to get out and get in that contest. After so long the jailer saw his way to take me out and take me up there. I played as hard as I could and I's playing with the best of 'em. I won third place. I'll tell ye what I played to win. I played Rovin' Gambler [No. 16]. The jedge of the contest come around and put a dollar and fifteen cents in my hand!"

Tom kept the banjo ringing for fifty years, picking up songs as he went about, bringing them home and handing them down to his children. His hearing had begun to deteriorate by the time I met him, and as a consequence he could no longer stay on pitch. But, in the years that followed, Jim went to him often to get the full versions of songs, and, once, when I went with him, old Tom added a stanza to a song. Finally, toward the end of my collecting, there were two songs that neither Jim nor Dave knew fully, and the only hope again was the old man. Jim also wished that the family could have some record of Tom's singing, no matter how poor it had become. Accordingly, Jim had him come to the tape recorder, into which he sang our only complete versions of I Saw a Sight and Hiram Hubbard [Nos. 36 and 32].

Tom was not a good informant in the folktale, having left this field to his first wife and the boys. Apparently he had heard many of the family stories often; he named several that were familiar to him. And before I left, I had him run through the one that seemed to mean the most to him, Polly, Nancy, and Muncimeg [No. 108]. His visualization of the story was as clear as a bell, and his telling was delightfully naive. He believed the story himself and cackled out in the tense passages, some of which he savored on his tongue with a second telling. I noticed the sparseness of words in the telling and the complete lack of elaboration. The gestures, the wide range of voice inflection, the dramatic pauses—these filled that lack. On paper the story seemed eroded and bare, and I had Jim tell it in his own way for print.

So much for the old man Tom, one of the best and most noted banjo men of eastern Kentucky.

Another member of the Couch family I met by an indirect route. Early in Jim's recording sessions he related the One-Eyed Giant [No. 107], the old adventure of Ulysses and Sinbad the Sailor. This was the first American recording of this old epic fragment that I knew of, and I was anxious to trace it back as far as possible. Jim was willing to go with me into the Leatherwood country, across the Pine Mountain and to Clover Fork, to find old Basil Holbrook, who had told him the story.

Almost four years passed before we set out over the mountains on this quest. Jim pointed out the old big log house in a bend of Clover Fork. We stopped and went toward the rustic houseseat, with its rived board roof, puncheoned floor, and beamed and raftered interior. There was an old rock well with its high wellsweep behind a peachtree grove in the garden. We found old Basil at home, retired from strenuous day labor. He was ailing this morning, but he was in a good mood to talk over old times. He was a rather large, stoutish man of perhaps seventy years, dressed in brown pants and chambray shirt open at the neck. In his life he had worked at everything—sawmilling, farming, moonshining (best maker in the country, Jim always said), and, lastly, running a whiskey store up the creek. No, he hadn't told any stories in a long time; he had been too busy until his family was raised and gone. But he remembered clearly the very man who had told him the One-Eyed Giant.

"Now I heared that story," he said, "and a lot of others from old John Couch, your great-uncle [i.e., great-uncle's son], Jim. He was the very man told me that old story."

"Now is that a fact?" Jim asked, his mouth open.

And I said, "Well, Jim, looks as if this throws the old story right back into the family tree. You men trace his descendants, and we'll see if we can find out more about it and other stories."

"Why, that'll be easy," Basil said. "Jim, you orght to know most of 'em well. They allas said that the first Couch to come was old Lihew, and later two or three brothers. The brothers settled down in here, but old Lihew [Anse's eldest son] moved on down the river to the three forks of the Kentucky, around Beattyville. And then he moved on to Owsley County. One of his boys was John, and he used to come back in here, moved a time or two and lived off and on for years. That's when I heared them stories from him. When he died, some of his chillern lived down there and Virginia. You know most of 'em, don't you, Jim?"

"Yeaw, I knowed ever' one of 'em well."

"Well, you had a grandpa John and this great-uncle John. He's dead and didn't leave many chillern in here, but they's one. That's Joe C—Little Joe they called him. The last time I heared of him he was over yander at Appalachia, Virginia."

"Yeaw, I know he's over there," Jim said. "He lives over there, and I've got a great-uncle Tom still over there sommers."

"Jim," I said, "looks like we had better be on our way to Appalachia to trace this story and to see if Joe knows any others that didn't come down to you."

The small town in the gorge of old Big Stone Mountain was quiet when we drove into it at ten o'clock at night. All the information we had was a name—Joe Couch. Up on a lost trail above the town we shouted at the house of an old man, a relative of the Couches. The family tree was traced again and other friendly visiting before we got a new set of directions, this time to the old freight depot. With all our equipment we had neglected to bring along a simple flashlight, and now we faced a long row of houses. A voice directed us farther on. We backed away to the outside of a fence and stumbled on to another opening—shouting again, mentioning names. We were in a back path, calling into kitchens. A noise from a dark porch, and a man approached to within five feet of us huddled in a backyard. He flourished a big pistol and demanded who we were, what we wanted. I hurriedly mentioned the name of Couch—we were visitors, relatives. The figure wavered and looked at us before walking to the next kitchen door and pushing it open. "Hey, dad," he said, "some men out here want to see you. All right, I reckon."

We were directed through the kitchen to the living room, and at last we had a good look at Joe and his wife and the only son at home. The two men talked about kinship and adventures. Joe was the excitable, talkative type. He was a small man, rather dark complexioned, lame in both legs. Before very long he had told about putting most of his life into mining, until the almost fatal day came for him. He was caught under a slab of slate fourteen feet square and many inches thick. The men who could get to him worked for four hours breaking the rock up with sledge hammers to rescue him. His legs were broken, his pelvis crushed, most ribs smashed like crushing a basket—all consigning him to the hospital for years.

"Can't walk to do no good now," he said, throwing his leg out of place at the knee and at the hip. "I was as good as dead and ever'body thought I was out of this world, and I don't know how I lived, but I made it.

"Yeaw, I used to know all them stories, but I've forgot 'em, man. Buddy, I used to tell stories all the time, but people don't tell stories like they used to. I've not been in a storytelling crowd in years." But it did develop before we went to bed that he knew most of the old Indian, pioneering, and Civil War legends that Jim and Dave had related. He knew a version of the old One-Eyed Giant somewhat different from those of Jim and Dave. He called it Johnny Sore-Nabel [No. 161], a nickname given by the giant to the hero because he had skinned his belly. His twelve-year-old son helped to recall an Old World tale that the other tellers had forgotten. Joe called it The White Deer [No. 157]. Jim acknowledged having heard it but said that he might never have thought of it.

The next morning the family went to their job in town—cleaning the local bus station. Joe was anxious to show us his garden that he had rented down in the valley, where we went and found that he had undertaken a large garden project. We helped him gather young corn and beans and tomatoes to bring back. At last we had a long storytelling session, in which Joe was able to contribute some fine old fairytales and many local legends and shorter anecdotes.

By the time the stories were told, Joe's wife had dinner ready. We all sat down to a delicious meal of steaming vegetables and hot coffee. Jim and I had been out on the road for four days, and, anxious to get back over Big Black Mountain, we loaded our equipment and said goodbye.

The account of the Couch family would be incomplete if I did not mention all the members and reveal some negative results. There was Tom's oldest son, Lewis, who had stayed in the rural sections of Harlan and Perry counties all of his life, but at no time would Jim or Mandy name him as a good storyteller. I saw him and talked with him, and, although he seemed to have remembered some of the older fairytales and perhaps told them on occasion, he had laid them aside. His children had long ago grown up and left home, but he had two grandchildren living beside him on Laurel Fork, and they came to Pine Mountain School. I had one, a boy of thirteen, in the seventh grade. He thought a great deal of his grandfather and said that he could tell tales and liked to talk. But the only items that the boy could give me were local legends, hunting stories, and a few puzzles and riddles. Apparently the oldest son of Tom did not make the effort necessary to be a folklore performer, and Jim had said as much to me when we discussed the family members.

There was the daughter Sally, living two miles below Putney with her houseful of children. I was interested in her earlier banjo picking and performing days. She was entirely negative on the subject. She once liked to sing ballads but had not kept it up. "I don't know any no more," she would say; "Jim and Dave have kept on telling them tales and singing the ballads."

As for the two youngest sons, Alex and Harrison, I had two different reactions. Alex was the shy man of the group and apparently had never let a story or song pass his lips. He was a quiet, serious, hard worker. The youngest child of the family, Harrison, was evidently too young to have heard his mother tell tales in the home. The family, as we know, scattered when the mother died, and Harrison had never learned the family traditions. He had come to be looked on by the other members as the scholar of the group, and perhaps he had gone to high school. Through work in the church he had become a song leader and finally had made his way to song teacher and had conducted simple singing schools in the churches of the valley. Jim referred me to him for hymns and moral songs. But during collecting times I always found Harrison too busy to perform, and, if he had, I am not sure that he would have known many items of traditional lore. He was busy at his store by the roadside and at times taking jobs in the community and at times mining coal with his brothers. When I approached him on one occasion, he seemed to feel that Jim and Dave should have the credit for putting together the family lore and, he intimated, they should be the sharers in its success and in its monetary rewards.

4. Jim and Dave, Their Moonshining

"Hold it a minute," Jim stopped me one Sunday morning in the spring of 1952 when I was just ready to start the tape recorder. He reached into his inside coat pocket and pulled out a small bottle nearly full of clear, beady liquid. Taking a couple of gurgles, he smacked his lips and extended it to me. One little swallow went down me like a red-hot ball bearing and rolled around at the bottom of my stomach. Jim deliberately gave me time to decide if I had had enough before extending his hand for it, giving it another little dash on his tongue before replacing the bottle.

"Ready to go! Ahmmmmmmmm. Let me sorter study now about my long experiences with moonshining. I'll tell you the best un that ever happened when I was at a moonshine still—and the scariest un. My daddy was a-making whiskey over there in a holler on the Sang Branch. He never had till then let me go with him to his still because I's just eight or nine year old. He come in home and got supper for the men at the still, and I bagged to go back with him. He took me along and I got to see my first run o' moonshine.

"The reason I can remember it so well—we got back there to that old still, and they had it farred up and was a-running whiskey to beat the band. They set down and eat and got through and was having a big-eyed time, there under the timber. All was a-drinking and everything was a-going good. Then they all looked back toward the east and saw something a-coming through the evedence [elements]. When they saw it coming, somebody called it a great comic [comet], and they begin to say, 'Lord how [have] mercy, the end of time is a-coming.' They begin to draw the far out from under that old still—like that would save 'em, you know. We set there and couldn't move while it was passing on over. I was standing there holding on to a mash barrel and my knees just a-giving it that. But finally it went down kindly in the southwest. Oh, it was just like a big light, or the sun shining for a while. It looked to me about like a ball the size of a half bushel, and it had a tail to it that looked to be about twenty feet long.

"It disappeared in several minutes, down under the hill, and then we heared a big explosion, and that barrel shook where I was a-hold of it. They claimed it busted. After a while they all eased up and decided the end was not a-going to come, leastways not that night, and commenced to fanning the far back up. They went on and made a purty good run the rest of the night."

"Do you know now what that was?" I interjected. "That was Halley's comet, that visited the earth in 1910—it is due to come back in seventy-five years—"

"I don't care when she comes back," Jim countered. "I'll remember that night till she comes again, I guess. When I heared ever'body a-moaning and carrying on, I was about to have heart failure.

"Well, I hope my dad make liquor a lot after that, but I didn't actually learn how from him. That man that learnt me to make whiskey he was a professional moonshiner. He was give up to be the best in the mountain parts. That was old Hiram Holbrooks over on Leatherwood.

"Now the way you begin making whiskey, you carry your old barrels to the place, in some holler where they are plenty of water. A still is a thing you can make. You take and get you a sheet of copper the size you want to make your still, large or small, and you take some brass brads and put that thing in the form of a barrel. Then you take plank and make a head for this still. After that you want a hole in this head, so you take a auger and a handsaw and saw a round hole in the head for your cap, whatever cap you want. It's a kag about twelve inches, I guess.

"But start with your mash first. Take and heat your water boiling,

then you take meal. Pour your meal in the barrel, and then you pour in
your water. You stir this meal up until you cook it good. You keep
right on adding meal and water until you cook it right into a mush.
Well, when you get it cooked to your notion, you take about a quart of
flour to ever' barrel, and put it right down on top of your mash to hold
your heat in. 'Ell, we let that set over to the next day, let it get good
and cool.

"And then we take an old sausage mill to grind our malt corn.
We'd sprout what was called malt corn. Take and put corn in a coffee
sack in water until it sprouted good, until good long sprouts come on
it. Then we'd take this mill and grind this malt corn up, about a kag
to a barrel. And we'd go back and put this malt corn in that barrel.
And then you take your hands like making dough, and you bust ever'
lump in there. Stir just like making gravy, to get it all dissolved just
like milk. And then you cover your barrel real good, and in about
three days this meal will go to working. You've seen slop, now, be setting in a bucket in hot times, come up in big bubbles and bust. That's
the way mash works. It'll work in about three or four days sometimes.

"Then it'll clear off, and all that meal will settle back in the bottom.
And then we'll go ahead and get a forked stick, and we'll get into
them barrels, and we'll stir all that up together. We'll take and build
us a far and heat that until it turns into a simmer, beginning to get
ready to boil. Then we take our cap, put a stick with a hole in it down
in the cap, and put it in that hole in the still. And then we'll take clay
mud and daub all the steam in there. The steam is coming out the hole
in your cap. We have a piece of wood, oh, usually about two feet long,
sourwood. Take it and bore me a hole in it. Start in at one end and bore
as fer as I can, and then start at the other end and bore the hole out.
We use that fer an arm. We put that in that still cap, and we'll daub it
in there. Well, we'll put a worm in it if we're making the old-fashioned way—we'll take our worm then and put in the other end of that
arm, and we'll daub her in there good. And of course if we're making
it with a crooked worm, we'll have a barrel to put that worm in; and
if we're making with a straight worm, we'll have a trough made and
a hole bored in each end of it, and the worm would run through it for
our water to pour in on.

"That goes to boiling in the still, and the steam comes out into that worm and evaporates in the worm, and when it comes out to the end, we catch it and call it singlings. It's an alkiehol, but not high-powered alkiehol. It runs a stream about the size of a number-eight nail. Well, we'll run these singlings off, about eight or ten gallons, sometimes twelve.

"I'll have this still full of singlings and go back and pour 'em in a barrel. I'll go right back and repeat it over and over till I'll get me a barrel of this what I call singlings. Well, now I'll take my old still apart and wash and scrub it. Have to wash ever'thing thoroughly clean —worm, arm, still, cap, and ever'thing. Take you about three hours or three hours and a half to get it cleaned up ready for your second run.

"Then I'll put these singlings back in the still. Get 'em on the far now and get 'em to boiling, just up in the center, like you was a-making sorghum, you know, when they go to foaming up in the pan. I'll cap 'em up like I did in the first place. Well, I'll pull my far down to a very small far—you wouldn't want to overheat it. Just heat it enough to get it started to boil good enough, and then just keep a small steady far under it. Keep about one temperature all the time. About an hour after you capped your still up again, your first shots of alkiehol begin to run. Two hundred proof. You'd catch that in a jar or jug, whatever you wanted to catch 'em in. Set it around. I always mark mine—number one, two, three, four, like that. Catch it in a gallon fruit jar or gallon jug. Sometimes I'd catch it in a gallon jug.

"When I'd get this run off down to where it gets so weak it wouldn't bead—you see, it is too strong to bead when it first comes out of a run like we're speaking of; sometimes you can catch ten or twelve gallons too strong to bead—well, then you catch you so much and this is good beading whiskey, about ninety to a hundred to hundred and ten proof. Then it runs down until it won't bead a-tall. And we call that backings. Then I'll catch a half a bushel of these backings, and then I'll cut it all off and get ready to make my whiskey.

"Take my first shots, my middle batch, and my weak batch, and I'll get me two old washtubs. I'll put me so much of one kind in there and so much of another. Take me a stick and keep it stirred up good. I'll keep a-tasting, you know, clear down in the bottom, and shaking it.

I'd put some in a bottle and give it three shakes and turn it back upright. Get the bead of the whiskey till it would be the size of a squirrel's eye—that's the way I allas judged it. I'd have a hundred and ten proof whiskey. And I'd keep on that way till I got my whole batch o' whiskey just the way I wanted it. Jar it up and go to selling it then.

"That's the way I started making whiskey and the way I run it when I didn't have more than five barrels of mash to run off. But if I was making up to thirty barrel and making in a big fashion, I'd have to have two stills, a hundred gallon and a thirty. I'd take this hundred-gallon still, and of course I sugared that time—put sugar in it and that made a lot more and stronger singlings. I'd run this big still full into singlings and put that in the little still, and I'd have both going at oncet. Build me a furnace on the left and a furnace on the right, and each one meeting the other. I have at times used the same trough for both worms. Take the singlings from the big still and put in the little, and keep 'em both going that a-way.

"I saw some big stills in Louisville a few months ago, but I couldn't tell what they was trying to do. Went down there to see my two sons. Had a purty good time and found my boys working ever' day and one of 'em took me out to see a big 'stillery. They make plenty o' whiskey down there, but when we went through we didn't see a thing in there but old big barrels and vats. Of course, they color their whiskey— bonded, it is called—and cut down on the proof. I never did see a man in here but wouldn't druther have moonshine—if it is made right— than bonded colored stuff. Now buddy, I guess I've made in my lifetime about as much as they had mashed up in there and in stock.

"Well, the stuff I've just told you to make was straight corn whiskey. For it you don't put a thing in it but just your meal and malt corn and the flour on top to keep in the heat. There is as much difference between corn and sugar whiskey as they are in between sweet milk and sour milk. Straight corn whiskey has got a sweet mellow mild taste. You can drink all of it you want and hardly ever get a headache. You can drink it and get too much on your stomach, and you can belch and spit it up. You take sugar whiskey, and, if you get too much of that, it comes back the hard way; you think your stomach and all is coming up with it. Straight corn sells for about four times what you get for sugar liquor. Sometimes if you have good luck, you get two gallons and a quart of straight out of one barrel.

"Now we are going to put up some sugar mash. Get you a sixty-gallon barrel and make her full up of meal and water like we done before, but instid of putting malt in it, you put in fifty pounds of sugar and stir that up good and let it set. And when you run it, you can get about eight gallons of sugartop whiskey. Now I never did run sugartop in the old-fashioned way. Takes too much time handling all them singlings. For the other way a-making, then, we put in what is called a thumping kag. The way a thumping kag works, you hook your old still up just like I explained, but you would have your thumping kag at the end of the arm where the worm connected in the old-fashioned still. You have you a ten-gallon barrel a-setting there and drill you a hole in it, and let your arm reach down in it about six or eight inches. On the other side of this kag we drill another hole down in the top and make us another chuck [wooden pipe]. This reaches to the bottom of the kag. We put an arm on this chuck a foot or two long and connect our worm to it. Use a coil worm and put it in your flake barrel. This gives us a thumping kag between our worm and our still.

"The steam runs from that still into this thumping kag, and we catch about four gallons of singlings and take them and pour 'em in the thumping kag. And then when the steam goes into that thumping kag, it comes out of there good whiskey from then on as long as you run, you see. You don't have to take it out and clean up ever'thing the way we did the other way. If you've got fifty barrels of mash, you can run all of 'em ever'time you put that still up.

"I learned most about a still by going and helping my dad. But over there on Leatherwood I got to helping old Hiram Holbrooks, and he was a regular old moonshiner, the best in there. I was purty well experienced before I went off to the army. After I come back, I made with my brothers a right smart. An old man of Evarts town was a regular old drinker. My brothers-in-law went over there on a timber job and found out I's making, and they would get some on weekends and take it back. That old man got hold of some of that and wanted more. They had taken some in an old bottle. I called it a turtle shell, the only one I had seen in my life like it.

"Well, I was setting up there on the railroad track. Looked down the road and saw five men a-coming up, and I didn't know one of them from sight. I said to myself, 'They're damn revenues right now.' They come up and set down beside me and asked me about some whiskey. I told them hell about whiskey, I didn't know anything about whiskey.

"The signal was that bottle I had let the boys have. They told me who they was, but I didn't believe them. Showed me that bottle. 'Well,' I said, 'you must be telling the truth.' I said, 'If you hain't, you must be sons o' bitches.'

"They said they wasn't no law. I showed 'em I had my forty-five on. I said, 'I've got whiskey—a-plenty.'

"I went off down the road with 'em and sold twenty-five gallons that night. It was sugar, and I got five dollars a gallon for it.

"One time my brother was making and had a feller helping him. They heared the revenues was hunting for 'em in that country, and they was scared to go to their still. They told me if I would run that run off for 'em, they'd pay me five dollars a day and ten dollars a night. They had sebemteen barrels mashed up. I didn't have no fambly, single, and about fourteen or fifteen years old. I took 'em up.

"I went to running that whiskey, and I had sixty-eight gallons run off. Stored it back in the hill. I was a-setting there, and the old thumping kag was just a-clucking. Seemed to me you could hear it thirty yards off. Making right in the edge of an old field, where a little holler came, and they had dug out in the bank and you could look over there from the field and couldn't see a thing. I was a-setting there one night running, just about done anyhow. I had a 30-30 marlin rifle gun setting beside me. I knowed I's a-bucking the law and weren't afraid of nothing.

"They'd hunted in that branch about all day. I peeped out in that old field, and there was one of them revenues, so clost to me I could see him bat his eyes. He was looking right up the holler. And he never did spy me. I scooted around the hill and got hold of my rifle. I thinks to myself, 'Old feller, if you come on up here, I'll drop you right here.'

"I had that right in my mind. The old feller turned off and went back down the hill about thirty yards. They was six or eight of them, and they come that nigh a-getting my whiskey and mash. I'd got away. I'd went right over a little bank and could have been gone if they had ventured up. They never did see no smoke. You can't see any steam from a still but only of the morning or late about dusky dark. You can't smell it or the still coming up, but you can coming down. They's in below it.

"I'll now tell you about how I got along back in Hoover's administration. You know, times got awful hard. We's logging at the time, but they had to shet down. We couldn't sell lumber, and ever'body just quit and nobody had no money saved.

"Some of the boys went to Evarts and took a timber job, just to make enough to feed their stock. They wanted me to go with 'em, but I had a purty good sized crop out that year. I couldn't leave it, and I took a notion to crop and make whiskey. It was selling for four dollars a gallon—when you could sell it.

"Now I went to making it. Put me up some mash and went and borrowed me an old still and worm. Mashed up one barrel and run that off. I think I made a gallon and three quarts of whiskey. Well, I turned right around and mashed that barrel up and set my whiskey back. I sawed me two old holler linn gums and reamed 'em out for barrels to mash in. The next run I made twenty-eight gallons. I kept on making it and storing it away, couldn't sell it much. I'd buy back materials and make whiskey, 'cause I knowed the times weren't going to stay that bad allas. I made the most I ever had on hand at one time: I'd salted away 168 gallons.

"I found out that the revenue men was looking for me. A boy down at Barbourville—I had soldiered with him—turned me in. They come up there on Greasy Creek and talked with a feller. He told 'em, 'He's making somewhere on that branch, but I don't know exactly where.' They looked all day and up into the night. I knowed it, but made right on.

"I was standing there by the old still, putting jars under the worm and taking the full ones out. I'd drunk all the beer [mash] I wanted, nearly made me high. I's standing there, and I heard a noise out through the tree tops where old timber had been cut. I clomb up on a little hickory pole that I had cut right at the mouth of the dreen [drain], just sawed him down and never cut him plumb off. Left it on the stump with green leaves on it so they couldn't see in there. The rest of my still was surrounded with earth. I was ready with my pistol, standing there ready, and that noise kept on coming right at me and my still and all that whiskey stored away there. It was getting about dusky dark, and I couldn't see good. I was peeping through the underbrush, and all at once an old white-faced hog peeked his head through there. Tell you the truth, I never come more nigh fainting in all my life. I never thought about my pistol when that damn hog stuck his head through that bresh.

"I'll tell you one more, and it will give you an idea how we carried on in our whiskey making. Back when I was young, we made whiskey along a little 'cause it was about the only way we had to collect up any money to keep ourselves in clothing and ever'thing. We made our eats on the farm, and we'd get out and 'still up some whiskey for tax money, you know, and so forth. We'd play jokes on one another. Maybe they'd be one still in this holler and maybe a half a mile away would be another in that holler. It'd just be a chance and time that a revenue would come around to hunt up our still. We had signals worked out to warn us. If the people at the mouth of a creek spied any revenues coming into the valley, they was supposed to ring the old dinner bell or shoot three shots. If we heared ary one, we knowed to sail out of there across the point.

"Two fellers was making in a holler when I was staying with my sister Mandy, and I took a notion to make me a run or two with 'em and mashed me up an old barrel or two. One of these men didn't care for nothing, but the other was awful scary. He was all the time looking for the law. One night they sunt me to get the supper. We'd been running for about three days. And I went and got the supper and took a notion I'd play a prank on them two fellers. I got one of the womenfolk to promise to toll the bell after so long. Most of the time the women wouldn't want to shoot a gun. Instid of me going back up the holler, I went out across the point and up in behind them. It was getting about dusky dark. The timber was green, but they'd been a storm blowed out an old limb and the leaves had dried on it. It was nearly right straight off to where they's at. That old bell begun to toll out, and I laid holt of that old bresh and started running down the hill. It went like a army a-coming.

"That scary fellow jumped up and left there, and he never come back there that night. The other one he run out to the mouth of the holler, it scared him so bad. I went down there and laughed all I wanted to and stayed with the old still. Along late in the night he took a notion he'd come back. I looked down the holler—the moon was kindly shining—and I'd see him peep up out of the branch next to the timber line. He'd come out and peep and then slink back a piece. When they found out it was me, you talk about a ragging, boy, I got it.

"Well, sir, I never was caught at a still, what time I was making, and I've made as much as any man in these hills. The law wa'n't bad to hunt us down, even if they knowed we was making. They knowed they couldn't enforce the law, and, if a man kept it quiet, they never bothered him. I've even had the local forces to tell me to stay outten the hills—when they heared some revenue was coming to get up a raid. Course they knowed I's a-making, but they knowed that I's a law-abiding man in ever'thing else, had a fambly, and had to eat and pay taxes. They never did ketch me." I had a similar interview with Dave.

"Now I've made a good lot of moonshine in my time," Dave said in his turn. "I begun when we lived back in Perry County. My dad was making then, but I learnt from old Hiram Holbrooks. He was the moonshiningest man that ever made in Perry County and was said to make the best whiskey that was made anywhere in the state. I started with him. He liked me and wanted me to learn how. He give me three bushel of corn to start on. I took it to the mill and had it ground into meal. Then he give me a half a bushel of corn to sprout and make into malt corn to use in my mash. And I mashed with him, put up a run with him on the Clover Fork of Leatherwood Creek, the first moon-shining I ever done. He was the one that made it. I just stayed with him, packed water and stuff for him, and done whatever he wanted me to. He was the man that made that batch ,'cause I was only about fif-teen, going on sixteen then. My part was about forty gallons that time. I stayed away from my mother and tried to keep it hid from her. She found out I's a-making, and she bagged and convinced me to sell what I had made and go out to the Pine Mountain School and work and not make moonshine. Well, I wanted to mind my mother, something I allas tried to do. Well, after she died, then, I didn't have nobody to 'suade me not to make moonshine, and I went back, through bad company and 'suaded by violators, to making whiskey again on Gabe's Branch.

"I made there for fourteen months in one place, and hoping old man Holbrooks learnt me how to make. Well, we had three stills up and outfits in the same holler. It was in a cleared field except a brush thicket by a watercourse. We made right in the middle of that brush thicket. I didn't do anything but make; the other party he carried it off and done the selling. He allowed his men to come to where I's making so I could load 'em up there, somebody we knowed. I stayed there and made day and night. In the daytime we would have a watch to look out for us for revenues. The watch would get out in a place where he could see fairly everywheres and not let 'em get on us too close. We had a sign for 'em, and we'd know what it meant. If they farred one shot, it would mean that bootlaggers was coming after whiskey, and not be afeared. Well, two shots meant that some people was going by the road and no harm in them. But with three shots it was the revenues, and watch out. And when they would far three shots, we grabbed everything setting loose and lit out of there. Any whiskey setting around we would get away to the bushes, and sometimes we could get everything out. If it was a false alarm, or if they missed us and went to some other place, we would stay low for a day or two and keep an eye on the revenues and see where they went to and when they got out of there before we went back to making.

"I made there for fourteen months and never got raided till a certain party who was making with us got mad. He told me he was going to have me cut up. He was going to bring 'em and show 'em the place. Well, I had my watchman out and was trying to run off what I had mashed up. I would run a barrel off and have the barrel carried off and saved. I had it all run off but two barrel and had forty-some gallons of whiskey carried off and hid. I got the alarm that the revenue was in. I had to leave there and also leave sebem gallons of whiskey and my still there. I didn't have much there 'cause I's not going to mash back when I's going to get raided and cut up. I got in the clear,

and they come and cut up what was left and taken the moonshine. I
guess they thought they got all I had, but they didn't. You see, we had
three stills that we run at the same time to get along faster, and we had
two of them out of the way and nearly all of the other'n. They got two
of my barrels and them full of beer—I was going to run them that
night. Well, after they cut that un up and left, I went back the next
day and went to putting me up a furnace at another place, about three
hundred yards above where I had been making, but in another holler.
I made there for about five months without any trouble. But some parties from over on Bailey's Creek, bootlaggers, got so bad with it they
got indicted all over the place. Then they lit into us. Old man Wright
Winn indicted me on five counts—operating moonshine still, selling
moonshine whiskey, transporting moonshine whiskey. The law was
hard on moonshining then, and, if they handled ye, they could give
ye two year. Well, I studied it would be better for me to leave there
then and not be 'rested on them cases than to have trial. So I left.

"I went to the C. & O. Railroad and got me a job about sebem mile
from Hazard. I worked on the railroad and bootlagged all the time,
but I didn't make any. Bootlaggers would come in there with a load,
and I'd buy 'em out and peddle it out of a night while I worked of a
day, or peddle of a day while I worked of a night. Made a profit on it.
Bootlagged all the time I was there for twenty-sebem months and never got turned up for it. I come back acrost the Pine Mountains to my
brother's and stayed there and bootlaged awhile. The law didn't run
out for five year, and I still had them indictments again me, you see. I
dodged for nearly five year, and the old feller that indicted me died
and passed on. I went to Bailey's Creek then and got me a job loading
coal. But I still sold whiskey, sold it right on. Loaded coal of a day,
come back acrost Pine Mountain where I moonshined and bootlagged
all the time, buy me a load of whiskey and pack it over there and boot-
lag it out. I carried it on my back, four gallon in a sack, across Pine
Mountain, then across Gabe's Mountain, and on to Bailey's Creek.
Most of the time I'd carry it across three mountains—Cutshin Mountain, Gabe's Mountain, and Pine Mountain. Even sometimes I'd go on
through Bailey's Creek and carry it across Black Mountain.

"I remember they's a cornival [carnival] in at Evarts in below Bailey's Creek one time. I was working at the Bailey's Creek mine and found out about that cornival to come in there, and I made three trips across them mountains, carried twelve gallon of whiskey over there, and hid it. And the night of the cornival I sold all them twelve gallon of moonshine. Sold it for forty dollars a gallon.

"But my money never did do me no good I got out of whiskey. It come easy and it went easy. And I believe today the reason I never got nothing out of whiskey making was 'cause my mother was all the time again' it and she told me never to do it and she bagged me not to. But I went ahead, after she left here, going again' her will. And I think that is the reason the money I got out of whiskey never done me no good.

"Well sir, I guess I made over 10,000 gallon of whiskey all told. I wouldn't have no ideas, but I know I've made more than that. And I sold five times more than I made. But I don't make none now; I hain't drunk a drap of whiskey in sixteen year, won't fool with it no way, makes me mad ever' time I see it, can't stand to smell it, can't stand to be where it's at—I don't want a thing to do with it. After I got up in my late years I realized what I'd done back in the first part of my days, spent all the good part of my life violating the law and doing things that my mother didn't want me to. I see where I missed it. And my father he is ninety-sebem years old and living today, and I have had several nar' ex-capes from the law. After I was first married and living on Bailey's Creek, I had a lot of whiskey in the house. Had sebem gallon in a box and had a few layers of empty fruit jars on top. They were searching for goods that had been stole from camp. They went all over my house and finally come to that box and commenced setting them empties out of there. Got down through some of the last layer and one of 'em said, 'Well, I don't reckon he's got anything in there. They look like they are all empty.' I come that nigh getting catched and taken off then.

"I went to work—"

Dave's wife had heard what he was recording and came hurriedly to the door at this moment. Just as he finished the last paragraph, she spoke up, "I'd be ashamed to tell it. I would, I'd be ashamed to tell it, to let my younguns hear me tell sech stuff as that."

The session was over.

Jim's and Dave's stories of making whiskey give us a rather vivid picture of the process, as well as some of the danger and trouble involved. To look at their record alone we may be prompted to condemn them for contributing to the problems of the region and for disregarding the law. But perhaps their case can be lightened, or at least partially explained, by sketching in the background of whiskey making among the people of Kentucky.

Whiskey making has always been a handicraft among the English, Scottish, and Irish from the Middle Ages, as names like Brewer and Bracer still testify. The process has been handed down from household to household as have other crafts and skills. Settlers of the land west of the Appalachians, largely peoples from the British Isles, brought their habits and folkways with them. As soon as the people found a valley to their liking in eastern Kentucky, they continued their self-sufficient way of life, making by hand all that they possessed. When they had more of any commodity than they needed for themselves, they sold it for money to pay taxes and to buy "brought on" necessities. The marketing of timber alone, with the struggles and hardships involved, makes a sagalike story. The men had to cut the timber and run it to the bottom of the hill, where they built a splashdam across the creek to make a flood when needed to carry the logs out to the larger streams. Here the logs were made up into rafts with rudder and tiller and were left until the spring rises and floods. Men then guided the crafts down winding, flooded rivers to the lowland markets.

Enterprising men who had a little money ahead bought up the people's cattle and drove them in large herds over winding upland trails to the railheads in the Bluegrass, a distance of sometimes 150 miles. They drove herds of sheep and hogs and flocks of turkeys and geese out of the mountains in the same way. They were able in this way to make their produce walk to market.

This could not be done with grain, fruit, and vegetables. The latter two commodities were preserved in profusion for home use and for barter among the neighbors. As for the grain, it helped to fatten the stock, and what was left over was turned into whiskey, put up in barrels, and hauled out. In the Bluegrass it found its way to the keelboat wharves and went down the rivers to New Orleans. By the time of the Civil War whiskey had become one of the chief sources of money income, pincipally because it was a steady source of income, whereas the timber, the herds, and the flocks were seasonal products. But dating from the time of that war, whiskey has been taxed, at times so heavily as to be punitive. The tax most of the time has equaled or exceeded the manufacturing cost of the product. And from that day to this, more and more whiskey has gone underground: it has been made by moonlight in hidden places, put up in smaller containers, transported in the bootlegs and saddlepockets of "blockaders," and sold outside the usual channels of trade.

The control of unlicensed whiskey makers up until 1918 was in the hands of state officials. The officers of the smallest unit of government, the county, were the county judge, the high sheriff, and his district subordinates, the constables. These men, especially the sheriff and his deputies, were acquainted with every family in the county—they had to assess property, issue various licenses, collect taxes, and keep records of the people from births to deaths. When we realize that the county officials were often related to many families in the county, had to rely on the citizens for election, and in many other ways were in sympathy with the men of the county and their large families, we should not expect that all laws were rigidly enforced, especially one so seemingly unjust and exorbitant as the whiskey tax.

This state of affairs prevailed in most mountain counties when the Prohibition Amendment was passed in 1918. The burden of enforcement was then shifted to the federal government. The smallest unit of federal government became the state district, comprising several counties. The staff was extremely small, made up of a judge and a district marshal or two. The marshal had authority to ask for help from county officers. When a marshal had evidence of whiskey making in a county (from reports and confessions made by bootleggers and drunks), he organized a "raid" for a county and called on the sheriff and constables for help.

Now we can see how Jim and Dave could make whiskey for many years and almost never be molested, never be arrested, and therefore never be involved in killing and being killed. The constables of their districts often sent them word beforehand of an organized raid. The men set watches and prepared to get away from the vicinity of a still, always taking the most valuable items (worms and other hardware) and the most damning evidence (whiskey and personal belongings). When the officers came upon a still, they could not make any arrests, but they always carried with them pickaxes and hammers. With these they proceeded to smash the jugs and fruitjars, pour out the barrels of mash, cut the hoops off the barrels, and stave pick holes in the cooker, still, and other vessels.

No two raiding parties were ever alike, I suppose, but they varied between two extremes, from orderly to violent, depending largely upon the marshal and his attitude. The distillers as a rule had but one desire, and that was to escape arrest. The story of the little boy who, when offered fifty cents to tell where his parents were, asked for the money in advance and explained by saying, "If you go up there, you ain't coming back," is highly exaggerated. Most men at a still, though they carried guns, did not want the crime of murder upon them.

Some marshals conducted orderly raids into mountain counties. They were aware of the fact that they had an unpopular and almost impossible law to enforce. Some were human enough to know that the county officials sympathized with an old farmer (sincere, honest, law-abiding in every way except moonshining) who had a large family and very little income. The marshals knew also that hunting a law-breaker did not give them the right to commit murder. Thus, when the officers made their approach on a still in some dark hollow, the rule of conduct was to arrest the operators if they were present and arrestable. But if one had a fair start in the other direction, he was not their man and should not be shot unlawfully in the back. If he were identified, he could be arrested later and handled by due process of law.

On the other hand, some marshals might be out to get their man, or the county officials might have political or personal scores to settle. The raiding party would go armed with Winchesters and pistols and steal upon the scene from all sides. They would accost the still opera-tor with threats and shouts. Upon one involuntary move on his part the armed men would riddle his body with bullets. Many men in the mountains thus have been shot down in violent and unlawful ways. The officers can easily say, and usually do say, that the man resisted arrest or offered violence or attempted to run from the scene of an illicit still. But no matter what the alibi given for such a crime, the entire citizenry of the county is so shocked by such a sordid murder that they tend to show less respect for law and its brutal enforcement.

When Jim Couch said that he made whiskey to pay his taxes and buy food and clothing, he was giving his side as he saw it. He and Dave made whiskey through the 1930's because there was almost no other source of income. The fact that they and others do not make it now is a sign of the times. The Second World War brought many changes. With it came a revival of mining, lumbering, and other industries. Moonshining among the Couches and over the whole region almost ceased, because the people had easier, more honorable, and better paying jobs for supporting their families.

5. Dave and Jim, Their Folkways

"Oncet my grandfather was a-thrashing wheat in the cove," Dave began when I started the recorder for a session of pioneer legends, "and he heared a hog squealing 'way up towards the top of the hill under a clift. He was thrashing that wheat with a big frailpole, what they allas used for it. He just laid his pole on his shoulder and broke in a run up the side of the mountain to find out what was wrong with his hog. Got up there, and they was a bear had it hugged right up in its arms a-gnawing it in the top of the head. He lit in on that bear with his frailpole, and he beat that bear to death before it would turn the hog loose. He took the bear in and skinned him and had him a good warm bearhide and some meat.

"He went again into the woods, him and his boys, and they holded a bear in the holler of an old chestnut tree. They was a hole went in just above the top of the ground, and the bear went in there. The dogs pushed right on in on it, and they fit the bear till they finally killed it. It had hurt a dog so bad they had to go on and leave the dog there. So they skinned the bear and took the hide and all the meat they could carry and went on.

"It got late on 'em, and they decided to lay out under a clift that night. They had 'em some of that bear meat br'iled for supper, and then they laid down. In that day and time the painters [panthers] were so thick you couldn't hardly do nothing like handle fresh meat in the hills for 'em; they would come to you and try to take it. A whole gang of them painters surrounded that clift that night, coming up, trying to get at that bear meat. Grandpa said he'd throw great chunks of far at them painters and scatter 'em off down the hill. They [Dave often pronounced *they* with a long *e*] had to fight them painters all night to keep 'em from coming in and taking their bear meat and maybe hurting somebody. Fit 'em off with far chunks.

"An old bear got to using around clost to my grandpa's house one time. He had some bee gums, and they would try to tear into them and rob 'em. Well, he thought he'd set a trap for that old bear. He got a trough and took him out about a half a gallon of honey from a gum and got about a quart of moonshine whiskey. He mixed the two up and poured it all into that trough. Went out there next morning and saw he had that old bear. There he was—laying drunk. He was just laying there flat on his back playing with his feet. Grandpa shot his brains out and got him another pile of meat and a good bearhide.

"This is another true bear story, and it goes back to my mother's grandfather. His wife went to her neighbor's house, about a mile and a half from one house to the other. People was thin settled in that day and time, and they was plenty of bear. She was there with her baby four months old and had to start back home. There was some clivves on the way. And the clift on one side of her was close, and they was a big bear a-laying out under there. As she passed, why it retch out and bit her little baby's head off and swallered it. She had to go on in home crying with the rest of her baby. And the old man he got him another man or two and went and killed the bear and cut it open and got the little baby's head back. They buried it with the baby. Now that was a true story, happened over there on Greasy Creek.

"My mother was borned and raised in Harlan County and my father in Perry County. When they married, they settled down over there in the Sang Branch. There wasn't very many bear and deer at that time—about all had scattered off and left. But anyhow, down in the Dollar Branch of Greasy some feller had a cornfield and something got to using in it, and it come out to be an old she-bear and her one little cub. They got out to hunting for these bears—my father, Ed Barnes, Will Minyard, John Huff, Willis Turner—they was a whole passel of 'em started hunting. And they all had their favorite dogs—my father had one he called Punk and another he called Nigger. They bayed up in a swag, and when they got up clost, they thought the dogs had cornered a gang of hogs. When they went in on 'em, the bears commenced to running ever which way, and the men follered their dogs after a bear. Some of the men went to the top of the ridge so they could get a shot at one if he crossed the point.

"My dad's and Tom Harris's dogs treed out on a flat, and when they got there they was barking up an old crooked water-oak. Up in that tree was an old bear behind some water sprouts, just hunkered down up there like somebody would. Come to find out they never had a gun, and Tom had nothing but an old thirty-two bulldog pistol, and it was so old it throwed the balls crossways. Tom up with that old pistol two shots and never tipped the bear. He just had one shot left. Dad said he got the gun from Tom and with that last shot he hit that bear right between the eyes. That old bear just sunk down, and they didn't know if they had killed him or not.

"Said they watched him around there for a little while, but he never would fall out of the tree. Dad said he pulled off his shoes and skinned that tree to kick the bear out. About the time he got up in there, why, here come another old bear right through there, scared Tom away because he didn't have no gun. And said that old bear stopped at the roots of the tree and looked up in it, and if it hadn't been for the dogs pressing him by now, he might have come up in there. Guess that was one time dad was betwixt a rock and a hard place.

"He kicked that old bear out of there and give chase to the other un. It run through Alex's Branch and got old Lewis Turner after it with an old muzzle-loading shotgun loaded with rifle bullets. They chased it from there into Rockhouse Branch of Greasy and back into Alex's Branch. Dad said they could have killed it a dozen times if they hadn't been afeared to kill the dogs. Will Minyard had a dog a-hanging right onto the old bear's jaw most of the time. Willis Turner got holt of that old muzzle-loader and cracked down at it. Well, he killed the bear and the dog too. It made Will so mad he wouldn't let Willis have nary bite of that bear meat.

"Purty soon they was all after another old big un, and run it plumb into Dollar Branch. Rob Turner lived up in there and got after it, and he didn't have no gun, only an old forty-four cap-and-ball pistol. He caught up with it and run it out of Dollar Branch into Greasy Creek and waded the water right by its side. He snapped his pistol six times right into that bear's head, and that gun wouldn't go off. That bear got away from them.

"One time my mother went to stay with her granny while the old man was gone. They lived in a log house, and for protection he had built a palin' fence around the yard about four feet high. A bear come that night and got inside that palin'. The dog barked at something all night, but the old lady was scared to get up and see what it was. Next morning there was a big bear right in the yard. It would start to climb them palin's, and the dog would grab it by the rump and it'd have to jump back on the dog. He had kept that up all night. My grandmother got the rifle-gun and killed it. That made one she killed. They allas skinned them bear and stocked up on meat for the winter. Dry the meat out like we allas do hog meat and eat it. They say bear meat was awful good. They would sell the hides or make shoes out of 'em. They made what they called moccasins. That was about all the kind of shoes they had back in my grandma's raising up.

"When my mother was just a little girl, deers was purty frequent in that country. One day the dogs got after a deer and run it right into a big hole of water below her house. The menfolks was all out hunting down to the mouth of Greasy. And mother said her mother said for her to go down there on a rock over the waterhole and see if she could see a way to get that deer. She said she went down there and got on that rock. The old deer kept swimming around and around in there. And one time when it come around under that ledge of rock, why, she just hauled off and jumped right astraddle of its neck, took it to the bottom, and helt it there till it drownded.

"I don't know about telling this un or not. Some men was hunting in Abner's Branch one time, trying to get after some bear that was using in there. They hunted all day, and the dogs was running bear and deer all over the place. One run a deer out of there and plumb out to the mouth of the branch and right across the road. Old Rock Minyard was going along the road at that time, and when that deer started up the hill away from him, he cracked down and killed that deer and never even busted the hide on it nowhere. He hit it right in the center of the bunghole."

Dave went into his pocket after his crooked briar pipe, letting me understand that his pioneering legends were exhausted. But I knew he had more, especially some old yarns about the Civil War. These I requested after he had had a good smoke.

"Well, back in the old Civil War my grandfather John Couch was a soldier, and he used to tell us boys about their ventures with the Rebels and how they fit 'em. Said one time him and a bunch of men knowed the Rebels was a-coming over a certain path, and they way-laid 'em on the top of a clift. They come riding along, and one of the Rebels in front was carrying a flag, a Rebel flag. They all picked 'em out a man to shoot offen his horse. Said he picked the flagsman. They come riding along, and they cracked down on 'em with their muskets. Killed sebem or eight of them. The rest of the Rebels jumped off their horses and took atter 'em.

"Run 'em all over the hills and plumb to the top of the mountain. Said he got away and run on till he got so hot he couldn't go no further. He rolled over behind a big chestnut log to rest. Said they got so clost on him he could hear 'em a-getting their breath—they come so nigh a-getting him.

"The next battle they had was over around Big Stone Gap, Virginia. They run into the Rebels over there, and the Rebels got too hot for them and scattered 'em. Captured one of my grandmother's brothers. My grandfather and another one of my great-uncles got away. Said they come back toward Lynch there on the Virginia side of the mountain and set there all night. He had got separated from my great-uncle and didn't know where nobody was at. Next morning, time day got to breaking, he could hear something thrashing in the sticks out from him. He got to peeping around, with his old musket ready to kill it. Thought it was a Rebel. When he spied it, it turned out to be Uncle

Hen Shepherd. Said they had set in about thirty foot of one another all night and didn't know one another was there that clost.

"Old man Arie Shepherd got captured, but he begin to try his best to get away before they took him off somewhere to prison. The Rebels had a lot of sheep gathered up where they had driven them off from the people's fields for the last few days. Arie got down amongst their sheep in a lot there, and he would baa like a sheep and move around in them till he found a way to get out and ex-cape the guards around their camp. Finally he saw his chance, and he broke through and run. Thought they was after him, and he run across that Black Mountain and run plumb on in home on Big Leatherwood. And he was so hot and give out, he laid down and never got up again. Laid there and died, he had got so overheated.

"The Rebels come through the Greasy Creek country. And they surrounded the home of old man Alex Turner's. Robbed him, took what he had, all the grub he had to eat. Then they all told him they wanted his gun. He told 'em he never had no gun. They got to searching and hunting all over the place, and finally found his old hog rifle—hid betwixt the feather bed and straw bed. They took it and started off with him too. Said they were going to kill him. His wife follered 'em with their babies and cried and bagged. And finally they turned him loose.

"That's about all I know of the Civil War stories. People don't tell them old legends much any more, and I've about forgot the most of them. But I used to hear them from just about anybody around where I growed up, and they could make them things sound so scary and dangerous the hair would stand up on my head. It was mostly the women and the old men who was left in here to take care of theirselves. Nearly everybody in here was called Republicans; that means they was for Lincoln and the North. But just any bunch o' soldiers passing through would want to take everything they seen. People had to hide out their cattle and horses—take 'em to the woods and tie 'em up—had to hide out their belongings like guns and quilts and tools, dig holes in the gyardens or in the stalls of their barns, and bury 'em. They would hide their meat and cans of lard in holes under the floor or just anywhere to preserve it. And every man that could carry a gun was allas under suspicion. If the Rebels couldn't get a man to go with 'em to join their forces, they would be just as apt to hang him as anything else. When my mother's father was still under age, he was laid under suspicion, and for the last year of the war he laid out under a clift and let the folks slip food to him of a night to keep 'em from taking him out of here.

"I guess you have heared about Rebel Rock up here on the road crossing Pine Mountain. I can tell ye about how that happened, but they are several ideas about the details of it. They was a bunch of Union soldiers come up through the Pore Fork here looking for Rebels that would slip over here from Virginia and make raids on the people and carry off their food stuff and drive off their cattle. They run into a purty good sized detachment of the Rebels right in here. They went to fighting and shooting one another, and the Union boys got the best of the other side and put 'em on the run. And naturally they took to the hills. If you have ever noticed, you see the rocks and ridges in the Pine Mountain stick out up the hill and not down it. The Rebels broke into groups, ever' man for hisself, and about three of 'em took up the spur of the point and some Union soldiers right after 'em. They come up to the upper end of that spur and couldn't get no further. They was cornered on the edge of that clift, about seventy-five feet high. They had to turn and fight and risk being killed, or jump off that high clift and take their chances. Two of the Rebels turned and tried to shoot their way back down the spur, but they got killed and the Union men throwed the corpses off. The other man thought he could make it off 'cause they was a purty good sized fir tree just off the clift and retch up nearly to the top. He jumped into that tree, and, as luck would have it, he landed in the top limbs and skinned down and got away. They say the frames of them dead Rebels laid up there in the crevices till the meat dropped offen their frames. Nobody would take a chance to bury 'em, afeared somebody would think they favored the other side."

Dave became quiet and reached for his pipe, a signal for me to stop the recorder. Some of the interesting pioneering folktales that he told during this and other sessions were Indian Binge, We Killed a Bear, and Seven Dead Indians [Nos. 152, 153, 151].

Jim had begun to show a great deal of interest in this collecting project, especially after I came back from Georgia in 1954 and pursued him to help me get a complete sampling of the family's lore. I had become increasingly aware of the exhaustless nature of a family's traditions. Since Jim believed in remedies and practiced bloodstopping, I let him talk at some length on these two folkways.

"I am going to tell you a whole string of witchcrafts," Jim said as he settled down to recording, "that happened up and down Cutshin and Greasy creeks, and most of them I saw with my own eyes.

"One of my great-great-uncles was named Mat Layson [fictitious], and he was a witch. His brother had a boy named Henry, and he told me this happened to him. Old Mat taken him out one time to train him to be a witch. Well, Henry said he took him out one morning just as the sun was rising over the hill. Said he set a silver plate he had down on the ground behind him. He cursed the Lord and blessed the Devil and then shot at the sunball. Said he farred three shots, and every time he would shoot, a drop of clear blood would fall in that silver plate behind him.

"He told Henry, 'Now put your hand on top of your head and the other'n at the bottom of your feet. Now swear that you'll give all between those hands to the Devil to do with you just as he pleases.' Henry, being a boy, did what he told him. Old Mat said, 'Now we'll go right over to the old lick and kill us a deer.'

"Well, Henry said he went on over to the old lick with him, and he told him to be quiet. Said Mat said some kind of ceremony and made some kind of noise, and the deer was coming through there just like a gang of sheep. He ra'red up and said, 'Lord how mercy!' and when he said that, they just vanished and were gone. The old man cussed him out and told him never to call on the Lord again. He told him he wouldn't.

"They went on up to the top of another ridge, and old Mat said, 'Now we are going to kill us a turkey.' He said his ceremony again and some talking, and he said forty or fifty big turkeys flew in there and flopped right down and lit all over the ground around them. He said he just ra'red up again and said, 'Lord how mercy!' He said when he said that, all the turkeys disappeared.

"He said old Mat told him, 'For a little I'd kill you right here. You don't know how to be a witch.' Uncle Henry said he was afraid to tell that for a long time after, afraid he would die.

"Weren't long after that old Mat went to Henry Shepherd's father's house to try and get some milk. And they told him they didn't have milk to spare. Just enough for the fambly. Well, in a little while it got so their cows wouldn't give no milk. They'd just run into the gap a-bawling and cutting a shine. They wouldn't give no milk. They got to inquiring about it, and they found an old feller over there who was a kind of witch doctor, and he told Henry's mother that a man would come there between this time and tomor' night. Says, 'Don't you let him have a thing offen this place. Don't even let him have a drink of water.' He said, 'If you don't, your cows will be all right and never be bothered again.' Well, the next day she looked out and saw the old man Mat a-coming. Said he come over and set around a few minutes, and he asked her to let him borrey some salt. She told him that she didn't have it. And he asked her to let him borrey some coffee, and she said she didn't have that. Everything he would ask for, she would tell him she didn't have it. He said, 'I believe I want a drink of water.' And she said, 'They hain't a drop of water in the house.' He went out and got that water bucket and took the dipper and turned it up and drained the water bucket enough to get him a swaller of water before he left there.

"Another time old Mat showed his witchcrafts. Back in Leatherwood in Perry County it was awful thin settled in there and in Greasy and along the Harlan County line. An old man there by the name of Ransom Turner nearly allas kept a bunch of dogs. And they would get over on Big Laurel Creek and in that section and jump a deer and bring it over to Leatherwood, and then they would lose it in the creek where old Mat lived.

"Uncle Henry said one time he heared the dogs coming down the old House Branch of Leatherwood and said his daddy jumped on a horse and took down the creek lickety-split to see what they's after. They was a big waterhole there on Leatherwood. The deers when they got run in there they would generally run in that waterhole for protection from the dogs. He rode his horse like a ball of far down there. Got purty close to the place, and he saw the deer come in across the road. And all at once the dogs turned right back the other way, just bawling every breath in their back tracks. Said he rode a few paces further where a hornbean bush growed right next to the small creek. He stopped and saw old Mat right in the top of that hornbean bush just a-wringing and twisting and a-tying them limbs in knots, and them dogs every one turning on the back track. He said the ugliest word he ever heared his daddy say in his life he said right then. He said he looked up at old Mat and said, 'Mat, if they was no hell and if I had a gun, damned if I didn't kill you, you old turkey cock.'

"His daddy went to the waterhole and got him a deer anyway. You see, old Mat witched the dogs and turned them on their back tracks toward home soon as the deer run off in there, so's he could get the deer. But they had seen the dogs after them and saw the deer run to the waterhole this time and got their deer.

"That's all I care to tell on Mat Layson, but they was another old feller down there on Greasy Creek name of Charles Isaacs [fictitious] who was a witch and a doctor and a preacher all in one. I have heared different people tell about his witchcrafts, and some instances I know are true because I saw them myself. I was coming from Hyden one time, me and a man by the name of Carter Turner. And old Ike Whitaker they called him lived at the mouth of Maggard's Branch. It got up in the night, and me and Carter put up to stay all night with him. He was Carter's uncle, and old Charles was there. Carter had a dog that he bought off of Coon Creek and had him chained with a chain, and we tied him to the palin' fence outside of the house.

"We was setting around and weren't noticing Charles too much. He was an old funny feller. He raised up and said, 'If I'm not mistaken, your dog is loose.' Well, Carter got up and we went out and, sure enough, the dog was loose. We put the chain back around the dog's neck and wired it with a wire, and it was impossible for the dog to get loose.

"We went back in and was setting there talking, and in about thirty minutes old Charles said, 'Your dog is loose again.' We started up and got on the outside of the door, and I told Carter, said, 'You know he told a lie.' We went out there, and that old dog was loose again. We just tied him back up and went in again.

"Set around a few more minutes. Now old Ike Whitaker never had a chicken on the place. Charles raised up and started talking about chickens. Ike said, 'I hain't got a chicken on the place.' 'Why, I know you have,' Charles said. Ike said, 'I know I hain't.' Old Charles slapped his leg and crowed right big. An old rooster under the floor r'ared up and crowed just as big as you please. Ike said they weren't a chicken on that place.

"I have heared a dozen suchlike incidents on him. Old Charles had all of his cattle named. He'd go out in the yard, and if he wanted one of his cattle in, ever which one he wanted in from the field to the house, he would call its name, and that thing would throw its tail over its back and it never stopped till it got there, bawling ever' breath. He had a big gang of hogs. Other people had hogs that run right along with his'n. And he'd go out and feed his hogs, and nobody else's hogs wouldn't take a bite.

"Another thing I saw him do one time with my own eyes. I was down on Cutshin one time at a man's house, and we's out in the corn-field, big bottom of corn waist high. Old Charles rode up and rode right out into that cornfield, set down, and turned his horse loose among that corn. I was wondering if that old horse wouldn't start eating that corn. Nobody never said nothing, and Charles said that old horse could stay in there a month and he'd never crack a blade nor he wouldn't step on none. That old horse picked on around there as long as I stayed. If he ever cracked a blade, I never saw it, and he never would step on a hill of corn.

"Old Charles peddled all the time, and he would stop at people's houses and sometimes show 'em what he could do. They would go out in the barnyard, and, if they was a sheep there, he would tell it to butt the chimley, and it would draw back and butt that chimley with all power. He'd flop his arms and crow like a rooster, and ever' rooster on the place would start crowing. He witched a man's cow one time and got it to walk up a ladder into the barn loft, and they liked to never got it outten there again. He would doctor the people and take warts and wens offen them ever'where he went. He had some kind of religious beliefs, and one time he took a notion to sacrifice his son. He dug a big hole in the gyarden and put some logs and chunks in there and some far, and had his son get down in there and lay down on them burning logs. It weren't burning to do no good, and he went back in the house for another shovelful of far, and the boy jumped out of there and run off.

"What caused old Charles to die, he had a wen to come on his side and he operated on it. It set up gangerine [gangrene], and he died from it. He was a man that could do without sleep all the time, I have heared tell. They said that he never averaged more than four hours' sleep of a night. My brother-in-law tells this on him. He was with Charles one time, and they was talking about going hunting. And all at once a big fine dog run right by him and took up the hill. Charles weren't to be seen anywheres. That dog went up the hill and treed a coon and got up in that tree some way and caught it. By the time my brother-in-law got there, it was back down on the ground, and then it turned itself back into a man and there stood old Charles. Now who would believe a tale like that? I have heared my brother-in-law tell that time and again. I don't recollect another like that.

"They was an old feller there on Greasy Creek name of Ed Horner [fictitious] that ever'body called a witch. Them fellers that lived over there allas had dogs, and they hunted coons a lot, you know. They'd take their dogs and see who had the best one. They'd get out a coon hunting, and old Ed would spell their dogs, they called it, and make them bark up trees and weren't nothing in 'em. On one occasion they went hunting back in Gabe's Branch in there in the wilderness. Said their dogs run about an hour and treed, and they went to 'em and said they got up there to them and something flew out of that tree went like a load of chains and everything. They allas called it the devil flew out. They got to where they couldn't catch nothing with their dogs. A man by the name of Jake Howard lived over there on Baxter claimed he was a repeller, a feller that could turn your tricks on you. They went over to Jake's and told him about their dogs, told him Ed was spelling their dogs and their dogs weren't no 'count. Old Jake asked them, 'Now just what do you want done to him? Do you want him killed?' They said, 'No, we don't want him killed.' 'Well,' he said, 'what about putting one of his eyes out—do you reckon that would help 'him?' They finally agreed to have Ed's eye put out. Well, they come on back home and their dogs was all right, and Ed had one eye from then on. I knowed him well.

"They said he would go to their matches where they used to have these old hog-rifle shooting matches, and he would get around and tell them fellers, 'Well, your gun won't far this time.' They'd crack down and their cap would bust, but their gun wouldn't go off. They would start putting powder in the tubes of their guns. He'd take his knife out and open it and put it back between 'his lags and say it wouldn't shoot, and when he would take it out and say, 'Now your gun is all right if you will far.' I don't know how he done it. He'd hold his knife back between his legs and tell them their gun wouldn't far, and shore enough it woudn't. Then he'd take it out and tell them it would far, and she would far off so clear and purty.

"My mother told me one time when she was just a small girl a bunch of people lived in there on Greasy Creek by the name of Yates, and there was one widder woman named Hester. Said ever' time she would pass, she would want them girls, her and her sister, to go up in Rockhouse Branch and stay all night with her. Then one night her mother finally agreed to let 'em go. Said they went up there, and they done up the work. Getting supper, and the old lady never had a cow on the place. Said she told them, 'Well, I'll churn and we'll have supper ready.' She grabbed the old churn and the dishrag, and right behind the door she went. Said she stayed in there about five minutes, and she come out of there with the awfulest bowl of butter that she had taken out of that churn. She knowed she didn't have no cow, but she didn't know where she got that butter. Of course they are a lot of these things.

"They was another feller over there called old man Saw Adams. They called him a charm doctor. I have seen his miracles work. My dad had a wen, they called it, on his knee-cap one time, and it was about the size of a good-sized goose egg. He went to the regular doctors with it. They claimed they would have to pull it out, take it off— operate on it. He was passing one day, and 'he heared about how Uncle Saw Adams was a charm doctor. He was hoeing corn out in the field, and my dad just rode up and hollered out at him. Talking to him, and then Uncle Saw said to him, 'Pull your britches lag up and let me take a look at it.' He pulled his britches lag up, and he looked at it from over in the field away from it. Told him to go on. In three days there weren't a sign of a scratch on him where that wen was. That was charm. These charms is true, because I can do 'em myself. It's a secret and can't be told. If I was to tell you my secret, then it would be no good to me. I learned it from my mother. It's bloodstopping."

I said, "Maybe you should tell us about your herb remedies and then finish up with your secret bloodstopping cure."

"Well, when I was growing up, they weren't no chance to get a regular doctor to the house when you needed him. Never but one doctor inside our house that I can remember of until I got grown. My mother would gather different things in the mountains just according to how you was sick. If you had the old grips, we called it, and what the fancy doctors called pneumonia, we would go to the fields with mother, and she would gather stuff that she called horsemint, wintergreen, hornbean bark, and pine top, and boil that all together and make a tea out of it. When that don't break up a fever on you, brother, you might just as well quit.

"We never did have no colds to speak of in them days, and not near the diseases people have now'days. For colds and stuff we had nothing but quinine and calamy we bought at the drugstores. They called it Sagame Calamy, in powder form. A dose was what you could get on the point of a knife. For croup we used groundhog grease or coal oil for a medicine for that. Now if one had the misfortune of catching something like the eetch, she would take this old pokeroot and make a ooze out of it and boil it and wash you with it and kill that eetch dead as a nit, buddy. We used gunpowder for the sore mouth and salt water for the eyes.

"We used a medicine called sweet oil for the yearache. My dad got it over in Virginia. Virginia Lee I think he called it. He would put that ooze in our years to take care of a yearache. For any kind of stomach trouble or disorder we would drink sody water or vinegar. For a running off of the bowels we had three or four remedies. Most of the time we would go out and dig us some blackberry roots, steam and heat 'em, and make a syrup out of that. Make a starch out of flour sometimes. But you know when I was growing up, you didn't see much of that running off 'cause people eat hard foods all the time, such as milk, butter, meat, cabbage, and beans, stuff like that. People weren't sick not one-third of the time like they are now'days.

"Another thing for the sick stomach—we would allas try to throw up and get it offen our stomachs. We would take a little whiskey out in a pan and set it afar and burn it down to a black scum and drink the results of that. It was an awful funny tasting stuff, and I've drunk a lot of it. For the cramps, stomach ache, or bellyache, take gunpowder and mix it with cold water and throw it up off your stomach. Another thing was hookle berries—not huckleberies you know in the hills. This grows up like a sunflower and have a head on 'em. I ain't seen any in a long time. They'd grow in the gyarden. Two things for a snakebite was whiskey and what they called Japanese oil. Both good for snakebite. My dad got a bottle of Japanese oil one time when my brother got snake-bit. He couldn't get the seal cap off the top. Couldn't get it off, and he jobbed the stopper down in there, and the stuff flew and hit him in the eye, and it come in a hair causing him to go blind, when that strong medicine hit him in the eye.

"Now this bloodstopping remedy I was telling you about, I learnt it from my mother. I don't know where she come into possession of it, but they can't but one know it in the fambly. I can tell it to my fambly, but I can't never operate it no more. It's a bloodstopping method. I have tried it, and it works. I tried it up on Leatherwood one time, and an old preacher and them made fun of me. We was working together, and I was talking about it to some fellers, and about that time my brother got a piece of steel in his hand. The blood was streaming off his hand just as big as it could stream, running off his fingers, where he had cut the artery in the top of his hand. He come up and said, 'Lord how mercy, do something to stop it.' I said, 'Don't you touch it!' I told my brother, I said, 'You walk off the top of the hill and set down on that log.' He walked off and set down on that log, and in about ten minutes it stopped and cleared up. That old preacher told me, said, 'It just quit itself—you never done it. You're not a Christian, and you can't work miracles like that.' I said, 'It's not a miracle—it's only a charm.'

"Passed on a week or two, and they's a Campbell boy there had his nose bust and was bleeding him to death, already had him bleeded so weak he couldn't hardly walk. I come in from work about four o'clock. That Campbell boy's nose had been bleeding since about two o'clock. It went on till about five-thirty. Couldn't get nobody to take him out of there to Hazard to the doctor. This Holiness preacher was there, and all the men that worked there. I said, 'Uncle Jason, you don't believe what I's telling you.' I said, 'If you was to see something happen, would you believe it?' He said, 'I certainly would.' I called the boy out of the washroom, where he was holding his head with a washcloth with his nose bleeding. I hollered and said, 'Straighten up.' I said, 'Turn around.' He turned around. I said, 'Uncle Jason, do you see any blood?' He said, 'No.' I said, 'Do you believe it now?' He said, 'Yes.' That was Uncle Jason Smith.

"Another time I was coming home from work over there, and Rile Hendrix had a wife that something had happened to her. They called it the flux. Had a doctor with her two or three times, and he hadn't done her no good. Rile told me, come out in the road and stopped me, and we was talking. I said, 'Rile, I never had an experience of a thing like that, but I'll do what I can.' I put on my charm. While we was there, before I left, his wife come to the door. She come out there and said, 'You know, I'm all right now.' Rile told me she had been that way for about two days.

"Then my time come in 1918 in the World War. I don't doubt if I didn't save a thousand lives. Boys would get wounded in the war and be bleeding bad. I'd do all the same; if I got a German, I'd administrate with him the same as I would with the Americans. It can be done, and don't let nobody tell you it can't be. If nobody don't believe it, come to me and I'll show 'em that it can be.

"It is a charm and can't be used for nothing but to stop blood. It's handed down from the Old Testament in the Bible. It has come from Ezekiel. I've knowed members of other famblies that could do it too. There was an old man by the name of Jim Koontz could do it, 'cause he performed it on me. I know it worked.

"I fell off a train one time when I was small and stuck a stake in my face, and my nose bled me so weak I couldn't get to my feet. Weren't a chance to get a doctor. Jim Koontz lived about a mile away, and the saying was that Jim could stop blood. Well, when my dad come in from work, he sent another boy just as hard as he could go to Jim Koontz. When he got there, he said Jim said, the first word was, 'Has his nose bled long?' He told him yeaw, he didn't know how long though. He said, 'Well, he's wet his head.' That boy told him he didn't know whether I had or not. But by the time that boy got to Jim Koontz, my nose had never bled another drop. My nose hain't bled since that time I don't guess a half a teacupful.

"Then another man I can prove I 'formed the charm on is old man Hampton Turner. His boy came to me about one o'clock in the night and said his dad had a cat-tar in his head, he called it. The doctors claimed, or the nurse—they didn't have no doctors then—his nose was bleeding out of both nose-holes just about as free as it could bleed. The boy stopped in the middle of the road and hollered me up and wanted me to come down there. I said, 'What's the matter?' He said, 'Pap's nose is a-bleeding him to death.' I said, 'It's no sech a thing.' He said, 'It is; it's a-bleeding him to death.' I said, 'I bet you his nose hain't bleeding a drop.' I jerked my clothes on, tore out, and went to the house. When I got there, the old man's nose wa'n't bleeding a drop."

Jim came to a halt as if he had proved his point and there was nothing else to record. I asked him about the mystery of the charm, if it took faith, if he said words, or if he just thought of something. All he would say was that it could not be divulged without losing it, and he finally quieted me and finished the session by saying, "Well, I can't explore it no further with you."

These reminiscences of Jim, Dave, and other members of the family touch on many aspects of mountain life that perhaps can be summarized. From their accounts of earning a living and of enjoying their leisure we can comment upon the society of which they were a part, with its unique family, social, and environmental conditions.

The family in a rural community still remains the unit of culture.

The unit, from two to a dozen or more, lives under one roof and provides everything it needs, and, what it cannot provide, it does without. The bigger the family the better. Most family heads go forth to multiply and replenish the earth under biblical command. They have as many children as nature provides, and they welcome each and every one. Mrs. Mary Breckinridge, director of the Frontier Nursing Service in Leslie County, says that the easiest births and the healthiest and most wanted babies in the world are in eastern Kentucky. As the family grows, each member has a place and a status, and each one has work to do in keeping the unit self-sustaining.

The most important member and the undisputed head of the family unit is the father. Almost without exception he controls, directs, and leads the family like the Patriarchs of old. When called upon or referred to in any way, he is usually called "the man of the house." While he is talking business with another man, the wife and children stay in the background, the mother usually collecting the children into a back room and going on with her work. If the business concerns the father only, he will take his time and consider the whole unit, but in the end he will make his own decision. If the business involves other members, the mother, for instance, the father will state the gist of it to her and leave her alone to think it over. She will reach a decision, mention it to the father conditionally, and he will accept, modify, or reject it as he sees fit. This dominant status of the father is in no way peculiar to Kentucky mountain people. It is somewhat typical of family units over the world and especially our forebears of Scotch-Irish background. Their hardships on poor acres and their dark and fatalistic outlook on life under Calvinism have made them stern and undemonstrative.

The position of the wife and mother in a mountain home has always been a trying and difficult one. Her endless chores around a household without conveniences wear her down and bring her to an early grave. She is expected to take care of the clothing from making to mending and of the food from tending the pigs and garden to preserving the meat and vegetables and serving them on the table three times a day. Meanwhile, she is giving her life day by day to her growing children and her strength to the bearing of more. It is not uncommon to find a man of the mountains who has worn out two or three wives in this round of endless sacrifice.

The undemonstrative nature of mountain people is completely dissolved with children. As was said above, each child is wanted, and, when one comes, he or she is treated with an indulgence that surpasses understanding. The grandparents come and dandle the child and "make over" him, and, perhaps before he is standing alone, one or the other has claimed him and even given him a nickname that he will bear for life. The parents fondle him with unfeigned love, as do the older children. The baby is breastfed until the next one is on the way, and he is allowed to sleep with the mother or with both parents. When old enough, he is allowed to crawl throughout the house, next to toddle indoors and out, and finally, when he can run about, he is allowed to follow the older people to the fields and about the neighborhood. All this applies to girls also.

But at six or seven he begins to make himself useful at running errands and performing other duties suitable to his age. If he is the oldest child in the home, he will soon take on responsibilities that make him seem older than he actually is. By young adulthood he has taken on a kind of fierce individuality among the other members of the group. Each succeeding child struggles for and is given a great deal of personal liberty and respect. Certain traits, abilities, and talents appear in each, and each is free to shine in them. One child can handle the horses better than another; one can manage the mowing machine better; one can better grind the ax and sharpen the saws; one shows up early in school and is called the learner. But also one may be a little hard to manage, be balky and "contrary," and become the Cinderella with feet in the ashes most of the time. Most large families have one who is known to all as the "black sheep."

There is a close parallel between such a mountain household and the Couch family. The parallel need not be drawn at all points. Tom Couch had an average-to-large family, as sizes go in the mountains. He was the leader, and the mother was the counselor of the unit. The children developed along natural lines and came out as distinct personalities in adult life.

But this family appears to me to be a little unusual in some respects. They seem to have got along better than the average, their life having a little more quality and distinction than the typical. The father was not so stern and forbidding as some; on the contrary, he put more life and zest into living and had ways that drew his children out. He had a skill that was looked up to in the home and community —playing the banjo and singing. And all of his children tried to emulate him. The indelible little picture given by Jim may illustrate his way with them. Jim began to pick up the banjo when he was seven or eight, too short to reach both head and neck of the instrument. His father fingered the strings while he beat out the tune and the rhythm. A similar illustration may suffice for the mother's ways. While waiting for the father to come home at night, she beguiled the children and held them from the table with animal and giant stories.

One other factor making the Couch family different appears to me to be that of good native intelligence. Of book learning they had very little, for the simple reason that it was not to be had. But the fact that the members of the family were able to adapt themselves to one another and to the larger community, to draw into the family unit most of the skills of farming, mining, and lumbering, and to retain most of the inherited lore, to add to it, and to pass it on indicates above-average mental powers. A few instances of clearheaded powers of retention may be given. Old Tom actually sang from beginning to end every song we asked him to recall, though he was ninety-two at the time and had not played the banjo in twenty years. Dave recalled and told a long story that he had not heard or even thought of in thirty-five years. When Jim was ten years old, he went with his father to a still in the woods, and on that night the great Halley's Comet appeared. He remembered not only the event but also the look in the men's eyes, the words they said, and how the mash barrel he was grasping seemed to tremble as he shivered. Such sensitive and unclouded minds as these are able to respond to the stimuli about them.

Another condition that must be taken into account for understanding a Kentucky mountain family, such as the Couches, is the environment. The earliest Couches came into Kentucky when it was still the Promised Land, when there was still an abundance of free or cheap land to be taken up by simple patent. They built their cabins in isolated creeks and branches, and lived by farming and hunting. One of their largest problems was to clear the land and to dig in some corn and beans by hand. Neighbors were few and far between, and their isolation threw them upon their own resources. The first generations fought the bears and panthers that later generations told about in chimney corners. All communication, all knowledge, and all recreation were handed down orally. Up until the First World War there were no distractions from passing cars, from phonographs, from radios; at the present time, of course, these are in common use, as is the telephone.

The people lived in the quiet, peaceful valley. They were in tune with the changing days and the changing seasons. Each hour of the day had its significance, from the break of dawn and the crowing of the cock to late evening with the flicker of fireflies and the croaking of frogs. Indoors before early retirement all was still except for the crackling of the fire and the ticking of the clock. Chores that went on then were handicrafts—smoothing an ax handle, fashioning a rag doll, carding the wool, spinning, knitting. Any recreation was performed by the family members from the store of lore and folkways handed down from the old folks—hul-gul with grains of parched corn, tales, legends, fox and geese with homemade board, ballads that told some tragic story.

Nights and days like these were lived by the Couches. And whatever lore they retained as they scattered to the settlements and to the more populated areas was learned by repeating it and reliving it in their isolated cabins on Sang Branch, on the Clover Fork of Big Leatherwood, and in other quiet valleys.

Though such families as the Couches lived in isolation, especially in the earlier generations, they did get together in many ways. They suffered isolation because of circumstances, and they broke that isolation as often and as long as possible. The three greatest socializing forces were religion, labor, and recreation, the people sometimes combining two, or even all three, of them.

Old Tom Couch was not a churchgoer and apparently never joined any church. When he was growing up, there was perhaps no church for him to join, because organized religion came late to the long-isolated valleys of eastern Kentucky. At first the people had only visiting preachers who held meetings at the forks of the creek once a month when weather permitted and crops were "laid by." Through the long winters they came not at all, and this gave rise to long protracted meetings in the spring, annual associations, and what came to be called funeralizings. Simply stated, this last custom was the preaching of the funerals in good weather of all those who had died during the long winters when ministers could not be called. (It also meant a series of weddings—for those who had been married by a civil officer and also wanted a religious wedding, for those who had been waiting for a minister to show up, and for those who had not waited.)

As time went on, more preachers appeared, church was held on Sundays, laymen felt the call, and churches were built, especially in the lower, more thickly settled river valleys. But to this day many isolated valleys have no regular or lay preacher, and some do not have a churchhouse.

The fact that Tom Couch was not overly religious was apparently a favorable factor in the preservation of the lore of the family. He did not govern its members with too many *dont's* and *thou shalt nots*. As Jim put it, "We just worked all day and played all night, about it." Although the mother went to church with the children and at times stayed all day, with dinner on the ground, she told the old stories to the family and welcomed a party at her house after a bean-stringing bee.

These bees were indeed an important socializing force among eastern Kentucky people. In early, laborious days they were true communal exchanges of labor. Six or eight families in a portion of a valley had about the same phases of work to do at about the same time. The able-bodied hands went to each other's homes and worked the crop, raised a house or barn, cleared a patch of land, or harvested the corn and wheat. The women took baskets of food and prepared it at the host's house for all to eat together. A game time by the younger set for part of the night was almost as necessary as the main task. When the beans were to be strung, the apples to be peeled, or the corn to be husked, the folk assembled to these lighter tasks as a pretext for a playparty the remainder of the night.

At these gatherings the Couches, some of them at least, had a chance to shine. Old Tom played the banjo for the sets and other musical games until he raised a son to take his place. Dave early became the favorite son with the banjo, and the fact that he never learned to dance a set attests to his long and faithful service as musician. Jim apparently preferred to be down among the lasses, since he became adept at organizing games and calling squares and other folkdance sets.

Thus, we see how one family inherited a store of oral traditions and through their own intelligence, industry, and desire for social acceptance and approval made the most of it. Old Tom gathered songs from all sources and fed them into the heritage. Mandy married and settled into another isolated valley. Soon she was telling the mother's stories to her own children, and, when Jim came to live with her, she refreshed his memory with their haunting mystery. Jim in turn began to excel as a story teller with the family store, to which he added the legends and yarns of many other men. Dave, continuing to play the banjo for dances long after he was married, kept the title as favorite banjo picker. He contributed most of the hundred folksongs to this collection, while Jim recorded most of the sixty stories.

NOTE: The material in the introduction appears in reduced and rearranged form from *Up Cutshin and Down Greasy* (1959), reprinted here with permission from the University of Kentucky Press.

II. Folksongs and Hymns

1. The Devil and the School Child

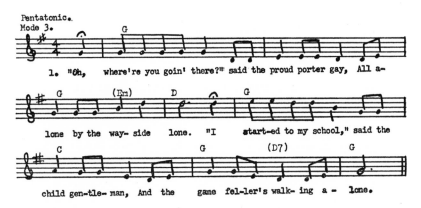

Pentatonic.
Mode 3.

1. "Oh, where're you goin' there?" said the proud porter gay, All a-
lone by the way-side lone. "I start-ed to my school," said the
child gen-tle-man, And the game fel-ler's walk-ing a - lone.

2. "What do you have in your bucket?" said the proud porter gay,
   All alone by the wayside lone.
   "It's vittles for my dinner," said the child gentleman,
   And the game feller's walking alone.

3. "O won't you give me some?" said the proud porter gay,
   All alone by the wayside lone.
   "No, not a bite o' crumbs," said the child gentleman,
   And the game feller's walking alone.

4. "I wished I had you in the woods," said the proud porter gay,
   All alone by the wayside lone.
   "With a good gun under my arm," said the child gentleman,
   And the game feller's walking alone.

5. "With your head broke in two," said the proud porter gay,
   all alone by the wayside lone.
   "O a fence rail jobbed down your neck," said the child gentleman,
   And the game feller's walking alone.

6. "Wished I had you in the sea," said the proud porter gay.
   All alone by the wayside lone.
   "Good board under me," said the child gentleman,
   And the game feller's walking alone.

7. "Your head turned bottom up," said the proud porter gay,

All alone by the wayside lone.
"Yes, and you under the bottom," said the child gentleman.
And the game feller's walking alone.

8. "I wished I had you in the well," said the proud porter gay.
   All alone by the wayside lone.
   "But the Devil's chained in Hell," said the child gentleman,
   And the game feller's walking alone.

2. Lord Batesman

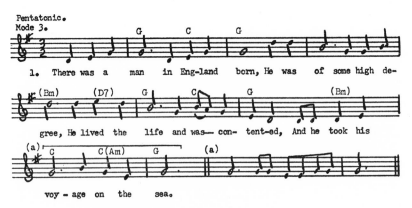

2. He sailed the East and he sailed west,
   He sailed over to the Turkish shore,
   And there he was caught and put in prison,
   And he never expected his freedom any more.

3. That Turkish had a love-lie lady,
   She was of some high degree,
   She stol'd the keys from her father's castle
   And said, "Lord Batesman, I'll set you free."

4. "Have you houses and rich land?
   Are you of some high degree?
   Will you will it all to the Turkish lady,
   If out of this prison she'll set you free?"

5. "I have houses and rich land,
   I am of some high degree,
   I'll will it all to the Turkish lady,
   If out of this prison she'll set me free."

6. She took him down to her father's hall,
   She drew a glass of the strongest wine.
   And there she gave and drink unto him,
   And said, "Lord Batesman, you are mine."

3. Joseph and Mary

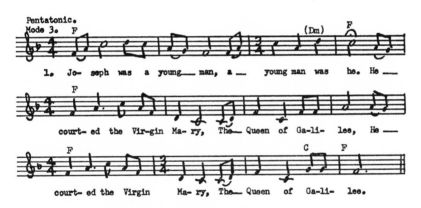

2. Joseph and Mary was walking one day,
   When Joseph spoke to Mary both neat and so bold,
   Said, "Here is plenty cherries, Mary,
   A sight to behold."

3. Mary spoke to Joseph both meek and so mild,
   Said, "Gather me some cherries, Joseph,
   For I am with child,
   Gather me some cherries, Joseph, for I am with child."

4. Joseph flew in anger and angry he flew,
   Said, "Let the father of your baby
   Gather cherries for you,

Let the father of your baby gather cherries for you."

5. Then Jesus bent the cherry tree all over on the ground,
   And Mary she gathers cherries
   While Joseph stood around,
   Mary she gathers cherries while Joseph stood around.

6. Joseph he took Mary all on his left knee,
   And he cried, "O Lord, how mercy,
   What have I done?"
   And he cried, "O Lord, how mercy, what have I done?"

7. Then Joseph he took Mary all on his right knee,
   And he said, "Pray tell me, little baby,
   When your birthday will be,
   Pray tell me, little baby, when your birthday will be.

8. "Next January my birthday will be,
   When the stars all in the elements
   They're trembling with fear,
   When the stars all in the elements are trembling with fear."

4. Little Matty Gross

2. He said to Lord Barne's wife,
   "Won't you come and join our band,

I know that you are Lord Barne's wife
By the rings that's on your hands, hands,
By the rings that's on your hands."

3. Little Foot Spaid was standing by,
   Hearing those words they say,
   And he said, "Lord Barnes will hear this news
   Before the break of day, day,
   Before the break of day."

4. He had fifteen miles to go,
   He ran twelve of them there,
   He come to Broad Waters,
   He smoothed his breast and swimmed, swimmed,
   He smoothed his breast and swimmed.

5. He went up to the captain's gate,
   He dingled down his ring.
   Who was it but Lord Barnes
   To rise and let him in, in,
   To rise and let him in.

6. "My fine houses is burned down?
   Down are my tower?" "No, your
   Fine houses aren't burned down
   Nor tower either are, are,
   Nor tower either are."

7. He called to his daughter and said,
   "Come, daughter dear."
   And he put his trumpet to his mouth
   And he blowed it loud and clear, clear,
   And he blowed it loud and clear.

8. Little Matty Gross was standing by,
   Hearing those words that sound,
   Saying, "I am in bed with another wife
   And time to leave this town, town,
   And time to leave this town."

9. "Lay still, lay still," said Lord Barne's wife,

"Lay still and go to sleep,
It's nobody but my father's boys
Herding home their sheep, sheep,
Herding home their sheep."

10. They first was talking
And then was asleep.
And when he awoke
Lord Barnes stood at his feet, feet,
Lord Barnes stood at his feet.

11. "Arise up, Little Matty Gross,
Arise and put on your clothes,
There is nothing a-shame in this wide world
As to slay a naked man, man,
As to slay a naked man."

12. "No, no," said Little Matty Gross,
"You must spare my life,
You have two keen-edged swords
And I don't have a knife, knife,
And I don't have a knife."

13. "Yes, I have two keen-edged swords
And you shall have the best one of them."
And the second lick he struck little Matty
He never stroke no more, more,
He never stroke no more.

14. He took his wife all on his knee and said,
    "How do you like his bedden? how do you like his cheeks?
And do you like his rhubarb lips
Better than me or my kind, kind,
Better than me or my kind?"

15. "Very well I like his bedden, sir,
Very well I like his cheeks and
Much better I love a kiss from his lips
Better than you and all your kind, kind,
Better than you and all your kind."

5. Barbary Allen

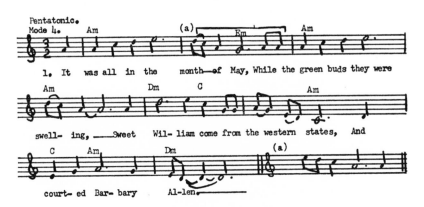

Pentatonic.
Mode 4.

1. It was all in the month—of May, While the green buds they were swell- ing, ——Sweet Wil- liam come from the western states, And court- ed Bar- bary Al-len.——

2. He wrote a sentence to the town,
   The place where she was a-dwellin',
   Saying, "Master's sick and sent for you
   If your name be Barbary Allen."

3. So slowly, slowly she got up
   And hated to deny him,
   All she said when she got there,
   "Young man, I see you lying."

4. "I am sick and very sick
   And feel so much like dying,
   No better, no better will I ever get
   Till I get Barbary Allen."

5. So slowly, slowly she got up
   And started off to leave him,
   He turned his pale face toward the wall
   And bursted out to crying.

6. When she was on her highway home,
   Little birds kept singing around her,
   They sang so sweetly and heartful joy,
   "Hardhearted Barbary Allen."

7. She looked to the east and then to the west,

She saw some cold corpse standing,
"Lie down, lie down, cold corpse," she said,
"And let me look upon you."

8. "I can't lie down, I can't lie down,
I can't lie down to save you,
I am a cold corpse of clay,
I can't let you look upon me."

9. She turned her face all down the road
And bursted out to crying,
"O mother, O mother, you're the one to blame,
You would not let him marry him."

10. "Mother, mother, go make my bed,
Go make it long and narrow,
Sweet William died for me today,
I'll die for him tomorrow."

11. Sweet William died on Saturday night,
And Barbary died on Sunday,
Her mother died for the love of both,
And all were buried on Monday.

12. Sweet William was buried in one church door,
And Barbary buried in the other,
A red rose sprung from Barbary's grave,
And a green briar sprung from William's.

13. They growed to the top of the old church house,
They could not grow any higher,
They lapped and tied in a truelove knot,
And then they died for loving.

6. Hangman

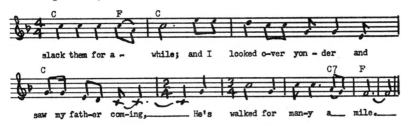

slack them for a - while; and I looked o-ver yon - der and

saw my fath-er com-ing,_____ He's walked for man-y a___ mile._____

2. O father, O father, did you bring me any gold,
   Any money to pay my fine;
   Or did you dist come here for to see me hang,
   Hang on this old gallows line?

3. No, son, no, son, I never brought you no gold,
   No money for you to pay your fine;
   I dist come here for to see you hang,
   Hang on this old gallows line.

4-6. saw my mother coming
7-9. saw my brother coming
10-12. saw my sister coming
13-14. saw my sweet heart coming

15. Yes, sir, yes, sir, I've brought your gold,
    Plenty money for to pay your fine;
    I never come here for to see you hang;
    Hang on this old gallows line.

7. Drunkard Blues

Pentatonic.
Mode 1.

1. Old man rolled in one even-ing Just as drunk as he could be, And he

seed a horse a-stand-ing Where _____ his horse ought to be. I'm goin' to

leave,——— yes, I'm goin' to   leave.

2. You're drunk and you're crazy,
   You're blind and you can't see,
   That's only a milk cow
   Mommy sent to me.
   I'm goin' to leave, yes, I'm goin' to leave.

3. Through this wide world I've been
   Forty-odd times or more,
   Never I seen a milk cow
   Have a saddle on before.
   I'm goin' to leave, yes, I'm goin' to leave.

4. Old man rolled in one evening
   Just as drunk as he could be,
   He seed some shoes a-setting
   Where his shoes ought to be.
   I'm goin' to leave, yes, I'm goin' to leave.

5. You're drunk and you're crazy,
   You're blind and you can't see,
   That's only a milk churn
   Mommy sent to me.
   I'm goin' to leave, yes, I'm goin' to leave.

6. Through this world I've been
   Forty-odd times or more,
   Never I saw a milk churn
   Have boot heels on before.
   I'm goin' to leave, yes, I'm goin' to leave.

7. Old man rolled in one evening
   Just as drunk as he could be,
   He seed a head a-laying
   Where his head ought to be.
   I'm goin' to leave, yes, I'm goin' to leave.

8. You're drunk and you're crazy,
   You're blind and you can't see,
   That's only a new-born baby
   Mommy sent to me.
   I'm goin' to leave, yes, I'm goin' to leave.

9. Through this wide world I've been
   Forty-odd times or more,
   Never I seen a new-born baby
   Have a mustache on before.
   I'm goin' to leave, yes, I'm goin' to leave.

8. The Devil and the Farmer's Wife

1. I went down in the fields to plow, the Devil flew o-ver my old grey mare, Come a- ti- i- idle ding-a- ding dum- a-ding, Come a-ti-i-idle ding-a day.

2. Old man drapped his plow and run,
   Said, "The Devil's after my oldest son."
   Come a-ti-i-idle ding-a-ding dum-a-ding,
   Come a-ti-i-idle ding-a-day.

3. "I hain't after your oldest son, I pray,
   I'm after that scolding wife o' yourn I say."
   Come a-ti-i-idle ding-a-ding dum-a-ding,
   Come a-ti-i-idle ding-a-day.

4. "Take her on all on your heart,
   I hope you and her will never part."
   Come a-ti-i-idle ding-a-ding dum-a-ding,
   Come a-ti-i-idle ding-a-day.

5. He took her up to the gates of hell,
   And give her a kick, says, "Lady, go there."
   Come a-ti-i-idle ding-a-ding dum-a-ding,
   Come a-ti-i-idle ding-a day.

6. Three little devils come a-running by,
   She up with her foot kicked one in the fire.
   Come a-ti-i-idle ding-a-ding dum-a-ding,
   Come a-ti-i-idle ding-a day.

7. Two little devils come peeping through the wall,
   Said, "Take her back, Daddy, before she kills us all." [spoken]
   Come a-ti-i-idle ding-a-ding dum-a-ding,
   Come a-ti-i-idle ding-a day.

8. He picked her up in an old tow sack,
   And the darned old fool went waggin' her back [spoken]
   Come a-ti-i-idle ding-a-ding dum-a-ding,
   Come a-ti-i-idle ding-a day.

9 She was six months a-goin' and sebem comin' back,
   And she called for her pipe she left in the crack.
   Come a-ti-i-idle ding-a-ding dum-a-ding,
   Come a-ti-i-idle ding-a day.

10. She hain't fit for heabem and she can't stay in hell
    So I guess on earth she'll have to dwell.
    Come a-ti-i-idle ding-a-ding dum-a-ding,
    Come a-ti-i-idle ding-a day.

9. Swappin' Boy

Pentatonic, Mode 3.

1. There was a lit-tle boy and he lived by him- self,

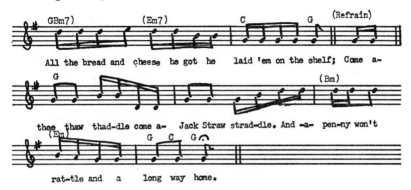

2. The rats and mice they led him such a life,
   He had to go to London to buy him a wife;
   [Refrain after each stanza]

3. The roads was muddy and the lanes was nar,
   He had to bring her back in an old wheelbar;

4. The wheelbar broke and his wife got a fall,
   Go it, wheelbar, wife and all;

5. He took his wife and he swapped her to a cow,
   And in that trade he just learnt how;

6. He took his cow and he swapped her to a calf,
   And in that trade he just lost half;

7. And he took his calf and he swapped it to a mule,
   And in that trade he wa'n't nothing but a fool;

8. And he took his mule and he swapped it to a mouse,
   And the danged old thing went straight to the fodder house.

10. The Old Big Ram

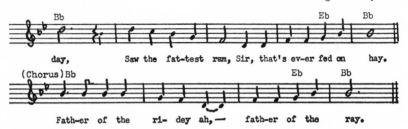

day,   Saw the fat-test ram, Sir, that's ev-er fed on   hay.

(Chorus) Bb   Eb   Bb

Fath-er of the   ri- dey ah, —   fath-er of the   ray.

2. The hoofs on that ram's foot
   Covered ten acres of ground,
   And the horns 'ats on that ram's head
   will hold ten bushels of corn.
   Father of the ridey ah, father of the ray.

3. The wool that's on that ram's back
   It growed to reach the sky,
   For the eagles built their nests in it
   And I could hear their young uns cry.
   Father of the ridey ah, father of the ray.

4. The man that butchered that sheep, sir,
   He waded to his neck in blood,
   The man that held the light, sir,
   Was washed away in the flood.
   Father of the ridey ah, father of the ray.

5. The man that owned that ram, sir,
   He owned mighty rich,
   The boy that made that song, sir,
   Is the son of a lying bitch.
   Father of the ridey ah, father of the ray.

11. Purty Polly

Pentatonic,
Mode 2,   Em   G(Bm)

1. Come   on, pur-ty Pol-ly and   go with — me, Come   on, Pur-ty

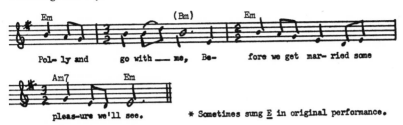

Pol- ly and   go with ___ me,   Be-   fore we get mar- ried some

pleas-ure we'll see.   * Sometimes sung <u>E</u> in original performance.

2. O Willy, O Willy, I'm afeard of your ways,
   O Willy, O Willy, I'm afeard of your ways,
   Afeard that you will leave my pore body a slave.

3. He led her over the hills and the valleys so deep,
   He led her over the hills and the valleys so deep,
   Purty Polly got dishearted and agin to weep.

4. He went a piece furder, what do you spy?
   He went a piece furder, what do you spy?
   A new-dug grave and a spade a-layin' by.

5. She threw her arms around him saying, "Willie, my dear,"
   She threw her arms around him saying, "Willie, my dear,"
   How can you kill the only friend you've got here?"

6. "No time to study, no time to stand,
   No time to study, no time to stand,"
   He come with his knife all in his right hand.

7. He stobbed her to the heart and the blood agin to flow,
   He stobbed her to the heart and the blood agin to flow,
   Down in the grave Purty Polly did go.

8. He threw dirt over her and on he did go,
   He jumped on his boat and on did he row,
   His boat struck a rock, to the bottom it did go.

9. Now where's Purty Polly? O yander she stands,
   Now where's Purty Polly? Over yander she stands,
   Them rings on her fingers, her lily white hands.

10. What a debt to the Devil pore Willy'll have to pay,

What a debt to the Devil pore Willy'll have to pay,
For killin' Purty Polly and runnin' away.

12. The Bachelor Boy

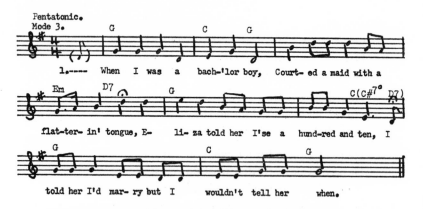

On Monday morning I married me a wife,
Fiddlin' and a-dancin' I never saw the like,
She tuned up her fiddle and merry she could play,
And I thought to my soul it'd never come day.

3. On Tuesday morning to my sus-sprise,
   About half an hour before the sun did rise,
   She tuned up her fife and scolded me more
   Than ever I was scolded in my lifetime before.

4. On Wednesday morning I went to the woods,
   Thinks to myself she'll do me no good,
   I cut me some hickories and a hornbean green,
   I thought it was the toughest I ever had seen.

5. On Thursday morning I carried them home,
   Thinking to myself she's a wife of my own,
   And thought to myself as I laid them by,
   I's expectin' next morning to have them to try.

6. On Friday morning I banged her well,
   Her tongue did rattle like a clapper in a bell,
   I told her the terms and the terms mought be,
   The Devil might have her next morning for me.

7. On Saturday morning the Devil came,
   Took her off in a shower of rain,
   Pass around your brandy bottle, my best friends,
   My hardships have come to an end.

13. Rich and Rambling Boy

2. Then I married me a lovin' little wife,
   I loved her dear as I loved my life,
   She proved to me both true and gay
   And caused me to rob on the broad highway.

3. Robbed them all they had to spare,
   I robbed them all they could declare,
   I robbed them of ten thousand pounds

In the nights that I was a-ramblin' around.

4. O give me a chear and I'll set down,
   I'll write a few lines to the Governor Brown,
   Every line will be the truth,
   If you're a free boy I'll turn you loose.

5. I've got enough dry goods to carry me through,
   Two glitterin' swords and a pistol, too,
   Colts forty-five, she'd never fail,
   My truelove come to go my bail.

6. Bought me a ticket in the London town,
   Got up on a train and I set down,
   The wheels they rolled and the whistle did blow,
   And five more days I'll land back home.

7. Roses are red and the stems are green,
   The days have passed that we all have seen,
   More comin' on but they may be few,
   I hope I can spend them all with you.

14. Sweetheart in the Army

* Circular ending; tonal center on G.

2. Perhaps he's in some river a-drowndin',
   Perhaps he's on some battlefield slain,
   Perhaps he took some poor girl and married,
   I'll love that girl for marrying him.

3. I've got a sweetheart lives in the army,
   He is the one I'll never see.
   But if he's gone for seven years longer
   No man on earth can't marry me.

15. The Knoxville Girl

2. She fell upon her bended knees, for mercy she did cry,
   "Willie, my dear, don't kill me here, I'm unprepared to die."

She never spoke another word, I only beat her more,
She never spoke another word, I beat her in her gore.

3. I took her by her golden curls, I drug her round and round,
   I took her by her golden curls, I drug her round and round,
   I took her by her golden curls, I drug her round and round,
   I threw her in the river that flows to Knoxville town.

4. I went in home about 12 o'clock, about 12 o'clock at night,
   My mother she was worried and woke up in a fright.
   "Son, O son, what have you done to bloody your poor soul?"
   The answer that I gave her, "Been bleeding from my nose."

5. The sheriff he come and got me and put me in the cell,
   My friends all turned against me and none will go my bail.
   They're goin' to hang me up so high between the earth and sky,
   They're goin' to hang me up so high between the earth and sky.

16. Rovin' Gambler

2. I had not been in Washington
   Many more weeks than three,
   Till I fell in love with a pretty little girl
   And she fell in love with me.

3. She got me in her parlor,
   She cooled me with her fan,
   She whispered low in mother's ear

I love that gambling man.

4. Daughter, dear daughter,
   Why do you treat me so?
   Leave your dear old mother,
   And away with a gambler go?

5. I know I love you, mother,
   I know I love you well,
   But the love I have for the gamblin' man
   No human tongue can tell.

6. Hear that train a comin'
   It's comin' on the curve,
   She's a whistlin' and a blowin'
   And straining every nerve.

7. Tell you, lovin' mother,
   Let me tell you if I can,
   If you ever see it comin' again
   It'll be with the gamblin' man.

8. I've gambled down to Washington,
   I've gambled out in Spain,
   I'm goin' now to Georgie,
   To gamble my last game.

17. The Wagoner Boy

(Stanzas 2,3,7.)   (Stanzas 4,5,6,8.)

2. You used to wouldn't have me
   Because I was pore,
   But now I have money plenty
   And a wagoner boy.

3. Go put up your horses
   And feed them some hay,
   Come and set down by me
   As long as you stay.

4. My horses is not hungry
   And won't eat your hay,
   Fare-you-well, purty Nancy,
   I'll feed on my way.

5. It's rainin' and a-hailin'
   And the moon gives no light,
   You can't see to travel
   This dark and rainy night.

6. My raincoat's on my shoulder,
   My whip's in my hand,
   I'll drive on tonight, love,
   No time to stand.

7. Go build me a castle
   On yonder mountain high,
   Where the wild geese can see me
   When they're passing by.

8. Where the turtle doves can hear me
   And can help me to mourn,
   For I am a pore girl
   And a long ways from home.

18. Wild Bill Jones

1. I went out walk-in' one —— morn-ing, And I met with that wild Bill Jones, He's a-walkin' and a-talk-in' with —— my —true love, And I told— him to leave— her a- lone.

2. He said his age was twenty-one,
   Too old to be controlled,
   I drew my revolver from my side
   And shot that wild Bill Jones.

3. That wild Bill Jones was a very bad man,
   He carried two guns at a time,
   I beat him to mine and shot him in time
   And destroyed that pore boy's life.

4. He reeled, he staggered, he stumbled as he fell,
   And he gave one dying groan,
   The very last words I heard him say was
   "Darling, you are left alone."

5. The engineer said to his black-featured fireman,
   "Shovel in a little more coal,
   We're 'way behind but we'll put her on time
   And pull her in some lonesome home."

19. Willow Garden

1. Down by the wil-low gar-den Where me and my love—did meet,

We set there a— court—ting, my— love fell off to —— sleep.

(Opening bars of stanzas 2,4,5,6.)

2. I had a bottle of that burglar wine
   In which I did not know
   That there I'd murder my old truelove
   Down on the banks so cold.

3. 'S I drew a dagger to her,
   Which was a bloody knife,
   And down by the willow garden
   I took that pore girl's life.

4. My father always told me
   That money would set me free,
   If I would murder that purty little girl,
   Her name Rose Anna Lee.

5. Now he's standing in his cabin door
   With teardrops in his eyes,
   Looking on his only son
   Upon the scaffold high.

6. My work is done beneath the sun
   And hell is waiting for me,
   Because I murdered that purty little girl,
   Her name is Rose Anna Lee.

20. Frankie and Albert

Hexachordal.

1. Frank-ie was a good lit-tle wo-man   ev-'ry bo- dy knows,

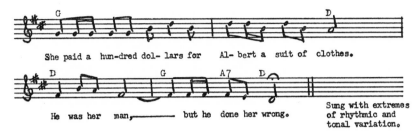

She paid a hun-dred dol- lars for Al- bert a suit of clothes.

He was her man,———— but he done her wrong.

Sung with extremes
of rhythmic and
tonal variation.

2. She paid for him a hat, dollar walkin' cane,
   She paid five thousand to go his bail and she loved him just the
   same.
   O he's my man, but he done me wrong.

3. Frankie went down to the corner, to have a bottle of beer,
   Said to the bartender, "Has Albert ever been here?
   He was my man, but he done me wrong."

4. "I hain't a-goin' to tell ye no story, hain't a-goin' to tell ye no lies,
   He left here about an hour ago with a girl named Nelly Spies.
   He was your man, but he done you wrong."

5. Frankie walked down the street, with a snow-white apron on,
   All under that little white apron she carried a .41.
   "O goin' to kill me a man who's doin' me wrong."

6. Frankie stepped up to Albert, Albert broke and run,
   Out from under that snow-white apron come a smokin' gun.
   To kill a man who has done her wrong.

7. Shot through Albert one shoot, shot through Albert twicet,
   The third shoot she shot him she took her husband's life.
   "O I killed me a man, but he's doin' me wrong."

8. "O turn me over, doctor, turn me over slow,
   Don't tetch my right side, O God, it hurts me so.
   I was her man, but I done her wrong."

9. Took old Frank to the graveyard, there no tears was shed,
   All she said when she got there, "Nail down the coffin lead.
   O I killed me a man, but he done me wrong."

21. Those Brown Eyes

2. One night we met upon the street,
   I bowed my head but could not speak;
   With another by her side,
   And I thought would be his bride.
   [Refrain]

3. One year ago just from today,
   They laid my darling Brown Eyes away;
   Up in heaven I know she be,

My brown-eyed angel waiting for me.
[Refrain]

22. Jack Was a Lonely Cowboy

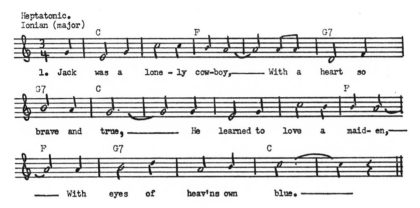

2. They learned to love each other
   And named the wedding day,
   When a quarrel came out between them,
   And Jack he rolled away.

3. He joined a band of cowboys
   Just to try to forget her name,
   But out on the lone prairie,
   She waits for him the same.

4. Your sweetheart waits for you, Jack,
   Your sweetheart's waiting for you,
   Out on the lone prairie,
   Your sweetheart waits for you.

5. Jack retched the lone prairie,
   He found a new-made mound,
   And his friends so sadly told him,
   That they laid his loved one there.

6. Your sweetheart waits for you, Jack,
   Your sweetheart's waiting for you,
   Out on the lone prairie,
   Where the skies are always blue.

23. The Orphant Girl

2. Her clothes were thin, her feet was bare,
   The snow had covered her head,
   "O give me a home," so feeble as she cried,
   "A home and a bit of bread."

3. The night was dark and the snow still fell,
   The rich man closed his door,
   His proud lips quivered so scornful he said,
   "No room nor bread for the pore."

4. The night rolled over like a midnight storm,
   Rolled over like a funeral song,
   The sky were white as a linen sheet,
   And the drifts of snow still fell.

5. The rich man lie on his velvet sheets,
   He was dreaming of his silver and his gold,
   While the orphant lies on a bed of snow

And cried, "So cold, so cold."

6. The morning light shoned over the earth,
   She was a-lying at the rich man's door,
   Her soul had fled to the heavens above,
   Where they's room and bread for the pore.

24. Brother Green

2. O sister Mary, don't you weep for me,
   For the loss of your dear brother,
   I am going to heaven to live,
   To meet my old dear mother.

3. O sister Ann, O take my children,
   And teach them up to heaven,
   O teach them up and arrive some day,
   To sing farewell forever.

4. I've got two brothers that I can't forget,
   They're fighting for the Union,
   The old Rebel foe has laid me low,
   On this cold ground to suffer.

25. James A. Garfield

1. I — killed James A. Gar-field,— I — killed him with two shots, And if you don't be- lieve me,—I'll—show you the ver-y spot.

*Tempo somewhat speeded up

2. 'Ts I rambled around the depot
To make my excape,
The circumstances was against me,
I found I was too late.

3. My name is Charleston Guitoff,
My name I won't deny,
I killed James A. Garfield,
I scaled the scaffold high.

26. Ellen Smith

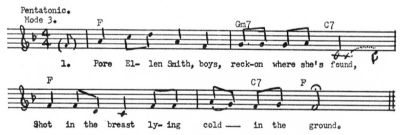

1. Pore El- len Smith, boys, reck-on where she's found, Shot in the breast ly- ing cold — in the ground.

2. My baby's in the cradle,
I'm sick and in my bed,
My truelove's off a-gambling,
I'd ruther I were dead.

3. I am all ragged,
   And they all treat me wrong,
   Come and get me, mommy,
   Don't stay away so long.

4. Last Monday morning,
   Before the break of day,
   They come and got pore Ellener,
   And carried her away.

5. I'm going back to Cuby,
   To fight them Spanish men,
   Before I reached that open boat,
   I wished I never had been.

6. Content yourself, my darling,
   Content yourself, my dear,
   I'm going to join the army,
   To be a volunteer.

7. Your fingers is too slender,
   Your body is too small,
   Your cheeks too red and rosy,
   To face them cannon balls.

8. I know my fingers are slender,
   And I know my body is small,
   But I don't believe I'd tremble,
   To see a thousand fall.

27. Mines of Coal Creek

1. I —— worked in the mines last Tues- day,—— I —— worked the

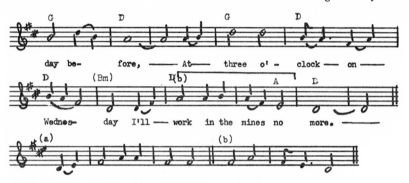

day be-   fore, ——— At—— three o' - clock —— on ——
Wednes-   day I'll —— work   in the mines no   more. ———

2. Shet up in the mines of Coal Creek,
   You know you have to die,
   Just put your trust in Jesus,
   To heaven your soul shall fly.

3. I got on a train last Wednesday,
   And 'way to the mines did go,
   I come out at 4 o'clock,
   I never did hear her blow.

4. What hills, what hills, my old truelove,
   That looks so bright and gay?
   That is the hills of sweet heaven,
   Where all good people live.

5. What hills, what hills, my old truelove,
   That looks so dark and blue?
   That is the hills of a burning hell,
   Where all mean people go.

6. I hain't grieving over my silver nor gold,
   Neither studying about my home,
   All in the world that's on my mind,
   My darling I left alone.

28. Wreck of the Old Ninety-Seven

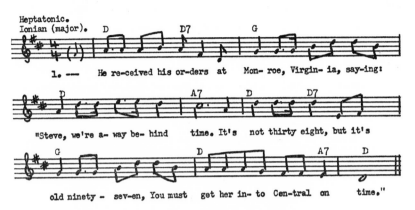

Heptatonic.
Ionian (major).

1. — He re-ceived his or-ders at Mon- roe, Virgin- ia, say-ing:

"Steve, we're a- way be- hind time. It's not thirty eight, but it's

old ninety - sev-en, You must get her in- to Cen-tral on time."

2. Turned around to his black old fireman
   Saying, "Shovel on a little more coal;
   When we get to the top of White Oak Mountain
   We will watch old Ninety-seven roll."

3. Going down grade making ninety miles an hour
   When the whistle broke into a scream;
   He was found in the wreck with his hand on the throttle
   And was scalded to death by the steam.

4. Come around, all you women,
   And listen from this day and on;
   Never speak false words to your true husband
   He may leave you and never return.

29. When I Left the Blue Ridge Mountains

Pentatonic.
Mode 2.

1. Left the Blue Ridge Moun - tains of old Vir- gin-ia,——— South Caro-

lin -   a I — did   go,   Court-in' with —— a   fair—young

la- dy, —— Her   age or name   I nev- er   knowed.——

2. Her hair was of a dark brown color,
   Her cheeks was a rosy red,
   On her breast she wore a white lily,
   Through the night the tears she shed.

3. When I'm asleep I'm dreamin' about her,
   When I wake I find no rest,
   Every moment seems like an hour,
   Aching pains all through my breast.

4. Her poppy said that we could marry,
   Her mommy said it'd never do,
   But if you say so, honey,
   I will run away with you.

5. I'd druther be dead and in my coffin,
   My face is turned towards thy sun,
   As to lay here and study,
   Thinkin' of the way you've done.

6. Druther be in some dark holler,
   Where thy bright sun never shines,
   As for you to be another man's darlin',
   And to know you can't be mine.

30. John Hardy

Heptatonic.
Ionian(major) mode.

1. John Har-dy was a   ve-ry bad_ man, He   carried two guns ev'ry

day; He shot two shoots, and he killed him a man. John Har-dy you better get a-

way, Lord, Lord, John   Hardy you bet-ter get a-   way.

2. John Hardy went down to the gambling house,
   Where the niggers was havin' a game,
   A yaller gal give him fifteen cents
   And shoved John Hardy in a game, Lord, Lord,
   And shoved John Hardy in a game.

3. John Hardy went down to Big Stone Gap,
   He thought he was out of the way,
   Along come a police-man
   Said, "Johnny, won't you go my way, poor boy,
   John Hardy, won't you go my way."

4. John Hardy's mother said to John Hardy,
   "John Hardy, what have you done?"
   "I killed me a man in Johnny town
   Hain't a-goin' to lie to my gun, Lord, Lord,
   Hain't a-goin' to lie to my gun.

5. "I been to the east, I been to the west,
   I been this wide world around,
   Now take me to the river let me be baptized,
   Then take me to my hangin' ground, Lord, Lord,
   Take me to my hangin' ground."

31. Floyd Frazier

1. Come— all you bless- ed — peo- ple From —ev-'ry na-tion —

fair, And— hear the cir- cum- stan - ces Of —what Floyd Fraz-ier—done.

2. He killed poor Ellen Flannery
   And he knew that he had done wrong,
   He prayed for it to rain
   And wash away the blood.

3. Oh, she had seven little chillern
   From door to door they run,
   They's crying for their mother,
   Yet no mother never come.

4. Their little hearts were hungry
   And they all did fall asleep,
   The morning waked them breaking
   But no mother never come.

5. He crept into his cabin
   There for to stay all night,
   He thought his crime was hidden
   From everybody's sight.

6. Fare-you-well, Floyd Frazier,
   Ask God what you have done,
   You killed an innocent woman,
   But you've got the race to run.

7. Floyd Frazier used to be a young man
   And the girls all knowed him well,
   They hugged and they kissed his cheeks,
   They bid him now farewell.

8. They took him down to the jailhouse,
   They locked him in a cell,
   He killed an innocent woman
   And sent his poor soul to hell.

32. Hiram Hubbard

2. They first robbed him of his money,
   His shoes they did take off,
   They first robbed him of his money,
   His shoes they did take off,
   And they drove him on before them
   Until the road was stained with blood.

3. Then they took him to the Cumberland River
   And there they tried his life,
   Then they took him to the Cumberland River
   And there they tried his life,
   They swore so hard against him
   That he was condemned to die.

4. Then they lashed their cord around him
   And they driv him up a hill,
   Then they lashed their cord around him

And they driv him up a hill,
To the place of execution
And there he begged to write his will.

5. "Fare-you-well my dear companion,
   Likewise my tender child,
   Fare-you-well my dear companion,
   Likewise my tender child,
   I will leave this letter with you
   For I am going to die."

6. Then they lashed their cords around him,
   They tied him to a tree,
   Then they lashed their cords around him,
   They tied him to a tree,
   And eleven balls did pierce him
   And his body did swank away.

7. "Farewell my friend and neighbors,
   You all I want to tell,
   Farewell my friend and neighbors,
   You all I want to tell,
   For I am leaving this letter with you
   Because it is my last farewell."

8. Hiram Hubbard was not guilty,
   I have heard great many say,
   Hiram Hubbard was not guilty,
   I have heard great many say,
   For he was not in this country,
   He was many miles away.

33. Kaiser and the Hindenberger

Hexatonic.

1. Well the Kai-ser said to the Hindenberg-er Le's go to the fight-in'

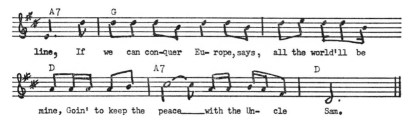

line, If we can con-quer Eu- rope, says, all the world'll be

mine, Goin' to keep the peace with the Un- cle Sam.

2. Well, the Hindenberger said to the soldiers,
   "Come on, boys, le's go,
   If we can conquer Europe, says, the world'll be ours you know,
   If we're goin' to keep peace with the Uncle Sam."

3. When the Kaiser seen the foodstuff
   Come transportin' over the sea,
   Kaiser said to the U-boat crew, said, "This no longer be,
   You'll have to run the bluff on the Uncle Sam."

4. Commenced sinkin' the vessels
   Of the grand old U.S.A.,
   Woodrow said to the Kaiser, "This's a game we'll help you play,
   You can't run your bluff on the Uncle Sam."

5. "Well, the war in Belgium, France, and England,
   We can hold them all in hand,
   But the marksmanship of the U.S. boys we Germans cannot stand,
   We'll have to skidoo from the Uncle Sam."

6. The Kaiser said to the Woodrow,
   "We'll pay you billions back,"
   Woodrow said to the Kaiser, "But you're goin' t' have to ball the jack,
   You've gone too far with the Uncle Sam."

7. The Kaiser went up to the trenches,
   All to his sus-prise,
   Well the brell'ance of Old Glory almost put out his eyes,
   He saw the flag of the Uncle Sam.

8. The Kaiser said to the Hindenberger,
   "Put a pad between my knees,

Send after my physician, I've got the heart disease,
I seen them boys of the Uncle Sam."

34. Young Lady in the Bloom of Youth

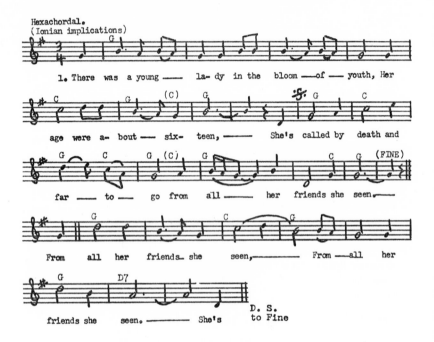

1. There was a young ——— la- dy in the bloom ——of —— youth, Her
age were a- bout —— six- teen, ——— She's called by death and
far —— to —— go from all ——— her friends she seen.———
From all her friends— she seen,——— From ——all her
friends she seen. ——— She's   D. S. to Fine

2. Her playmates gathered from far and near,
   They seemed to bow their heads,
   I heard her mother's pitiful groans
   That her poor child were dead.
   That her poor child were dea-e-ed,
   That her poor child were dead,
   I heard her mother's pitiful groans
   That her poor child were dead.

3. Her oldest brother were standing by,

His hand upon his breast,
O pity, Lord, O Lord, forgive
And take her home to rest.
And take her home to re-e-est,
And take her home to rest,
O pity, Lord, O Lord, forgive
And take her home to rest.

4. The people gathered from far and near
To carry away the dead,
They carried her body to a tomb
Where many of a tear were shed.
Where many of a tear were she-e-ed,
Where many of a tear were shed,
They carried her body to a tomb
Where many of a tear were shed.

5. O ain't this enough to break friends' hearts,
To break friends' hearts below?
To think a that we all must die
And into judgment go.
And into judgment go-o-o,
And into judgment go,
To think a that we all must die
And into judgment go.

35. O Those Tombs

Pentatonic.
Mode 3.

1. I was strol-lin' one day in a lone-ly graveyard, When a voice from the
tombs___ seemed to say, I once lived as you live , walked and talked as you

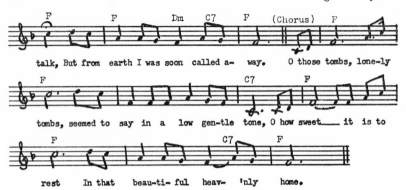

talk, But from earth I was soon called a- way. O those tombs, lone-ly

tombs, seemed to say in a low gen-tle tone, O how sweet it is to

rest   In that beau-ti-ful heav-'nly home.

2. Every voice from the tomb seemed to whisper and say,
   Up in the mansion, my son, follow me,
   O I stood and gazed on those cold marble slabs,
   What a dark lonesome place that must be.
       O those tombs, lonely tombs,
       Seemed to say in a low gentle tone,
       O how sweet it is to rest
       In that beautiful heavenly home.

3. Then I came to the place where my mother was laid,
   In that silence I stood by her tomb,
   And her voice seemed to say in a low gentle tone,
   I am safe with my Savior at home.
       O those tombs, lonely tombs,
       Seemed to say in a low gentle tone,
       O how sweet it is to rest
       In that beautiful heavenly home.

36. I Saw a Sight All in a Dream

Hexatonic.
(Dorian implications)

1. I saw a sight, all in a dream, There's things before —

I nev- er seen; I saw my compan- ion——— tra-'v'llin' on the

way my bless - ed Re- deem- er's gone.

2. I saw my husband away behind,
   Him who I love so tender and kind,
   With seven little chillern around her bed
   Remending for their mother kind.

3. A mother kind indeed was she,
   A loving wife she's been to me,
   She called her companion to her bed,
   Ten thousand tears for her he shed.

4. "Companion dear, come pity me,
   Come take my two little babes away,
   Take both my twins all in your care,
   And teach them up in God to fear.

5. "And teach them both to sing and pray
   And to serve the Lord till endless day."
   The sharpest pain run through her breast,
   A-worrying for her two little babes.

6. Poor little babes must cry and weep,
   No breast to suck, cuddle them to sleep;
   It's come, great God, look down and view,
   See what a kind mother has went through.

7. She is paid the debt we all must pay,
   She's left this world to sleep in the clay;
   Come friends and neighbors from all around
   And see her laid in the cold ground.

8. A warning to the human race,
   A warning of the human race,
   We all must go to that cold place.

37. The Twelve Apostles

1. Come and let us sing.   [1st voice]
   What will we sing?   [2nd voice]
   Sing you one.   [two, three, etc., for each stanza]
   What'll be the one?
   The one, the one that's left alone
   Is long to be alone.

2. Come and let us sing.
   What will we sing?
   Sing you two.

What'll be the two?
Two, two the little white babes,
O my dear Savior,
The one, the one that's left alone
Is long to be alone.

3. Three, three are weeping
4. Four, four are rumble [humble?]
5. Five, five all on the board
6. Six, six are rekal [regal?]
7. Seven angels singing bright
8. Eight, eight are mansions white
9. Nine the Gab'el [Gabriel] angel
10. Ten commandments given
11. Eleven went to heaven
12. Twelve, twelve the Apostles

38. Bright and Shining City

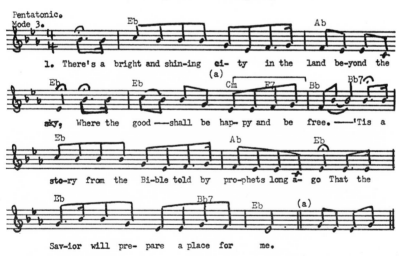

2. We are drifting, yes, we're drifting and our days are passing by,
   We are drifting down the rugged streams of time;

Jesus suffered an' died on Calvary for the opening of the way,
Yes, I'm drifting to the happy home of mine.

3. O sinners, take this warning, Christ is pleading now for you,
   As He warns the end of time will surely come;
   You have to face the Judgment on the Resurrection morn,
   You'll have to meet the deeds that you have done.

4. We are drifting, yes, we're drifting and our days are passing by,
   We are drifting down the rugged streams of time;
   Jesus suffered and died on Calvary for the opening of the way,
   Yes, I'm drifting to that happy home of mine.

5. You will have to face the Judgment on that Resurrection morn,
   When your sinful life here on earth is over;
   You will look to him for mercy but he'll only shake his head,
   And say, "Depart from me forever more."

6. We are drifting, yes, we're drifting and our days are passing by,
   We are drifting down the rugged streams of time;
   Jesus suffered an' died on Calvary for the opening of the way,
   Yes, I'm drifting to that happy home of mine.

39. Glory Land

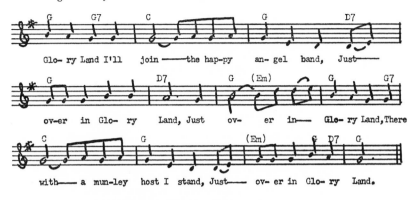

2. I'm on my way to those mansions fair
   Just over in Glory Land,
   To sing God's praise, yes, his glory share
   Just over in Glory Land.
       Just over in Glory Land, etc.

3. With that blood-washed throng I will shout and sing
   Just over in Glory Land,
   I'll stand there by Christ, my Lord and King
   Just over in Glory Land.
       Just over in Glory Land, etc.

4. What a wonderful thought when my Savior I see
   Just over in Glory Land,
   With my kindred safe forever I'll be
   Just over in Glory Land.
       Just over in Glory Land, etc.

40. Father Took a Light

light and ___ gone to heav- en, Father took a light and ___

gone to heav- en, ___ Bright an-gels wait-ing at the door.

2. Some bright day we shall go and see him,
   Some bright day we shall go and see him,
   Some bright day we shall go and see him,
   Over on that other shore.

3. Then let us all try to meet and rejoice 'ith him,
   Then let us all try to meet and rejoice 'ith him,
   Then let us all try to meet and rejoice 'ith him,
   Over on that other shore.

4. Our Mother took a light and gone to heaven, etc.
5. Some bright day we shall go and see her, etc.
6. Then let us all try to meet and rejoice 'ith her, etc.

7–9. Sister took a light, etc.

10–12. Brother took a light, etc.

13–15. Children took a light, etc.

16–18. I'm goin' to lay down my Bible and go home to be with them.

41. Climbing Up Zion's Hills

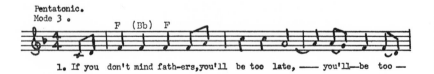

1. If you don't mind fath-ers, you'll be too late, ___ you'll ― be too ―

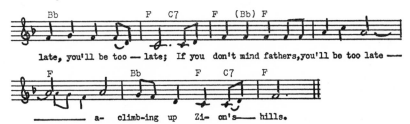

late, you'll be too — late; If you don't mind fathers,you'll be too late —

a- climb-ing up Zi- on's— hills.

2. Heaven bells are ringing, I'm a-going home,
   Yes, I'm a-going home, I'm a-going home;
   Heaven bells are ringing, I'm a-going home,
   A-climbing up Zion's hills.

3. Bless the Lord, I'm al-a-most there,
   I'm there, I'm there;
   Bless the Lord, I'm al-a-most there,
   A-climbing up Zion's hills.

4. If you don't mind, mothers, you'll be too late, etc.
5. Heaven bells are ringing, I'm a-going home, etc.
6. Bless the Lord, I'm al-a-most there, etc.
7–9. If you don't mind, brothers, you'll be too late, etc.
10–12. If you don't mind, sisters, you'll be too late, etc.
13–15. If you don't mind, children, you'll be too late, etc.

42. The Lifeboat Is Coming

Pentatonic.
Mode 3.

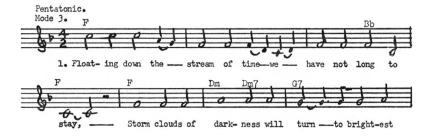

1. Float- ing down the — stream of time—we — have not long to

stay, ——— Storm clouds of dark- ness will turn —to bright-est

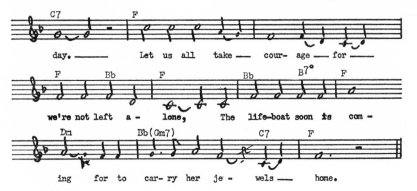

day. _____ Let us all take _____ cour- age _____ for _____
we're not left a - lone, The life-boat soon is com -
ing for to car- ry her je - wels _____ home.

2. Then, cheer, my brothers, cheer, our trials will soon be o'er,
   Our loved ones we shall meet, shall meet upon that golden shore.
   Let us all take courage for we're not left alone,
   The lifeboat soon is coming for to carry her jewels home.

3. Sometimes the devil tempt-es me, he says it's all in vain,
   Trying to live a Christian life and walk in Jesus' name.
   But then I heard my Master say I'll lend you a helping hand,
   If you will but trust in me I'll guide you to that land.

4. Then cheer, my brothers, cheer, our trials will soon be o'er,
   Our loved ones we shall meet, shall meet upon that golden shore.
   We're pilgrims and we're strangers here, we're seeking a city to
   come,
   The lifeboat soon is coming for to gather her jewels home.

5. The lifeboat soon is coming by a higher faith I see,
   As she sploshed through the waters to rescue you and me.
   The fairest peace for one and all and the Master bids you come,
   Get on board the lifeboat, she'll carry you safely home.

6. Then cheer, my brothers, cheer (etc., as stanza 4)

7. Get on board the lifeboat while she is passing by,
   If you stand and wait too long you must forever die.
   She'll carry you safely to the port where friends you love so dear,
   O love, love, the lifeboat, O love, she's almost here.

8. Then cheer, my brothers, cheer (etc., as stanza 4)

43. Lord, I've Started for the Kingdom

Pentatonic.
Mode 3.

1. Lord, I've start- ed for the Kingdom, Lord, I've start -ed for the King-dom,——— Lord, I've start- ed for the King- dom,———

— And I won't turn back,— and I won't turn— back.

2. If my father he won't go with me,
   If my father he won't go with me,
   If my father he won't go with me,
   I won't turn back, Lord, I won't turn back.

3. Lord, I've started for the Kingdom, etc.

4. If my mother she won't go with me,
   If my mother she won't go with me,
   If my mother she won't go with me,
   I won't turn back, Lord, I won't turn back.

5. Lord, I've started for the Kingdom, etc.
6. If my brother he won't go with me, etc.
7. Lord, I've started for the Kingdom, etc.
8. If my sister she won't go with me, etc.
9. Lord, I've started for the Kingdom, etc.

10. Take this world and give me Jesus,
    Take this world and give me Jesus,
    Take this world and give me Jesus,
    And I won't turn back, and I won't turn back.

44. I'm All Alone in This World

Pentatonic.
Mode 3.

1. O my father's gone to glo-ry, I'm a- lone in this world, O my
fath-er's gone to glo- ry, I'm a- lone; I'm a- lone in this world, Je-sus
knows I'm a- lone, Take me home, bless-ed Sav-ior, take me home.

(a)

2. O my mother's gone to glory, I'm alone in this world, etc.
3. O my brother's gone to glory, I'm alone in this world, etc.
4. O my sister's gone to glory, I'm alone in this world, etc.

5. I'm alone in this world, I am weary of life,
   I'm alone in this world, I'm alone;
   I'm alone in this world, Jesus knows I'm alone,
   Take me home, blessed Savior, take me home.

45. O Sinner Man

Hexatonic.
Suggests mixolydian mode.

1. O sin-ner man, where you goin' to run to? O sin-ner man,
where you goin' to run to? O sin-ner man, where you goin' to run to

all   in that   day?

2. Run to the rocks, pray rocks won't you hide me,
   Run to the rocks, pray rocks won't you hide me,
   Run to the rocks, pray rocks won't you hide me
   All in that day.

3. Lord says, sinner man, the rocks be a-rollin', etc.
4. O sinner man, where will you run to? etc.
5. Run to the moon, pray moon won't you hide me, etc.
6. Lord said, sinner man, the moon be a-bleedin', etc.
7. O sinner man, where you goin to run to? etc.
8. Run to the sun, pray sun won't you hide me, etc.
9. Lord said, sinner man, the sun be a-darkened, etc.
10. O sinner man, where will you run to? etc.
11. Run to the stars, pray stars won't you hide me, etc.
12. Lord said, sinner man, the stars be a-fallin', etc.
13. O sinner man, where you goin' to run to? etc.
14. Run to the Lord, pray Lord, won't you hide me, etc.
15. The Lord said, sinner man, you ought to be a-prayin', etc.
16. Sinner man said, Lord I been a-prayin', etc.
17. Lord said, sinner man, you prayed too late, etc.
18. O sinner man, where you goin' to run to? etc.
19. Run to Satan, pray Satan won't you hide me, etc.
20. Satan says, yes, dest come right in, sir, etc.

46. I Got a Hope in That Rock

Pentatonic.
Mode 3.

1. I got a   hope   in that rock,_ don't you   see,   I got a

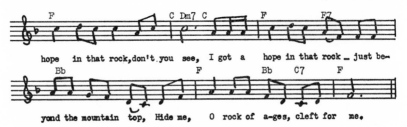

hope in that rock, don't you see, I got a hope in that rock — just be-

yond the mountain top, Hide me, O rock of a-ges, cleft for me.

ヿ. East and west the fire shall roll, hide by me,
   East and west the fire will roll, hide by me,
   East and west the fire will roll,
   What shall become of my pore soul,
   Hide me, O rock of ages, cleft for me.

3. I got a hope in that rock, don't you see, etc.

4. O the rich man lived he fared so well, don't you see,
   The rich man lived he fared so well, don't you see,
   When the rich man lived he fared so well,
   Waitin' God his home in hell,
   Hide me, O rock of ages, cleft for me.

5. I got a hope in that rock, don't you see, etc.

6. Lazrus was buried right where he lie, don't you see,
   Lazrus was buried right where he lie, don't you see,
   Lazrus was buried right where he lie,
   When he died his home's on high,
   Hide me, O rock of ages, cleft for me.

47. Will the Circle Be Unbroken?

Pentatonic.
Mode 3.

1. I were stand-ing by my win- dow one — cold De- cem- ber

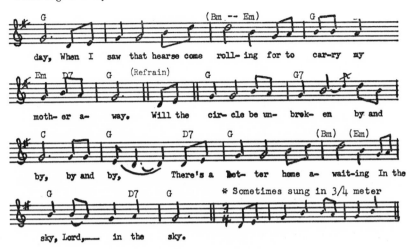

day, When I saw that hearse come roll-ing for to car-ry my moth-er a-way. Will the cir-cle be un-brok-en by and by, by and by, There's a bet-ter home a-wait-ing In the sky, Lord,— in the sky.

(Refrain)

* Sometimes sung in 3/4 meter

2. Then I said to the undertaker,
   Undertaker, please drive slow,
   For this lady you are hauling,
   Lord, I hate to see her go.
   > Will the circle be unbroken, etc.

3. Lord, I followed along behind her
   Until we come to the family grave,
   But I could not hide my sorrow
   When they laid her in the grave.
   > Will the circle be unbroken, etc.

4. Went back home and home was lonesome,
   O yes, my mother she was gone,
   Brothers and sisters all was cryin',
   What a home so sad and lone.
   > Will the circle be unbroken, etc.

5. One by one our family is leaving,
   One by one they're gone away,
   But some day I hope to meet them
   In that coming Judgment Day.
   > Will the circle be unbroken, etc.

48. Praise the Lord, I Saw the Light

Pentatonic.
Mode 3.

1. I wan-dered so aim-less, my life filled with sin That I would not let my dear Savior in, But Je-sus he come like a stranger in the night, O praise the Lord, I —— saw the light. Saw the light, I saw the light, No more dark- ness, no more—— night. I am so hap-py, no sor-row in sight, O praise the Lord, I —— saw the light.

2. Just like a blind man I wandered alone,
   Nearest and dearest I claimed for my own,
   Just like a blind man who God gave his sight,
   O praise the Lord, I saw the light.
   Saw the light, I saw the light, etc.

3. O what a fool to wander astray,
   Straight is the gates and narrow the way,
   But now I have traded the wrong for the right,
   O praise the Lord, I saw the light.
   Saw the light, I saw the light, etc.

49. Kingdom a-Comin'

1. O the mar-ster looked down the road, Seed the smoke to my link to my gun-boat laid; He grabbed his hat in a great big hur-ry and I guess he run a- way.

2. The marster's run away
   And the darkies stayed at home;
   They must a been down to the Kingdom a-comin'
   For to hear the bugle blow.

3. The wine's a sight all under the cellar,
   The darkies they wanted some;
   They must a been down to the Kingdom a-comin'
   To hear the bugle blow.

50. Yankee Song

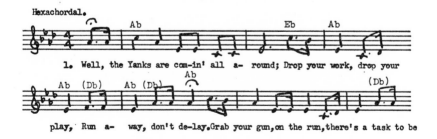

1. Well, the Yanks are com-in' all a- round; Drop your work, drop your play, Run a- way, don't de-lay. Grab your gun, on the run, there's a task to be

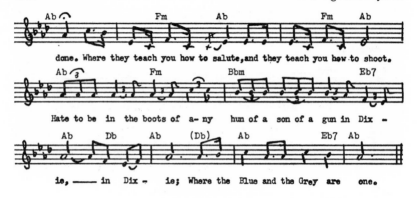

done. Where they teach you how to salute, and they teach you how to shoot.

Hate to be in the boots of a-ny hum of a son of a gun in Dix -

ie, —— in Dix - ie; Where the Blue and the Grey are one.

[No other stanzas]

51. Cumberland Gap

Tetratonic.

1. Lay down boys and take a lit-tle nap, Lay down boys and take a little nap,

Lay down boys and take a little nap, We'll have a battle at the Cumberland Gap.

2. Cumberland Gap it hain't very far,
   Cumberland Gap it hain't very far,
   Cumberland Gap it hain't very far,
   Just a little piece above Middlebar.

3. Lay down your gripsack, hang up your cap, [three times]
   We're goin' to have trouble at the Cumberland Gap.

4. Cumberland Gap, it's mighty cold, [three times]
   Can't make a nickel for to save your soul.

5. Rub your cannons bright and clean, [three times]
   Goin' to whup them Rebels out o' Bowlin' Green.

6. Lay down your gripsack, hang up your cap, [three times]
We'll beat them Rebels at the Big Stone Gap.

7. Come on, boys, listen to me, [three times]
Whup them Rebels out o' Washington, D.C.

8. Come on, boys, le's play fair, [three times]
Beat them Rebels on the Delaware.

52. Big Stone Gap

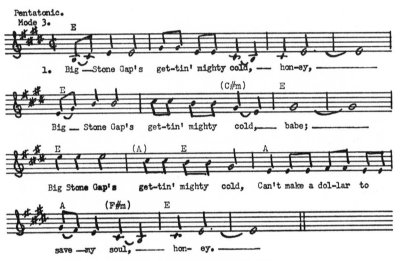

2. I got on a dummy and I had no fare, baby,
I got on a dummy and I had no fare, honey;
I got on a dummy and I had no fare,
Doggone police took me by the hair, baby.

3. Took me by the hair and he led me to the door, honey,
Took me by the hair and he led me to the door, baby;
Took me by the hair and he led me to the door,
And I betcha I don't ride that dummy no more, honey.

4. I got a forty-five shoots six straight, baby,

I got a forty-five shoots six straight, honey;
I got a forty-five shoots six straight,
You can't bluff me with your thirty-eight, honey.

5. What're you goin' to do when the po-lice comes, baby?
   What're you goin' to do when the po-lice comes, honey?
   What're you goin' to do when the po-lice comes?
   Hide in the corner, break and run, baby.

6. Got no razor and I got no gun, honey,
   Got no razor and I got no gun, baby;
   Got no razor and I got no gun,
   Got no woman and I don't need none, honey.

7. 'Ts I'm goin' back to Jellico, baby,
   'Ts I'm goin' back to Jellico, honey,
   'Ts I'm goin' back to Jellico,
   'Ts I'm goin' back to marry before I go, baby.

53. Back in the Hills

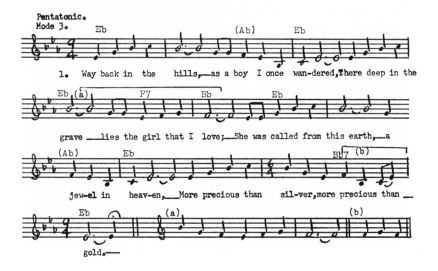

2. She was a jewel on earth, she is a jewel for heaven,
   She'll brighten the kingdom all around God's great throne;
   May the angels have peace, God bless her in heaven,
   They have broken my heart and caused me to roam.

3. When a girl of sixteen we courted each other,
   She promised some day to become my sweet wife;
   I bought her the ring to wear on her finger,
   But the angels they called her to heaven one night.

4. She was a jewel on earth, she is a jewel for heaven, etc.

5. This world has its wealth, its trials and troubles,
   The mother earth has treasures of diamonds and gold;
   But you can't hold the soul of one precious jewel,
   She's resting at peace in her heavenly home.

6. She was a jewel on earth, she is a jewel in heaven, etc.

54. My Daddy Was a Gambler

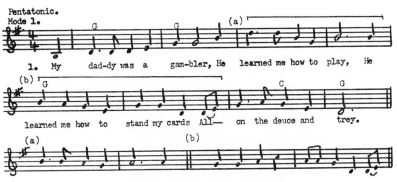

2. 'Ts I played cards on the steamboat,
   'Ts I played cards on the train,
   If there's a man can beat me
   I want to know his name.

3. Gambled on my pocketbooks,
   Gambled on my comb,

Gambled all my money away
And now I'm a-goin' home.

4. Old jack of diamonds,
   It's you I know so well,
   Gambled all my money away
   And sent my soul to hell.

55. Icy Mountain

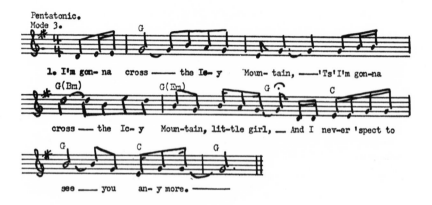

2. Rock and feed my baby candy,
   Rock and feed my baby candy, little girl,
   I never expect to see it any more.

3. 'Ts I'm gonna to cross the Icy Mountain,
   'Ts I'm gonna to cross the Icy Mountain, little girl,
   And I never expect to see you any more.

4. Stop and tell my mommy howdy,
   Stop and tell my mommy howdy, little girl,
   I never expect to see her any more.

5. 'Ts I'm gonna cross the Icy Mountain,
   'Ts I'm gonna cross the Icy Mountain, little girl,
   And I never expect to come back any more.

56. Moonshiner

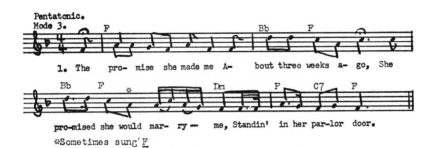

1. The pro- mise she made me A- bout three weeks a- go, She
pro-mised she would mar- ry — me, Standin' in her par-lor door.

*Sometimes sung 'F

2. I'll walk up on the mountain and put up a still,
   I'll make you one gallon for a two-dollar bill.

3. I go to the grocery and drink to my friends,
   No woman to follow to see what I spend.

4. I oft-times have wondered how women loved men,
   Many a time I've studied how men did love them.

5. Come all you purty women and stand in a row,
   You look so sadly, you're lonesome I know.

6. You caused me to see trouble and many a downfall,
   If you want to live happy don't marry a-tall.

57. Short Life of Trouble

1. I've been a moon- shin- er for sev- en- teen years,——
I've spent all my mon - ey for whis- key and beer.——

* Sometimes sung G in original performance.

2. Short life and trouble,
   A few more words and part,
   Short life and trouble, girl,
   A boy with a broken heart.

3. Now you've broke your promise,
   Can marry who you please,
   All the girl I ever loved,
   She's turned her back on me.

4. Short life and trouble, etc.

5. I cannot be your sweetheart,
   I'll tell you the reason why,
   My mother always taught me
   To pass a drunkard by.

6. Said it would be dangerous
   For a young girl as I
   To fall in love with a boy
   Who carried a drunkard's life.

7. Short life and trouble, etc.

8. My father he's in heaven,
   And my mother's by his side,
   I never took to drinking
   Till my dear old mother died.

9. First thing I owned was a pistol,
   The next was cards to play,
   Then go down to the gambling hall
   I gambled my life away.

10. Short life and trouble, etc.

11. I hear the train a-comin',
    She give a station blow,
    Rather see my casket come in
    As to see my darling go.

12. Short life and trouble, etc.
13. See my casket coming,

All over lined with black,
It takes me to the graveyard
But it hain't a-goin' to bring me back.

14. Short life and trouble, etc.

58. Chilly Wind

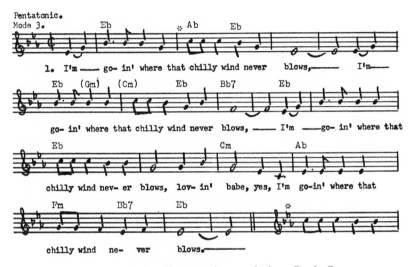

2. I'm goin' where the climate suits me clothes, [twice]
   I'm goin' where the climate suits me clothes, lovin' babe,
   Yes, I'm goin' where the climate suits me clothes.

3. I'm goin' if I have to ride the rods, [twice]
   I'm goin' if I have to ride the rods, lovin' babe,
   Yes, I'm goin' if I have to ride the rods.

4. I'm goin' if I never come back, [twice]
   I'm goin' if I never come back, lovin' babe,
   Yes, I'm goin' if I never come back.

5. Them blue-eyed girls they don't treat me right, [twice]
   Them blue-eyed girls they don't treat me right, lovin' babe,

Yes, them blue-eyed girls they don't treat me right.

6. I'm goin' if I have to ride a mule, [twice]
   I'm goin' if I have to ride a mule, lovin' babe,
   Yes, I'm goin' if I have to ride a mule.

59. Darlin' Cory

2. Wake up, wake up, darlin' Cory,
   How can you lay and snore?
   The marshall's got you 'rested,
   O baby, I hate to go.

3. Go dig a hole in the meadow,
   Go dig my hole in the ground,
   Go dig a hole in the meadow
   And lay darlin' Cory down.

4. Last time I seen darlin' Cory,
   Had a dram glass in her hand,
   She was drinkin' down her troubles
   With a low-down drunken man.

5. How can I live and stand it
   For to see her purty blue eyes?

She's a-courtin' some other fellow
And she's a-tellin' me all her lies.

6. Corn whiskey'll run a man crazy,
   Will bake ever' brain in his head,
   Corn whiskey'll run a man crazy,
   Purty women will kill him stone dead.

7. Last time I seen darlin' Cory,
   She was standin' on the bank of the sea,
   With a forty-four special round her,
   She was wavin' her hand at me.

8. When I am dead and buried,
   Purty women all ought to know,
   Take the lid off of my coffin
   And let darlin' Cory know.

9. When I am dead and in my coffin
   And my face laid toward the sun,
   You can set down by me, darlin',
   And think of the way you have done.

60. Greenback Dollar

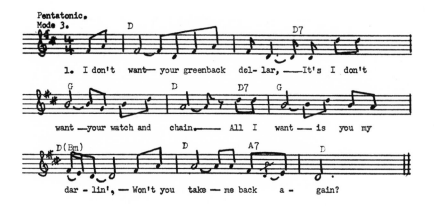

Pentatonic. Mode 3.

1. I don't want— your greenback del- lar, ——It's I don't
want —your watch and chain.—— All I want — is you my
dar - lin', — Won't you take — me back a - gain?

2. Don't that road look rough and rocky,
   Don't that sea look wide and deep,
   Don't my darling look much sweeter
   When she's in my arms asleep?

3. Rather be in some dark hollar
   Where the sun don't never shine,
   Than to hear you call another darling
   When you promised to be mine.

4. I don't want your greenback dollar,
   It's I don't want your watch and chain,
   All I want is you, my darling,
   Say you'll take me back again.

5. Many of a night I've set and rambled
   On the banks of the deep blue sea,
   In your heart you call another darling,
   In my grave I'd rather be.

6. I don't want your greenback dollar, etc.

61. In the Pines

2. I stayed in the pines where the sun never shines,
   And shivered when the cold wind blows.

3. The long steel rails and short cross-ties
   I wandered my way back home.

4. In the pines, in the pines, where the sun never shines,
   Where I shiver when the cold wind blows.

5. The longest train I ever saw
   Come running from the Coal Creek mines.

6. The engine passed at four o'clock,
   The caboose went by at nine.

7. The longest train I ever saw
   Come running from the Coal Creek mines.

8. The lonesomest day I ever experienced,
   When I left my girl behind.

9. Truelove, truelove, what have I done
   To turn your back on me?

10. I've killed no man, I've robbed no train,
    I've done no hanging crime.

11. The purtiest girl I ever saw
    Lived a mile and a half from town.

12. Her head was found in the driver's wheels
    And her body was never found.

13. In the pines, in the pines, where the sun never shines,
    Where I shiver when the cold wind blows.

62. Little Birdie

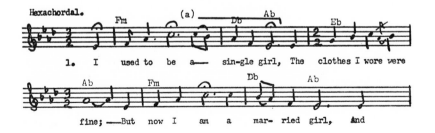

wear just an- y   old   thing. ———

2. Little birdie, little birdie,
   Sing to me your song,
   Sing a song, little birdie,
   Sing a song to me.

3. I used to be a single girl,
   To go with whom I pleased,
   But now I am a married girl,
   With a baby on my knee.

4. I wished I had a cedar bow,
   Arrow tied by a string,
   I'd shoot it through the little bird's heart,
   No longer would she sing.

5. Big white house in Baltimore,
   Sixteen stories high,
   Got my wife in an upper room,
   I hope she'll never die.

6. Little birdie, little birdie,
   Come and set down on my knee,
   Sing a song, little birdie,
   Sing a song to me.

63. My Trunk Is Packed

1. My —— true love may be ——flirt- ing, But I know I've treat-ed her kind, What—— can I do or—— say ——dar-ling, That'll ever change her mind.

2. There's nothing you can do or say
That'll ever change my mind,
My trunk is packed in the depot,
And it's getting almost train time.

3. I'll make my escape by the winder,
And I'll beat her down the line,
My trunk is packed and in the depot,
My train is almost due.

4. I've spent my last day, darlin',
I'll ever spend with you,
You'll see me here today, darlin',
Tomorrow I'll be gone.

5. I'll beat her across the ocean,
I'll beat 'her across the sea,
I'll beat 'her across the ocean
Where she never can see me.

6. I went to see my girl last night,
I stayed till one, two, three,
I hugged and kissed them purty sweet lips,
She hugged and kissed me.

7. I went to see my girl last night,
I stayed till almost four,
I hugged and kissed them purty sweet lips,
But I hain't a-comin' back no more.

64. Old Reuben

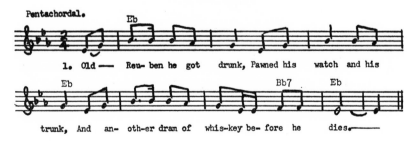

Pentachordal.

1. Old — Reu- ben he got drunk, Pawned his watch and his trunk, And an- oth-er dram of whis-key be- fore he dies.———

2. If you say so I'll railroad no more,
   I'll sidetrack my engine and go home.

3. The train's off the track and I can't get her back,
   And I can't get a letter from my home.

4. If you say yes we'll marry I guess,
   We'll leave on the next train that goes down.

5. If you say no I'll railroad no more,
   I'll lay down my hammer and go home.

6. You can count the days I'm gone, you can tell the train I'm on,
   You can hear the whistle blow a hundred miles.

7. Where did you get them brand-new shoes
   And that dress you wear so fine?

8. I got my shoes from a railroad man,
   And I got my dress from a driver in the mines.

9. I'll pawn you my watch, I'll pawn you my chain,
   I'll pawn you my gold diamond ring.

10. If that don't pay my baby's way,
    I'll pawn you my wagon and team.

11. If I die a railroad boy bury me under the tie,
    I can hear old Number Nine go rolling by.

12. When I die, the railroad boys will build my casket out of pine,
    And bury me in that tunnel Number Nine.

65. Good-bye, My Lover

Pentatonic.
Mode 3.

1. The   day is long and   lone-some, The nights is get- tin' cold, I'm

goin' to see my true love, Be- fore she gets too old.
(Refrain)
Good- bye my lov-er I'm gone, Good- bye my lover I'm gone, Good-
bye my lo-ver I'm gone, Oh — yes, I'm goin' to leave you now.

2. I'm goin' on that mountain,
   Mountain high and tall,
   Broad-ax on my shoulder,
   Hew that mountain small.
   Good-bye, my lover, I'm gone, etc.

3. I'm goin' on that mountain
   To plant me a patch of cane,
   Raise me a barrel of 'lasses
   To sweeten Liza Jane.
   Good-bye, my lover, I'm gone, etc.

4. I'm goin' on yon mountain,
   I'll look back and say,
   "Feel so sad and lonesome
   Goin' away to stay."
   Good-bye, my lover, I'm gone, etc.

5. I'm goin' on yon mountain
   To give my horn a blow,
   Purtiest girl in that town
   Says, "Yander comes my beau."
   Good-bye, my lover, I'm gone, etc.

66. Bald Eagle

Pentatonic.
Mode 3.

1. Well I wish I was an old bald eagle, long —time a- go, ——I'd
fly a- way down to Ok-la- ho- ma, Long time a- go.———— Whooo
wheee, ———— Whooo - ooo.————

2. Well a darkie said he'd hug my Sally, long time ago,
   Darkie said he'd hug my Sally, long time ago.
   Whooo whee whooo.

3. I cocked my gun and pulled the trigger, long time ago,
   Shot that darkie through the liver, long time ago.
   Whooo whee whooo.

4. She ought been there to see him kickin' and quiverin', long time ago,
   She ought been there to see him kickin' and quiverin', long time ago.
   Whooo whee whooo.

5. Oh, what's in the pot, my good granny, long time ago?
   Oh, what's in the pot, my good granny, long time ago?
   Whooo whee whooo.

6. Sheep shank and a husky dumplin', long time ago,
   Sheep shank and a husky dumplin', long time ago.
   Whooo whee whooo.

67. Paper of Pins

Hexatonic.
Ionian(major) implications.

1. I will buy you a pa-per of pins, It may be for the first begin, If

you'll be my true lov- er.   Old Rack-A-man- der with-out a reason   deed,

I love a girl and she don't love me; Then for love I die;Jack the money will gain.

3. I will buy you a dress of red,
   It's stitched around with golden thread,
   If you'll be my true lover.

4. I won't accept your dress of red,
   It's stitched around with golden thread,
   I won't be your true lover.
   [Refrain]

5. I will buy you a little pacin' horse,
   Pace these hills and mountains across,
   If you'll be my true lover.

6. I won't accept your little pacin' horse,
   Pace these hills and mountains across,
   I won't be your true lover.
   [Refrain]

7. I will buy you a little happy dog
   To stay with you when you go abroad,
   If you'll be my true lover.

8. I won't accept your little happy dog
   Stay with me when I go abroad,
   I won't be your true lover.
   [Refrain]

9. I will buy you a little handmaid
   Stay with you when you are afraid,
   If you'll be my true lover.

10. I won't accept your little handmaid
    Stay with me when I'm afraid,

I won't be your true lover.
[Refrain]

11. I will give you the key to my desk
    To get your money at your own request,
    If you'll be my true lover.

12. I'll accept the key of the desk
    To get my money at my own request,
    I'll be your true lover.

13. If you think I'm blind and cannot see,
    It's for my money and not for me,
    I won't be your true lover.
    [Refrain]

68. Soldier, Won't You Marry Me?

2. She run away to the miller shop
   Just as hard as she could run,
   Brung him back the finest hat—
   Soldier, won't you put this on?

3. Soldier, soldier won't you marry me?
   Musket fife and drum.
   How can I marry such a purty little girl
   And me no shirt to put on?

4. She run away to the apartment store
   Just as hard as she could run,

Brung him back the finest shirt—
Soldier, won't you put this on?

5. And me no pants to put on?
6. She run away to the tailor shop
7. And me no coat to put on?
8. She run away to the tailor shop
9. And me no underwear to put on?
10. She run away to the apartment store
11. And me no tie to put on?
12. She run away to the apartment store
13. And me no socks to put on?
14. She run away to the apartment store
15. And me no shoes to put on?
16. She run away to the shoe shop

17. Soldier, soldier, won't you marry me?
    Musket fife and drum.
    How can I marry such an ugly old girl
    With a pretty little wife at home?

69. Down the Road

Pentatonic.
Mode 3.

1. Way down yan-der as far as I have been, All them women love row-dy men.
(Refrain)
Down the road, down the road, 'Ts can't get a let-ter from down the road.

2. Way down yander far as I can see,
   'Ts everybody looks alike to me.
   [Refrain]

3. When the moon went down so I couldn't see,
   The first I knowed the sheriff had me.
   [Refrain]

70. Cindy

Pentatonic.
Mode 3.

1. 'Ts you go up the new-dug road, 'Ts I'll go 'round the lane. If you get there be- fore I do, Good morn-ing, Li - za Jane.

(Refrain)

Run a- long home, home, ____ git a-long home, home, ____ Git a-long home, home, Cin-dy, Down the ri- ver road.

* In performance, sung as a quarter note.

2. 'Ts if I had no horse to ride,
   'Ts I'd be found a-crawlin',
   Up and down the rocky road
   A-huntin' for my darling.
   [Refrain after each stanza]

3. You may ride the big bay horse,
   'Ts you may ride the roan,
   You go see your own truelove
   And leave my gal alone.

4. 'Ts I went to see my Cindy
And I never was there before,
Shoes and stockin's in her hand
And her foot all over the floor.

5. Her chin looked like a punkin pie,
Her nose looked like a squash,
Every time she opened her mouth
So I laughed, by gosh.

6. Her chin looked like a punkin,
Her nose looked like a spout,
Her mouth looked like an old fireplace
With the ashes just tuck out.

71. Black-Eyed Susie

2. Rain come and wet me, sun come and dry me,
Look out, purty girls, don't you come a-nigh me,
Hop up, purty little black-eyed Susie,
Hop up, purty little black-eyed Susie.

72. Blue-Eyed Girl

1. Fly a-round, my blue-eyed girl, Fly a-round my dai-sy,
Fly a-round my blue-eyed girl, you dang nigh run me cra-zy.

2. The higher you climb the cherry tree,
   The riper grows the berries,
   The more you court and kiss them girls,
   The sooner you will marry.

3. Cincinnati is a purty place
   And so is Philadelphia,
   The streets is lined with the dollar bill
   And the purty girls a-plenty.

4. Black-eyed girl went back on me,
   The blue-eyed girl won't have me,
   Before I'd marry the cross-eyed girl
   A-single I would tarry.

5. I went to see my old truelove,
   I never was there before,
   She lay on the old straw bed,
   And I lay on the floor.

6. She took me by the hand
   And she led me in to supper,
   Stumped my toe on the table lag
   And stove my nose in the butter.

73. Georgia Buck

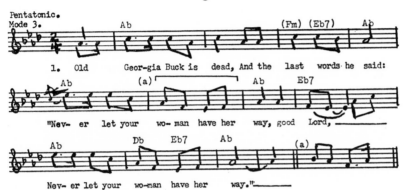

2. If you let her have her way,
   She will whup you ever' day,
   Never let your woman have her way, good Lord,
   Never let your woman have her way.

3. I get upon the dumps
   And act like I'm drunk,
   And it's nobody's business but my own, Lord, Lord,
   And it's nobody's business but my own.

4. I get up in the loft
   And I pull my britches off,
   And I'll dance in my long shirt-tail, Lord, Lord,
   Well I'll dance in my long shirt-tail.

74. Idy Red

2. Buy me a horse, goin' to make me a sled
   To take a little ride with Idy Red;
   Idy Red, Idy Blue, I'm in love with Idy too,
   Idy Red, Idy Red, I'm in love with Idy Red.

3. Goin' to buy me a horse, goin' to make me a hack,
   Goin' to get Idy, goin' to bring her back;
   Idy Red, Idy Blue, I'm in love with Idy too,
   Idy Red, Idy Red, I'm in love with Idy Red.

4. Idy Red, Idy Green, prettiest little thing I ever seen,
   Idy Red, Idy Red, I'm in love with Idy Red;
   Idy Red, Idy Blue, I'm in love with Idy too,
   Idy Red, Idy Red, I'm in love with Idy Red.

75. I'm a-Longin' for to Go This Road

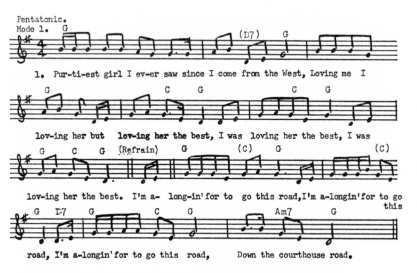

2. When she saw me coming she wrung her hands and cried,
   When she saw me leaving she fainted away and died,
   Fainted away and died,

When she fainted away and died.
[Refrain]

3. Her nose looked like a punkin vine, her chin looked like a squash,
Every time she opened her mouth and so I laughed, by gosh,
So I laughed, by gosh,
And so I laughed, by gosh.
[Refrain]

4. Her chin looked like a coffee pot, her nose looked like a spout,
Her mouth looked like a fireplace and the ashes fresh took out,
And the ashes fresh took out,
With the ashes fresh took out.
[Refrain]

76. Sourwood Mountain

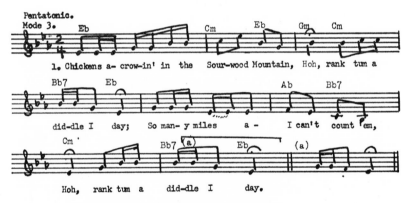

2. My truelove in the head o' the hollar,
Hoh, rank tum a diddle I day,
She won't come and I won't foller,
Hoh, rank tum a diddle I day.

3. Big dog'll bark and the little un'll bite ye,
Hoh, rank tum a diddle I day,
Big girls'll spark and the little uns'll fight ye,

Hoh, rank tum a diddle I day.

4. My truelove in the bend of the river,
   Hoh, rank tum a diddle I day,
   A few more jumps and I'll be with her,
   Hoh, rank tum a diddle I day.

5. Chickens a-crowin' in the Sourwood Mountain,
   Hoh, rank tum a diddle I day,
   So many miles I can't count 'em,
   Hoh, rank tum a diddle I day.

6. My truelove lives in Magoffin,
   Hoh, rank tum a diddle I day,
   Too fer there and I can't go often,
   Hoh, rank tum a diddle I day.

7. My truelove she's a daisy,
   Hoh, rank tum a diddle I day,
   She won't work, she's too lazy,
   Hoh, rank tum a diddle I day.

77. Yonder Comes My Love

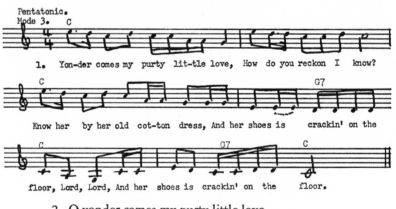

2. O yonder comes my purty little love,
   She's all dressed in yaller,

Looking down at her purty little feet,
And her shoes all greased with taller, Lord, Lord,
And her shoes all greased with taller.

3. O yonder comes my purty little love,
She's all dressed in red,
Looking down at her purty little feet,
And she wished my wife was dead, Lord, Lord,
And she wished my wife was dead.

4. I went upon the mountain
And give my horn a blow,
Purtiest girl in that town,
"Yonder comes my beau, Lord, Lord,
Look yonder comes my beau."

78. Little Brown Jug

Pentachordal.

1. Me and my wife went o-ver my farm, A lit-tle brown jug stuck un-der my arm. Ha, ha, ha, you and me, Little brown jug, don't I love thee.

2. 'Ts I laid down in the shade of a tree,
Little brown jug in the shade of me.
Ha, ha, ha, you and me,
Little brown jug, don't I love thee.

3. 'Ts I raised up and give it a pull,
Little brown jug was about half full,
Ha, ha, ha, you and me,
Little brown jug, don't I love thee.

4. Me and my wife and a stump-tail dog

Went across the river on a hickory log.
Ha, ha, ha, you and me,
Little brown jug, don't I love thee.

5. Bark it slipped and I fell in,
   Broke my jug and spilled my gin.
   Ha, ha, ha, you and me,
   Little brown jug, don't I love thee.

6. Bought me a cow from Farmer Jones,
   It wouldn't nothing but skin and bones.
   Ha, ha, ha, you and me,
   Little brown jug, don't I love thee.

7. I fed her on the choicest hay
   And milked her forty times a day.
   Ha, ha, ha, you and me,
   Little brown jug, don't I love thee.

79. Sugar Hill

2. 'Ts if you want your freedom,
   If you want your fill,
   If you want your eye knocked out,
   Just look on the Sugar Hill.

3. Saw the jaybirds in the mountain
   Flopping up and down,
   Purty girl in the sugar tree

Shaking the sugar down.

4. 'Ts I set my mill to the grinding,
   Water poured over the dam,
   Thought I'd made a fortune,
   And I married poor Julie Ann.

5. I thought I'd made a fortune
   And never could be sunk,
   I lost it all a-gambling
   The night that I got drunk.

6. O a jaybird in the mountain,
   Jaybird's trying to crow,
   Dead man's trying to shave himself,
   Blind man's a-trying to sew.

7. O the little bee makes the honey,
   And the big bee makes the comb,
   Poor man fights the battle,
   And the big man stays at home.

8. Jaybird pulls a two-horse load,
   Sparrow, why don't you?
   My neck's so long and slender,
   I'm afraid it'll pull in two.

9. When you go a-courtin',
   I'll tell you what to do,
   When you go down to the tailor shop,
   Put on your long-tail blue.

10. When you go a-courting,
    I'll tell you what to say,
    When you go down to the tailor shop,
    Put on your Rebel gray.

11. If I had the money,
    Half that I have lost,
    Buy my wife a shoo-fly dress,
    And I wouldn't care what the cost.

80. Shoo Fly

2. Daddy bought a yaller girl,
   He brought her from the South,
   Her hair was so kinky,
   She could not shet her mouth;
   Shoo fly, don't you bother me.

3. Well, he took her to the tailor shop
   To have her mouth made small,
   Was no screws she 'scaped the vise
   And swallered the tailor and all;
   Shoo fly, don't you bother me.

81. Cripple Creek

Goin' up Crip-ple Creek to   have a lit- tle fun.

2. The girls over Cripple about half-grown, (three times)
   Jump on a boy like a dog on a bone.
   [Refrain]

3. The girls on the Cripple Creek a-layin' in the shade, (three times)
   A-waitin' for the dollar the poor boy made.

82. Old Corn Whiskey

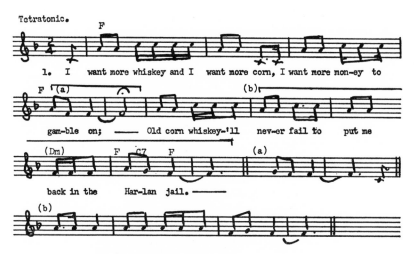

1. I want more whiskey and I want more corn, I want more mon-ey to
gam-ble on; —— Old corn whiskey-'ll nev-er fail to put me
back in the Har-lan jail. ——

2. Harlan jail is no jail a-tall,
   Watch them graybacks scale the wall;
   I want more whiskey and I want more corn,
   I want more money to gamble on.

3. Shout, Little Luly, shout and shout,
   What in the devil're you shoutin' about?
   Sift your meal and save your bran,

Shake that little foot, Sally Ann.

4. Who're you goin' to marry, Jake and Nan,
   Who're you goin' to dance for, ring-eyed Sam?
   Shake that little foot, Sally Ann,
   Put that left foot on the ground.

83. Old Coon Dog

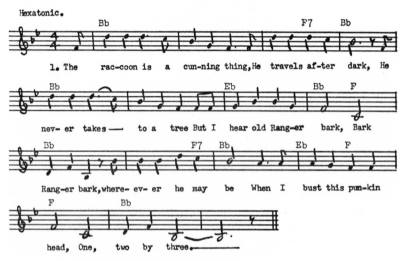

2. Somebody stole my old coon dog,
   They better bring him back,
   He run the big hogs over the fence
   And the little hogs through the crack,
   Wherever he may be,
   Wherever he may be
   When I bust this punkin head,
   One, two by three.

3. Somebody stole my little bunny pullet,
   They better let her be,
   Ever'day she laid two eggs,

Wherever she may be,
Wherever she may be
When I bust this punkin head,
One, two by three.

4. My daddy had an old grey horse,
   Called him Charlie Brown,
   The least tooth was in his head
   Was sixteen inches around,
   Wherever he may be,
   Wherever he may be
   When I bust this punkin head,
   One, two by three.

5. There was a little girl she lived in town,
   Her name was Sally Brown,
   She courted and married
   Before the sun went down,
   Before the sun went down,
   Wherever she may be
   When I bust this punkin head,
   One, two by three.

84. Mule Skinner Blues

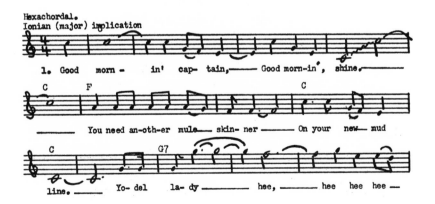

hee. ——————

2. When I hain't workin',
   I'm ramblin' all the time,
   I could cut my 'nitials
   On a mule just any old time.
   Yodel lady, hee, hee, hee, hee, he-ee.

3. Say, little waterboy,
   Pass your water around,
   If you don't like your job,
   Set your water bucket down.
   Yodel lady, hee, hee, hee, hee, he-ee.

4. I'm goin' to town,
   What'd ye want me to bring you back?
   A walkin' cane
   And a John B. Stetson hat.
   Yodel lady, hee, hee, hee, hee, he-ee.

5. Workin' on the railroad,
   A dollar and a dime a day,
   Purty little girl in town Saturday night
   A-waitin' to draw my pay.
   Yodel lady, hee, hee, hee, hee, he-ee.

6. Smell your bread burnin',
   Good gal, turn your damper down,
   If you have no damper, good gal,
   Turn your bread around.
   Yodel lady, hee, hee, hee, hee, he-ee.

85. Chisholm Trail

1. Come, boys, and listen to my tale, The sto-ry I'll tell you 'bout the

old Chisholm trail, Come a ty yi yip-pi yip-pi yi yip-pi ya, Come a

ty yi yip-pi yip-pi yo.

2. Way down yonder on the ole Chisholm trail,
   Rope in my hand and a calf by the tail,
   Come a ty yi yippi yippi yi yippi ya,
   Come a ty yi yippi yippi yo.

3. Well I went to the boss to get me some roll,
   He had it figured up nine dollars in the hole, etc.

4. Well a ten-dollar hoss and a twenty-dollar saddle,
   I'm going to quit punching them long-horn cattle, etc.

5. Well a twenty-dollar saddle and a forty-dollar hoss,
   I won't work for that durn boss, etc.

6. Went to the boss to draw my money,
   I'm going to town to see my honey,
   Come a ty yi yippi yippi yi yippi ya,
   Come a ty yi yippi yippi yo.

86. Groundhog

Hexatonic. Suggests Mixolydian Mode.

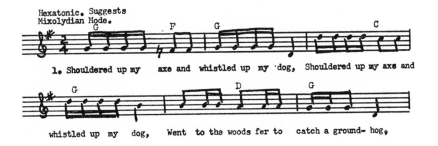

1. Shouldered up my axe and whistled up my dog, Shouldered up my axe and

whistled up my dog, Went to the woods fer to catch a ground-hog,

Ground- hog.

* Sung toward the sharp side

2. Two on the ground and one on the log,
   Two on the ground and one on the log,
   Two for me and one for my dog,
   Groundhog.

3. Run that groundhog in his hole,
   Run that groundhog in his hole,
   Couldn't tetch a tail with a ten-foot pole,
   Groundhog.

4. Joe and Kate kept prizing about,
   Joe and Kate kept prizing about,
   At last they prized that groundhog out,
   Groundhog.

5. Put 'im in the pot and he begin to bile,
   Put 'im in the pot and he begin to bile,
   I bet five dollars you could smell him a mile,
   Groundhog.

6. Up run Kate with a snigger and a grin,
   Up run Kate with a snigger and a grin,
   Groundhog grease all over her chin,
   Groundhog.

7. The meat's in the cupboard and the hide's in the churn,
   The meat's in the cupboard and the hide's in the churn,
   If that hain't groundhog I'll be durned,
   Groundhog.

8. Old Aunt Sal come hoppin' on a cane,
   Old Aunt Sal come hoppin' on a cane,
   Said she'd have that groundhog's brain,
   Groundhog.

9. Up jumped granny and she replied,
   Up jumped granny and she replied

She loved groundhog cooked or fried,
Groundhog.

10. Some did laugh and some did cry,
Some did laugh and some did cry,
To see 'em eat groundhog punkin pie,
Groundhog.

11. Took that hog and they tanned his hide,
Took that hog and they tanned his hide,
Made the best shoestrings ever was tied,
Groundhog.

87. Arkansas Traveler

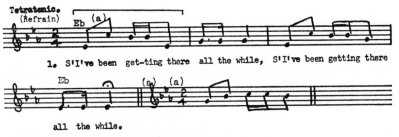

"Hello, stranger. How long has this road been here?"
"I don't know. It's here every morning when I get up."
[Refrain between each exchange]

"Hello, stranger. How far is it down to the forks?"
"I don't know. I keep my forks in the shelf."

"Hello, stranger. Does this river ford above?"
"Yes, sir, my ducks forded it this morning."

"Hello, stranger. Did you ever see or hear any spirits in this country?"
"Yes, sir, Sal heared something a-kickin' up its heels in the loft t'other
night."

"Hello, stranger. How many chillern have you got?"

"I don't know. Sal, roll a punkin unner the bed and run 'em out and count 'em."

"Stranger, what's your chillern all named?"

"They're all named Sal but the little foolish un, and it's named Sal too."

"Hello, stranger. How did your 'taters turn out?"
"They never turned out, the old sow rooted 'em out."

"Hello, traveler, what'll you take, tea or coffee?"
"Take tea."
"Sal, get the grubbing hoe and go dig some sassafack."

"Stranger, is squirrels much thick in this country?"
"Yes, sir, they're about as thick as your wrist."

88. Old Dan Tucker

Pentatonic.
Mode 3.

(Chorus)
1. Clear the way for Old Dan Tuck-er, Clear the way for Old Dan Tucker,

Clear the way for Old Dan Tuck-er, You come too late for to get an-y

(FINE) (Stanza 1)
sup- per.   Old Dan Tuck-er   He got drunk, Fell in the far and

kicked up a chunk. A red hot coal hopped in his shoe; Good God-a -

might-y how the ash- es flew.

D. C.
to Fine

2. Old Dan Tucker clomb a tree,
    The Lord did save him for to see,
    The limb did break and he did fall,
        Killed old Cally with a buckeye ball.
            Get out of the way, it's old Dan Tucker, [three times]
            You come too late for to get your supper.

3. Old Dan Tucker was a fine old man,
    He swapped his wife to a bob-tailed ram,
    Rode him over a big high clift,
    If she hadn't got up been layin' there yit.
        Clear the way, it's old Dan Tucker, etc.

4. Old Dan Tucker he went to town,
    He swallered a barrel of molasses down,
    The hoops did swell and the barrel did bust,
    Sent him to hell in a thunderglust.
        Get out of the way, it's old Dan Tucker, etc.

5. Old Dan Tucker he went out a-huntin',
    The first thing he spied was a big bar a-rootin',
    Its back was bent and its tail was a-shakin',
    He cocked his gun and he saved his bacon.
        Clear the way, it's old Dan Tucker, etc.

6. Old Dan Tucker was a fine old man,
    He washed his face in a frying pan,
    Combed his head with a wagon wheel,
    And died with a toothache in his heel.
        Clear the way, it's old Dan Tucker, etc.

89. Cold Frosty Morning

_____ with an   ax on his shoulder and   not a bit o' shirt.

2. One frosty morning the Nigger's mighty good,
   His ax on his shoulder and not a stick of wood.

3. One cold frosty morning when the meat's mighty fat,
   Look out, Nigger, don't you eat too much of that.

4. Out of the big house into the kitchen,
   There came a little Nigger, he's a-r'arin' and a-pitchin'.
   He's a-r'arin' and a-pitchin'.

90. Did You Ever See the Devil, Uncle Joe?

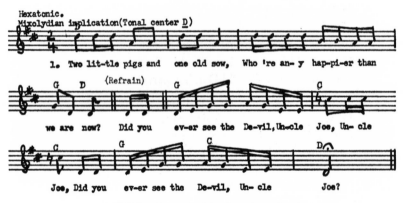

Hexatonic.
Mixolydian implication(Tonal center D)

1. Two lit-tle pigs and one old sow, Who're an- y hap-pi-er than

we are now? Did you   ev-er see the De-vil,Un-cle Joe, Un- cle

Joe, Did you   ev-er see the De-vil, Un- cle   Joe?

2. Make them darkies laugh and grin
   To see Uncle Joe come steppin' in.
   [Refrain after each stanza]

3. Make them darkies laugh and cry
   To see old Joe come ridin' by.

4. The old man come ridin' by,
   Said, "Old man, your horse will die."

5. If he dies I'll get his skin,
   If he lives I'll ride him again.

91. Do Johnny Booger

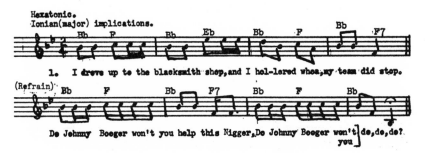

Hexatonic.
Ionian(major) implications.

1. I drove up to the blacksmith shop, and I hol-lered whoa, my team did stop.

(Refrain)

Do Johnny Booger won't you help this Nigger, Do Johnny Booger won't you de, de, de?

2. Axed that Nigger for to mend my yoke,
   He jumped to the bellows and blowed him up a smoke.
   [Refrain after each stanza]

3. I drove up to the foot of the hill,
   I hollered whoa, my team stopped still.

4. Axed that Nigger to mend my ring,
   He jumped to the anvil tang tang tang.

5. Hollered whoa, and my horse bucked around,
   Broke my tongue right even with the hound.

6. Put my shoulder against the wheel,
   I mashed the mud with my big heel.

7. I went down to that old field,
   A black snake got me by the heel.

8. Went a little faster and I run my best,
   And I stove my head in a hornet's nest.

9. The hornets they went boo, boo, boo,
   You better been there to see the Niggers flew.

10. Run, Nigger, run, run your best,

Run, Nigger, run the patteroles will ketch ye.
Don't go away, child, you can't fool me.
Do, Johnny Booger, won't you do, do, do.

11. I went off and I come back again,
    The white man scared me in an old sheep skin.

12. Run and I run and I almost flew,
    An' I tore my shirt-tail slap in two.

92. Cock Robin

2. Who seen him die?
   Me, said the Fly
   With my little yaller eye,
   It was me, it was I.

3. Who caught his blood?
   Me, said the Fish
   With my little silver dish,
   I was me, it was I.

4. Who dug his grave?
   Me, said the Crow
   With my little spade an' hoe,
   It was me, it was I.

5. Who hauled him off?
   Me, said the Lark
   With my little hoss an' cart,

It was me, it was I.

6. Who covered him up?
   Me, said the Duck
   With my little flatter foot,
   It was me, it was I.

7. Who preached his funeral?
   Me, said the Swaller
   Dist as loud as I could holler,
   It was me, it was I.

93. Tree in the Mountains

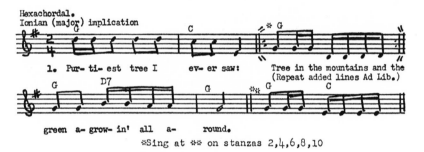

2. Purtiest limb I ever saw,
   Limb on the tree
   And the tree in the mountains
   And the green a-growin' all around.

3. Purtiest nest I ever saw,
   Nest on the limb, etc.

4. Purtiest egg I ever saw,
   The egg in the nest, etc.

5. Purtiest elk [yolk] I ever saw,
   The elk in the egg, etc.

6. Purtiest bird I ever saw,

Bird in the elk, etc.

7. Purtiest feather I ever saw,
   Feather on the bird, etc.

8. Purtiest bed I ever saw,
   Bed on the feather, etc.

9. Purtiest woman I ever saw,
   Woman on the bed, etc.

10. Purtiest cover I ever saw,
    Cover on the woman
    And the woman on the bed
    And the bed on the feather
    And the feather on the bird
    And the bird in the elk
    And the elk in the egg
    And the egg in the nest
    And the nest on the limb
    And the limb on the tree
    And the tree in the mountains
    And the green a-growin' all around.

94. The Old Grey Mare

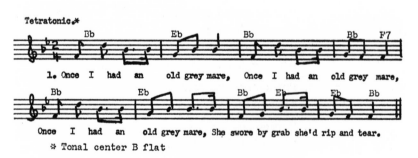

Tetratonic.*

1. Once I had an old grey mare, Once I had an old grey mare,

Once I had an old grey mare, She swore by grab she'd rip and tear.

* Tonal center B flat

2. Took her and I put her in the field to plow,
   Took her and I put her in the field to plow,
   Took her and I put her in the field to plow,

She swore by grab she didn't know how.

3. I kneeled down in the field to pray,   [three times]
   The danged old mare she run away.

4. Tuck my bridle and I tuck her tracks,   [three times]
   Found her in a mudhole flat of her back.

5. Says, "Old gal, do you think I'm mighty stout?"   [three times]
   Tuck her by the tail and I pulled her out.

6. Boys, old boys, do you think it any sin?   [three times]
   Hauled my knife and I begin to skin.

7. Tuck her hide and put it in the ooze,   [three times]
   Purpose to make my winter shoes.

8. Tuck it out and I hung it in the loft,   [two times]
   Some danged old rogue come stold it off.
   Left my old bare toes to take the frost.

95. The Fox and the Goose

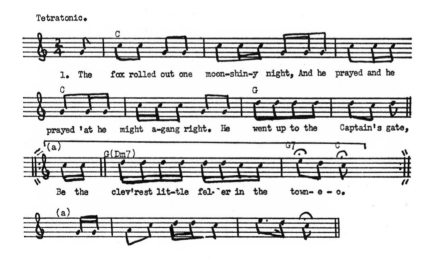

Tetratonic.

1. The fox rolled out one moon-shin-y night, And he prayed and he
prayed 'at he might a-gang right. He went up to the Captain's gate,
Be the clev'rest lit-tle fel-'er in the town- e - o.

2. There he spied an old black drake,
    O drake, O drake, come go along with me,
    And he never eat meat till he eat meat o' mine,
    He'll never eat no meat in no town-e-o,
    He'll never eat no meat in no town-e-o.

3. And the fox stepped back and he made a very tack,
    And he took the old grey goose by the back,
    A wing flip-flop up over her back,
    And her heels hanged dingle dangle down-e-o,
    And her heels hanged dingle dangle down-e-o.

4. The old woman tipple toppled in her bed,
    Out to the winder she poked her head,
    "Old man, old man, our grey goose is dead,
    I heared her going quim quam-e-o,
    I heared her going quim quam-e-o."

5. The old man tipple toppled in his bed,
    Out to the winder he poked his head,
    "Old woman, old woman, if your grey goose's dead,
    I never heared such music behind her,
    I never heared such music behind her."

6. And the fox went back to his old den,
    Where he had younguns nine or ten,
    The younguns eat the meat and the olduns eat the bones,
    "O father, father, when you go again
    Be the cleverest little feller in the town-e-o."

96. The Fox Chase

Pentatonic. Mode 3.

One time the fox come to the house to ketch one o' man's old hens.

Next morning pa said, "Son git your rifle and le's go up top of the ridge and give that fox a-chasing'."

Well, I called up old Queen and old Bounce; old Drum and old Rattler went along too.

We go up on top of the ridge and we heared old Queen let out 'way down in the ivy spur—yelpin' along a little bit.

Pa said, "There, she started 'im! She's gettin' a little hotter now. Watch out fer him."

We got up in the gap where the old fox supposed to go through. Pa said, "Now be still, son—set and watch fer him."

I heared old Bounce bark—gettin' a little bit hotter—there goes Drum.

Old Rattler's let out now and they're gittin' real hot.

Well, they chased that old fox all over that ridge—back'ards and forwards—Pa said, "Now son, keep right quiet and it'll come right back this way."

They got so hot on that old fox I said, "Pa, I just can't hep it but I'm goin' to holler if they do turn back."

I hollered, "WhoooooOOOOOOoooooweeeeEEEEEEEeeeeee—take me to his hole, lightning hound."

The old fox had a den over on the next ridge and he made straight for his hole.

The dogs was just about to git him when he got there.

But he got there and turned around, looked back down the hill and

said, "HaaaaaaAAAAAy, youuuuuu, old Rattler, you can't ketch me
noooow."

97. Froggy Went A-Courtin'

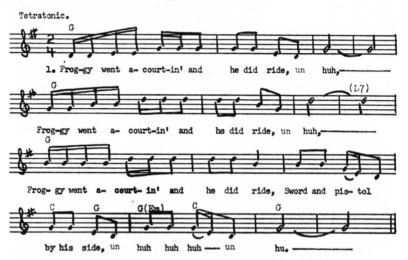

2. He went up to Miss Mousey's door, un huh,
   He went up to Miss Mousey's door, un huh,
   He went up to Miss Mousey's door,
   He hit it so hard he made it roar, un huh huh huh un huh.

3. He took Miss Mousey on his knee, un huh, etc.
   He said, Miss Mousey, won't you marry me, un huh huh huh un
   huh.

4. No, no, I can't answer that, un huh, etc.
   You'll have to ask my Uncle Rat, un huh huh huh un huh.

5. Old Uncle Rat give his consent, un huh, etc.
   Away for the license he did went, un huh huh huh un huh.

6. Old Uncle Rat he went to town, un huh, etc.
   He bought Miss Mousey a wedding gown, un huh huh huh un
   huh.

7. Where will the wedding supper be, un huh, etc.
   Way down yander in a holler tree, un huh huh huh un huh.

8. First come in was a little flea, un huh, etc.
   Tuned his fiddle all on his knee, un huh huh huh un huh.

9. Next come in was a bessy bug, un huh, etc.
   Had a little whiskey in his jug, un huh huh huh un huh.

10. Old Uncle Frog went across the lake, un huh, etc.
    He got swallered by a big black snake, un huh huh huh un huh.

11. All the bread and cheese I got I got 'em in the shelf, un huh, etc.
    If you want any more you can tell it yourself, un huh huh huh un huh.

98. Funniest Is the Frog

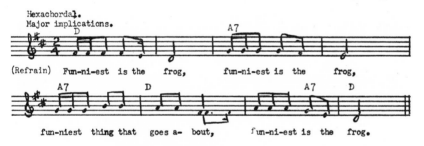

Hexachordal.
Major implications.

(Refrain) Fun-ni-est is the frog, fun-ni-est is the frog,
fun-niest thing that goes a- bout, fun-ni-est is the frog.

1. Setting on a log,
   With his little rusty mug,
   Before he gets half way down,
   Then he goes ka-chug.
   [Refrain after each stanza]

2. Funniest is the frog,
   He won't stay by work,
   Ever' time he goes about
   He goes it with a jerk.

3. Funniest is the frog,

His only daily quest,
Sploshin' through the rain and mud,
But he loves the sun the best.

4. Times is a-gettin' hard,
Money is gettin' skace,
If I can't sell my old banjo
I'm sure to leave this place.

5. Goin' down to town,
Goin' down to town,
Goin' down to Linburg town
To take my tobaccer down.

99. The Little Piggee

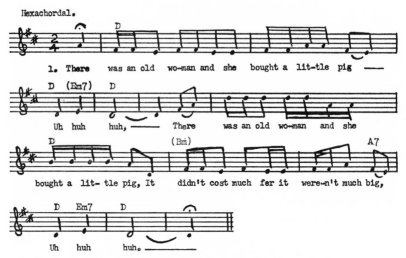

2. That little old woman put the pig in the barn,
Uh huh huh,
That little old woman put the pig in the barn,
It made little tracks all over the farm,
Uh huh huh.

3. That little old woman turned the pig outside,
Uh huh huh,
That little old woman turned the pig outside,
The pore little thing laid down and died,
Uh huh huh.

4. That little old woman fed the pig on clover,
Uh huh huh,
That little old woman fed the pig on clover,
It got so fat and it died all over,
Uh huh huh.

5. O that was the last of the one, two, three,
Uh huh huh,
That was the last of the one, two, three,
The man and the woman and the little piggee,
Uh huh huh.

6. O the good old book lies on the shelf,
Uh huh huh,
O the good old book lies on the shelf,
If you want any more you can tell it yourself,
Uh huh huh.

100. The Cat Played Fiddie on My Fee

2. I bought me a hen and my hen played me,
   And I fed my hen on Dando's lea,
   And my hen went shim shank, shim shank,
   And my cat played fiddie on my fee.

3. I bought me a duck and my duck played me,
   And I fed my duck on Dando's lea,
   And my duck went quow quow, quow quow,
   And my hen went shim shank, shim shank,
   And my cat played fiddie on my fee.

4. And my goose went slee slaa, slee slaa
5. And my hog went squee squaa, squee squaa
6. And my dog went bew bew, bew bew
7. And my horse went whee whaa, whee whaa
8. And my baby went mam mam, mam mam

9. And I bought me a mommy and my mommy played me,
   And I fed my mommy on Dando's lea,
   And my mommy went hon hon, hon hon,
   My baby went mam mam, mam mam,
   My horse went whee whaa, whee whaa,
   My dog went bew bew, bew bew,
   My hog went squee squaa, squee squaa,
   My goose went slee slaa, slee slaa,
   My duck went quow quow, quow quow,
   My hen went shim shank, shim shank,
   And my cat played fiddie on my fee.

III. Folktales and Riddles

101. Jack and the Beanstalk

Once there was a pore mother and her boy a-living by themselves out in the mountains. She had this here boy Jack a-shoveling up ashes and packing them out and while he was out in the yard he found him a bean. He come back in and said, "Mommy, give me a piece of bread-an-butter and I'll go and plant my bean."

She give him a piece of bread-an-butter and he went out and he planted the bean in the garden. He come back in and he packed out a few more buckets of ashes. Shoveled and shoveled awhile and he went to his mother and said, "Mommy, give me a piece of bread-an-butter and I'll go out and see iffen my bean has come up."

She give him another piece of bread-an-butter and he went out. Here he come back in a-running, said, "Law me, Mommy, my bean is knee high!"

"Why, you little old lying pup, you are telling something that hain't so. You go to shoveling out them ashes."

Well, he went to shoveling up ashes and packing them out. After he had shoveled and shoveled awhile he run to her again. "Give me another piece of bread-an-butter, Mommy, and I'll go out and see how my bean is a-doing."

She give him a piece and he went out. Come back just a-tearing, said, "Law me, Mommy, that bean, hit's as high as my head!"

She said, "You little old lying pup, I said for you to take all them ashes out." She thought Jack was just a-teasing her. Well, he shoveled at his ashes awhile longer and he asked her for some more bread-an-butter so's he could go out and see about his bean. Went out there and come back just a-flying, called out, "Lawsy me, Mommy, that bean's as high as this house!" He couldn't get her to believe him a-tall. He went back to the living room and took up another bucket of ashes, and he asked her for more bread-an-butter so's he could go out and see about his bean. Come back just as hard as he could run, said, "Law me, Mommy, I'll swear my bean is as high as a tree!"

She was just about to whup him this time, said, "I told you if you didn't quit that telling me a pack o' lies I was going to dust your jacket. You get all them ashes packed out this minute."

He shoveled and shoveled and got all the ashes packed out and he come to his mother, said, "I got 'em all packed out. Now give me another piece of bread-an-butter and I'll go out and see iffen I can see the top of my bean."

She give him some more bread-an-butter and he went out. Come back in so fast his shirttail was standing right straight out. "Law me, Mommy, I wush I may die if my bean hain't as high as the sky."

"I told you you little lying pup, I'd whup you for telling me that again. You get out of here so's I can rede the house up."

He played out there awhile and come back in and said, "Mommy, give me a piece of bread-an-butter and I'll go climb my bean."

She give him a piece and he went out there and he started climbing. He clomb and he clomb. Finally he clomb up into a new world and he got out of the bean and traveled around till he came to an old giant's house. The giant was gone, but his wife was there. The boy told her he was hungry and cold and he would like to stay all night there.

She said, "My old man is a giant and I don't want to keep you." Said, "He kills everybody he can get and eats 'em. It wouldn't do for you to be here when he comes in tonight." But said, "I guess I'll keep you. I've got a big kittle here and I'll turn it over you and let you stay till tomor'. You be quiet till he gets gone."

She put him under that kittle and he laid there till dark come. Along after dark the old giant come. By the time he got to the door he smelt the boy and he commenced saying:

> "Thee, thaw, thumb,
> I smell the blood of an Englishmun,
> I'll have his heart and liver and lights
> For my supper tonight!"

The old woman said, "Ah, hush, old man, hit's a raven a-flying over the house with a bone in its mouth."

She fed him and fixed his bed down before the fire and he ordered his wife to bring his hen to him that laid golden eggs. She brought the hen to him and he told it to lay some golden eggs. She laid just as many golden eggs as he wanted that night. And by the time she had quit laying the old giant was dead asleep. Just as soon as Jack heard him begin to snore he stold that hen and run to the beanstalk and clomb back down to his mother. He said, "Mommy, I've got the best hen here you ever saw. She can lay golden eggs."

They kept the hen there for a few days and Jack told her he wanted to go back up into this other world. He changed clothes so that the old woman wouldn't know him and he clomb back up. Come to her house and told her he was hungry and cold and he'd like to stay all night with her.

She said, "No," said, "I don't want to keep you. They's a boy come here t'other night and I kept him and he got away with my old man's hen that laid golden eggs." Said, "If he finds out you're here he'll just scrush your bones. He lives on human meat anyway, when he can get it."

Well, he 'sisted and begged to let him stay. She fixed him something to eat and she said, "I've got a chest here. I'll fasten you up in it. You be still when the old man comes. He'll be 'quiring where you're at because he can smell fresh meat."

Jack laid in that chest till dark and he heard the old giant coming shaking the earth at every step. He got to the door and begin to say:

> "Thee, thaw, thumb,
> I smell the blood of an Englishmun,
> Though he may be alive or he may be dead
> I'll grind his bones to make my bread."

The old woman said, "Ah, be quiet, old man, "Hit's just a raven or a dog dropped a bone around the house you smell."

Well, he laid down on his pallet before the fire and he asked his wife to bring him the golden harp. She brung it to him and he played and played that harp till he went sound asleep. The boy lifted the lid of the chest and kindly watched out till he saw him breathing heavy. And he jumped out and got that harp and back down the beanstalk he went and took the harp to his mother. He said, "Mother, I've got

his harp now. I'm going back up again and see if I can get his gold
in a few days."

A few days later he disfigured himself till the wife wouldn't know
him and he went back up. He 'sisted on her to let him stay all night.
She took the boy in when he complained how cold and hungry he
was. She fed him and said, "Now my husband's a giant and if he
comes in and finds you here he'll kill you." Said, "I took two boys
in and one stold his hen and the other his harp, and if he finds you
here he'll scrush your bones into powder."

He said, "Well, I'll take a chance and I won't bother nothing you
got. I won't touch nothing if you'll let me stay."

She was tender-hearted and she let him stay. She had a big box
there and she said, "You get in this box and I'll shet the lid down on
ye and when he comes 'quiring about human flesh you be still as you
can lay till tomor'."

He got in the box and waited till dark. He heard the old giant
coming. When he got to the door he begin to say:

> "Thee, thaw, thumb,
> I smell the blood of an Englishmun,
> I'll have his heart and liver and lights
> For my supper tonight."

She said, "Ah, hush, old man, it's nothing but just a raven flying
over the house with a piece of cyarne [carrion] in its mouth."

Well, he laid down after supper and called for his gold. She
brought out his big bag of gold and he started counting it, and counted and counted till he got sleepy. He dropped over and went to sleep
and when he got to snoring the boy slipped out of his box and
grabbed that bag of gold and run to the beanstalk and down to his
mother. He said, "Mommy, I've brung us a big bag of gold."

His mommy was pleased with Jack, and she bought food and stuff
with all that money. And Jack he waited about a week before he took
a notion to go back up. He had seen a banjer hanging on the wall he
wanted to get and that's all he wanted to bring down from the old
giant's house.

He told his mother he was going back up again. He clomb and

clomb till he got there and he turned his coat wrong-side out and disguised himself so she wouldn't know him. He went up to the door and asked to stay all night. The old woman wouldn't hardly take him in a-tall. Said, "My old man's a giant and he's been a-roaring around here about to shake the house because some other boys have come here and stold about all the valuables he's got. If he finds you here he'll scrush your bones into powder and eat you raw."

Jack begged her so pitiful that she took him in. She said, "I've got an oven here that he never does look in. I'll put you up tonight. Don't you make a sound till he gets gone tomor'."

The boy got in the oven and stayed in there till dark. He felt the earth jarring when the old giant arrived. He come to the door and roared out:

> "Thee, thaw, thumb,
> I smell the blood of an Englishmun,
> Though he may be alive or he may be dead
> I'll grind his bones to make my bread!"

The old woman said, "Ah, hush, old man, it's just a dog dropped a bone around the house or a raven flying over with a bone in its mouth you smell."

The old giant looked through the house for that fresh meat and when he got close to Jack he roared out again:

> "Thee, thaw, thumb,
> I smell the blood of an Englishmun,
> I'll have his heart and liver and lights
> For my supper tonight."

The old woman said, "Why, old man, that's just a raven flying over with a piece of cyarne in its mouth. Why don't you hush?"

She fed him and got him quiet. He laid down on his pallet before the fire and called for his banjer hanging on the wall. She brought it to him and he played several pieces. Got to dozing and Jack peeped out of that oven. The old giant had the banjer on his chest. He made a break for it, grabbed it off the old giant's chest, and hit for the door. That woke the old giant up and he come up from there a-roaring. Jack made for his beanstalk and started climbing down with this old giant right after him. By the time he got down over his house he commenced to hollering, "Mommy, hack the bean down, mommy, hack the bean down, MOMMY! HACK THE BEAN DOWN!"

His mother heard the racket up over the house and she come out with her big butcher knife and started hacking the beanstalk down. It commenced falling and that old giant fell a hundred feet and his head went in betwixt two big rocks and broke his neck.

And them pore people was the richest people in that country from then on.

102. The Two Gals

Once upon a time there was a man who married and him and his old woman had a purty gal. The old woman died and the man married again. This time they had an ugly gal. The stepmother was mean to the purty gal and made her do all the work, and she was good to her gal and let her set around and play with her purties. One day the old woman sent the purty gal to the well to draw a bucket of drinking water. The bucket was so heavy she couldn't hardly draw it up and she slipped and fell in the well. And when she come to the bottom she raised up and saw she was in another world.

She got up and started walking down the road to see where it went to and what and all she could see down there. And she come to a big log acrost the road. Hit was holler and she heared it say, "Go around me, little gal," and she went around it.

Then she come to an apple tree just a-hanging full of purty red apples and she wanted some. When she started to get some, the apple tree said, "Climb me and get all the apples you want, but don't break any of my sprouts."

She never broke no sprouts. Got her some apples and went on. She come to a cow, and that cow needed milking. She said, "Milk me, milk me, little gal. Get all the milk you want and hang the bucket back on my horns."

She milked the cow and got all the milk she could drink and hung the bucket back on her horns. Then she come to a sheep and it was just as wooly as it could be. It said, "Shear me, shear me, little gal, and get all the wool you want and hang the shears back on my horns."

She sheared the sheep and took some of the wool and hung the shears back on its horns. She went on along the road and come to a house. A witch lived there but the gal didn't know it. She asked the woman if she could get a job of work with her. The witch said, "Yes, but you have to rake up ten bales of hay ever' day and milk sebem head of cows."

She went to work for the old woman and she put up the hay ever' day and milked sebem head of cattle. After awhile the gal decided to go back home and told the woman to pay her wages. The witch didn't pay her in money, but she set out some colored boxes and said, "Take your su'prize box whenever you're ready to go."

The little gal finished up her work and when she was about to start a little bird flew up in her winder and commenced to sing:

> Pee wee, take the blue,
> Pee wee, take the blue.

She took the blue box and started out. This box had the witch's gold and silver in it, and the witch took out after her. The little gal saw her a-coming and run on till she come to the sheep. She said, "Sheep, sheep, hide me, the old witch's coming."

The sheep said, "All right, crawl up in my wool."

She crawled up in the sheep's wool and hid. And the old witch come up to the sheep and said, "Sheep o' mine, sheep o' mine, have you seen ary gal go up through here with my little blue box?"

The sheep said, "Yeaw, she went by here about an hour ago. You can't catch her."

The witch turned around and started back to the house. The little gal crawled out of the sheep's wool and started on. The witch saw her and took out after her again. The little gal saw her a-coming and run on till she come to the apple tree.

Said, "Apple tree, apple tree, hide me, I see the old witch coming."

The apple tree said, "All right, climb up in my sprouts."

The little gal clomb up in the sprouts and hid. Soon the old woman come up to the tree and said, "Apple tree o' mine, apple tree o' mine, have you seen ary gal go up through here with my little blue box?"

The apple tree said, "Yeaw, she went up through here about an hour ago. You can't catch her."

The old witch looked around the apple tree and didn't see nothing so she started back home. The little gal come out of the tree and started on up the road. And the witch seen her and come on after her again. The little gal run on till she come to the log and said, "Log, log, hide me, I see the old witch a-coming."

The log said, "All right, crawl up in my holler then and she can't find ye." She crawled up in the log.

The old witch come up and said, "Log o' mine, log o' mine, have you seen ary gal go up through here with my little blue box?"

The log said, "Yeaw, she went up through here about an hour ago. You can't catch her."

The old witch went up to the end of the log and looked up in there but the little gal stopped the holler up and it was so dark the old witch couldn't see nothing. So she went back home.

The little gal got out of the log and went on home. When she got there and didn't have nothing her stepmother got mad at her and put her out in the hogpen to live. She washed up the hogpen and made her a clean place to live, and then she opened up her su'prize box and found it was full of gold and silver. She took it and started counting it. The other ugly gal slipped around and saw her and went and told her mommy. The mother come out there and saw it and she said, "If you done that good I'll send my gal off to work."

So she told her ugly gal to take off and hunt her a job of work. She went out there and jumped in the well. And she come to the log in the road and the log said, "Go around me, go around me, little gal."

But the ugly gal just stepped on the log and went on. She come to the apple tree and started to climb it and get some apples. The apple tree said, "Get all the apples you want but don't break my sprouts."

Well, she clomb around in the tree and broke ever' sprout offen it. She went on and come to the cow and started milking it. The cow said, "Get all the milk you want and hang the bucket back on my horns."

But she drunk all the milk she wanted and throwed the bucket on the ground. Went on till she come to the sheep. She started shearing the sheep. The sheep said, "Get all the wool you want and hang the shears back on my horns."

But she took all the wool the sheep had and throwed the shears on the ground. She went on till she come to the house and she hollered and told the woman she wanted a job of work. The witch said, "You can work here but you have to put up ten bales of hay and milk my sebem cows ever' day."

The ugly gal started working but she never ruck up enough hay and she never milked all the cows. The old witch never could get her to do up all the work. And when the time come for her to go home she asked for her pay, and the old witch set out a lot of pretty boxes and said, "You can take your su'prize box whenever you're ready and I'm going to whup you all the way home."

The little ugly gal got ready to go and a little bird flew up in her winder and said:

Pee wee, take the red,
Pee wee, take the red.

The ugly gal come out and took the red box and lit out for home. She looked back and saw the old witch coming with a big long switch. She run till she come to the sheep and begged it to hide her but the sheep said, "I can't, my wool is too short." She come to the cow and begged it to hide her but the cow said, "I can't, my sack is empty and I have to pick grass." She come to the apple tree and begged it to hide her but the apple tree said, "I can't, I hain't got no sprouts." About that time the witch come up to her. She run on to the log and begged it to hide her but the log said, "I can't, my holler is stopped up." The old witch give her two big licks with that switch as she jumped over the log and run to the well.

She come up the well and went home and her mother grabbed that red su'prize box and opened it up. And out of the box come rattlesnakes and copperheads and eat the mother and the little ugly gal up.

That purty gal lived there happy ever after.

103. Johnny Conscience

They was a fambly one time their last names was Conscience and they had one son. This boy weren't afraid a nothing. His father tried to bluff him and skeer him but he wouldn't skeer to do no good.

Father couldn't do nothing with him. He just didn't know how to make the boy afraid.

Well, they was a man died in the neighborhood and they taken him over to the funeral home and when they come back this boy's father took a notion he'd try to skeer Johnny with this corpse. He taken this corpse and set him up in a chear and placed a hime [hymn] book in his hand, made him look right natural. He come back and found Johnny and told him to go over there to the funeral home and bring his hime book back to him. They'd be a man there a-reading it, he guessed. Johnny he went down there and went in and saw this corpse a-setting there r'ared up in a chear with the hime book in his hand. Johnny said, "Father sunt me atter his hime book."

The corpse just kept a-setting there and didn't answer him. Johnny looked at him a little closter and said, "Father sunt me atter his hime book. You let me have it now."

Of course the corpse wouldn't answer the boy and he just hauled off with his fist and he knocked the corpse over and the hime book flew outten his hand. He grabbed it up and run back home with it. He come to the house with it and handed it to his daddy, and the father said, "Well, I see you got my hime book."

He said, "Yeaw."

Said, " 'Ell, how did you get it?"

"I knocked him down and tuck it."

The father knowed right then that he couldn't do nothing with his boy and that he'd grow up to be a brave un or a fool, one.

Old Johnny he growed on up and got to be a purty good-sized man. And they was an old ha'nted house in the neighborhood. Nobody could live in the house it was ha'nted so bad. Knowing that Johnny weren't afraid of nothing, the owners of the house asked Johnny one day how much he'd take to go down there and stay all night in that old house. Johnny didn't care to go and said, "I'll take me a bed, three blankets, a Bible, and a good fat goose."

Well, they give Johnny his equipment and he went down to the old ha'nted house, built him up a far. They was a hole through the back of the chimley and Johnny noticed it while he was a-setting there br'iling his goose and reading his Bible. Along in the night an old man come and peeped through that hole in the chimley. Johnny said, "Look out here, old man. Don't you nasty that goose."

In a few minutes there come an old lady and she peeped through the hole at him. Johnny looked up from his reading and said, "Look out here, old lady. Don't you nasty that goose!"

A little boy come next and looked through that hole at him. And Johnny said, "Look here, little boy. Don't you nasty that goose!"

They had come there to scare Johnny and he weren't the scary kind. They went on out. He set there and read his Bible and eat his goose, and then took a notion he would go to bed. He went back in the floor and made him a pallet out of one of them bankets. Laying there and something come in and commenced to pulling at his cover. He r'ared up on his bed and tuck his knife and he split that cover open in the middle and said, "Equally divide." He tuck a half and give that haint the other half. It went away and come back after awhile, started pulling at his second quilt. He just r'ared up again, tuck out his knife and split it open, said, "Equally divide." That thing went away but come right back in a few minutes and started pulling the third quilt right out from under him. Well, he tuck out his knife again and cut it open and said, "Now you've got half and I've got half. Now go away and don't come back again."

It never come back. But as soon as he got to dozing in his sleep he heared a racket and looked up and there shot a coffin down the stairs, painted in white. He jumped up and he knocked the lid offen it. There laid a boy and a bulldog. He nailed it right back up and away the thing went out the door. He laid back down, tried to go to sleep and he heared another racket and down the stairs come another coffin, painted in purple. He jumped up and knocked the lid offen it, and in there laid an old lady. He nailed her back up and away it went out the door. He laid back down trying to get a nap of sleep, rested there awhile and down the stairs shot another coffin, painted in black. He jumped up and went to knocking the lid offen it, and out of it raised an old man with no head on and a big sword in his hand.

Well, old Johnny stepped back two or three steps, spoke to it in the three highest names—"By the Father, the Son, and the Holy Ghost—what are you a-doing here?"

That give him power over all them ghostes, and that man let his sword down and said, "Me and my family's been murdered here, and I've got one son left in the world somewhere. And I've got a pot o' gold hid in under this house. I want you to dig that gold out and go find my son. Divide that gold with him, give him half and you keep half."

Well, old Johnny he dug the gold out and he found the old man's son and divided up his gold. That house was never ha'nted no more and Johnny lived well from there on.

104. Little Black Hunchety Hunch

Once upon a time there was a family of a father and a mother and three sons. When the father and mother died the three boys decided to housekeep right on. The oldest boy was named Tom, the middle-sized one was named Will, and the youngest one was named Jack. They always called him the Foolish Jack.

They lived out in the mountains at that time and follered farming. In the spring when they got the fields ready for working, Jack and Will went out to work one morning and they left Tom there to cook the dinner. Tom got his dinner ready and went out in the yard and blowed his horn. He looked down the road and saw a little black thing coming hunching up the road. It was the little black Hunchety Hunch. It come right on to the house and run up to Tom and grabbed up a handful of ashes and throwed in Tom's eyes. He jumped up on the table and got their dinner under his coat and run off with it.

Tom was a-trying to get the ashes outten his eyes when Will and Jack come in. They went to the table and didn't find nothing on it. They asked Tom about dinner and why he blowed the horn. Tom said, "The little black Hunchety Hunch come in and throwed ashes in my eyes and run off with it."

They laughed at Tom, standing there with his eyes a-watering. Will said, "Well," said, "I'll cook dinner tomor' and that little black thing won't get my dinner." They eat the scraps that was left and went back to the fields.

Next day Will stayed there and begin to cook him a big dinner. He got it about ready and went out and blowed the horn. Looked down

the road and saw the little black Hunchety Hunch coming just a-
hustling up to the house. It come right on in, grabbed up a handful
of ashes, and throwed in Will's eyes. Jumped up on the table and
took up his dinner and run off with it. The other boys come in and
saw Will standing there rubbing his eyes. He said the same thing,
"That little black thing come in here and throwed ashes in my eyes
and run off with my dinner."

They had to eat the scraps or go hungry back to the fields. Jack
said, "Next time let me get the dinner." Said, "It'll not get mine."
They laughed at Foolish Jack, but said he may as well get him a dost
of ashes tomor'.

Next day they decided to let Jack cook dinner. He got him a big
dinner about ready and went out and blowed the horn. Looked out
and he saw the little black Hunchety Hunch coming hunching up the
road. It come right on in, grabbed up a handful of ashes, and throwed
at Jack's eyes, but Jack hundered down and let 'em fly over the house.
It jumped up on the table and started picking up their grub. Jack
grabbed up the broomstick, and he knocked it offen the table. It got a
chance and grabbed up another handful of ashes and throwed 'em at
Jack's eyes. Got some in his eyes this time and so it grabbed up all his
dinner and took out of there. Jack rubbed the ashes outten his eyes
and put out atter the little black thing. Went down the road a good
piece, Jack a-gaining on it, when it come to a big hole in the ground
and went down in there out of sight.

The other boys come in to dinner and saw Jack coming back up the
road rubbing the ashes offen his face. "Well, have you got our dinner
ready?"

Jack said, "I got it ready all right but that little black thing come
and took it away from me in spite of all I could do. But I run it down
the road till it went in a big hole. You boys get some rope and let me
down in there to see where it went to."

They gathered up a long piece or two of rope and went down there
and Tom and Will let Foolish Jack down in there. He told 'em he'd
jerk the rope when he wanted out. Got down in that hole and come
into a new world. Traveled around a little and come into a awful lot
of purty girls. Old Jack just got him a girl and went to the rope and

give it a jerk. They pulled them out to the top and Tom took his girl away from him. Will made him go back and get him one. They let Foolish Jack back down and he got another purty girl and jerked the rope. They hossed 'em out and Will took that un.

Jack said, "Now, boys, let me back so's I can get one of them purty girls." They said they would. Let Jack back down and he found the purtiest one in the bunch and jerked the rope. They pulled him up a piece and cut the rope and let 'em fall back.

Him and his girl stayed down in there a considerable time. And an old raven flew along, saw Jack looking up through that hole, and said, "Jack, what will you give me to take you all outten here?"

Jack said, "I wouldn't know. Most anything, I reckon."

The old raven said, "If you will fill my mouth full of meat ever' time I squawk," said, "I'll carry you out of here."

Well, Jack said, "All right." So he took him up on it and got him a middling and a half of meat and tied it to his back. The raven started out with 'em, Jack in front holding to his neck and his girl holding him around the waist. The old raven would squawk and Jack would job a strip of meat in his mouth. He'd squawk and Jack would job his mouth full of meat. They got almost to the top again, just about to land, and Jack run out of meat. That old raven squawked and Jack saw he didn't have a thing to feed him. So he just whipped out his knife and cut a big piece of meat out of his own thigh and jobbed it in the raven's mouth. And he carried them out and landed on top of the earth.

Well, that was the purtiest girl Jack had ever seen. Then he took her and hit out for home. When he got there the other boys begin to claim his girl and one of them took her away from him and tried to give him the other uglier girl. Jack wouldn't hear to it and they teamed up and run him off from home.

Foolish Jack went along the road for a few miles. Come to an old pasture field where some men had killed some beeves and left the hides on the fence to dry. Old Jack crawled in under one of them hides to rest and take a nap of sleep, and some crows flew along and lit on them hides. Jack caught him one. He begin to pet that crow and it tamed up right good, got used to him, and Jack decided to take it along with him to seek his fortune. Called that pet crow his fortune-teller.

He went ahead with his crow and come to a house, stopped and rested awhile. The old lady of the house was alone and she baked up a fine pig and put it away in the cupboard. Wanted to save it and have a feast with her lover supposed to come in. Her old man come in about that time and told his old woman he was awful hungry. She said, "They hain't nothing to eat on this place."

Jack spoke up and said, "For fifty dollars I'll tell your fortune with my crow."

The old feller decided to have Jack tell his fortune. Jack reached up and pinched his old crow's toe and that old crow let out a big squawk. The man said, "Well, what did he say, Foolish Jack?"

Said he said, "Baked pig in the cupboard."

The old feller was su'prized, said, "I know that hain't so." He went and opened up the cupboard and there was that baked pig. He paid Jack off and they set down and eat all they wanted of that pork.

Jack started on along the road, got hungry and started looking for another place to tell fortunes. He stopped at another place and while he was there talking he saw the old lady cork up a big jug of rum and hide it in under the floor. She wanted to have a good time with it later. But her old man come in about that time and said he was wanting a drink awful bad. The old woman said, "They hain't a drop to drink on this place."

Jack said to him, "For fifty dollars I'll tell your fortune with my pet crow."

The man decided to take Jack up on it. Jack pinched the old crow's toe and he let out a squall. He said, "Well, Foolish Jack, what did he say?"

Said it said, "They are a big jug a rum under the floor."

The old feller was badly su'prized, said, "Now I know that hain't so." He went and looked under the floor and drug out that jug of rum.

Jack collected his money and they had about all they wanted out of that jug. Jack went on and took up at another place. And they was a man there a-sparking with the old woman. Jack didn't know the difference till another man come up the road, and this old lady put that feller in the cotton barrel as fast as she could. The man of the house come in and asked about supper. The old woman said, "I've been a-working and hain't had time to fix any."

Jack spoke up and said, "For fifty dollars I'll tell your fortune with my crow."

The man took him up on it and told Jack to go ahead. Jack pinched the old crow's toe and the crow let out a squawk. "What did he say, Foolish Jack?"

He said, "It said they was a man over there in that cotton barrel."

The old man said, "I know that hain't so." He went toward the cotton barrel to see, and the feller in there jumped out with cotton sticking all over him and run off down the road.

Jack collected his money and went on telling fortunes through the land and country till he was rich. He decided to go back in home. When he got there his brothers was having a hard time and when they saw Jack with some money they got jealous of him, tried to take it away from him. Jack kept it around his middle. And they caught him and decided to destroy him, get shet of him for good. They crammed him down in a big sack, tied it up and went down and throwed him in the river. Went off and left him, live or die. Jack started kicking around in that sack and finally got it untied and swum out of the water. He set down on the river bank and thought he'd count it. While he was doing that the boys dropped down on him and saw him with all that money. They was awful su'prized and said, "Well, Foolish Jack, where did you get all that money?"

He said, "I kicked it out of the river."

They said, "Suppose if you tie us up and throw us in there we can get us some money?"

Jack said, "Yeaw, you will shore get rich."

Old Jack tied them up and throwed them in the river. They started kicking and spluttering in there and couldn't get the sacks untied. They kicked and they kicked till they drownded. They never did come back. And Jack had the purtiest girl and the money all to himself from then on.

105. The Old Woman and Her Pig

Once upon a time there was an old lady lived by herself, and she finally got a little boy to come and stay with her. She treated him good 'cause he was good company to her. She was sweeping the floor of her house one day and she found a pin. And she said to the little boy, "You stay here and keep house and I'll go to town with this pin and swap it to us a pig." The little boy said he'd stay if she would hurry right back.

She took her pin and went to market and swapped it to a pig. Coming back home they come to a bridge and the pig wouldn't go over it. They was a dog come along.

She said, "Hey, dog, bite pig, pig won't jump the bridge, I can't get to my little boy tonight, It's almost dark but the moon shines."

Well, the dog wouldn't bite the pig. She saw a stick laying there. She said, "Hey, stick, bang dog, dog won't bite pig, pig won't jump the bridge,

> I can't get to my little boy tonight,
> It's almost dark but the moon shines."

The stick wouldn't bang the dog. She got some far, said, "Hey, far, burn stick, stick won't bang dog, dog won't bite pig, pig won't jump the bridge,

> I can't get to my little boy tonight,
> It's almost dark but the moon shines."

The far wouldn't burn the stick. She got some water, said, "Hey, water, squinch far, far won't burn stick, stick won't bang dog, dog won't bite pig, pig won't jump the bridge,

> I can't get to my little boy tonight,
> It's almost dark but the moon shines."

The water wouldn't squinch the far. She got an ox, said, "Hey, ox, drink water, water won't squinch far, far won't burn stick, stick won't bang dog, dog won't bite pig, pig won't jump the bridge,

> I can't get to my little boy tonight,
> It's almost dark but the moon shines."

The ox wouldn't drink the water. She said to the butcher, "Hey, butcher, kill the ox, ox won't drink the water, water won't squinch the far, far won't burn the stick, stick won't bang the dog, dog won't bite the pig, pig won't jump the bridge,

> I can't get to my little boy tonight,
> It's almost dark but the moon shines."

The butcher wouldn't kill the ox. She said to the rope, "Hey, rope, hang butcher, butcher won't kill ox, ox won't drink the water, water won't squinch far, far won't burn the stick, stick won't bang dog, dog won't bite the pig, pig won't jump the bridge,

> I can't get to my little boy tonight,
> It's almost dark but the moon shines."

The rope wouldn't hang the butcher. She said to the rat, "Hey, rat, gnaw rope, rope won't hang the butcher, butcher won't kill the ox, ox won't drink the water, water won't squinch the far, far won't burn the stick, stick won't bang the dog, dog won't bite the pig, pig won't jump the bridge,

> I can't get to my little boy tonight,
> It's almost dark but the moon shines."

The rat wouldn't gnaw the rope. She said to the cat, "Hey, cat, catch the rat, rat won't gnaw the rope, rope won't hang the butcher, butcher won't kill the ox, ox won't drink the water, water won't squinch the far, far won't burn the stick, stick won't bang the dog, dog won't bite the pig, pig won't jump the bridge,

> I can't get to my little boy tonight,
> It's almost dark but the moon shines."

The cat wouldn't catch the rat. She said to the gun, "Hey, gun, shoot the cat, cat won't catch the rat, rat won't gnaw the rope, rope won't hang the butcher, butcher won't kill the ox, ox won't drink the water, water won't squinch the far, far won't burn the stick, stick won't bang the dog, dog won't bite the pig, pig won't jump the bridge,

> I can't get to my little boy tonight,
> It's almost dark but the moon shines."

The gun wouldn't shoot the cat. She said to the hammer, "Hey, hammer, break the gun, gun won't shoot the cat, cat won't catch the rat, rat won't gnaw the rope, rope won't hang the butcher, butcher won't kill the ox, ox won't drink the water, water won't squinch the far, far won't burn the stick, stick won't bang the dog, dog won't bite the pig, pig won't jump the bridge,

> I can't get to my little boy tonight,
> It's almost dark but the moon shines."

Well, the hammer flew to breaking the gun, the gun flew to shooting the cat, the cat flew to catching the rat, the rat flew to gnawing the rope, the rope flew to hanging the butcher, the butcher flew to killing the ox, the ox flew to drinking the water, the water flew to squinching the far, the far flew to burning the stick, the stick flew to banging the dog, the dog flew to biting the pig, the pig flew to jumping the bridge.

> And she got to her little boy that night,
> It was almost dark but the moon shined."

106. Jack and the Bull Strap

Once there was a married man and he had one son, and his wife died, and he married again. And his second wife had three daughters and didn't like his son Jack. So she took a notion she would starve him to death. His father would come in and Jack would be a-setting out behind the house on a rock. He'd be a-crying, and his father would say, "What's the matter, Jack?"

He said, "I'm a-starving to death."

His wife would say, "Look at his little old greasy mouth!" Said, "He's been eating and stuffing all day."

His father said, "Well, I guess you've had enough today, Jack."

The second time when the father was about to come home, the

stepmother caught him and greased his mouth and made it appear like he'd been a-eating. His father come in and found him out on that rock a-crying. He said, "What's the matter, son?"

He said, "I'm a-starving to death."

She said, "Hit's not so," said, "look at his little old greasy mouth. He's been eating and stuffing around all day."

The next day he was out on his rock setting and crying, and his little bull come along, said, "What's the matter, Jack?"

He said, "I'm a-starving to death."

He said, "You knock off one of my horns and eat." Said, "If you don't get enough out of it, you knock off the other'n and help yourself. They's plenty more in it."

Jack knocked the horn off the bull's head and he eat all he wanted. Put it back on. The bull said, "Now when you get hungry you get out here and whistle and I'll come."

Jack said he would. He eat a few days and got to feeling good and his stepmother noticed it. She asked him, said, "What are you livin' offen, Jack?"

Jack said, "For all you know I'm livin' offen the fat o' my guts."

She let him go but the next morning she sent old One Eye to watch him all day. Jack went out in the pasture and when he got good and hungry he set down on a rock and cut loose to whistling. Old One Eye listened for a while and she fell a-sleep. The old bull come up and Jack took off his horn and he eat.

Old One Eye went back in the house and the woman said, "Well, One Eye, what's he livin' offen?"

Old One Eye said, "Law me, mommy, I don't know." Said, "He whistled the purtiest whistling I ever heared and whistled me to sleep."

She said, "Never mind, I'll send old Two Eyes to watch him."

Next day when Jack went out of the house she set old Two Eyes on his trail. Jack wandered out in the fields and when it come dinnertime he set down on a rock and cut loose to whistling. He whistled and he whistled and Two Eyes went to sleep. The old bull come up and he took off one of the horns and he eat again.

That evening when old Two Eyes went in the old woman said, "Well, Two Eyes, what is he livin' offen?"

She said, "Law me, Mommy, I don't know." Said, "He whistled the purtiest whistling I ever heared and whistled me to sleep."

"Never mind," she grouched at her. "I'll send old Three Eyes to watch him tomorr'."

Next day old Three Eyes follered him to the pasture and come dinnertime Jack set down and cut loose to whistling. He whistled two of the girl's eyes asleep and the other'n almost shot. Up come his little bull and he took off a horn and he eat. Well, old Three Eyes went back to the house and the old woman asked her, "What did he live on, old Three Eyes?"

She told her, "He eat all he wanted out of one horn of his little bull."

Well, this old lady took a notion to fool him and so she got down sick. Jack asked her, "What's the matter?"

She said, "Oh, it wouldn't do no good to tell you."

He said, "It might," said, "tell me what it is ails ye."

She said, "I'm a-longing for your bull's heart."

Jack knowed what was the matter but he never let on. He says, "All right," says, "you make me up the last of the wheat dough to cap over his eyes and hold him for me and I'll knock him in the head and you shall have his heart."

Well, she fixed up her wheat dough and took it to Jack. He caught his little bull and had her hold it and he took the dough and he capped them wheat plasters over *her* eyes and knocked *her* in the head.

He jumped on his bull and took off. He rode till dark and decided to spend the night by the edge of the woods. Jack he clomb a tree and his little bull slept at the roots. They got up the next morning and the little bull said to Jack, said, "Jack, I had an awful dream last night."

Jack asked him, "What did ye dream?"

The bull said,

> "I dreamed that me and a bear fit and fit
> It almost killed me, but I killed it.

But if it kills me you take three raw straps out of my back, and whoever asks your name tell 'em Jack and the Bull Strap."

Well, Jack said he would and he got on his bull's back and he rode on till about ten o'clock and he looked out and he saw the bear a-coming. He got off of his bull and clomb a tree.

The bull and the bear fit and fought and fit
The bear almost killed the bull, but the bull killed it.

Jack got down and he rode his bull on till dark overtuck him again. He clomb a tree and his bull slept at the roots. Well, the next morning when he clomb down the bull said, "Jack, I had a worser dream than ever last night."

He said, "What did you dream?"

It said,

"I dreamt that me and a lion fit and fit and fit
It al-most killed me, but at last I killed it.

But if it kills me you do this, you take three raw straps out of my back and whoever asks your name you tell them Jack and the Bull Strap."

They went on till it got up in the day and Jack looked out and saw the lion a-coming. He jumped off and clomb a tree.

They fit and they fit and fit
The lion almost killed the bull, but the bull killed it.

They rode on till dark overtaken them again. Jack he clomb a tree and the bull he slept at the roots. The next morning the bull said, "Jack," said, "I had a *nawful* dream last night."

Jack said, "Why, what did you dream last night?"

Said,

"I dreamt that me and a pant'er fit and fit and fit
I almost killed the pant'er, but it killed me.

And if it kills me, Jack, you take three raw straps out of my back and whoever asks your name tell 'em Jack and the Bull Strap."

They went on till about ten o'clock and Jack looked off and he saw the pant'er a-coming. Jack jumped off the bull's back and clomb a tree. An' they fit and they fit. The bull almost killed the pant'er but the pant'er killed the bull. Jack he got down and he cut him three raw straps out of the bull's back and went on.

He went on and on and he met a man driving a wagon. He said, "What's your name, Son?"

He said, "Jack and the Bull Strap."

Said, "If you don't tell me better than that," said, "I'll cut you in two with this ox whip."

"Tie him down," said Jack, "and wring his head twicet around."

He said, "Spare my life, Jack, and I'll give you my wagon and team."

Jack put his straps away, took his wagon and team on and went on till he come to a king's house. He hired to herd the king's sheep. The king said, "Well, Jack," said, "They are an old two-headed giant lives down there." Said, "He kills ever'body I hire to herd sheep."

Jack said, "He won't kill me."

"Yes, he will; you're the smallest feller I ever hired to do it."

He hired Jack just the same and sent him over there. Jack was herding the sheep around and up the road come the old giant with two heads. He said, "What're you a-doing here?"

Jack said, "Letting my sheep eat grass."

He said, "Get outten here, I'll kill you and your sheep, too."

"Tie him down," said Jack, "and wring one of his heads off and the other'n twicet around."

The old giant said, "Spare my life, Jack, and I'll give you a hoss, bridle, saddle, and a fine suit of clothes."

Jack said, "Deliver 'em up here, sir!"

He took up his straps and collected his rewards from the old giant and went on off. Got a job working for another king. Hired out to herd sheep again. The old king said, "They're an old three-headed giant lives down there. He'll kill you. He kills ever' man I get to herd sheep."

Jack said, "He won't kill me."

King said, "Yes, he will, you're no bigger than the others."

He hired Jack to herd the sheep. Jack went down to the place and was herding sheep all right and the old giant rode up. Said, "What're you a-doing here?"

He said, "I'm a-letting my sheep eat grass."

He said, "If you don't get out of here I'll kill you and your sheep, too."

"Tie him down," said Jack, "and wring two of his heads off and the other'n twicet around."

"Spare my life, Jack, and I'll give you a hoss, bridle, saddle, and a fine suit of clothes."

Jack said, "Deliver 'em up here, sir!"

He took his goods and he went on to another old king's house. Hired to herd sheep with him. The old king said, "They're a four-headed giant lives down yander. He kills ever' man I hire to herd my sheep."

Jack said, "He won't kill me."

King said, "Yes, he will, you're a runtier man than the others."

Jack was a-herding his sheep and the old giant rode up. Said, "What're you a-doing here?"

"Letting my sheep eat grass."

"Get out of here, I'll kill you and your sheep, too."

"Tie him down," said Jack, "and wring three of his heads off and the other'n twicet around."

"Spare my life, Jack, and I'll give you a hoss, bridle, saddle, and a fine suit of clothes."

Jack said, "Deliver 'em up here, sir!"

Jack got his goods, took up his bull straps, and rode on. He went to another old king's house and fell in love with the king's daughter. They're about to get married, and this old king didn't approve of it. He set a day to kill his girl by drownding her. She was out crying. Jack rode up, said, "What's the matter?"

"Won't do me any good to tell ye."

"Yes, it will."

She said, "They've set a day to drownd me."

Jack said, "No, they won't," said, "I've got horses that'll beat far and squirt water into the briny ocean."

The day come that he had set to drown her, and they put her out and the water was all up around her. Jack run in with his horses, beat the far, and squirted the water into the briny ocean.

Well, the next day she was out a-crying again and Jack rode up, said, "What's the matter?"

She said, "They've set a day to burn me."

Jack said, "No, they won't."

She said, "Yes, they will."

He said, "No, they won't." Said, "I've got horses that'll beat the far and squirt water into the briny ocean."

Well, when the day come they'd set to burn her, she was out and the far was roaring up all around her. And Jack rode in with his horses. He beat the far and squirted water into the briny ocean.

He took the king's daughter up behind him and rode off with her. They's married and lived happy thereafter.

107. The One-Eyed Giant

Back in 1901 I was down in Mississippi, at Camp Shelby. I had me two companions down there and we took a notion we would go on a fishin' trip down the Mississippi River. It was an awful wilderness down there where we went, and time we got down to where we wanted to go we was lost. We looked away acrost the river and saw a little blue smoke boiling up out of a little shack. We got to callin' and hollerin' for help. Well, we called and called and after while they was an ol' one-eyed giant—lived over there—after while he got his boat and come over and got us.

He took us over to his shack or cave where he lived. Now on the trip down the river we three men had to climb trees to get away from the snakes of a night and other varmints, and I had a skinned place on my belly. Purty bad sore. The old giant took us in to his cave and welcomed us. He started feedin' and fattenin' us up mighty good. I didn't know what it was for and they didn't neither. But it looked like he was fattenin' us up like a farmer a-fattenin' his hogs. He was goin' to eat us.

Well, it come a time, one of my buddies was good and fat. The old giant come and took him out. We never heard a thing of him again. And in a few days he come and took the other'n out and left me alone in his cave. Next time he come back I asked him, said, "Why, where's my buddies?"

He laughed and said, "Hawr, hawr, hawr. You needn't mind your buddies." Said, "They make good steak," and said, "when that sore's cured on your belly you'll make good steak, too!"

Now he'd go out of a day and he'd herd his goats. He had an awful good herd of goats. And he'd come back in of a night and herd his goats in the cave and then lay down out front and sleep. I knowed my time was short when I saw that sore on my belly healin' up purty good. I had a notion one day that I would ex-cape. But when he'd come in to the cave and get ready to sleep he'd set a big rock up in the cave door, after he'd herd his goats in. And they weren't no way for me to ex-cape out through it.

He went to sleep one evenin' in the front of the cave and I took my chance. They was a big bunch of arn a-layin' around there, like pokin' sticks for his far. They was kindly sharp on one end. I took and chunked up the far and helt them arns in that far till they got good and red. You know, he was a one-eyed giant. His eye was right in the middle of his forehead. I het them arns good and hot and I slipped up to him and I rammed about four of them right down that big eye. He raised from there a-buttin' them walls and a-carryin' on. He got right in the entrance of the cave and he roared out, "YOU WON'T GET AWAY WITH THIS!"

I managed to stay out of his way till he hushed and then he moved the rock from over the cave door. And he set right in it. Well, he had one old goat there he called his pet. I picked that very old goat because he was the biggest and got right up between that goat's legs, right under the bottom of his belly and got a-hold of his wool. I tried to stampede that goat herd out of there, but he stopped 'em and let 'em out one at a time. They kept a-goin' out of the cave, and this very old particular goat that I was on—or under, I mean—when he come up to the old giant he stopped. That old giant rubbed him over. He said, "I knowed you'd never fail me." Said, "You're my pet and I love ye." Was I scared! But it happened that he didn't find me, and the old goat passed on through.

When all of them passed on through and got out he knowed that

I'd somehow ex-caped. When I got out from there I made for the river, and he come out of there a-squallin'. And when I looked around and down the river I saw seven other big giants a-comin'. I made my getaway and got to the boat in the river and hopped in it. I felt awful anxious by the time I hit the water. And by the time they all got up there why I was two-thirds of the way acrost. Now there was some great big high mountains standin' on that side of the river bank, clifts there that weighed tons. Well, they grabbed one of them clifts and throwed it at me. In the place of sinkin' me they just shoved me on all the way acrost.

When I come out of that danger I had an old hog rifle-gun, but I just had one bullet. I took up the river bank and had to climb trees at night from the snakes and wild varmints. One day about noon I was settin' on the bank of the river, and of course I was lost. There come along a great big flock of wild geese and flew up in a water-birch right over where I was a-settin' and lit on a limb. I managed and studied how I would get that flock with one bullet. Well, I finally thought of a way to get all them geese at one shot. I shot right up through the middle of that limb and split it and it clamped back and caught all them geese's toes. I clomb up the tree, took my old galluses and tied all them geese together and tied myself to them. I thought I'd jump off with 'em to the ground. But instid, them geese flew off with me.

They flew on and on with me, and when they got to goin' further than I wanted to go I just ripped out my knife and cut the old strings that I had tied to 'em and myself. That dropped me, and the luck was I fell right down in an old holler snag. I felt something under my feet and rubbin' against my britches legs. Felt awful soft but I couldn't find out for awhile what it was. I soon found out it was some cub bears. I heard a racket all at once comin' down the holler of that tree, just rip, rip, rip. I reached up with my hand—I couldn't see— and just happened to clinch an old bear right by the tail. Well, I had that old rusty Barlow knife with the blade about half broke off. I tuck that knife and I commenced jobbin' that bear, and she tuck right back up that holler tree and carried me out the top.

I clomb down and started on. I didn't have any bullets left in my old hog rifle-gun, but you know we always carried a wiper-an-ramrod. As I was goin' along I loaded my old rifle with powder and with that wiper. Purty soon I come upon one of these old Russian wild boars and a bear a-fightin'. I taken aim with that wiper and killed that bear. And then me and the boar had it around a few trees. I took around a little sugar maple, about six, eight inches at the stump, and that boar made a lunge at me and hit that tree. His tush went plumb through it and come out on the other side. I grabbed me up a rock and bradded that tush on the other side and there I had that old boar, too.

Well, I went on home for a horse to come and get my meat. When I started to go across an old field by the river I got tangled up in some old sawbriars and down I come. I fell on a whole flock of pateridges and killed 'em. Gathered up my pateridges and went on till I come to the river. I had to wade it and I was so dirty and ragged I just left on my huntin' shirt. I waded that river and when I come out I'd caught a whole shirttail full of fish. I just rolled up my shirt like a poke and took 'em on.

I moved on in home. Well, the old horse I had he was awful pore, and he had a purty sore back from a saddle scald. But I got that old horse ready and started back with him to get my bear and boar. Got over in the woods purty close to where my wild meat was at and that old horse slidded up and fell and hurt hisself, and he wasn't able to carry no bear in. I just stripped him and turned him loose in the woods, live or die.

You know, in about fifteen years after that I was back in that same place again a-huntin'. I saw a tree a-shake, shake, shakin' up toward the top of the mountains. I decided to investigate and see what it was. I went up there and saw what it was. A acorn had fallen in the horse's back and made an acorn tree. A big gang o' wild hogs was follerin' that old horse around, bitin' his heels, making him kick up and shake off them acorns for 'em.

108. Polly, Nancy, and Muncimeg

Once upon a time there was an old widder-woman, and she had three daughters. One was named Polly, one was named Nancy, and one was named Muncimeg. The old lady taken sick and she divided up her inheritance. She give Polly her house and garden, she give Nancy the rest of her land, and she give Muncimeg her old pocket penknife and gold ring. Muncimeg thought she was cheated and she said, "Law me, Mommy, you just give me this old pocket penknife and gold ring."

The mother said, "You keep 'em and they'll come in handy when you are in trouble." And she died.

Well, they made it up to go on a journey to seek their fortune, Polly and Nancy did. And Polly said, "Well, what shall we do with Muncimeg?"

Nancy said, "We'll lock her up in the house."

They locked her up in the house and started out on their journey. After they got down the road apiece, Muncimeg started to worrying and taking on about her fortune. She said, "Law me, my mommy's old pocket penknife and gold ring." The door flew open and she had nothing to do but take out after 'em.

Polly looked back and said, "Law me, sister Nancy, I see sister Muncimeg a-coming." Said, "What will we do with her?"

Nancy said, "Le's kill her!"

"No," said Polly, "le's take her with us."

"No, le's not," said Nancy, "le's stop her up here in this old holler log."

They put her in the old holler log, stopped her up good and went on. Muncimeg was crying and taking on.

She didn't let them get far along till she said, "Law me, my mommy's old pocket penknife and gold ring." The stopping come out of that old log. Out she come and after 'em she went again.

Polly heared her coming and stopped and said, "Law me, sister Nancy, I see sister Muncimeg a-coming again." Said, "What will we do with her this time?"

"Le's kill her."

"No, le's let her go with us."

"No, le's stop her here in this old holler tree."

Well, they stopped her up in the old holler tree and went on. Muncimeg let 'em get gone and she said, "Law me, mommy's old pocket penknife and gold ring." Out come the stopping and out she come and away she went after 'em.

Nancy heared her behind 'em and said, "Law me, sister Polly, I see sister Muncimeg a-coming. What will we do with her!"

"Le's kill her."

"No, le's let her go with us."

Well, they agreed to let her go along with them. They went along till they come to an old giant's house and stopped to stay all night. The old giant had three girls and they put these three girls in a room to sleep with his three girls. The old giant was up 'way in the night whetting his knife. And Muncimeg, who had stayed awake, raised up and asked him, says, "What are you whetting that knife for?"

"Aah, go to sleep. Cut meat in the morning."

He whetted right on on his knife and then went to his old lady and asked her, "How can I tell our three girls from them three girls?"

The giant's old lady said, "Why, our three girls wears nightcaps."

Well, old Muncimeg heared 'em talking and she eased up and slipped the nightcaps off the giant's girls' heads and put 'em on her head and her two sisters' heads. The old giant come in and he cut his three girls' heads off in place of the others'. Old Muncimeg knowed all about it, of course, and early next morning she waked Polly and Nancy and helped 'em escape before the giant and his wife waked up.

They wandered along the road that day and come to the king's house. He put 'em up for the night, and while they's a-talking the old king told them about the old giant living across the way a piece. He told them he had three sons and said, "I'll give you my oldest son for the oldest girl if one of you will go to that old giant's house and drownd his old lady."

Well, next morning they talked around and bagged Muncimeg into taking him up on it. She went to the old giant's house and laywayed the well. When the old lady come out to draw water she headed her in the well—drownded her—and the old giant heared the racket and come running out there. Saw who it was and took after Muncimeg just a-roaring, "I'm going to pay you for this, Muncimeg. You caused me to kill my three girls and now you've drownded my old woman. I'm going to pay you for this!"

Muncimeg come to the river and couldn't make it across. She said, "Law me, my mommy's old pocket penknife and gold ring." And she leaped the river and went back to the king's house. The king give his oldest son to her oldest sister Polly.

"Well," he said, "I'll give you my next oldest son for your other sister if you'll steal his horse, and the horse the giant has is covered with gold bells."

Muncimeg agreed to go back again and steal his horse. She got him out of the barn and she started riding him, and them bells started rattling. The old giant woke and jumped out of bed and run out there after it.

Muncimeg saw him a-coming and said, "Law me, my mommy's old pocket penknife and gold ring." And she become small and jumped in the horse's year and hid. Well, the giant tuck the horse and put him back in the barn, went back to sleep. She come outten his year and started riding him off again. The bells started rattling. The old giant heared 'em and he jumped out to see about his horse.

Muncimeg heared him and she said, "Law me, my mommy's old pocket penknife and gold ring." And she become small and jumped under his mane and hid. Giant tuck him and put him back in the barn and went back and got in bed and went to sleep. Muncimeg come out from under his mane and started off. The giant took after her but she was too far gone. He called out, "Hey, Muncimeg, I'll pay you for this. You caused me to kill my three girls, you drownded my old woman, and now you've stole my horse. I told you I'd pay you for this!"

Muncimeg come to the river with the old giant right in behind her. She said, "Law me, my mommy's old pocket penknife and gold ring." And the horse jumped the river with her and she rode in to the king's house.

The king was glad to see her come in with it and give her his next oldest son for her older sister Nancy. He said, "Now I'll give you my youngest son for yourself if you'll steal his gold. He sleeps with it under his head."

Muncimeg went back over there, found the gold sack under the old giant's head, and while he was asleep she slipped it out and started to run away from there. She slipped and fell and the old giant come up from there and caught her. He took her in the house and tied her up in a sack and hung her up to the joist. He said, "I told you, Muncimeg, I'd pay you for this. You caused me to kill my three girls, you drownded my old woman, you stold my horse, and now you're trying to steal my gold. I told you I'd pay you for it. I'm going to make you mew like a cat, bew like a dog, and I'm going to make your old bones ring like teacups and saucers, knives and forks."

He went out to get him a frail to frail her with. She said, "Law me, my mommy's old pocket penknife and gold ring," and down come the sack and out she come. She caught his old dog and cat and put 'em in the sack and rounded up all his knives and forks, teacups and saucers. Put 'em all in the sack and hung it back up to the joist. She got out beside the house and listened for him. The old giant come back with a big frail, and the first lick he warped the sack, "Mew" went his cat. The next lick he warped, "Bew" went his old dog. The next lick he warped it he broke up his dishes and teacups and saucers. "I told you, Muncimeg, I'd pay you for it!"

When he tuck the sack down he poured out his old cat and his old dog and all of his broke-up dishes. And he looked out and saw Muncimeg making it for the river. He tuck out after her, calling, "I told you, Muncimeg, I'd pay you for this. You caused me to kill my three girls, you drownded my old woman, stold my horse, stold my gold, you caused me to kill my dog and cat and caused me to break all my dishes. I told you I'd pay you for this."

He was gaining on her by the time she got to the river. She said, "Law me, my mommy's old pocket penknife and gold ring." And over the river she went, safe from the old giant. She took the gold back to the old king's house. She got the king's youngest son for a husband, and they all went back home and lived happy.

109. Daub It with Clay

One time they was an old guy and he had a girl. Her mother died and he married again. This other woman had two girls. That made 'em three.

They told these girls that if they would go to the spring and bring back a sifter of water why they would turn 'em free to marry. The old lady sunt her oldest girl first. She went to the spring. A little bird flew up in a tree and he said,

"Peewee, daub it with clay
Peewee, daub it with clay."

She wouldn't pay no attention. She dipped and she dipped. She had to take the sifter back empty, couldn't get no water.

Well, she let her next girl go and try it. The little bird flew down and said,

"Peewee, daub it with clay
Peewee, daub it with clay."

She wouldn't pay no attention to the bird. She went back to the house with an empty sifter.

Well, she finally agreed to let her man's girl go and try it. She went down to the spring to get the water. The little bird flew up and said,

"Peewee, daub it with clay
Peewee, daub it with clay."

She listened to the little bird, and she got clay and daubed the sifter good and tight and she took the sifter back full of water. This old mother turned her loose.

She started down the road and a little butterfly flew out in front of her. It'd fly out in front of her and dance around and wait for her. She'd catch up with it and it'd fly on a piece furder. She took a notion she'd foller that butterfly. She follered it on till it come to a big hole down in the ground. That little butterfly he'd fly down in that hole and it'd fly out, he'd fly down and he'd fly out. That old girl took a notion she'd go down there and see what she could find.

She went down in that place and they was a house down in under there. She knocked on the door and a big cat meowed. He says, "Cemmmmm in."

She went in and there laid a big cat stretched out before the far. That old cat said when she went in, said, "Meow, yeee heengeery?"

She said, "Yes."

He said, "Over there in the cupboard and get you something to eat."

She eat her supper, setting around by the far, and directly that old cat said, "Meow, yeee sleeeepy?"

She said, "Yes."

He said, "Back there is a bed fixed."

Well, they was an old boy in that catskin and he throwed that old catskin off and jumped out of it. He told that old girl that they would get married. That old guy he'd been using that catskin to cover up his robberies and his roguing around to keep from getting caught. He told her, said, "Now if your oldest sister comes here," he said, "don't you let her in." Said, "She'll be here before night," and said, "don't you let her in and don't you let nobody in."

Well, along that evening her oldest stepsister come. She bagged her to let her in and she wouldn't let her in. She said, "Well, you won't let me in," said, "let me see just the end of your little finger through the keyhole."

Well, that old girl she didn't see where there was any wrong to let her see the end of her finger. She just jobbed her finger out and that old girl rammed a needle in it. She just fell back in the floor.

She laid there till that man come in. He come in and he got her to and said, "I told you not to let nobody in and not to see nobody."

And they got married and lived there from then on.

110. Corpse in Pieces

Once they was an old hainted house and nobody wouldn't live in it. They was an old feller—he was a purty big coward, they thought—and they wanted to hire him to stay all night in that old hainted house. They made him up some money to go there and stay for a night. He said, "Well, I'll go stay there. Bake me a pone of corn-bread and give me a gallon of sweet milk."

They give that grub to him, and he went down there and built him up a big far and just set down before it and started eating his milk and cornbread. And 'way long in the night he heared a noise. Hit was on the roof and all to once down the chimley come a big shoe. He grabbed it outten the far and sot it over in the corner. He set there awhile eating his bread and milk and then here comes another big shoe down, made the soot fly ever'where. He grabbed it and sot it over in the corner with the other un.

Setting there eating and listening for more noises, and heared another racket coming and this time down the chimley come a big old leg. He grabbed that leg outten the far and sot it over in the corner in one of them shoes. In a minute down come another big leg and he grabbed it and popped it over in the other shoe.

Hadn't eat but a few bites and down come a big body. He pulled the body out of the grate and sot it over there on them legs. Directly down come a big arm, and he grabbed that arm and stuck it on the body. Down come another arm and he stuck it on the body, too. Tried to eat again and down come a big neck. He knowed where it went so he stuck it on the body. He set there a few minutes and down come a big head. He took up that head and sot it up on the neck. He set around awhile, never heared nothing more for a time, and then here come down the chimley a big mustache. He grabbed that mustache and stuck it on the man's lip. Then he grabbed his milk and bread and went to feeding it.

111. The Devil's Big Toe

Once they was an old lady out in the 'tater patch digging 'taters. She dug up something she didn't know what it was. She tuck it to the house and the old man said it was the devil's big toe.

Well, she cooked that big toe and eat it. Then along in the night they was laying in the bed, and they heared a voice, said, "Where's my big toe at?"

She said, "Jump up, old man, and look in the cellar and out-a-doors!"

The old man he got up and looked under the cellar and out-a-doors and he couldn't see nothing. He laid back down. The voice come again, "Where's my big toe at?"

"Jump up, old man, and look under the bed and up in the loft."

He got up and he looked under the bed and up in the loft and he never seen nothing. He laid back down. The voice come again, "Where's my big toe at?"

"Get up, old lady, and look under the bed and up in the loft and up in the chimley."

She got up and she looked under the bed and up in the loft and up in the chimley and there it set. She said, "What's them big eyes for?"

It said, "To see you, madam!"

"What's them big ears for?"

"To hear you, madam."

"What's that big nose for?"

"To smell you, madam."

"What's that big beard for?"

"To sweep down your chimley."

"What's them big claws for?"

"To tear you all to pieces."

He jumped down on the old lady and tore her all to pieces for eating his big toe.

112. Animals and Robbers

One time they was a farmer that had a mule and he kept him till he got so old he wasn't able to do nothing, and he took his old mule out of the barn and turned him out to die. The old mule he took off and got down the road a piece and he met an old dog. The old dog said, "Where are you going?"

He said, "I'm a-going to seek my fortune." Said, "I got too old for the farm and they turned me out to die."

Well, the old dog said, "I've got so old they won't let me stay under the bed no more and so they run me off." Said, "I'll go with you."

They went down the road a piece and they met an old cat. The old cat asked them where they's a-going. They told him. The cat said, "I'm so old they won't let me stay in the kitchen no more." Said, "I'll just go with ye."

They went on a little piece furder and they met an old sheep. The sheep asked them where they's going and they told him. And the sheep said, "I'll just go with ye." Said, "I'm old, too."

They went on and they passed a barnyard and an old rooster come out. "Where are you going?" They told him. He said, "Well, I'll just go with ye."

They traveled on and on, and come to a house in the woods. They decided to take up there and rest. The house had been used by robbers but they was out. Well, the old mule he laid down in the edge of the yard and the sheep he got up by the door and the cat got up in the fireplace and the dog in under the bed and the old rooster flew up on the joist. 'Way in the night them old robbers come in. First place they went was to the bed. The dog run out and bit 'em. Well, they went to the fireplace and the old cat reached out and scratched 'em. They started to run out the door and the old sheep butted 'em. Got out in the yard and the old mule r'ared up and kicked 'em. The old rooster let out a squall upon the joist.

They run off and wouldn't come back no more. They said they was a gang of devils up there in that house. Said one devil was under the bed and he flew out and bit 'em. Another was in the fireplace and he flew out and scratched 'em. Said they was another at the door and he hit 'em with a maul. Said they was another one out in the yard and he knocked 'em down with a sledge hammer. But said best of all was one little feller, setting upon the joist hollering ever breath, said, "Hand him up to me, boys, hand him up to me!"

They left that neck of the woods and the animals lived there in peace.

113. Nip, Kink, and Curly

They was three boys once by the names of Nip, Kink, and Curly. Their parents died off and left them, and they decided to housekeep and live on there together. Nip and Kink thought they was wise and they thought Curly was a fool.

Well, they took a notion after so long to turn out to be outlaws and go stealing for a living. They got together and made it up one night to go and steal 'em a goose. And old Curly said, "Boys," says, "let me go with you."

They said, "No," said, "we don't want you—you're too dumb."

Now Curly had heard what they said and what they was up to, so he took out another way and beat them through the woods to where they was figuring on stealing the goose. He asked that old feller, "What'll you give me to mind your goose pen tonight?" Said, "I know of two fellers a-going to steal your geese."

He said, "I wouldn't know," said, "what's your price?"

He said, "A big fat goose."

"All right."

"Give me a pair of pincers and show me to your goose pen."

He give Curly a pair of pincers and he went and crawled in the goose pen. Along in the night here come old Nip and Kink. Kink said, "I'll watch and you go get one."

Nip he went and he rammed his hand into the goose pen and old Curly pinched him with them pincers. He run back out. He says, "I can't get nary un," says, "that gander bites so hard." Says, "Suppose you get one."

He said, "All right, you watch and I'll try it."

He went and run his hand in to get him a goose, and old Curly he clinched him with the pincers. He come out of there, said, "That old gander bites so hard I can't get nary-un." Said, "Le's call it off and go back home, huh?"

They called it off for that night and went on back home without nothing. Next morning about sunrise here come old Curly carrying his big fat goose under his arm. They called, "Hey, Curly, where did you get that fat goose?"

He said, "Eh, I stold him last night."

Well, they got together that day and made it up, says, "Tomor' we'll go steal us a mutton." Curly heared 'em and come around, said, "Well, shall I go with ye?"

They said, "Nope, you can't go."

Well, old Curly went on another way and come to the feller's house and said, "I know of two fellers is going to steal your sheep tonight." Said, "What'll you give me to mind your sheep pen?"

He said, "I wouldn't know. What's your price?"

He said, "A good fat mutton."

He said, "All right."

"Give me a maul and show me to your sheep pen."

Old Curly took the maul and swung it up in the sheep pen. Along in the night here come Nip and Kink. Nip said, "Kink, you watch and I'll go in and get us one."

He says, "All right."

He went in and old Curly he drew back with that maul and swung it and out he put him. Nip run back and said, "Kink, that old ram butts so hard I can't get nary un. Supposen you try it."

He said, "All right," said, "you watch and I'll try it."

He walked in the door and he got a-holt of him a sheep and he started toward the door with it, and old Curly he drawed back with that maul and he pounded him right in the setter and out he put him. He went back.

"Well," said, "that old ram butted me so hard I can't get nary un." Said, "Le's just go back home."

They went on back home, and next morning old Curly he come leading a fat sheep in. They said, "Where did you get him at?"

"Ah, I stold him last night."

Well, they said, "Now tomor 'night we'll go steal something that can't butt nor bite."

Curly said, "Shall I go with ye?"

They said, "Yeaw," said, "we'll take you along with us tonight." Said, "I know of a man that's got a big smokehouse full of meat." Said, "We'll go steal us a big load a meat."

Well, they went to that man's smokehouse and Curly watched while Nip and Kink went in and shouldered 'em up a big load of meat, and they got purt near all of it. When they come out they told Curly to get a few pieces and bring the door to. Curly went in and got a few pieces and just took the door off the hinges and come on after 'em, and away they went. When they saw Curly with the door they asked him, said, "What are you doing with the door, Curly?"

Curly said, "You fellers took nearly all the meat, so I just brung the door, too."

They got on their way home and they heard a racket, and it was some fellers coming. They was a pine tree there by the side of the road. One of 'em said, "What shall we do? We don't want anybody to see us on the road with a load of meat this time a night."

Curly said, "Le's climb this pine tree."

They clomb up the pine tree, and Curly said, "Take my door up." They took his door up and got in the top of the tree. Directly they come two old robbers along and they was tired and hungry. They set right down under that tree, rested, and then went to counting their loot that they robbed. One of them said, "I'm so hungry I could tie my belly in a knot."

The boys heared it, and Curly sliced off a nice piece of meat and pitched it down to 'em. He pitched it down right where they was at. One of 'em grabbed it and looked at it, said, "Glory be, some good old meat—come down from heaven. Now if we could just have a little bread to go with it."

Old Curly had a little piece of bread in his pocket. So he broke some off and he pitched it down.

"Glory be to God, the Lord has answered our prayer. He has sent us some bread," said the old robber. Said, "Now if He'll just send us a table eat it off of," said, "we'll be all right."

Curly he just turned his door to, and down through them limbs it went. Made sech a racket it skeered the robbers off. Well, old Curly jumped down and gathered up their loot. They divided it up and all of 'em was rich, and they didn't have to steal no more for a living.

114. Arshman and the Watch

Once they was two Arshmen. They come over from England to America and was a-traveling along the road. One was named Pat and the other'n was named Mike. Come to the forks of the road and one took one fork of the road and the other'n took t'other. They had been advised by fellers who had been over here and went back that they was awful big ticks and varments over here, and if they found such a thing they was supposed to kill it.

Well, old Pat come along and he found a watch laying in the road a feller had lost. Had a chain on it. He picked that old watch up and helt it to his year and the watch went tick, tick. The old Arshman said, "Fat o' me Jesus," he said, "this is a tick and I'll smash him up."

He laid it down on a rock and took another rock and he smashed the watch all to pieces. He went on down the road and he met the man that lost the watch hunting for it. The man said, "Did you find ary watch along the road?"

He said, "No, fat o' me Jesus," said, "I found a big tick back up yander."

Said, "What did you do with it?"

He said, "I smash him up."

"Go show me where it was."

He went and showed him and it was his watch. He give him a string and said, "Now next thing you find like that on the road," said, "you tie this string to it and put it in your bosom pocket."

Old Pat went along the road, come to a mudhole in the road, and he went to cross it and he saw a little old young turkle [turtle] about the size of a watch. He reached down and picked it up, tied it by the leg with his string and stuck it in his bosom. Went on a mile or two and old Mike and him run together again. Mike looked at him a minute, saw that string said, "Pat, fat o' me Jesus," said, "what time is it?"

Old Pat pulled that little turkle out, kicking, and looked at it awhile. "Fat o' me Jesus, I don't know," he said. Pulled it out and had that old turkle by the leg. "Must be twelve, scratching for thirteen."

115. Frog or Moose?

They went on along the road, both of 'em was broke. They tried to manage a plan to get 'em some rum. While they was going along they found a big frog by the road. Old Pat said, "Mike, I'll take this frog along and call him a moose." Said, "I'll go in that saloon down yander and I'll bet that man a dollar again a quart of rum this is a moose. And he'll bet it's a frog." Said, "And we'll leave it to the next man comes in." Said, "You be by the side of the door and step in and say it's a moose."

Well, they went down and old Pat went in. He was holding that old frog by the leg. Directly he said, "Mister, what is this?"

He said, "Why, it's a frog."

"No," he said, "this is a moose."

"No, it's nothing but a frog."

"I know it's a moose. I bet you a dollar again a quart of rum this is a moose, and we'll leave it to the next man steps in."

The old bartender said, "Well, I'll bet with ye."

They made their bet and in a few minutes in stepped old Mike. Pat said, "Say pardner, what is this, a frog or a moose?"

He said, "Why, that's a moose!"

That old bartender couldn't do nothing but hand him over a quart of rum.

116. Frogs and the Rum

Pat and Mike took their quart of rum and went on down the road. They come to a creek and walked along it a piece. Soon they heared a big bullfrog calling across the water, "Rum, rum, rum!" One of them old Arshmen said, "Fat o' my Christ, Pat, there that man is wanting some rum." Said, "Give him a drink."

He went and poured some rum in the creek where that old bullfrog was a-hollering. Went on. Drunk it all but a little. Went along beside the stream and one of these here little bullfrogs heared 'em a-coming and he jumped into the creek and went, "Jug, jug, jug." Old Mike said, "By fat and by Jesus, Pat, he's wanting jug and all." Pat just throwed the whole jug in the creek.

117. The Mon a-Coming

They went on through the country till they got awful hungry. They come to some apple trees with purty good apples on them. Mike clomb over the orchard fence to get some, and old Pat he was a-watching. About then the moon begin to raise. Pat said, "Hey, Mike, I see the mon a-coming—"

Old mike jumped out of that tree and tore out of there, and right down through the field he went. Thought it was a man coming after him. Went on down through there as fast as he could split it and passed a pasture field where some men had been raking hay and left an old rake a-lying on the ground. He stepped on that old rake and the handle of it flew up and hit.him in the back. He let out a yell and run on till he give out. He stopped till Pat come up and then called and asked him, said, "Is the mon still a-coming?"

He said, "Yeaw, it's still a-coming."

Old Mike said, "Fat o' my Jesus, I want to stay out of his way," said, "he already give me one good whop as I went."

118. Picking Mulberries

They went on, stayed all night with a fambly, and set out the next day. Got hungry again, and come to some mulberry trees. They had some berries on 'em. Old Pat he clomb the tree to shake some mulberries off and left old Mike on the ground gathering them up an eating them. Cows had laid out under the trees and they was a lot of tumblebugs rolling their loads outten there. And old Mike was a-eatever'thing that looked black, tumblebugs and all. He hollered up at Pat and said, "Hey, Pat, fat o' my Jesus, has mullems got laggums?"

Old Pat said, "Why no, they don't have no laggums."

He said, "Fat o' my Jesus, I've eat my belly full of spradling bugs then."

119. I've Got the Job

They went on for another day or two, trying to get 'em a job of work along at the houses. After a few days Pat got a job from an old farmer to cut up a piece of corn. Told him he would give him two dollars to cut corn and shock it. He turned around to Mike and said, "Mike," said, "I'll give you two dollars if you'll help me cut up this piece of corn."

Mike said, "All right, I want a job here too, but," said, "tell me what you're going to get out of it?"

He said, "By fat and by Christ," said, "I've got the job, hain't I?"

120. Arshman and the Kraut

Once they was an Arshman come over from England to America. He was traveling around to seek his fortune. He got broke and hungry and was looking for something to eat. Come to a house and he called and wanted something to eat. This old guy he told him, "Well, come in," said, "we're pore people, but we'll give ye sech as we got."

Well, the old Arshman he went in and they never had nothing to eat but sauerkraut and bread. This old Arshman couldn't eat that kraut. He wasn't used to it, and so he got up and went on. Went to another house four or five miles down the road and called for something to eat. They told him the same thing. "We're pore people, but come in and we'll give ye sech as we got."

"No," said the old Arshman, said, "fat o' my Christ," said, "I tried that sech-as-we-got at the other house and I can't eat it."

121. Arshmen and the Gold Mine

He went along the road and run into some more Arshmens seeking a gold mine. They's going along 'side the brook and saw the moon in the bottom of a hole of water in the creek. They stopped and managed how to get to that gold mine in the creek. Finally one of them said, "Why, I know a way," said, "I'll get a-holt of this limb on this tree. You fellers hang onto my lags and form a line down there and the lower man can reach down in there and get it."

They was sebem of 'em and they started stringing out a-holt of each other's lags. Time they all got on there the weight got on him at the top and his hand got tard. He hollered out to the lower man, said, "Hold on below till I spat in my hands up above."

He turned loose to spit on his hands and they all went in.

122. Arshmen Counting

They all finally got out on the other side and went to counting to see how many come out alive. The first feller counting never counted hisself and he come up with one missing. Well, another'n would count and he'd leave hisself out and find one missing. They went along worrying and counting, till one feller said he knowed of a plan. They come to a big cowpile in the road and he said, "Le's all get down here and stick our noses in this old cowpile and count the holes," said, "then we can tell whether we're all here or not."

They done that, laid down and stuck their noses in the cowpile and counted the holes and found they was all sebem there.

123. Arshmen Squirrel Hunting

They went on and split up along the way, and Pat and Mike found themselves together. They got hungry on the trail. Saw a squirrel run up a tree and Pat said, "Mike, you go borrey us a skillet to fry it in," said, "and I'll climb up the tree and ketch it while you're gone."

Well, Mike took off to get the skillet and Pat clomb the tree to ketch it. He got up in the tree and the squirrel it jumped out. Old Pat looked over the way that squirrel jumped and said, "Fat o' my Christ, where your little legs can go my big long uns can." He jumped out of that tree and broke his neck. The other Arshman he come back. Blood was all around Pat's mouth and he looked at him and said, "Well, fat o' my Christ, you tried to eat it blood raw and got choked to death on it, did ye?"

124. Arshmen and the Red Pepper

Mike went along the road till he run into another old Arshman and they decided to stay together, and did for some time. They was allas hungry and trying to get enough to eat some way. They come to a gyarden with a lot of red pepper in it. They didn't know what it was, of course, but they was hungry enough to try to get 'em a bait of it. Mike said, "Sam, you go up there and watch for the mon and I'll climb through in and get us some of that nice red fruit."

Sam watched and Mike jumped in the gyarden and got him a few pods of that red pepper, poked one or two pods in his mouth. Come on out with water running outten his eyes, like he was crying. The other'n said, "Well, what are you crying about?"

He said, "I'm crying because my pore old granny didn't get none of this good fruit before she died."

Well, Sam took a pod and poked it in his mouth. Chawed a-while, tears come to his eyes. He said, "Well, fat o' my Christ, if your old granny liked this stuff she orght to a been dead forty year ago."

125. Arshman and the Gun

They went on till they come to a little town and walked along looking in the store windows. Come to a hardware store. They hadn't never seen no guns, and this old hardware clerk had an old double-barrel shotgun setting here. This old Ashman wanted to find out what it was. The clerk told him it was a gun, kill anything with it. Showed him how it worked. Old Mike bought the gun and they started on down the road looking for something to shoot at. Directly he saw a fly light on his buddy's back. He said, "Hupe, hupe, stop here. They's a fly on your back. Let me kill it."

He cracked down with that old gun and killed his buddy. Took it back to the hardware man and said, "Here," said, "I don't want this thing."

He said, "Why, what's the matter with it?"

He said, "Fat o' my Christ, I started to kill a fly with it on my buddy's back and killed him."

The clerk said, "Well, I told you it would kill anything you pointed at." And he took the gun and went on.

126. Arshman Splitting Rails

Mike went on by himself and got him a job finally splitting rails. So he cut down a blackgum, the hardest thing to bust they is, and he spent all morning till dinner getting the first log busted open. When he got in for dinner the old farmer asked him, says, "Well, pardner, how did you make out today?"

"Well," said, "fat o' my Jesus, I've got two of their little white bellies turned up."

The man told him what to cut and said, "Now when you see that light up there go out you come in." It was the sun he was speaking of.

He went back out and by the time the sun went down the moon loomed up on the other side of the ridge. He just worked right on. Never quit and the old farmer had to go out and see about him. Found him still a-working. He said, "I thought I told you to come in when that light went out up there."

The old Arshman says, "Well, fat o' my Christ, when He took that un down He hung another one and I thought He wanted me to work right on."

127. Arshman Never Tard nor Hungry

Old Mike went on and got work from another farmer. This farmer asked him when he wanted his meals. And Mike said, "Well, I'll tell ye, I never get hungry nor tard. I can work and never get tard or hungry."

This old farmer was anxious to get him to work for him. He weren't in no hurry to feed him nohow. Hired him and along about nine o'clock this old Arshman come in for his dinner. He set around till the old lady got his dinner ready. Eat his dinner and went back. Along about two o'clock the old farmer thought he'd go out and see about him. And he went out and found him a-setting out there. He come up to him and said, "Pardner, when you hired to me I thought you told me you never got tard nor hungry."

"Well," he said, "I'll just tell you, mister," said, "I allas rest before I get tard and I allas eat before I get hungry. So that's the reason I never get tard nor hungry."

128. I Up the Chimley

One time they was three women. They all lived together and they's all witches. They'd get out of a night and steal and rob and come back in and never get caught. Go through locked doors and such and people couldn't catch 'em.

After so long an old boy went and took up with 'em. Them three women they had nightcaps they'd put on. They slipped up one night and put them nightcaps on and said their little rigamarole. One said, "I up the chimley like a spark of far."

The other'n said, "I up the chimley like a spark of far."

The other'n said, "I up the chimley like a spark of far."

They went out and that old boy he found him a nightcap. He socked it on and said, "I up the chimley like a spark of far," and he follered 'em. They all went out and them old witches brought him back. The next night them old witches made it up to go out and rob the bank. That old boy he laid and listened at 'em. They all got up and got started and he took after 'em. They went to the bank and he

follered 'em there. One of them old witches said, "I into the keyhole."

Another one said, "I into the keyhole."

The other one said, "I into the keyhole."

That old boy said, "I into the keyhole," and he went with 'em.
They gathered up all their loot and all their money.

One said, "I out through the keyhole."

The other recognized this man among 'em and she snatched the
old boy's cap and said, "I out through the keyhole." That left the old
boy in there to take the rap.

129. Bridling the Witch

Once they was two young men working at a place. One of them he
got to looking awful thin and bad. The other'n asked him what was
wrong with him. He told his buddy, he said, "if you went through of
a night what I did," said, "you'd look bad, too."

The other guy said, "Let me sleep in front tonight and see if it will
happen to me."

Well, he laid in front that night. Got up along in the night and
in come a woman. Stood up over him, said a little ceremony she used.
Had a little bridle in her hand and when she was done she popped
that bridle on him and turned him into a horse. Took him out, riding
him around. Went to an old place where they's having a big time, fid-
dling and dancing. Hitched him up and went in.

He went to trying to slip the bridle off of him. He'd rub and get it
about off and she'd know about it and run back out there and put it
on and hook him back up to the fence. He kept on rubbing, and finally he got the bridle off. And after he got the bridle off he turned back
into his natural self again. He just grabbed the bridle and went in
there where she's at and said the same words over her that she said
over him and popped the bridle on her, jumped on her and rode her.

He rode her to a blacksmith's shop and had her shod, and he rode
her then to her husband's house. Told him he wanted to trade horses
with him. They agreed to trade. He said, "Now, this filly's kindly
skittish. You'll haft to lead her inside the born before you take the
bridle off of her."

He saddled this other horse and rode it off. This old guy he led the filly back into the born and pulled the bridle off of her and there stood his wife with horseshoes on her hands. He took his gun and shot her brains out. And that was the last of the witch.

130. To the End of the World

There was a man married and he had a girl. And his wife died and he married again and she had a girl. The one he had by his last wife was awful ugly; the one he had by his first wife was purty. She wanted to destroy his girl. And she had heard that there were a lot of animals betwixt their home and the end of the world where they went to get their water. So she sent her stepdaughter out after some water to try to get her destroyed.

And the first thing she met on her way after her water was a bull. And she spoke friendly to it, it spoke friendly to her, and she went on. She went on and she met a bear, and she spoke friendly to it, it spoke friendly to her, and she went on. She met a pant'er. She spoke friendly to it, it spoke friendly to her, and she went on. Well, went on and met a wild boar and spoke friendly to it, and it spoke friendly to her. Went on and met a hackle a-layin' in the road, and she surrounded it and went on. She met an old man and she called him grandfather. It pleased him and he made her go in and eat dinner with him. She went on and she found three little red foxes layin' in the road. One said, "Pick me up and wash my face and lay me down right easy."

So she picked it up and she washed its face and she laid it down right easy. The next one said, "Pick me up and wash my face and lay me down right easy."

So she picked it up and washed its face and she laid it down right easy. The third un said, "Pick me up and wash my face and lay me down right easy."

So she picked it up and washed it and laid it down right easy.

They said, "Le's all three make wishes."

The first un wished that ever' time she'd blow her nose she would blow out silver.

The next un wished that ever' time she spit she would spit up gold.

The third one wished that ever' time she washed her face she would get ten times purtier.

She got her water and went back home. She begin to tell her stepmother what had happened and she happened to blow her nose and out of her mouth come a lot of silver pieces. The very moment she started telling about it out of her mouth come pieces of gold. And when she washed her face she was the purtiest thing they had ever seen.

The stepmother was mad and said, "If that be so I'll send my girl."

She sent her girl. Her girl was kindly high-headed. She met the bull and she spoke ill to it and it horned and hooked her and knocked her all around the road. She went on and met the bear. She spoke ill to it and it liked to tore her up. Went on and met a wild boar, spoke ill to him and he jumped on her and liked to tore her up. Also met a pant'er and it liked to tore her up. She met a hackle and she kicked it out of the road and it jumped back and liked to tore her all to pieces. She went on and met an old man. She spoke ill to him, and he cut him a limb and give her a good whuppin'. She went on and found three little foxes layin' in the road. One said, "Pick me up and wash my face and lay me down right easy."

She picked it up and washed its face and throwed it down again' the ground.

The other'n said, "Pick me up and wash my face and lay me down right easy."

She picked it up and washed its face and throwed it down again' the ground.

The third'n said, "Pick me up and wash my face and lay me down right easy."

She picked it up and washed its face, and she throwed it down again' the ground.

They said, "Le's all make us three wishes."

The first one said, "I wish ever' time she'd blow her nose she would blow out cyarne."

The second one said, "I wish ever' time she spit she'd spit up blood."

The third one said, "I wish ever' time she washes her face she will get ten times uglier."

She went on and got her water and went back home. Her mother met her and begin to pet her and talk to her. The girl blowed her nose and out come cyarne. She begin to talk and spit and out come blood. When she washed her face in the water she was ten times uglier than she was, and you know she was a purty thing then.

When the husband come in that night and saw what a mess the house was in and what an ugly girl his old woman had brought in he threatened to have her hanged for a witch. She and her ugly daughter run away into the forest and the wild animals eat 'em up. The purty girl and her father lived there happily forever after.

131. Cat and Rat

Cat and rat playin' dirt-up and the cat bit off the rat's tail. The rat said, "Give my long tail back again."

Cat said, "I shan't do it lessen you go to the cow and get me some milk."

The rat run to the cow and said, "Pray, cow, give me milk, I give catty milk, catty give my long tail back again."

Cow said, "Won't do it lessen you go to the born and get me some hay."

"Pray, barn, give me hay, I give cow hay, cow give me milk, I give catty milk, catty give my long tail back again."

"Can't do it lessen you go to the shop and get me a key."

"Pray, shop, give me key, I give barn key, barn give me hay, I give cow hay, cow give me milk, I give catty milk, catty give my long tail back again."

"Can't do it lessen you go to the bank and get me some coal."

"Pray, bank, give me some coal, I give shop coal, shop give me key, I give barn key, barn give me hay, I give cow hay, cow give me milk, I give catty milk, catty give my long tail back again."

"Can't do it lessen you go to the eagle and get me a feather."

"Pray, eagle, give me feather, I give bank feather, bank give me coal, I give shop coal, shop give me key, I give barn key, barn give me hay, I give cow hay, cow give me milk, I give catty milk, catty give my long tail back again."

"Can't do it lessen you go to the sow and get me a pig."

"Pray sow, give me pig, I give eagle pig, eagle give me feather, I give bank feather, bank give me coal, I give shop coal, shop give me key, I give barn key, barn give me hay, I give cow hay, cow give me milk, I give catty milk, catty give my long tail back again."

"Can't do it lessen you go to the crib and get me a year of corn."

"Pray, crib, give me year o' corn, I give sow corn, sow give me pig, I give eagle pig, eagle give me feather, I give bank feather, bank give me coal, I give shop coal, shop give me key, I give barn key, barn give me hay, I give cow hay, cow give me milk, I give catty milk, catty give my long tail back again."

"Can't do it lessen you go to the man and get me a key."

"Pray, Man, give me key, I give crib key, crib give me corn, I give sow corn, sow give me pig, I give eagle pig, eagle give me feather, I give bank feather, bank give me coal, I give shop coal, shop give me key, I give barn key, barn give me hay, I give cow hay, cow give me milk, I give catty milk, catty give my long tail back again."

The man give the rat the key, the rat give the crib the key, the crib give the rat the corn, the rat give the sow the corn, the sow give the rat the pig, the rat give the eagle the pig, the eagle give the rat the feather, the rat give the bank the feather, the bank give the rat the coal, the rat give the shop the coal, the shop give the rat the key, the rat give the barn the key, the barn give the rat the hay, the rat give the cow the hay, the cow give the rat the milk, the rat give the cat the milk, the cat give the rat his tail. And he wiggled it on and away he went.

132. The Fox and the Cat

Once there was a fox started out of the woods to hunt him something to eat, and he went along the road and met a cat. The cat said to the fox, "Where you goin'?"

"To seek my fortune."

"May I go, too?"

"Yeaw, company's good sometimes."

The fox and the cat then went on and on till they met a hen. The hen said, "Where are you goin'?"

"We're goin' to seek our fortune."

"May I go, too?"

"Company's good sometimes."

The three of 'em went on and on till they met a duck.

The duck said, "Where are you goin'?"

"To seek our fortune."

"May I go, too?"

"Yeaw, company's good sometimes."

They traveled on and traveled on and met a drake.

"Where are you goin'?"

"To seek our fortune."

"May I go, too?"

"Yeaw, company's good sometimes."

All the animals went on and on till they met a goose. Goose said, "Where are you goin'?"

"To seek our fortune."

"May I go, too?"

"Yeaw, company's good sometimes."

Took the old goose along and went on till they met an old gander. Gander said, "Where are you all goin'?"

"Goin' to seek our fortune."

"May I go, too?"

Company's good sometimes."

They all went along the road till they met a turkey and a gobbler. Gobbler asked them, "Where are you goin'?"

"To seek our fortune."

"May I go, too?"

"Yeaw, company's good sometimes."

Well, the fox thought they was ready to travel by now, and so he led the whole gang along the road and off into the fields. Purty soon it was up in the day and they all commenced to get hungry, and the fox started studying how he was goin' to get to eat one of them travers. Finally they come to a log, and the fox said, "Well, le's all set down on this log and tell our fortunes. I'll give your names and which one has the ugliest name will have to die." They all agreed and set down in a row on the log. The old fox begin:

"Foxy Loxy purty name, Catty Latty purty name, Henny Penny purty name, Ducky Lucky purty name, Drakey Lakey purty name, Goosey Loosey purty name, Gander Lander purty name, Turkey Lurkey purty name, Gobbler Lobbler—ugly name."

They all jumped on the old gobbler and eat him up.

They traveled on through the evening and made camp in a tree that night. Went on the next day till they begin to get hungry again. Come to a log and they set down on it to hear their fortune again. The fox said:

"Foxy Loxy purty name, Catty Latty purty name, Henny Penny purty name, Ducky Lucky purty name, Drakey Lakey purty name, Goose Loosey purty name, Gander Lander purty name, Turkey Lurkey—ugly name." So they all jumped on the old turkey and made a meal out of her.

They got goin' again and traveled on and traveled on. Stayed in a tree that night and went on till up in the day. Commenced gettin' hungry again. The fox said, "Here's another log. Le's set down and hear our fortune again." They set down and he started out:

"Foxy Loxy purty name, Catty Latty purty name, Henny Penny purty name, Ducky Lucky purty name, Drakey Lakey purty name, Goosey Loosey purty name, Gander Lander—ugly name." So they made a meal that day offen the old gander.

Went on till the next day and come to a log, set down to hear the fox tell their fortune again. He started out:

"Foxy Loxy purty name, Catty Latty purty name, Henny Penny purty name, Ducky Lucky purty name, Drakey Lakey purty name, Goose Loosey—ugly name." So they made their meal offen the old goose.

Went on and stayed all night and traveled till up in the day. They come to a log and set down to hear their fortune again. The fox started out:

"Foxy Loxy purty name, Catty Latty purty name, Henny Penny purty name, Ducky Lucky purty name, Drakey Lakey—ugly name." And so they eat up the old drake.

Well, they went on till it come night. Stayed in the woods and traveled till up in the day. When they begin to get hungry again the fox stopped 'em on a log and started:

"Foxy Loxy purty name, Catty Latty purty name, Henny Penny purty name, Ducky Lucky—ugly name." And they eat up the old duck.

Went on and when the next day come and they was hungry the fox stopped at a log and started telling fortunes:

"Foxy Loxy purty name, Catty Latty purty name, Henny Penny— ugly name." The fox and the cat eat up the old hen.

So the fox and the cat went on and on. Got along good together that night and traveled till way up in the day. Finally they come to a log and they climbed upon it and the fox started telling the cat's fortune:

'Foxy Loxy purty name, Catty Latty—ugly—"

Cat jumped off the log and started telling the old fox's fortune:

"Catty Latty purty name, Foxy Loxy—ugly name."

Fox said, "Foxy Loxy purty name, Catty Latty—ugly name."

They fell into a quarrel about which one had the ugliest name, and they fit and they fought and they fit and finally they eat each other up. The fox eat the cat and the cat eat the fox. And that was the fortune of all them animals.

133. Tailipoe

I'll tell you a tale now about an old lady who lived by herself near the forest. She had two dogs and the name of one was old You Know and the other was named I Know. Something got to bothering her, prowling around her log house. She had a nawful bad door, made of old boards and she was always afraid something would get in at her old-time door. Of a cold time this strange varmint would get to freezing and it would try the house, and go around and around it and stop and try the door.

One night when it was prowling around the house it stopped at the door and worked around it and at the crack till it stuck its old big tail under the door. It was about sixteen feet long, I've allas heared, and she grabbed her ax and cut that old thing's tail off. Well, after she cut its tail off she set them dogs on that thing and they run it away down in the big timber woods, eight or ten miles down in the valley below her house. Them dogs treed that thing down there and barked and barked till they got tard. And they come back to the house. Soon as they got back they heared that thing coming up the valley moaning and crying. It was saying, "You Know, and I Know, all I want is my taaaail-iiii-pooooe—"

And they tell me that to this day down in them big timber woods where the dogs treed that animal, the wind blows through the trees and they hear a moaning voice, saying, "YouuuUUUuu KnoooOOOOO-oow, and IIIII KnoooOOOOOoow, alll IIIIII WaaaAAAAnt iss myyyYYYYyyy taaaaaAAAAAil-EEEEE-paOOOooe."

134. Fat Man, Fat Man

One time they was an old man, an old woman, a little boy and a little girl, and a little monkey. The old woman sent the little girl to the store to get a loaf of bread. And she went out there and she said, "Fat man, fat man, what makes you so fat?"

"I eat a bowl of gravy, drunk a cup of coffee, eat a loaf of bread. Eat you if I can catch ye." He caught that little girl and eat her.

That old woman sent that little boy out to get a loaf of bread. He went out there and he said, "Fat man, fat man, what makes you so fat?"

"I eat a bowl of gravy, drunk a cup of coffee, eat a loaf of bread, eat a little girl. I'll eat you if I can catch ye." He caught the little boy and eat him.

Well, that old woman she sent the old man to the store. Well, he went out there and he said, "Fat man, fat man, what makes you so fat?"

"I eat a bowl of gravy, drunk a cup of coffee, eat a loaf of bread, eat a little girl, and eat a little boy. I'll eat you if I can catch ye." He caught that old man and eat him.

Well, that little monkey sent that old woman to the store. She went out there and said, "Fat man, fat man, what makes you so fat?"

He said, "I eat a bowl of gravy, drunk a cup of coffee, eat a loaf of bread, eat a little girl, eat a little boy, eat an old man. I'll eat you if I can catch ye." Caught her and eat her.

Well, that little monkey he went to the store. He said, "Fat man, fat man, what makes you so fat?"

"I eat a bowl of gravy, drunk a cup of coffee, eat a loaf of bread, eat a litttle girl, eat a little boy, eat an old man, eat an old woman. I'll eat you if I can catch ye."

He took after that little monkey. And he run and climbed up a tree. And that old man went up after it and that old fat man fell and busted open.

The little girl said, "Tee, hee, I got out."

The little boy said, "Tee, hee, I got out."

The old man said, "Tee, hee, I got out."

The old woman said, "Tee, hee, I got out."

The little monkey said, "Tee, hee, I didn't get in to get out!"

135. Chew Tobaccer, Spit, Spit, Spit

One time they was an old man, a little boy, and a little girl. The old man sent the little girl out to the spring to get a bucket of water. She went out to the spring and got the bucket of water and she heared something going, "Chew tobaccer, spit, spit, spit."

She throwed the water bucket down and run back to the house. Said, "Daddy, they's something out there going, 'Chew tobaccer, spit, spit, spit."

Well, he sent that litttle boy. He went out there to get a bucket of water at the spring and he heared something going, "Chew tobaccer, spit, spit, spit; chew tobaccer, spit, spit, spit." And he throwed his water bucket down and run back to the house and said, "Daddy, I heared the same old thing."

And he sent that old woman. She went out there to the spring and she heared something going, "Chew tobaccer, spit, spit, spit; chew tobaccer, spit, spit, spit." She run back to the house and said she heared it too.

Well that old man he went. And he got out there and he heared something, "Chew tobaccer, spit, spit, spit." And he looked up in a tree and they's two little niggers up in there chewing tobaccer and spitting the juice.

136. Couch Family Riddles

a. World of Wiglam Waglam

As I went around my world of wiglam waglam,
There I found old Tom Tiglam Taglam;
I called old Hellum Bellum
To take Tom Tiglam Taglam
Out of my world of wiglam waglam.   (Dave Couch)

b. I Went Through the Woods Spin Spin

I went through the woods spin spin,
That little thing went grin grin,
To hoot the day the day to pop,
That little thing went johnny woodcock.   (Dave Couch)

c. Good Morning, Good Morning

This is the story of a king. He told his servant that if he would tell a riddle that he couldn't onriddle why he would free him. He was under bondage. He said:

Good morning, good morning, your cermony, king,
I drunk a drink out of your morning spring;
Through the gold the streams did run,
In your garden that was done,
If you onriddle that I'll be hung.   (Dave Couch)

d. King Met a King

King met a king in a long lane,
To the king, to the king, what is your name?
Silver is my saddle, brass is my bow,
I've told you my name three times in a row
And yet you don't know.   (Dave Couch)

e. Twelve Pear

Twelve pear hanging high,
Twelve men come riding by;
Each man took a pear
And left eleven hanging there.   (Virgil Couch)

f. Love I Set

Love I set, love I stand,
Love I hold in my right hand;
Love I see in yonders tree,
If you can onriddle that
You can hang me.   (Dave Couch)

g. Heely Veely

I went through heely veely,
I looked over and there believie,
Saw a colliver planting caniver,
Called to my nighest neighbor,
Lend me his euney cuney crow,
Kill a colliver I'd give him the calliverow.   (Jim Couch)

h. Highest Winder

I went up to my highest winder,
Called for my nighest neighbor,
To lend me his tittick and his tattick
His three-legged mattick,
His quick and go whirly over.   (Dave Couch)

i. Green as Grass

Green as grass and grass it hain't,
White as milk and milk it hain't,
Red as blood and blood it hain't,
Black as ink and ink it hain't,
What is that?   (Bige Couch)

The telling and unriddling mounted as the mike went around at this night session in 1952. The younger generation had not heard some of the tongue-twisters and the teller often recited them so fast that in some instances nobody could catch the words. On the other hand, most of us knew others, and the answers would pop out before the teller could finish. Jim and Frank came in and joined the fun.

j. Yaller Bank

I went down a yaller bank,
I seed something looked rough and rank,
Two thick lips and yaller beard,
Drat that thing how bad I got scared.   (Dave)

k. Five Bars

Five bars went over a bridge,
and they all went off sows.   (Dave)

l. Bone Eat a Bone

Bone eat a bone up a whiteoak tree,
If you can onriddle that you can hang me.   (Jim)

m. Whizzy Busy

Whizzy busy on the wall,
If you tetch whizzy busy
Whizzy busy will bite you all.   (Dave)

n. Humpy Bumpy

Humpy bumpy on the wall,
Humpy bumpy got a fall;
Ten men, a thousand more,
Can't fix humpy bumpy back
Like it was before.   (Dave)

o. Round as a Hoop

Round as a hoop, deep as a cup,
All the king's horses can't pull it up.   (Bige Couch)

p. Blacky

Blacky upon blacky,
And brown upon brown,
Three lags up
And six lags down.   (Dave)

q. Clank, Clank

Clank, clank under the bank,
Ten against four.   (Virgil Couch)

r. Two Lookers

Two lookers, two crookers, two flappers,
Four down-hangers and a switch-about.   (Dave)

s. Round as a Biscuit

Round as a biscuit, busy as a bee,
Purty little thing as ye ever did see.   (Jim)

t. High as a House

High as a house, low as a mouse,
Has as many rooms as any man's house.   (Jim)

u. All Over the Hills

I go all over the hills, mountains and valleys
Through the day, and at night I still gape
for the bones.   (Jim)

v. Under Water

Under water and over the water
And it never gets wet.   (Jim)

w. Over the Roads

Over the roads and through the fields
With its head down.   (Jim)

x. Goes to the River

Goes to the river and drinks and drinks
But it never drinks any.   (Jim)

y. Adam's Race

One time when I's working over yonder in Letcher County they
was a preacher over there having a revival, and he was all the time
holding questions and quizzes on the Bible. And he said nobody
could stick him on any facts in the Bible. I said to myself, "Huh uh,
old boy, I'm going to fix you." So I made me up a riddle and put it to
him one night there before all the meeting crowd and he couldn't answer it. Here it is:

Once I knew a man of Adam's race,
And he had a certain dwelling place,
It wa'n't in heaven nor it wa'n't in hell,
It wa'n't on the earth where the people dwell:
Who was this man and where did he dwell?   (Jim)

z. God Never Made

Well now, listen to me and I'll give you one. I have a show
to put on here tonight. I'm going to show all these people
something that God never made and man never saw. What
do you think it could be?   (Dave)

aa. Lives in the Barn

What is it lives in the barn,

Eats corn and hay and can see out a one end
As good as it can out a the other?   (Frank)

bb. Man That Made It

The man that made it never seen it,
The man that sold it never seen it,
I bought it and I seen it,
And nobody else never did see it.   (Dave)

cc. Born from a Woman

All right now, boys, what's this one?
Who was the man born from a woman that never was born,
Sucked the woman that never did suck,
He died and was buried in his grandmother's bosom?   (Jim)

dd. Battle Was Fought

And here's another one from the Bible:
What battle was fought when one fourth
of the people was slain in a day?   (Jim)

ee. The Devil

All right now, I know a Bible riddle.
The Devil was created when man was:
Where was the Devil in the time of the Flood?   (Dave)

ff. Big at the Bottom

Big at the bottom and little at the top,
A thing in the middle goes flippety flop.   (Jim)

gg. Patches on Patches

Patches on patches and a hole in the middle,
If you can guess that riddle I'll give you a fiddle.   (Dave)

hh. Red Pig

Now let me try you on this one. Back in the time when kings had slaves he'd tell 'em if they could make a riddle up that he couldn't on-riddle he'd free 'em. He sent a slave out to see about his old sow and he discovered he had found pigs.

He come back and told the king about her:

> She had a red pig and a dead pig,
> A boar pig and a pore pig—
> How many pigs is that?   (Dave)

ii. Fat Hog

> If a fat hog will sink four feet in the mud,
> How many feet will a pore hog sink?   (Frank)

jj. Across London Bridge

> As I went across London bridge
> There I met a London feller,
> I tipped my hat and drew my cane,
> And in that riddle I told my name.
> What is my name?   (Frank Couch)

kk. Cement Wall

Now get your pencils ready, boys, and see who can figure up this problem first. If you was building a cement wall ten feet high and four feet wide, how many brick would be in it?   (Frank)

ll. Electric Train

You don't need no pencil for this one but I bet some of you boys can't answer it. If you saw an electric train and it was going east and the wind was blowing north, which way would the smoke be going? (Frank)

mm. Crooked as a Rainbow

Ah, them's not riddles—them's puzzles to trick somebody. Let me give you another good riddle.

Crooked as a rainbow, teeth like a cat,
You can onriddle all things
But you can't onriddle that.   (Dave)

nn. Two Backbones

What has two backbones and ten thousand
ribs?   (Frank)

oo. Always a-Running

Always a-running and never walks,
Got a tongue and can't talk.   (Jim)

pp. East and West

East and west, north and south,
A thousand teeth and nary mouth.   (Jim)

qq. Black and White

What's black and white and red all over?   (Virgil)

rr. Blacky in Blacky

Blacky went in blacky,
come back out and left whitey.   (Dave)

ss. Heap a Steeple

I went up the heap a steeple,
There I saw a heap o' people;
Some was tick, some was tack,
Some was the color of brown toback.   (Jim)

The boys had thought of about all the riddles they knew, and now those who had not heard their voices on the recorder wanted to have a playback. This took some time, prolonging the session until far up in the night. Jim's family had gone to bed and the other boys were dozing. Before we forgot the subject of riddles I asked Dave the story of

137. The Magic Sausage Mill

I'll tell ye one about a rich brother and a pore brother. This here rich brother he had plenty of ever'thing that a man needed. The pore brother didn't have nothing much and worked for this rich brother, just a little hire every day. He'd take meat or about anything he could get.

Well, this rich brother heared of a place where a lot of goblins stayed and a woodcutter that stayed on the outside and cut wood. He told him he would have to be awful careful with his meat if they were there. Said them goblins would try to take it away from him. Well, he went by that place, and the old woodcutter asked him what did he have and he told him he had meat. "Well," he said, "if the goblins find it out they'll take it away from you," but said, "they got a mill, magic mill that'll grind anything you want it to grind, and it's a-setting behind the door." Said, "If you'll throw that meat in to 'em and while they're a-fighting over it, you can get that mill. Bring it out and I'll tell you how to operate it."

Well, so he did. He throwed the meat in to the goblins. They's onto the meat a-fightin' over it, and he got the mill and come back out to the woodcutter. That woodcutter said, "Now when you want to grind anything—it'll grind anything you want it to—you have to say, 'Hoky, spoky, foky, stop' hit'll stop."

He took the mill and he went home. His wife met him at the door, thinking he'd have something to eat. He told her that he tuck meat for his work but he swapped it on a mill. She stormed at him over takin' that old rusty-looking thing. "Well," he said, "you get ready now, and we'll have us plenty of forks and knives and things to eat out of," and then said, "we'll have food to eat in 'em."

He got ready and he told the mill, said, "Grind knives and forks." And the mill obeyed him and ground what they wanted of knifes and forks. He told it to stop from grinding them. Then he told it to grind out plates and teacups and all things they wanted to eat out of and then cooking vessels. And he told the mill now to grind sausage. And so the mill obeyed him and ground them a big meal af sausage, and he said the magic words to get it to stop, "Hoky, spoky, foky, stop!"

Well, he ground all kinds of food and anything he wanted, any kind of a mess, and he didn't have to work for his brother.

And his brother got kindly uneasy about him, and he went to see about him because he didn't have to work. The pore brother told him, said, "I've quit work." Said, "I've got a mill now." Said, "I can collect all the things I need without work."

Well, his brother 'sisted on him that he wanted to see some tricks that the mill could do. His brother told him to watch and he'd show him. He got the mill and he spoke the words in a low tone so his brother couldn't hear him start the mill and stop it. He started the mill out and ground sausage. And his brother said, "Well," said, "can you grind fish with the thing?"

He spoke the magic words and the big fish commenced flopping out and that sus-prised his brother. Then he ground gravy, and he ground bread, and he ground cornpone, just anything he wanted to eat. Well, his brother 'sisted on him to sell him that mill. His brother told him, said, "I don't want to."

Well, he said, "Sell it to me and you won't have to work. You let me have the mill."

His brother finally asked what would he give.

Said, "I'll give you two thousand dollars for the mill," and said, "you can come to the house whenever you want anything and I'll grind you whatever you want and need to eat along."

He traded with him.

His rich brother said, "You help me take the mill home and help me start it out till I can operate it, then I'll pay you your money."

The pore brother took the mill over and helped him set it up and got his money and come back to the house.

The rich brother took the mill and looked him over and then he told his wife, said, "You go to the field to work tomor' and I'll get dinner for us." Said, "I'll have fish and gravy and sausage and just have us a good dinner when you come in."

She said, "All right, if you can cook that a way." Said, "I'll go work."

She went to work. Now the pore brother had left the mill with him all right and he told him how to start the mill, but he didn't tell him how to stop it. The rich brother was so anxious to start he hurried up and got him a pan and he told the mill to grind fish and gravy and grind it fast.

Well, the mill went to grindin' and the big fish flopped out and in a minute he had the pan run over. He said, "Stop!" That wa'n't the magic words to stop the mill and the mill didn't stop. He said again, "Stop!" And the mill didn't stop. The pan run over and the fish and gravy was running into the house. Well, he called it again and he begin to cuss it but it wouldn't stop. He didn't know anything else but to throw the mill out. He throwed it out the door and still the mill kept on grinding. It run a big branch of gravy and fish, and they went a-floppin' on down toward town down in below him. The gravy kept on runnin' and the fish kept on floppin', and he saw it was a-goin' to run the town over. And he run back to his brother.

Said, "Brother," said, "I want you to go quick and stop that mill," said, "it's a-grindin' fish and gravy and it's a-goin' to have the town flooded if you don't do something with it."

His brother said, "Le's set down and talk awhile. Take you a chear and set down and we'll talk about that mill awhile." Said, "What did you say about that mill?"

Said, "Hurry." Said, "I'll give you two more thousand dollars if you'll go and stop that mill, do something with it, and I'll give you that old mill back."

Slowly he got up and went with his brother and got his two thousand dollars that his brother said he'd give him to get that mill and take it away. He stopped the mill and tuck it on home with him. He was wealthy then by his rich brother's money. He had paid him for the mill and then paid him for takin' the mill on hand.

They was an old storekeeper near there and he bought up all sorts of stuff, salt and wheat and sech, and he tuck it across the sea from one nation to another and sold it. And he heared about this pore man having this mill. His brother had told the storekeeper that he had it and that it would grind anything and any amount he wanted it to. So the storekeeper come and saw the pore brother about the mill. He told him, said, "What will you take for the mill?"

"Oh," he said, "I don't want to sell it. I want to keep it to grind my grub and stuff with."

"Well," he said, "I'll give you enough money so you won't have to grind it. You'll have enough money to buy anything you want."

He said, "Well, how much will you gi' me?"

He said, "I'll give you $10,000 in cash for the mill."

He said, "Hoky doh." Said, "I'll trade you the mill."

He took the mill and he put it on his ship and he got ready to grind. He was aimin' to grind a shipload of salt as he went acrost the sea and take it to another nation. Well, he started the mill to grinding salt and he told it to grind its best. The mill started to whir, whirrin' and the salt went to pourin'. Filled ever' bag he had full and ever' tub, ever' box. He said, "Stop!" And the mill wouldn't obey. That weren't the words to get it to stop and it kept on grindin' salt. By that time the salt was gettin' so heavy it was almost sinkin' the ship. He throwed the mill out into the sea. And if you don't think that the mill is grindin' today in the sea, you taste of the sea water and see if it ain't salty.

138. The Three Piggies

One time there was an old sow had three pigs, Tom, Will, and Jack. They got up great big and the old sow turned them out to live for themselves. Tom said, "Mommy, I'm goin' to build me a house."

She said, "I'm afeard you're goin' to get caught."

"No, I won't. I'll build it out of stick and straw."

He was building on his house one day, seed a fox a-comin'.

"What're you doin', little pig?"

"Buildin' me a house."

"Come to see ye when ye get it built."

"All right."

Got his house built and he looked out and seed the fox a-comin'. He jumped in the house and shet the door. The fox come and said, "Let me in, little pig."

"In my nose, in my tail, I shan't do it."

"If you don't let me in, I'll get on top of your house and I'll shickel and shackel and tear it down." He got on top of his house and he shickeled and he shackeled and tore it down and he caught the pig and eat it.

Well, Will said, "Mommy, I'm goin' to build me a house."

Said, "No, you'll get catched like your other brother."

"No, I won't. I'll build it out of wood."

He went out and he was buildin' on his house and looked and seed the fox a-comin'. Said, "What are you doin', little pig?"

"Buildin' me a house."

"Come to see you when you get it built."

"All right."

Got his house built and he seed the fox a-comin'. "Let me in, little pig."

"In my nose, in my tail, I shan't do it."

"Don't let me in, I'll get on top of your house and shickel and shackel and tear it down."

He got up on top of his house and he shickeled and he shackeled and he tore it down and caught the pig and eat it.

Jack said, "Mother, I'm goin' to build me a house."

Said, "No, you must not. You'll get catched like your other two brothers."

"No, I won't. I'll build it out of brick."

Buildin' on his house, looked and seed the fox a-comin'.

"What're you doin', little pig?"

"Buildin' me a house."

"Come to see you when you get it built."

"All right."

Got his house built, looked out and seed the fox a-comin'.

"Let me in, little pig."

"In my nose, in my tail, I shan't do it."

"If you don't let me in, I'll get on top of your house and I'll shickel and shackel and tear it down."

He got on top of his house and he shickeled and shackeled and he couldn't tear it down. He got back down and come to the door and said, "Let my nose in, little pig, I'm a-freezin'."

He let his nose in.

"Let my head in, little pig, I'm a-freezin'."
Let his head in.
"Let my forelegs in, little pig, I'm a-freezin'."
Let his forelegs in.
"Let my body in, little pig, I'm a-freezin'."
He let his body in.
"Let my hindlegs in, little pig, I'm a-freezin'."
He let his hindlegs in.
"Let my tail in, little pig, I'm a-freezin'."
He let his tail in.

The old fox jumped right up and down and shouted, "Piggie and peas for my supper, ha, ha, ha."

The little pig said to him, said, "Law me, Mr. Fox, I see a man and a gun, and he's got a great gang o' greyhounds a-comin'."

"Where will I go, where will I go?"

"Jump right here in my chest and I'll lock you up."

He jumped in his chest and Jack locked him up. He put him on a kittle of water. Getting the water hot, fox said, "What are you heatin' that water fer, little pig?"

"Goin' to make you some tea."

"That's right, little piggie, that's right."

The little pig went to borin' him a hole right down through the top of the chest.

"What are you borin' that hole fer, little pig?"

"To give you some air."

"That's right, little piggie, that's right."

He went to porin' that water to him. The fox yelled, "Fleas and chinches a-bitin' me. Fleas and chinches a-bitin'. Ouch, Jack, I'm gettin' hot, ouch, Jack, I'm gettin' hot! Fleas and chinches a-bitin' me!"

That was the last of the fox. Jack burnt him up.

139. The Tar Baby

One time they was a man set him out a big cabbage patch. 'Fore he knowed it they was a rabbit took to his gyarden, eating all of his cabbage up and he couldn't get up with it. He made him a man out of tar and put him up in his gyarden to catch the rabbit.

The old rabbit come jumping into the cabbage patch not long after that and he saw his little tar man a-standing there. He said, "What're you doing here?" Said, "You get out of here or I'll knock you down with my foot."

The tar man never offered to move, of course, and old Mr. Rabbit farred away into the old tar man with one of his feet and it stuck. "You turn my foot loose or," said, "I'll take my other foot and I'll knock you down with it."

Tar man never budged. He farred loose into the old tar man with his other forefoot and it stuck. He called out again, "Let loose o' my two forefeet or I'll take my hindfoot and I'll kick you out of here."

He cut loose with his hind foot and of course it stuck. "You let loose of my two forefeet and my hindfoot or I'll take my other hind-foot and kick the puddin' out of you." Nothing never moved, so he farred loose with his other hindfoot and it stuck. "You let go of my feet or I'll take my head and butt you down."

The tar man never did say anything, so he hauled back with his head and butted him and his head stuck. Up come the old man and said, "Ha, ha, rabbit," said, "now I've got ye. I got you just where I want ye now." Said, "I'm going to build me up a big far and burn ye."

"All right, Mr. Man, that's the very place I want to be."

"No, I won't put you there. Too good for ye." Said, "I'll take you to a big hole of water and drown ye."

"All right, old man, that's the very place I want to be."

"No, I won't put ye there. Not bad enough for ye." Said, "I'll tell ye what I'll do," said, "I'll take ye and put ye in a big briar patch where the briars will scratch ye and pick ye to death."

"Ooooo, noooo, old man, don't put me there," said, "them briars will scratch me and stick me to death."

He took the old rabbit and he whizzed him into the briar patch. The old rabbit said, "He, he he, thank you, old man," said, "this is pimeblank where I live, he, he, he—"

While the rabbit was laughing about it, the old man run up and grabbed the rabbit again. The rabbit looked around for another way to ex-cape and looked behind the old man and said, "Fool, fool," said, "you've got holt of a fence rail. That's not my back, you've got holt of a fence rail—"

The old man looked around suddenly to see what it was, and turned the rabbit loose. He run out through the briar patch. And so the man didn't get to catch the rabbit after the rabbit had eat all his cabbage up.

140. Granddaddy Bluebeard

There was oncet an old man lived out in the country and he was thought to be a robber. He found a neighbor out not far from him who was rich. Now he had him a trap fixed for killing all the people he could get to come and stay all night with him. He sent for this neighbor, and this neighbor decided to go and try him out. Said, "I believe I'll go and see what he wants tonight."

So he went to old Granddaddy Bluebeard's house and took his bull-dog with him. They eat supper, he had a fine meal, and they set around till 'way in the night. Old Mr. Bluebeard told this neighbor man where his bed was and the room he was to sleep in. He didn't have no light in it and he told him when he got ready to go ahead and lay down. He said he believed he'd go on to bed and went on to his room.

This neighbor started in to bed and went into this room. His bull-dog happened to get betwixt him and the bed and he started pushing his master back and growling. The master happened to suspicion something and he looked down on the far side of the bed on the floor and he seen some lights shining up like lightening through a glass trap the old man had set there. He struck him a match and saw that it was some kind of trap fixed there on the far side of the bed.

He got out of there as quiet as he could, went down below the house, and set down to see what happened next. This old Granddaddy Bluebeard along in the night, about eleven o'clock, got up and he lit his light and went in there and started peeping around and searching for this man. Couldn't find him.

Well, the neighbor went off and next day he got the law and they come back up there and tore the trap up and they found seven men, dead men, with their heads cut off in that trap. The law took old Bluebeard on off to jail.

Now this neighbor also knowed of two more fellers who lived by theirselves. They kept sending for him, and he thought they were up to the same thing. He decided to go up to their house and see what their plans might be.

When he got up there and had supper with 'em, they said, "We allas go a-coon hunting of a night." Said, "But you can stay here. Right there is your bed and you can go to bed when you are ready." They give him a newspaper to read till he got sleepy and went off.

After they was gone awhile he thought they might be aiming to shoot him, kill him some way before he had time to see what was going on, and so he went to hunting for a place to hide. He went in under the bed, and he crawled right up again' a dead man that had been killed, laying there under the bed. Well, he knowed then what was going to happen. They killed their guests in the bed asleep. So he taken this dead man and put him in the bed where he was supposed to sleep and covered him up. He got by the door where they had to come into the house, got down on his hands and knees like he would be a dog or something that would jump out when them men opened the door. The men come in and he jumped out and they never caught on 'cause they were coming in without no light. He stepped off a few steps from the house. D'rectly he heared a thump, thump, thump, beating on that old dead man. They thought they was killing him and him out there a-laughting at 'em.

So he called the law and they found the dead man in their house and other signs of robbery and had 'em throwed in jail. That was two gangs of robbers that he cleared up all by himself. I think that was a mighty nice deed that he done, clearing up them robberies and bringing them three men to jestice.

141. My Mommy Killed Me

This next un is one I never did care much about. My mother would tell it oncet in awhile when we would want to hear about that little dead baby.

There was some pore people, a man and his wife, and they had a hard way to get anything to eat and was on starvation biggest part of the time. They had three kids, had two little girls and a baby. The baby was a baby boy. The old man he was out a-workin'. And the old woman she didn't have anything to eat and she killed her baby and cooked it up for their supper.

The old man he come in and she got supper and tuck that baby up on the table, called the old man to his supper. He forked into the dish and got out his little baby's hand. He said to her, said, "This is my pore little baby's hand."

She said, "Ah, old fool," said, "that's a rabbit's hand."

He forked in again and he got its foot out. Said, "This is my pore little baby's foot."

She said, "Ah, old fool," said, "that's a rabbit's foot."

Well, he forked in again and he got its head the next time. And he said, "This is my pore little baby's head."

She said, "Ah, old fool," said, "eat on," said, "that's a rabbit's head."

Well, that night that little baby it come back and went to cryin'. It said,

> My mother killed me and my father eat me,
> I want my two little sisters to take my bones
> And bury 'em atween two marvel stones.

That's not all of it. Hit goes on and tells how the baby drops a millstone on the mommy and kills her, but that's all I want to tell of it.

142. Rat or Mouse?

Here's one that is just like old people and it might have happened far as I know.

I had an uncle and an aunt one time. The uncle was named John and the aunt named Betts. They were gettin' awful old and childish, but they had lived their life together and hadn't never had no quarrels. They was settin' by the fire one night, and they's a mouse run through the floor. Old Aunt Betts said, "Did you see that mouse?"

Uncle John said, "That was a rat."

Aunt Betts said, "It was a mouse."

Uncle John said, "No, it was a rat."

They brung up a quarrel and they separated. Stayed apart about two or three weeks, and all of us neighbors around we got 'em back together again. Told 'em they orght to be ashamed, in their old days let a little thing like that tear 'em up. We got 'em back together, and the same night that we got 'em together they's settin' there before the fire. Aunt Betts said to Uncle John, "That was a awful thing for us to separate over, us a-gettin' so old."

He said, "Yes, I know it was, but," said, "that was a rat."

She said, "You're a liar, it was a mouse."

They cut loose to quarreling and they separated again, and they are still apart today over that little rat-and-mouse tale.

That didn't happen to my people that I know of but it's just like some of 'em, so contrary they can't stand theirselves sometimes.

143. Sambo and Golder

This was back in the days when the kings had the Niggers all under bondage. And they'd give 'em riddles to make up when they was in trouble and if the kings couldn't guess the riddles why they'd free 'em.

Once the king had two Niggers under bondage and he sent them out horse hunting. These two Niggers was named Sambo and Golder. Golder he went out to horse hunt. And it was a-rainin' that day about all day. And he got under an old rock under a shelter. And he had him a gourd and he made him a banjer out of it. Well, when he sent Sambo to hunt for Golder he found him under that rock pickin' on that old banjer and a-singin', "Jango bum and a bungo jing; and a jango bum and a bungo jing."

Well he roused him out and they went on a-horse huntin'. And they found a cave in the ground. And Golder told Sambo for him to watch the hole and he'd go in and see what he could find in there. And so he went in there and he found some bears. He told Golder if the old bear come for him to ketch her and hold her, not let her in on him. He was in there and here come the old mammy bear and started in there after him. Sambo he grabbed the old bear by the tail to keep her from goin' in on him. Old Golder saw his light cut off and he called, "What darkened up the hole, Sambo?"

Sambo said, "If the taily holt breaks you'll find out what darkens up the hole."

144. Groundsow Huntin'

I used to hear another un about a hunt that turned all things around on themselves, but I bet I can't say half of it.

Me and my brother Jim we went a groundsow huntin' one day. We treed one up a buckeye sycibuck-amore sourwood saplin'. Hit was up in there about forty foot above the top. Jim he shot at it and missed it, and I shot pime blank where Jim shot and killed it stone dead. And it fell out of there a-straddle of a log, with both feet on one side, ha, ha. We took it to the house and let the old woman and chillern see it. We set it up on the j'ist and it was one more sight to hear Sal and the chillern laugh about that groundsow, ha, ha, ha.

Come home one day, my wife was standing right wide open, the door was sick in the bed. I looked out in the gyarden and I seen a cabbage head running around the side of the hill with a pig in its mouth. And my little dog Black he come running into the house and I pulled out my tail and cut its knife off. They was a lot more to that but I can't put it together any more.

And then there is the joke about

145. The Colored Preacher

They was an old colored man holding a revival meeting in a small town one time and he preached away every night and he took out his text on the Devil for several nights running. He preached again' the old Devil just as hard as he could lay his tongue to it for these nights. He had a small room upstairs above the church where he would go before the meeting started and rest and go over his text and his sermon.

Well, they was another old colored feller there ever' night hearing him, and he planned out a way to play a good prank on the old preacher. He slipped up there in his small room, had on some old ragged clothes, and disfigured himself. This old preacher come in and went up to his room to get his sermon ready, and there stood this old raggedy man. The preacher looked up at him and said, "Hody-de-do, who are you?"

He said, "I'm Mr. Devil." Said, "I come tonight to see you about bilifyin' me so bad." Said, "You've preached again' me purty hard now for a week, again' me just as hard as you could preach ever' night. What do you mean by it?"

The old preach began to stutter and said, "Yeaw," said, " 'pon my honor, Devil, I know I bilified you and preached again' you, but," said, "my heart's been for you the whole time."

146. Big Frait and Little Frait

They was an old man and an old woman had a little boy and a little monkey. That little boy had to go a-cow hunting all the time. Well, he went out one night and was gone late and the old man got uneasy about him and follered the boy. He was off playing and it plumb dusty dark and the man brought him in.

Next time he was out that late the old man said, "Well, I'll foller the boy and I bet ye a dollar he won't stay out no more this way."

He got him a sheet and started after the boy. The monkey seen the old man get a sheet and it got a sheet and put it over his head like the old man and started follering. Took right after the old man. The man got up purty clost to the little boy with that white sheet on him. The cow seen the ghosts there and she broke, but the boy just stood there. And the old man happened to look around and saw that little ghost by him and he broke to running. The old man passed the boy up and then the little monkey passed the boy. That boy started right out after them and he begin to holler, "Run, big frait, the little un will catch ye; run, big frait, the little un will catch ye."

That old man run home scared to death and the monkey come in just about to die. But the boy wa'n't scared half as bad as the old man nor the monkey nary one was.

147. Counting the Nuts

That reminded me of another un just about like it that I've heared all my life.

There was an old crippled-up man one time, got down so's he couldn't walk none, but he was all the time bragging what a brave man he was and that he wa'n't afraid of nothing. They was a graveyard up on the hill near there, and people claimed they was allas something to be heared up there. "I wouldn't be afraid to lay out on a grave." Well, some of his neighbors was there and they told him they would carry him up there if he would make good his brag and lay out there that night. He said he was ready to go.

Well, two of the men picked him up and carried him up there. Now they's a lot of big black warnut trees around the graveyard. Some boys was out there gathering up the warnuts, picking 'em up and dividing 'em. They was picking up and saying, "You take this one and I'll take the other un, you take this one and I'll take the other un." Well, the men all got scared and was ready to run by that time.

The boys went on counting and they had dropped two warnuts out at the gate where these men was and they wanted to count them in. They said, "And they's two out at the gate. You take one and I'll take the other un."

These here fellers throwed that old crippled man down and they broke out of there with their hair standing right straight up. They thought the boys was talking about the two of them. They tore on into the house and when they run in there was this old crippled man setting there cooling off. He had beat 'em back home. That's about all I know now for awhile.

Dave went after his pipe and had a good smoke while we played some of these jokes over again. They sounded funnier to the boys from the tapes than from the mouth, at least they laughed and reacted more sensitively to the strangely familiar voice on the playback. And now the boys began to show interest in recording anything they could think of. Bige was ready first with a poem he said he had heard a long time ago, and so we let him recite.

> I had a little dog and his name was trigger,
> He barked up a tree and down come a Nigger,
> An old Nigger woman and an old Nigger man,
> Playing "Yankee Doodle" in an old dishpan.

Now I know one of them jokes about Arshmen," Bige said. "Do you want to tell it?" We let him tell about the

148. The Arshmen and the Cushaw

One time they was two Arshmen coming along through the country asking for work. Well, an old man got 'em to do a little job for him. He told 'em to go up to the backside of a field and drive his hogs in. He told 'em to watch out for snakes. Been some big poisonous rattlesnakes killed in that field. Well, they agreed to go. They went back to the backside of the field. They didn't know what a snake looked like, and one of them saw a big long-necked cushaw laying on a stump. He called out, "Oh, I see a snake." Said, "Le's kill it. You get you two big rocks and get in below the stump and I'll take a fence rail and punch it off the stump." Said, "You can kill it then."

He took him a fence rail and got up there, and he punched that cushaw off the stump and it took off down the hill. The man below took off down the hill and the cushaw right after him. Scared him. The cushaw hit a stump and busted all to pieces and throwed the grines all over him. The one up above hollered and said, "Are you bit?"

He said, "Fat o' my Christ, no, but" said, "that thing throwed poison all over me."

"Well, I believe that I know a little short joke," the new listener Alvis said. We were glad for him to record his voice with

149. The Holy Ghost

One time they was an old feller wanted to get religion and maybe preach, and he'd go out under a 'simmon tree ever' night and pray for the Lord to let the Holy Ghost fall on him.

Another man caught on to what he was doing out there, heared him calling for the Holy Ghost to fall on him. So he slipped out there one night and clomb up the tree with a big punkin. A little bit later this old feller come out under his tree and he started praying. He got in a big way telling the Lord what and all he would do and ended up by saying, "Yes, Lord, I'll do all I can for you if you'll only let the Holy

Ghost fall on me." About that time the man up in the tree turned that punkin loose and dropped it right on him and it busted all over him. That old feller looked up and said, "O Lordy," said, "can't you take a joke?"

150. Seven Days' Journey

a. One time I was out traveling around, hoboing and hitching along the road, bumming and seeing if I could get along without work. I met up with another feller and we decided to go along together. We's bumming along and we went by a house where a lady was baking pies, and she had some of the nicest pies set out to cool I ever saw. We went on around the bend and I said, "I'm going back there and bum one of them pies." The other feller said, "Go ahead and do your best—see if you can get two of them."

I went back down there and was going to ax the old woman for one but she was out of sight, back in the house or somewhere. So I just reached over and picked up two of them biggest pies, plates and all, and hustled back out of the yard and hit it on up to where my buddy was. His eyes bugged out a foot and we set down and had us one more feast. We eat 'em and set down a while to let 'em settle, and I told my buddy, "I went and bummed these and I hold her we'd bring her plates back." Said, "It's your job to take 'em back and thank the lady."

He said, "Yeaw, sure, I'll be glad to do that." He went fetching it down the tracks and out of sight. About the time he got there I heared one of them plates crack over his head and a woman's tongue break loose on both ends. And such another scolding I never heared a man get and he come back around that bend with his shirt-tail standing straight out. Passed me up he was going so fast and I didn't catch up with him for a mile or two.

Well, we laid out that night and started on and along up in the day we's getting hungry again. Begin to plan a way to get something and finally we decided that I was to play off deef and dumb. We made a sign and put it on my chest, said, "Deef and Dumb."

We went along and purty soon come to a house clost to the road and they was setting in there eating dinner, old woman and man and a girl, awful nice girl there. I went up to the door and the girl come, said, "Mister, what can I do for you?"

I's trying to play deef and dumb and I said, "Bite me." I meant to ax her to give me a bite to eat and just said, "Bite me." She looked at me a minute, read my sign, and I knowed right then I'd made a mistake.

She said, "I can't bite ye but I've got something that will bite ye." I thought she went to get us a good hand-out, but she come back with a big bulldog and said, "Seek 'im, Boss!" I set out from there and run right at my pardner. He tried to get started but I passed him up but as I passed I said, "Kick at him and turn him off me." He started kicking at that dog and it turned on him and run him back'ards up a big high bank. He got away from it and come on up the tracks and passed me up before we stopped running.

b. Well, we got by all right that night and went on down the road. This time I persuaded him to try that deef and dumb trick and see what *he* could do. We saw a house setting up on a hill like and a man there on the porch. I got him to go up there and give 'em a try. He went up there, and he had some words written on a piece of paper— he was not supposed to talk, you know. He went up there and went on in the gate. Big palin' fence all around the house. He shet the gate and walked on up to the old man and handed him the paper. The man looked at it, read it, and said, "Deef and dumb, hey?"

He blurted right out and said, "Yeaw, and hungry, too."

The man looked at him again and at the paper, said, "Yeah!" He turned around and just dropped a big mean dog right on my pardner. He took right around the house and never did have time to open the gate. It run him around that house four or five times by the time I walked up to the gate. I called after him on one of his trips and said, "Anything I can do for you?"

He said, "Yes sir, just have that gate open again' I make another round."

I let him out the gate and we hit 'er down the road again.

c. Well, I went on and got separated from my buddy. Night come on and I stopped at a place and asked to stay all night. Just an old man and woman there. They finally agreed to let me stay. We set around and directly they begin to talk about going to bed when we hadn't had a bite of supper. I's so hungry it made me half mad. But they went on to their back room and fixed me a place in the front room.

Everything got right still in an hour and so I heared the old man say to his old woman, "Old woman, I've got to have something to eat—I'm about to starve to death."

She said, "Well, you go out there in the gyarden to our cabbage hole and get you a cabbage head and eat it."

The old man come slipping through my room and on out the door. I remembered seeing a big old ox whip hanging on the porch when I come in, and so I eased up and got that whip. About the time the old man got down on his hands and knees digging him out a cabbage I let him have it a few cracks with that whip and run him out of the gyarden.

Come back and went to my bed and purty soon he slipped back in and went to his room. I stayed awake to see what they would do next. Purty soon I heared the old man say again, "I've just got to have something to eat," said "I'm starving to death."

She said, "Well, they's a little dough in the pan in there. Go and get it and pour it in the ashes and make you an ash cake."

Here he come back through my room and went in the kitchen. Come back and puttered around the ashes. I raised up like I had been waked. He said, "Just fixing the far. Did I wake you?"

I said, "Yeaw, but I was sleeping light. Had something on my mind. I'm in a lawsuit over a piece of land. I want t' show you how my lines run and everything and see what you think about it." I took the poker and raked around in the ashes showing him how my lines run and tore his ash cake all to pieces. He went back to bed again.

Next morning they was a big fine breakfast on the table and we all eat like we hadn't had a bite in a week. When I finished and pushed back from the table I thanked them and said, "That was a fine breakfast and I hope I paid you some for it by doing you a good deed last night."

The old feller said, "What was that?"

I said, "I took your ox whip and whupped a rogue out of your cabbage hole last night." I left 'em setting there studying about that and took on off down the road.

d. Went on and went on till dark overtook me. I come to a big house and called to stay all night. The man said, "Yeaw, stranger, we'll take you in. Can't give ye nothing to eat. We have supper over."

I was awful hungry. Well, they put me in a room to sleep, and right over in the room from me was the kitchen and they's glass in the door twixt me and the kitchen. I could see all kind of things to eat, cake and good stuff setting in there on the table. I was starving to death. But they was a boy and a girl setting in there courting. Come to find out they was sitting up with a dead man, having a wake in the house that night. A lot of people stirring around. The courting people got up and went downstairs for something and I saw my chance. I jumped up and went through that door and begin to eat that cake and stuff. It was so good I didn't pay no 'ttention till I heared 'em coming back. I didn't have time to get back to my room so I jumped over behind the boards with that dead man. Covered up and laid there, as still as I could. That boy and girl got to loving it up right good, just hugging and kissing. I got tard laying there and I raised up to see how to get out of there. They saw me and tore out of there and looked to me like they both just rolled in a wad down them stairs. Went down there and told the people, said, "That dead man has come alive on us. He raised on the boards and looked around!"

While they's gone I got out of there and went back and jumped in my bed. A minute later the old man of the house come up there and said to me, "Stranger," said, "I'd like for you to get up and set up the rest of the night with us." Said, "We've got a dead man here, and that thing come alive and raised up on the cooling board awhile ago."

I knowed what had happened but I didn't let on. He offered me five dollars to set in the room with the corpse and I took him up. I done the setting up the rest of the night, and it suited me pimeblank 'cause I eat all I wanted till daylight. He give me all I wanted to take with me and the money and that set me off for a long time.

e. Went on and eat up my grub and spent that five dollars. Met up with Alvis Couch here and we decided to go down to a house and court some. We went down there and got to sparking with two purty girls and stayed up most of the night. They lived in an old log house, with the boards off of most of the cracks. They told us where we laid and we went to bed, Alvis over behind.

When we went to bed Alvis just laid his pants up in the crack of them logs. Next morning I got up and dressed but Alvis got to looking for his pants and couldn't find 'em. An old cow had drug them out through a crack and chewed 'em up. Well, I told Alvis I'd go home and get him some more pants, for him to lay in bed till I come back. The girls got breakfast ready and I eat. But Alvis laid right on, playing off like he was sick. The girls bagged and bagged him to get up and the old woman, too, but he wouldn't get up.

I got gone and didn't go back, left him a-laying there. Later on the old woman went off to milk and brung the milk back in and set it down on the foreside of his bed and went off to do something. Alvis took a notion he'd make a break for it and jumped up. Slipped and fell in the floor and got his head in that milk bucket. He went out of there with that bucket on his head. The old woman took right after him calling, "Here, here goes Dick with my milk bucket. Stop him, stop him!"

He run plumb on in home with that bucket on his head.

f. He got over that after so long and I took him with me again to do some sparking. We set up till 'way in the night and they all went to bed and told us where to sleep upstairs. And time we got in the chinches bit us so bad we couldn't sleep. The old man had a big pile of boards on the outside of the house and we decided we'd slip out and lay down on them boards and sleep till just before daylight and get back in and make like we'd slept good all night.

We got out there and made us a little pen out of them boards and stuck it out till near daylight. We started back in and run into a big bulldog they had around the house. It got to barking at us and wouldn't let us come in the house. There we was on top of that board pile and that old bulldog a-minding us up there. The old man heared the barking and come out there. We's in that pen of boards with our heads sticking out and didn't have no pants on. He never did know what in the nation caused us to be out there but he went in and got our pants and we sailed out home.

g. Well, this here is old D. Y. Couch—everybody knows him by that name. The story I'm telling is the last one of the seven days' journey and it is on J. D. and Harrison, my two brothers.

We's purty bad and mean when we's growing up. I was about sixteen I guess when we all went a-sparking, all of us to one place. We had three girls and all going to see 'em. Jim and Harrison was kindy sporty, but I never seem to had much. I never did care what I wore nor what I had. I'd go feeling just as sporty as they did. In getting there they had a fine horse apiece and I had an old jenny—had years about a foot long. These boys they would play ever' kind of prank on me they could, trying to down me. Thought I was foolish I reckon.

We took it time about going out and seeing about our horses. They's afraid theirn would get loose. Course I wa'n't afraid about mine getting loose, wouldn't a cared if it had and it wouldn't a gone far if it had. They went out one time and come back in a-laughing. I knowed they was something wrong. I set around a few minutes, but I's anxious to get to go out and see what the' had done. Well, I went out there and the' had cut my old jenny's mouth, split from year to year. Well, I didn't do a thing about it but take out my knife and cut both of their horses' tails and their years off, right ebem with their heads. I come back a-laughing.

The' said, "What are you laughing about?"

"Why," I said, "your fellers' horses got into a fight out there awhile ago," and I said, "they eat one another's tails and years off right ebem with their heads." And I said, "What do you think that old jenny o' mine done?" Said, "She split her mouth from year to year a-laughing at em."

151. Seven Dead Indians

Now I'll tell you a Indian story, and hit was a true story. When our people taken this nation away from the Indians and come in here we was thin settled in this country. More Indians in some places than they was American people.

They was an old woman she lived by herself and she had sebem chillern. The Indians had killed her man and she was trying to stay on and raise up her fambly. When she went out of an evening to get her wood in, she had to be on the lookout for Indians. All the people had to work in danger and the men-folks allas stood guard watching for 'em while the others worked. Well, this old woman was getting her wood and she seed sebem Indians hiding and slipping around and she heared 'em talking about coming in when it got dark. She rushed back quick and got her wood and got supper for her chillern. She got 'em all sebem in bed and lulled 'em asleep so they wouldn't get scared. Then she planned out a way to fight them Indians. Well, she had a hatchet-ax, a tommy hatchet they called it. And she opened the door just about big enough for one man to scrouge in at a time, and she spiked that door open, just leaving it so's it'd open no furder than that crack.

Well, along about dusty dark they come to make the attack on her. One crowded in that crack at the door and she hauled away and split its brains out with that hatchet-ax. She dragged that un back and pitched it back in the floor. It kept on, one come after another, scrouging in that door and she kept swinging that tommy hatchet till she killed all sebem of them, piled 'em all up in a pile together. That's the way the women used to have to fight for their children back then.

152. Old Indian Binge

Yes, Indians used to come in and out of here and keep the people scared to death all the time. They was an old runigade Indian—he was a mixed breed, wa'n't full-blooded Indian—used to get him a bunch of runigades and travel this country, robbing and stealing. He was called old Indian Binge. Went through here several trips. They'd start from Virginia and come down Cumberland here and cross Pine Mountain and then go back across maybe to Norton, Appalachia, and in there.

He come through Big Stone one time, had six more Indians with him. And them Indians kidnapped 'em a woman apiece and led 'em away, took 'em towards Norton above Appalachia. But the leader, old Indian Binge, he claimed he protected the women and kept the others from violating and killing 'em. Well, they took them women right up a rough creek into the hills. Them women would tear off bits of their dresses and throw down for their men to foller.

Their men come in that evening and heared the alarm and was directed the way they went. The Indians got back in what was later called Binge Branch where Binge had 'em to camp for the night, said it was for delay so the white men could overtake 'em. The men come upon them in their camp. Old Binge helped the whites and they killed all the other six Indians and got their women back. They let old Binge go because he did seem to know what was happening and tried to protect the women—at least he didn't do no violence that time.

Well, a little later than that happening old Binge was back in this country again, with two more Indians with him. And the people figured that if he wa'n't going to do no meanness he was coming back to hunt treasures that the Indians allas claimed was in here. Well, it was norrated that he was in here for a treasure hunt and a bunch of men got back in the Shell Gap of Pine Mountain and waylaid 'em. The Indians come along there. And right in the saddle of the mountain was a blackgum tree and old Binge clomb that blackgum to get some mistletoe. They farred away at the men on the ground and killed one. The other man with him, called the Runner, got away and excaped back to Virginia. They leveled down on Binge and one shot went right square through his head. They said old Indian Binge reached in his pocket and took out a silver cup and put it over the bullet hole and catched his brains in it. He fell dead at the roots of the blackgum tree. That was about the last Indians that ever come into this country. After that they left it all to the whites.

153. We Killed a Bear

Then another true bear tale I'll tell. They was a man and his wife off at their neighbor's house and had to come back along a wooded section. And a bear got atter 'em and run 'em plumb home. Run 'em right in the door and was trying to come in. They had some stairs going up in the loft and they run right on up in there and had a big box stored up there. The old man just jumped in that box and told his old woman to fasten him up from that bear. She fastened him up in there and that left the old woman and that bear to have it out. She got holt of her a hatchet-ax and got right on the top of the stairsteps.

That old bear he started right up these stairs. He come on up and got one foot on the top step, and the old woman she hacked that foot off. Well, he retch up with his other foot and she hacked it off. The old bear he tumbled back down the stairs and she went right down on him and got a chance and split his brains out with that hatchet-ax.

She let the old man out and he saw the dead bear there and he said, "Well, we've done purty good today," said, "we killed a bear." And him in that box, didn't have no hand in it a-tall.

154. The Hairy Woman

One time I's prowling in the wilderness, wandering about, kindly got lost and so weak and hungry I couldn't go. When it begin to get cool I found a big cave and crawled back in there to get warm. Crawled back in and come upon a leaf bed and I dozed off to sleep. I heared an awful racket coming into that cave, and something come in and crawled right over me and laid down like a big bear. It was a hairy thing and when it laid down it went chomp, chomp, chawing on something. I thought to myself, "I'll see what it is and find out what it is eating." I reached over and a hairy-like woman was eating chestnuts, had about a half a bushel there. I got me a big handful of them and went to chawing on them too. Well, in a few minutes she handed me over another big handful and I eat chestnuts until I was kindly full and wasn't hungry any more. D'rectly she got up and took off, and out of sight. Well, I stayed on there till next morning when she come in with a young deer. Brought it in and with her big long fingernails she ripped its hide and skinned it and then she sliced the good lean meat and handed me a bite to eat. I kindly slipped it behind me, afraid to eat it raw and afraid not to eat it being she give it to me. She'd cut off big pieces of deer meat raw and eat it. Well, I laid mine back and the other pieces she give over to me as she eat her'n. She was going to see I didn't starve.

When she got gone I built me up a little far and br'iled my meat. After being hungry for two or three days, it was good cooked, yes, buddy. She come in while I had my far built br'iling my meat, and she run right into that far. She couldn't understand because it kindly burnt her a little. She jumped back and looked at me like she was going to run through me. I said, "Huh oh, I'm going to get in trouble now."

Well, it was cold and bad out, so I stayed another night with her. She was a woman but was hairy all over. After several days I learnt her how to br'il meat and that far would burn her. She got shy of the fire and got so she liked br'iled meat and wouldn't eat it raw any more. We went on through the winter that way. She would go out and carry in deer and bear. So I lived there for about two year and when we had a little kid one side of it was hairy and the other side was slick.

I took a notion I would leave there and go back home. I begin to build me a boat to go 'way across the lake in. One time after I had left I took a notion I would slip back and see what she was doing. I went out to the edge of the cliff and looked down the mountain, and it looked like two or three dozen hairy people coming up the hill. They was all pressing her and she would push 'em back. And they wanted to come on up and come in. I was scared to death afraid they's going to kill me. She made them go back and would not let them come up and interfere.

Well, I took a notion to leave one day when my boat was ready. I told her I was going to leave. She follered me down to my boat and watched me get ready to go away. She was crying, wanting me to stay. I said, "No, I'm tired of the jungles. I'm going back to civilization again, going back."

When she knowed she wasn't going to keep me there she just grabbed that little youngun up and tore it right wide open with her nails. Throwed me the hairy part and she kept the slick part. That's the end of that story.

155. All at One Shot

Once in slack time I decided to get out and look for some game. I hunted all day and I come down to the river bank, didn't find no game at all that day. I set down on the river edge watching the big fish swim up and down the river. I was setting there and heard an awful racket up the river and here come 500 ducks sailing in and lit on the river. I was carrying a big old double-barrelled shotgun. I turned my gun up the river; I was going to shoot some of them ducks, get me a little game for the day. Well, just as I went to pull the hammer back I heard an awful noise down the river. And I looked and they was 500 wild geese landing on the river below me.

Well, I'd rather have wild goose than duck meat, so I turned my gun down the river. I was going to kill a few geese. I pulled the hammer back and I heard a fearful noise right clost to me, making the awfulest racket. I looked down and they was a big snake coming at me with its mouth opened looked like it could swaller a gallon bucket. So I said I would kill the snake first and turned my gun on the snake, pulled both hammers back and let both barrels go. That old gun busted and the right hand barrel went up the river and killed 500 wild ducks and the left hand barrel went down the river and killed the 500 wild geese. The ramrod went down the snake's throat and choked it to death. The stock kicked me over a bank into the river head over heels. I had on boots and when I come out I had 'em full of fish. So I gained a lot of game that day, after all.

156. Leaping Painter

I heared my grandfather tell how he went to hunt bears a lot. So one morning he said he got up early and he heard a gobbler, sounded like a turkey gobbler a-gobbling. He gobble-gobbled a few times and my grandfather said to his old woman, "Well, I'll slip up there and kill that turkey."

He slipped back in the mountain and never could locate him. Said to himself, "I'll go ahead of it this time—I'll get back up here before he comes in in the morning and I'll locate him."

He went back out there next morning before daylight and hid in a big sinkhole, and he said, "I set there till it got daylight and it never did come back no more, and I kindly dozed off, drapped off to sleep, and when I woke up a few minutes later I'm covered plumb over with leaves, covered over, hidden. Something had found me and wanted me for breakfast, so I scratched out of there and got holt of my gun again. I figured it had been a painter. I got out of there and piled them leaves back up just the way they was. I got up above them and laid my gun across a log right opposite them leaves. After while I saw a big old painter come down the hill and stretch out on a bank above that pile of leaves and then come two little ones and stretched out with her. Stayed there together awhile, all working their tails and then they all just made a leap and landed right in the leaves in that sinkhole. Them leaves was b'iling and flying for a time, and I knowed then they's looking for me. D'rectly the old one come out and looked all around trying to wind me. So I cracked down and I killed her and when the gun went off the little ones run off. I got me a painter but I didn't get that turkey. That's that.

157. The Magic White Deer

Once there was a couple of twin boys that favored—you couldn't tell one from the other they was so exactly alike. In their growing up one of them had cut off his big toe, maybe with an ax. He had a toe off of one foot, and that was the only way you could tell them apart.

They took a notion to set out and seek their fortune one day and traveled and traveled along the road a long ways, until they come to the forks of the road where it split up and went different ways. One of them said, "All right, brother, we are going to part here. We will stick this knife right here in the forks of the road in the grass." And he said, "You go your journey and if you happen to come back here and this knife is rusty it'll mean I'm in danger. You foller my direction and try to trace me down and I'll do you the same—so if something happens to either one of us the other can locate him."

The boys separated and went on their ways. One of the boys traveled till he come into a section of the country where there was a white deer that was going through killing all young girls and carrying them away. He come up and stayed all night with a rich farmer who had an awful good-looking girl. They was worrying about their girl, keeping her in and scared for her to get out where the white deer could find her and carry her off. She and the boy got to talking and soon were good friends, and he worried about it, too, and he said, "I think I'll get out and hunt it." Soon it passed through and he got a glimpse of it, and he said, "I believe I can kill it. Believe I can track it down."

Her daddy said, "If you'll kill it you can have my daughter." He said, "You can get my dogs—they's about five big hounds here—and get my rifle-gun, and I'll furnish you with ammunition."

Well, he started hunting after it. He got in sight of it once and the dogs were close on it. They run it up a big oak tree in a certain place on the mountain. Well, he come up under the tree and he could hear it up there shivering like it was freezing. He hollered and told it to come down and he shot at it, but it would shiver again and tremble like it was freezing. He said, "I'm freezing."

Twin said, "Well, come on down."

And he said, "No, I'm afraid of your dogs."

The twin said, "My dogs won't hurt you."

The deer said, "I'll drop a stick down and you tetch the dogs and then I'll come down."

And so he dropped a stick down, a little twig or branch from the tree, and the twin picked it up and tetched one of his dogs with it, and it turned into a rock. When he tetched 'em all they every one turned into rocks. When he dropped the stick at his feet he turned into a rock, too. And that was the end of them. The white deer come down and went on where it was going.

His brother made his journey out into the land and finally come back to the forks of the road where they parted. He went to the knife and it was rusty, the blade was. He said, "Well, something is wrong with my brother." He started down his fork of the road tracing him.

He come up to this farmer where his brother had been. When he come in they thought it was the same one and said they wanted to know about his hunt. "Where have you been, where are your dogs and gun?" He saw that they talked strange and he just shook his head and wouldn't talk much. They worried over him and thought his mind had changed. But that night when he pulled off his shoes and his toe was gone, they knowed this was another boy and mentioned it to him. He told them about his lost twin brother and how they had set out on different roads to seek their fortunes. They told him then about this white deer raging through the country, and said, "Your brother follered it and he has never returned." He told them he knowed his brother was in trouble and they said, "It passed through here and he got a glimpse of it."

The twin said, "I believe I can capture it if you'll furnish me the equipment I want." The man said he would furnish him with anything. He said, "Run me three silver bullets and put 'em in with the lead balls for my gun and give me five dogs and I'll trace it down."

He started with his dogs and gun, and chased it on and on till it come to its main hideout in the forest, up that big old oak tree. The boy walked under the tree and could tell it was up in there by the way the tree trembled, and the deer whined like it was freezing. He said, "Come on down."

It said, "No, I'm afraid of your dogs." Said, "I'll drop this stick down and if you'll touch your dogs—"Before it could finish talking the boy had loaded his gun with a lead ball and he cracked down at it. It just shivered and said, "Uuh, I'm a-freezing."

He said, "Well, maybe this will warm you up a little." He put a silver bullet and cracked down and shot the deer through the shoulder. He fell down a distance and lodged, and when he lodged he was taking on and saying, "I'm freezing, don't kill me."

"Well," the boy said, "tell me where my brother and his animals are."

The deer said, "If you promise you won't kill me I'll drop this stick down and you tetch certain rocks there you see." He dropped the stick down and when the twin tetched a rock it turned into a dog. He tetched another and another and turned all of the rocks back to dogs. And when he come to the last one and tetched it his brother rose up before him. They fell on one another's necks when they found they were alive and well again. And this second twin said, "You can have that rich farmer's daughter if you take back this deer. Here is the magic stick. You tetch it when I make it come on down with this silver bullet."

When he pointed the gun at it the deer promised to come down. When it landed on the ground the first twin touched it and it turned into the purtiest girl they had ever seen. And the first twin said, "Since I have a purty girl myself and you saved my life, I'll give this one that has been enchanted to you."

They come on in to the home of the rich farmer, and both married and settled down in that section and lived happy ever after.

"I have heared that story several times," Jim averred. "I remember just exactly who I heared tell it the first time. It was a Shepherd woman, one of my people on my father's side. You see, my grandmother was Sally Shepherd and she was Dutch."

"Yes, that's right," I remembered. "That puts the story on the Couch side, going back more directly to France and the Low Countries. Well, it was a good discovery. Do you have any more something like that, Joe?"

"Know two or three more," he said.

158. In the Cat Hide

There was a rich man had three daughters, the only chillern he had. He had a fortune to give to one. He couldn't give to all three but he would give one the fortune. So he told them, said, "I have a fortune to give to one of you and I'm going to start you out." He give the oldest one the sifter, that you sift meal through, and told her to go to the river and bring it back full of water. Well, she took the sifter and dipped and dipped and it would pour out as fast as she dipped it in. She worried with it a little longer and then come back and said, "Father, I can't get it."

Well, the next one went and she set and dipped for two hours, and she couldn't get no water to stay in the sifter. And she brought it back and said, "Dad, I can't get no water to stay in the sifter."

He told the youngest one to go. Well, she went down there, setting and dipping the water, pouring it in the sifter and it pouring out. In a few minutes a little bird flew up in a tree and said,

"Peewee, daub it with clay."

Well, she kept dipping the sifter in and after awhile she noticed the little bird in the tree, and it said again,

"Peewee, daub it with clay."

She went over to the bank and got some mud and daubbed the bottom of the sifter and filled it full of water and took it back to her daddy.

When she took it to him the old man went and got a loaf of bread and give it to her and said, "Now start—go off and seek your fortune."

She started with that loaf of bread. Thought it was a great fortune for her to inherit and said, "I can eat on my way, but what'll I do when it's gone? He said for me to go and not turn back." She traveled all day and eat up her bread and was getting purty hungry and weak.

All at once there was a little yaller butterfly got right in front of her, flying along in front and when she would go to turn the wrong way he'd come flying, flutter, flutter, in front of her and then turn off the other path again. She took a notion she would foller it and see where that little butterfly was leading her to. She follered it and finally she come to a big hole that went right down in the ground. Looked like it had been traveled a lot, and that butterfly flew down in there but she stopped. Scared her kindly. D'rectly he'd come back up to the surface and quiver and then go back. She said, "Well, I've follered you this far, I'll just foller you on and see where I go and where you lead me."

She follered him down in that hole to a cave of a place and come out in a fine house, furnished and everything set fine. When she come to the door that little butterfly flew through the keyhole. It come back out and flew in again. She said, "Well, I'll knock." She knocked and heard a voice tell her to come in. Opened the door and there was a big yaller cat setting there. It never said another word till she walked in and then he said, "You're hungry, ain't you?"

She said, "Well, I could eat."

The cat said, "Go in the kitchen there in the cupboard and get anything you want to eat. Everything cooked in there and just go ahead and eat a fine supper."

She eat and then set back down in the living room in front of the cat. Nobody to talk to because the old cat just set there. D'rectly he said, "You are sleepy." She said yes and he said, "Well, go back to bed."

She went back and laid down and went to sleep. It went on like that for a week. With nobody to talk to and the cat setting there telling her what to do when she was hungry or sleepy. But one morning he was leaving out and told her, "Now listen. Your oldest sister will be here to visit you today and don't let her see the end of your finger. If you do she will kill you."

She said, "I won't."

He had one room in the house that he wouldn't allow her in. He said, "You can go in all the rooms of the house but the one back there. I've got the key to that room. Don't try to go in it." She told him she wouldn't try.

That day her oldest sister shore enough come to the door and knocked. She said, "Who is it?"

She said, "It's your oldest sister come to visit you."

She said, "I can't let you in."

She said, "I want to see you for the last time, you must."

"No, no, I can't let you in."

She said, "Then let me see the end of your finger for the last time."

She stuck her finger up to the keyhole and she jobbed a poison needle under her fingernail. She fell back on the floor unconscious.

When the old cat come in he knowed what was up. He just pulled the needle out and doctored the wound up and she come to. "I told you what would happen." She stayed with him longer and got more interested in him, the way he acted and all. One night she thought she would watch him and see what he done. She played off like she was asleep. D'rectly that cat got down out of his rocking chair and got in front of the fire and commenced rolling and rolling, just like a cat does. All at once the old cat's hide opened up and out come a man, oh, a nice looking young man. He come back and took his clothes off and went to bed beside her.

She had seen it all right before her eyes and was wondering, "What will I do now?" Said, "I'll stop that cat hide." She eased out of the bed and run and kicked that cat hide into the far. When it went to burning he started howling, taking on, and making the awfulest to-do out of it, until after it burnt up. And then he quietened down and said, "Well, that finishes me and my work as a cat. I'll just settle down here in my home." He took her in and opened that forbidden room and there were trunks stacked on top of trunks full of greenbacks, which he had taken out of banks that he robbed as a cat. He told her, "You see, I would go to a bank as a cat and be friendly around the cashiers through the day and at night I would hide as they went out and locked the bank door." Said, "I would get all the money together I could get away with and hide right by the door of a morning and when the first cashier opened up I would dodge out. They would just think it was a cat going out."

Well, they had plenty of money and purty soon they got married. That was her fortune that her father sent her out to seek after.

"Well, I guess Jim recognized parts of that story," I began, "but yours has episodes that I have never heard with the story before. That ending about the robberies in the bank has a kind of modern sound. Do you know where you heard that one?"

"I guess my father told that un to me. He told about all of 'em at one time or 'nother."

"You and Jim might like to know that I have collected a good deal on Leatherwood where you people lived. I remember finding a short version of that one among the McDaniels there. Are you related to them?"

"No, not as we know of. But the people used to get together so much on a creek like that, they could have swapped stories just like they swapped seeds and stock and stuff."

Next, Joe had for us a haunted house story. I remembered Jim's story of Johnny Conscience and let Joe summarize this one before recording it. It seemed varied enough to enter here.

159. The Hainted House

Well, there was a young man who wanted to ramble, back in the olden days, and he got at his father to give him some money, wanted to go out west. "Well," his father said, "all right, if you think you want a trip, I'll give you a hundred dollars to start you, and good luck." The boy wasn't afraid, he was nervy, had plenty of nerve, so he started out, traveled through sections of the country that he knowed until he come to strange places he had never seen before.

Night come and he called to stay all night. Well, it seemed that every place he called there was something wrong—sick folks, or something had happened—company or something else kept them from putting him up for the night. It was getting good and dark and he was awful tired and hungry and he come to the last place on the road and said, "Well, maybe this is it—I've got to find a place to stay." He

called and an old gentleman come and told him he was sorry but he
was crowded. But he said, "I'll tell you now. I know of an old waste
house down from here about a quarter." He said, "It's equipped in
every way to stay in, but it's hainted and nobody could never stay
there."

The boy said, "Oh, I'll stay there."

He said, "Everybody who's tried to stay or forced theirselves to stay
all night was killed." He was a preacher, and said, "I allas go down
and hold inquest over 'em next morning—they're allas killed."

"Oh," the boy said, "that just suits me—I'll stay."

"Well," he said, "if you're going to stay all night I'll give you a
big fat goose to bake tonight. As I said, everything is ready for staying all night and for cooking and all, but it's just hainted."

So he went down, the boy did, and started up a far and he was having his goose on to bake in front of the far and he was setting there
reading the paper. So d'rectly he heard a little noise out behind the
house—heave and set and a grunt—sounded like rolling logs, trying
to roll something over, shaking the house. He run out there and
grabbed him a fence rail, jobbed it down under the house, and said,
"All right, boys, le's turn it over in the creek." And the noise hushed.

He went back in the house and was reading the paper and d'rectly
something begin to go, "yan, yan, yan." He said, "Get away, little
girl, you're after my goose, but I've got it right there a-baking." Said,
"Get out!" And it hushed.

He was setting there reading and all at once a man's leg fell down
the chimley, just cut off. He just retch in the far and pulled it out and
laid it in the corner. D'rectly down fell the other leg, and he set there
and pulled a man piece by piece out of the far and set him up in the
corner. He said to him, "A man staying all night with me orght to
have something to eat—I'll feed ye some." So he set him back up
piece by piece in a chear and went and got him some milk and bread
and was going to feed him. Well, naturally trying to feed a corpse,
putting the spoon in his mouth, he let the spoon slip out of his hand
and it just went on down the man's throat. It made him so mad that
he kicked him out in the road, said, "A man staying all night with me
and swaller the spoon when I feed him, I won't keep him."

Come time to go to bed and he laid down. Something broke loose
up in the loft and lambang, rous-bous, down in the floor and across
the room under his bed, went like barrels, log chains, and he didn't
know what else. Then it went to pulling off his cover. He retch in and
got his knife. He split a blanket open, said, "Equal-divide—you take
that part and I'll take this one." Cut up three or four blankets and
finally that quit.

D'rectly he heard someone knock on the door and he went and
opened it and there set a coffin. Well, that made him mad and he
kicked that out in the road, shut the door, and went back to bed.
D'rectly he heard the knock again and when he got up to open the
door that time the coffin slid in the room and right across the farplace.
Well, he set down right on the coffin and started studying, "What's
this all about? I don't know what to do about it." He said, "I believe
I'll open it and see what's in there." He went and got his hatchet and
prized the lid open, and when he done that there laid a man with no
head on and a bulldog laying beside him and a big long sword. He
said the three highest words and asked him, "Father, Son, and Holy
Ghost, what do you want?"

"Well," he said, "I want you to capture three men that killed me
and my bulldog and my old lady for my money. But they didn't get it.
My money is buried up in a big orchard at the roots of a big apple
tree, my handprint on the apple tree. When you arrest these men have
them prosecuted. I've got one brother living and I want you to let him
have a thousand dollars, and this farm and the rest of the money belongs to you."

"Well," he said, "I've got no witnesses."

He said, "You set your trial for any day around four o'clock and
I'll appear for a witness."

The next morning the preacher come down with the Bible under
his arm to hold an inquest on him. Knocked on the door. The man let
him in and he looked around surprised, said, "Did you hear anything
last night?"

He said, "No."

He said, "Didn't nothing haint you?"

"No, no nothing at all."

He went away surprised. The man went to hunt these three men that had killed the family. He found them and they said, "We don't know nothing about this feller, we don't know even these folks, we don't know nothing about it. We'll have the trial and get you for false arrest."

The hour of the trial come and he was setting around and these other men ready to swear they knowed nothing about no murder. At exactly four o'clock he heard something hit the top of the house and it come down through the ceiling and it was this casket dropped down in the courtroom on the floor. The lid come open and that man raised up and said, "Right here's the three men that killed me and my wife and my bulldog and for my money, but" said, "they didn't get it."

Two of the men fainted dead, and they took the other one out and hung him. The boy inherited the farm and all that money and he sent back and got his father and told him, "Now I'll pay you that hundred dollars back." That's the end of the story.

Jim was surprised to hear this one, so different from his. I am letting it stand here as the adaptation and variation of perhaps the same original story on its adventures within the family tree.

160. The Orphant Boys

Once they was two orphant boys and their parents died when they were young. They was just raised up here and there and didn't have much to go on and stayed only where people would keep 'em. They always planned and said, "If we live till we are grown we will go to the gold mines where we can dig gold." Well, they finally got about eighteen years old, made it up to leave, and struck out. They would work a day every so often as they went along for twenty-five cents a day, and they would take off the next day. They worked their way through, half and half, that way till they got to the gold mines where they could dig gold.

They got a job working for twenty-five cents a day and worked so long the company begin to give them a little nugget of gold for a day's work. They saved that gold and worked till they had got them quite a peck of gold each. Well, by that time they took a notion to quit and go back home to the settlements where the people knew them. So they bunched up their gold and put it in a leather bag, and as they went along they wouldn't let nobody know what they had, afraid somebody would rob them of their money.

When they got back to the section where they were raised they went to the man's house where they had stayed when they were small. This man had been cruel to them and had run them off sometimes, if his mood wasn't just right, and they would have to lay out some nights, and have no home at all. But they were grown now and had forgot about that. They called to stay all night and the man took them in. He told them who he was and asked them who they were and where they had been. Finally he asked them, "What have you boys got in that leather sack?"

Well, they didn't care to tell him, they knowed him and thought he was all right. They said, "That's gold. We dug this gold at twenty-five cents a day."

These boys heard the man and his family up all night, but they didn't know what they were talking about. The man was working up a plan to take their gold. He didn't bother them that night and they got up the next morning and started on their journey. It was raining and the road was awful muddy and rough. They walked on, maybe four or five hours, along the road, when they looked behind them and saw a man coming fast on a horse. He rode right on up with them and it was the high sheriff of the county. He stopped them and said, "Well, boys, you are under arrest."

"What for?"

"You know what for—stealing that man's gold back there where you stayed all night." He said, "The man was good enough to take you in and keep you and then you come along and steal his money." Said, "I have to take you back."

He took them back to the courthouse in a little village and got them ready to try 'em. Well, the boys were strangers and they had no proof that they had dug this gold and worked it out. This man they stayed with and his wife and son were ready to swear they stold their gold that night.

They had the trial at four o'clock that evening. The boys was setting around down-hearted and didn't know what to do. No witnesses or nothing. The man had taken the witness stand and was ready to swear again' 'em. They looked out and down the road and saw a big man coming, big red face, his cheeks were just like fire, riding a big bay horse. He rode up to the hitching post and throwed his reins over it and walked in through the crowds just like he had been there all day. Walked in and never spoke to nobody till he got in the courtroom. The man on the witness stand begin to swear what these boys done after he kept them all night.

So this strange man walked up to him and said, "Mister, you can't stand on my toes and swear that."

He said, "Yes, I can."

When he hopped over on the man's toes and went to say how they stold his gold, he went up in a blaze of far. So this man looked around and said, "Does anybody else want to swear that?"

Nobody spoke. This man's wife and son standing over there was going to swear it but they changed their minds when they saw what went on. Nobody spoke so he said, "All right." He looked at the high sheriff and said, "Where's the money?" He brought in the money. He said, "Now listen. You give it to these boys. And you take these boys back where you picked them up and you walk and let them ride."

The boys went back safe and got on their journey and went on where they was going. That's the end of it.

161. Johnny Sore-Nabel

One time there was a man who liked to hunt far away into the woods. He got some time off and decided he would go off on a long journey to the wilderness and hunt all he wanted to. He got his stuff ready and catched a boat to ride so far. The boat finally anchored at a port and he got off to find something to eat. The boat pulled out and left him, and so he decided to walk, take the dirt for it, on a nigh cut over the country.

He walked along all that day and he got worried and tard by the time night overtook him. He laid down behind a log in a thicket of a place to take him a night's rest. When he waked up again, it was light and there was a little man trying to ride him. He was right a-straddle of his neck, jobbing him with big spurs. It scared him and he raised up and started to run. Run along in the bushes for a ways and slowed down. This little hairy man hung right around his neck and cut loose to gigging him again with them sharp spurs. Every time he run apiece he would quit spurring, but when he got give out and slowed down to blow a minute, he would commence again jobbing them spurs in his sides. Well, he run and he run till he just about run himself to death.

He was studying how in the world he was going to get him off of his neck. He couldn't shake him off, he couldn't find out what he wanted nor where he was aiming to go to. Well, he finally rode the little hairy feller through some woods where there was a lot of wild grapevines, and he noticed the little man pulling off some big pods and eating them. So he decided he would pull some and have him a bite, he was starved too. He eat some as he run along and he put some in his flask to take along with him. First thing he knowed that grape juice had worked off into the best wine he ever drunk. Right then he hit on a way to get shet of them spurs. He reached that flask up to the little feller, and he tasted of it and turned up the flask and drunk it all down. And directly he commenced to getting drunk, reeling and swaying on his neck. He said, "Huh oh, now I'm going to fix you." And when the feller's legs begin to get a little loose around his neck, he rocked and bucked and throwed him off again' the ground. He couldn't get up, so the man just picked him up a rock and pecked that feller's brains out.

He went on into the wilderness. And there was a man coming out of the forest. He said, "Feller, how much farther is it to a house out this way?"

He said, "Mister, they hain't no houses back this way. It is wilderness." But he said, "I met a couple more men on the way going back into the jungles and I told them it was great danger laying out in this wilderness. Snakes come out of this ocean here that will swaller you. The only way to keep 'em from it is to build you a big far around a high tree and climb right in the top of it to sleep."

He said, "Well, I thank you for telling me how to excape them snakes." He said, "I met a little old hairy man coming in here and he about rode me to death. I got shet of him and thought I'd go further in the jungles."

When dark come and he took a notion to camp, he built him a big heap around a high tree, set it afar, and clumb right in the top of it. Long in the night he heared something coming out of the ocean. And he looked down and saw a big snake looking up at him. It r'ared up on its tail and 'peared like and reached up to get him. That far hit it in the belly and it rolled back into the ocean. They come on like that all night, reaching up to get him, but his far helt out and scorched their bellies and they would roll back into the water.

The next morning he woke up and climbed back down his tree, and as he slid down he skinned his nabel and the whole side of his belly. He went on and he seen where some big fars had been built around trees, and by that he knowed these men was not far ahead of him. He walked on purty brisk to catch up with them, and soon he did and talked to them about their night's lodging. They said, "Yeaw, we had an awful time with the snakes last night. Had to fight off the old sea snakes and swamp snakes."

They kept tramping on together further back into the jungles. Finally they seen a little bitty cabin, way out on a big island of a place, curly blue smoke coming out of the chimbly and all. They said, "Well, there's a chance to get us something to eat." They went on out there, got up to the door, and one of the men coughed to get attention. A big old man come to the door. He was a giant about nine-foot tall, and he had one big eye right in the middle of his for'head. They spoke to him and he talked awful coarse and said, "Come in, gentlemen."

They said, "We'd like to get a little something to eat, we're starving."

He said, "Come right in and I'll fix you up."

They went in, set down, and the old giant went into a back room and they could see men hanging in there. He'd cut 'em up and had 'em hanging up in there to dry. He sliced a big piece of meat offen one of them humans. He offered one of them a piece, and he backed off, said he didn't want none of that kind of meat.

Old giant said, "All right, just come in here, and I'll examine you all and see if you're fat enough to kill." Said, "If you're not fat enough, I'll keep you for a few days till you are fat enough."

They all looked at one another and knowed they was up again' it. When he examined 'em all, he come to the man with the skinned place on him. Said, "I can't kill you right now, you got that sore place on your nabel." Said, "I'll turn you out trusty and put them other two fellers in here, they'll do to kill." Said, "I'm going to call you Johnny Sore-Nabel. You run around till you get well, haw, haw."

Well, the feller who was trusty run around there a few days and helped the old giant all he could. And he noticed the old feller shut his door good and laid down to sleep right in front of it. He kept a far in his farplace and he laid down with his feet to that far. He noticed he had about three big iron poking sticks setting there to poke the far. He thought to himself, a feller could kill somebody with them iron pokers setting over there.

One night when the giant went to sleep, he eased over and got them pokers and put 'em in the far. Got 'em hot and he slipped the keys off his old clothes and went in the back room and waked his buddies. Said to 'em, "Now's the time." They come out and got 'em a poker apiece, and they stuck them red-hot poking sticks right down in the old giant's eye. He rose from there and knocked the door down with his head and thrashed around in the room.

They commenced dodging and trying to run out of there. He knocked one of them down, but he up from there and lit out. The old giant come out and run up into the mountain hollering and squalling. They stood there and laughed at him.

Finally he was out of sight. Directly they looked out and seen him a-coming with ten more giants just like him. They started away from there and run to the waterfront and hit it out into the ocean. They come some rafts floating by, and they got on a raft apiece. They commenced to paddling and rafting out into the ocean. Them giants come down there and started throwing big rocks, trying to sink their rafts. They sunk his two buddies and drowned them, but he was too far out. They couldn't sink him.

He made it on across and finally got back home. And this is the story he told about his journey to the wilderness.

IV. Appendix

1. Abbreviations Used

BSS   Bibliographical and Special Series (American Folklore Society)

FFC   Folklore Fellows Communications

JAF   Journal of American Folklore

JSFO   Journal de la Société Finno-ougrienne

MAFLS   Memoirs of the American Folklore Society

SFQ   Southern Folklore Quarterly

2. Notes to the Folksongs and Hymns

1. The Devil and the School Child
(The False Knight Upon the Road. Child No. 3)

Child printed only three texts of this rare ballad, all from Scotland. He summarized related items from Sweden and from Scottish nursery rhymes. As with his Nos. 1 and 2, this ballad has almost no narrative element. It is a flyting or wit-combat between a schoolboy and a false knight (Devil in disguise). The exchanges in the wit-combat remain fairly constant in the few texts: Where are you going? To my school. What do you carry? My books, or my dinner. A text from Maine (Barry, *Bulletin*, 9[1936]: 8) contains an interesting variation: "If the /fiddle/ bow should break?" "May the end stick in your throat." In Kentucky the fence rail jobbed down his throat seems to be more appropriate—and deadly.

The ballad has not often been collected in Britain since Motherwell (Child's source). In America, however, it has had more vitality in tradition, appearing in scattered collections from the Maritime Provinces to Oklahoma. Coffin, *British*, lists about 18 in Types A and B. Some selected references are these (in the order of our frontiers from the eastern seaboard to Florida, the Appalachian states from Pennsylvania to Alabama, the Midwest from the Lakes to Texas, and the West): Creighton, *Songs*, No. 1; Barry, *British*, p. 11 (from Scotland); Davis, *Traditional*, No. 2; Sharp and Karpeles, *English*, No. 2; Brewster, *Ballads*, No. 2; Belden, *Ballads*, p. 4; Moore and Moore, *Ballads*, No. 2 (from Scotland). The homiletic theme (developed by Barry, *Bulletin*, as above) of the piece seems to have appealed to the Scottish people.

The present text seems to be the only one thus far recovered in Kentucky. It is the one Jim Couch wrote me about (see Introduction) in the summer of 1955. After he had recorded it he could only say, "I heared my father sing this a long time ago—about the Devil and the School child. I got up there to him a week or two ago and he went plumb through it. I wrote it down here." He took out the tablet paper sheets and checked the stanzas before "putting it on record."

2. Lord Batesman
(Young Beichan. Child No. 53)

Child had 15 texts (A to N) of the ballad to include in his collection, all, except one, from Scotland. He traces it in the literature over Europe from Spain to Scandinavia. Because it is found in old metrical romance tradition, he finds it popular in southern Europe as well. In his Additions (II, 508) he prints a text to substitute for his broadside version. According to Coffin, *British*, this broadside has influenced later English variations and has led to some confusion in American texts. He lists 75 references to the ballad in North America, in two story types. Most of his listings come under Type A. His Type B is based on variations in the story line, such as the father's helping the Lady to prepare her boat or her convenient marriage arrangement with another of his family.

The ballad has been popular on most frontiers of North America from Canada to Oklahoma. Selected listings are these: MacKenzie, *Ballads*, No. 5; Barry, *British*, p. 106; Flanders *Ancient*, II (24 texts); Davis, *Traditional*, No. 12 (9 texts); Belden and Hudson, *Brown*, II, No. 14 (6 texts), Schinhan, IV (2 tunes); Morris, *Folksongs*, p. 269; Cox, *Folk-Songs*, No. 8; Cox, *Traditional*, No. 7; Gardner and Chickering, *Ballads*, No. 49; Randolph, *Ozark*, I, No. 12; Moore and Moore, *Ballads*, No. 15.

Perhaps more texts have been found in Kentucky than in any other state: Sharp and Karpeles, *English*, No. 13 (5 texts); my collection contains 5; Shearin and Combs, *Syllabus*, p. 7; Thomas, *Devil's*, p. 86; Ritchie, *Singing*, p. 109; Niles, *Ballad*, No. 22; Combs, *Folk-Songs du Midi*, p. 201 (23 listed); Wyman and Brockway, *Lonesome*, p. 58.

The present version was sung by Jim at our First Session in 1952; he had learned it from his father. It is in my *Tales*, No. 2, and entered in my Kentucky manuscript, No. 12.

3. Joseph and Mary
(The Cherry Tree Carol. Child No. 54)

This is now the most popular of the three carols Child included in his collection. He traces its probable source to Pseudo-Matthew, Chapter XX, in which is related Joseph's flight into Egypt. Resting on the third day, Mary sees fruit on a palm tree and, craving it, asks Joseph to get her some. Joseph rebukes her for the difficult task. The infant Jesus from her lap performs His first miracle by bidding the tree to bow down to her feet. In France it is an apple tree; in England and America it is usually a cherry tree.

Coffin in *British* lists about 35 references, in 7 types. Some English versions contain prophecies of Jesus speaking from the womb as the couple are journeying to Bethlehem. He announces His birth on Christmas, His death on Good Friday, His resurrection on Easter. In some American versions He specifies His birth to be on January 5 or 6. When England adopted the new calendar in 1752 by dropping 11 days from the old one, the folk adhered to the old style by having Christmas (later called Old Christmas) in January.

In America the carol has been recovered from Canada to Oklahoma. Selected listings are these: Fowke and Johnson, *Folk-Songs*, p. 128; Barry, *Bulletin*, 6 (1935):14; Flanders, *Ancient*, II, p. 70; Davis, *Traditional*, No. 13; Belden and Hudson, *Brown*, II, No. 15 (no tune); Sharp and Karpeles, *English*, I, No. 15 (6 texts); Gainer, *West Va.*, No. 74; Henry, *Folk-Songs*, No. 10; Niles, *Ballad*, No. 23; Thomas, *Ballad*, p. 223; Randolph, *Ozark*, I, No. 13; Moore and Moore, *Ballads*, No. 16.

By the time of my Ninth Session with Jim and Dave in the summer of 1955, Jim had begun to reflect on the earliest singing of his parents. He brought forward this one and some more of the oldest in their collection. With some difficulty he recorded it, and, when I showed him the transcription, he was reminded of the first stanza. It is in my *Tales*, No. 3, and No. 13 in my Kentucky manuscript.

4. Little Matty Gross
(Little Musgrave and Lady Barnard. Child No. 81)

Child had fourteen versions of this ballad for study (A to N). He includes many variants from English broadside collections, such as *Wit Restored* (1658), *Pepys*, *Roxburghe*, and an added O from Scotland. Child also discovered that it had been entered in the Stationers' Registers in 1630, and that fragments were sung in *The Knight of the Burning Pestle* (1611) and in later seventeenth-century plays.

The story varies only in details, such as the place of meeting: at the church or at a ball; as to messenger: a footpage overhears in secret or is bribed to keep quiet, or a friend of the lord's carries the news. The lord kills the two in various ways, bemoans the loss or one or both, and in some texts slays himself or is hanged. But the essential story is so unified that Coffin, *British*, with more than 60 references in America needs only three story types.

Although the ballad has been recovered in later British tradition, the above 60 references attest to its vigorous currency in America. It has been sung from eastern Canada to Jamaica and west to Oklahoma. Selected references are these: Creighton, *Songs*, p. 11; Barry, *British*, p. 150 (15 texts and fragments, with notes praising purer and more vigorous texts in America than in Europe); Davis, *Traditional*, No. 23 (7 texts); Davis, *More*, No. 24 (5 texts); Sharp and Karpeles, *English*, No. 23; Belden and Hudson, *Brown*, II, No. 26 (5 texts), Schinhan, IV (6 tunes); Smith, *South*, No. 7; Gardner and Chickering, *Ballads*, No. 7; Belden, *Ballads*, p. 57; Randolph, *Ozark*, I, No. 21. With over 20, Kentucky has yielded more texts than any other state. It appears in my *Tales*, No. 4, and in my Kentucky manuscript, No. 20.

When I motored up the Cumberland River on a Sunday in September 1955, I found a gathering in and about the house of some twenty-five people. Jim and Dave sang and played the numbers they had recalled and practiced on, and their kin reminded them of others and requested their favorites. The harvest that day was twenty-six songs. During a lull Jim produced from his pocket a ballad in his own hand on tablet paper. He said of it, "This is a song ballad of an old time song called 'The Little Matty Gross.' I've heard my father sing it when I's a kid and he give it to me t'other day—the words—he's 96 year old—and I wrote it down. I'm a-going to try to put the tune to the words. His voice is so bad he hain't got no tune."

5. Barbary Allen
(Child No. 84)

"Barbara Allen" is used by folklorists to introduce students to the old English and Scottish ballads. There are so many texts of the three fairly distinct versions that the items collected in America alone run into the hundreds. Davis had 118 items to edit in Virginia alone (*Traditional*, No. 24; *More*, No. 25). Some comments on the ballad are as follows:

It is a Scottish story, but was first mentioned by Pepys in his *Diary* for January 2, 1666. Pepys was a ladies' man and loved to go to plays. He said he was in perfect pleasure to hear Mrs. Knipp (an actress) sing her little Scotch song of Barbary Allen. On the strength of this remark some say that the song might have been a stage piece. Barry tries to go a step further and consider it a libel on Charles II and his mistress Barbara Villiers. See note of Belden and Hudson, *Brown*, II, No. 27 (18 texts), and Schinhan, IV (18 tunes).

The second historical fact about the ballad is its appearance in Ramsay's *Tea-Table Miscellany*, 1740 edition. The third is an allusion by Oliver Goldsmith, in an essay of 1765: "The music of the finest singer is dissonance to what I felt when an old dairymaid sang me into tears with 'Johnny Armstrong's Last Goodnight,' and 'The Cruelty of Barbara Allen'" (Child's Headnote).

Child admitted only three faulty short versions into his collection, those that he felt were authentic. Two have the tavern slighting, all have Barbara's remorse, but none have the rose-briar motif.

In the great number of American texts there are interesting, but not vital, variations. In some the lover dies cursing Barbara, or he heaps on her most of his possessions. In some Barbara does not die of remorse, but is still cruel: she curses the lover or her parents for interfering. These and many others are identified by Coffin, *British*, with over 100 references in 10 types.

Without cataloguing, we find the ballad in virtually all collections. This wide distribution has been aided by the songsters, the magazines, and the bulletins printing it. Kentucky seems to be second to Virginia in the number collected: Sharp and Karpeles, *English*, I, No. 24 (5 texts); Niles, *Ballad*, No. 36 (2 texts); Fuson, *Ballads*, p. 47; Combs, *Folk-Songs du Midi*, p. 204 (2 listed); Shearin and Combs, *Syllabus*, p. 81; McGill, *Folk Songs*, p. 40; Thomas, *Devil's*, p. 94; Thomas, *Singin'*, p. 6; Wyman and Brockway, *Lonesome*, p. 1. There are 67 texts in my archive and 2 in my Kentucky manuscript. It is No. 5 in my *Tales*.

The present ballad was recorded during the First Session in 1952, with Dave singing and Jim plucking the banjo, not a very successful plan. Dave said that he had learned "Barbary Allen" before he could play the banjo and had to change the tune when he did learn banjo accompaniment. Jim gave a similar experience: "Me and my sister Mandy worked out the tune of this one so we could play it on the banjo." Perhaps the least change was made by Dave; I am using his piece because of the older, more modal tune.

6. Hangman
(The Maid Freed from the Gallows. Child No. 95)

Child based his lengthy headnote upon eight versions of the ballad (A–H), most of them from England, the oldest from the Percy papers of 1770. His F is a children's game, and C and H, he says, are set to a popular tale in which the girl has lost a golden key or a golden ball. His E is from Scotland as well as his I (IV, 481). The end of this last is unique in that the freed girl hurls curses on her stingy kin. J and K are from England, the latter involving a man rather than a girl on the gallows. In V, 296, Child prints the earliest American text, recited by a North Carolina woman who said that her forebears brought it to Virginia before the Revolution.

In his scholarly way Child traces the ballad in European collections, such as Sicilian, Spanish, Faroe, Icelandic, Swedish, German, Russian. What he finds is a consistent story with infinite details: A wife in one, but girls in most, is seized by pirates (corsairs), usually from their ship, and is held for ransom. Father will not give up the household goods required; Mother the silver trinkets; brother the hats, coats, swords; sister the shoes, etc. The husband or lover gives up all asked and frees the victim. In the Wendish, Slovenian, and Russian versions the prisoner is a man.

The game played and the story told about the loss of a key or ball (G, H) precede the recitation or singing of the stanzas. This type of text (cante-fable) has been collected among Negroes of the West Indies and Missouri—reprinted by Barry, *British*, pp. 210–213. I have collected tales with similar motifs in Kentucky, *South*, pp. 27, 30, titled "The Little Blue Ball" and "The Golden Ball." These are classified as Type 311, The Three Sisters Rescued from the Power of an Ogre. Further collecting and study might reveal the nature of story and ballad kinship.

In America Coffin, *British*, lists some 80 references in 7 story types. It seems to be rare in Canada, but has been recovered from Maine to the West Indies, down Appalachia and the Mississippi Valley to Texas. Selected references are as follows: Barry, *British*, pp. 206–213 (4 texts, including "The Golden Ball," with Barry's extended discussion); Davis, *Traditional*, No. 27 (21 texts and 3 related ones); Sharp and Karpeles, *English*, I, No. 28; Belden and Hudson, *Brown*, II, No. 30 (8 texts), Schinhan, IV (8 tunes); Scarborough, *Song Catcher*, p. 196; Hudson, *Folksongs*, p. 111;

Owens, *Texas*, p. 45. Perhaps second to Virginia, Kentucky has provided about 20 texts, a few of which are these: Fuson, *Ballads*, p. 113; *Kentucky Folklore Record*, 6 (1960):127; Ritchie, *Singing*, p. 122; Thomas, *Devil's*, p. 164; Wyman and Brockway, *Lonesome*, p. 44; some 10 texts in my files; this one is in *Tales*, No. 6, and in my Kentucky manuscript, No. 23.

At my First Session in 1952, Dave had just had some fresh practice on the banjo and accompanied himself on most pieces. He then passed the instrument to Jim for their singing of "Barbary Allen," with unpleasant results, and on into this one. I suggested that he leave off—he was playing hob with Dave's slow tempo, his older modal tune, and the constant change of meter. Dave said he had heard the piece first from the singing of his mother.

7. Drunkard Blues
(Our Goodman. Child No. 274)

Child prints two versions of this humorous ballad: A, Scottish, from Herd of about 1776; and B, a London broadside. In tracing the ballad abroad he finds Gaelic and Flemish forms seemingly derived from his A. The B, he says, was turned into German in a very happy style, furnishing an ending in which the man gives his wife a beating ". . . as caresses which her mother has sent her." Child also identifies other European forms (Scandinavian, Magyar, French, Italian) but does not trace influences. The slight difference in the story elements is that in A (Coffin's A) the man returning finds one horse, hat, sword, etc., where his ought to be; in B (Coffin's B) the man finds evidence of three men in succession. Coffin has a Type C (perhaps more recent and nearer most American forms) in which a man, usually drunk, returns home on three or four successive nights; hence, the local titles "Three Nights' Experience" and "Drunkard Blues."

This ballad has been recovered not only in Canada and the eastern United States, but also in Iowa, Texas, Utah, and Oregon. Coffin, *British*, enters over 75 references, in 3 story types. Selected listings are these: MacKenzie, *Ballads*, No. 14; Barry, *British*, p. 315; Belden and Hudson, *Brown*, II, No. 42 (4 texts), Schinhan, IV (10 tunes); Morris, *Folksongs*, p. 317; Belden, *Ballads*, p. 89; Owen, *Texas*, p. 65. The Kentucky list of over 25 is fairly modest, since I have heard the ballad often and have 18 in my files. A few references are these: two in Sharp and Karpeles, *English*, No. 38 (D has the popular opening, "Old man came home . . ."); Niles, *Ballad*, No. 57; *Kentucky Folklore Record*, 3(1957):94, and 6(1960):127;

the present text in my *Tales*, No. 7, and entered in my Kentucky manuscript, No. 7.

During the Final Session, in November 1955, both Jim and Dave had variants and relished singing this humorous ballad. I have entered Dave's text and tune here because of the refrain line, "I'm goin' to leave, . . ." He said of it, "I'm going to sing one now I've heared ever since I's jest a little bitty boy. I've heared my mother sing it and the older folks, my grandfather and grandmother." Jim took the banjo, saying as he tuned up, "Now I've heared it different from what he sung about the drunkard. I have a different version than what he's got on it. But they both have been handed down I reckon."

8. The Devil and the Farmer's Wife
(The Farmer's Curst Wife. Child No. 278)

Child had only two texts of this humorous ballad for his collection, one English and one Scottish. He mentions others, one reworded by Robert Burns. He does not trace the ballad out of Britain, but cites related folktales from the *Panchatantra* and from W. R. Ralston's *Russian Folk-Tales*, p. 39. I discover that other European folktales contain some of the ballad motifs; Type 810 ff., The Man Promised to the Devil; and Type 1164, The Evil Woman Thrown in the Pit. The ballad is still current in Britain, as listed by Sharp and Karpeles, *English*, II, 315n, and by Davis, *More*, No. 40.

It has much more vigor and variation in America. Coffin, *British*, lists about 70 references, in 7 story types. Selected references are these: Creighton, *Songs*, p. 18; Barry, *British*, p. 325; Fowke and Johnson, *Folksongs*, p. 172; Davis, *Traditional*, No. 46; Belden and Hudson, *Brown*, II, No. 45, Schinhan, IV (4 tunes); Sharp and Karpeles, *English*, I, No. 40; Morris, *Folksongs*, p. 323; Gardner and Chickering, *Ballads*, No. 154; Moore and Moore, *Ballads*, No. 53 (one of 35 collected); Owens, *Texas*, p. 54. It has not flourished in Kentucky: Sharp and Karpeles (4 texts); Niles, *Ballad*, No. 60; Ritchie, *Singing*, p. 143; and I have two in my file. The present text is in *Tales*, No. 32, and is entered in my Kentucky manuscript, No. 32.

A version of the ballad was sung by Dave at the First Session in 1952 and contained the refrain, "Sing ti O rattle dumiday." Then in the summer of 1955 Jim had recalled a version (included here) with this sprightly air.

He said of it, "This here one I heared from my grandpa Harris. He was an Arshman and would mumble around on it and make it awful funny."

9. Swappin' Boy

In some of the collections this piece is called "Foolish Boy," but it is not to be confused with "The Farmyard Song" that usually starts out "I had me a cat and my cat pleased me . . ." (No. 100 below). The present "jingle about animals" (Belden and Hudson's title to vol. III, ch. 6), though they enter it in II, No. 196) has had an early British origin, perhaps harking back to Wat Tyler's rebellion of 1381 because of the Jack Straw and Bread and Cheese references. It appears in a number of British collections, such as Sharp and Karpeles, *English*, II, No. 217 ("The Foolish Boy"); Halliwell, *Nursery Rhymes*, p. 37; Baring-Gould, *Nursery Songs*, p. 17; Greig, *Folk-Song of the North-East*, I, 43, etc.

It has been only moderately reported in American collections: *JAF*, 26 (1913):143; Wyman and Brockway, *Twenty*, p. 10; Belden and Hudson, *Brown*, II, No. 196 (5 texts, not all printed), Schinhan, IV (tunes to A and E); Eddy, *Ballads*, No. 93; Cambiaire, *East Tennessee*, p. 78; Richardson, *American*, p. 48; *Bulletin of Tenn. Folklore Society*, 3(1925):4; Cox, *Traditional*, No. 19; Combs, *Folk-Songs du Midi*, p. 223 (listed).

Dave recorded a version of the piece in my First Session in 1952 without much comment. His does not have a refrain. Then at my Final Session in 1955 Jim had recalled this funny tongue-twister and proceeded to record it without trouble. I use Jim's here because of the refrain. He said of it, "This funny old thing used to be said by heart and then some of the old folks would sing it. I don't remember who sung it first."

10. The Old Big Ram

Usually called "The Derby Ram," the song about the gigantic ram has many off-color stanzas, other than the usual last line. The references I have seen show that the piece has long been in British tradition and is still popular (I heard an English lady on an American tour include it). The oldest dated appearance at hand seems to be in Kinloch, *The Ballad Book*, in 1827, but the era of lying goes back to Munchausen (Type 1889) of the eighteenth century and beyond. I have a song about a big deer hunt that features several motifs of Type 1889, such as the bent gun barrel, the fish in boots, riding on the horn of the moon, etc.

Aside from a few appearances in New England, it has been most often found in Appalachia and in the Midwest. Some selected references are these: *JAF*, 18(1905):51; 36(1923):377; 39(1936):173; Sharp and Karpeles, *English*, II, No. 141 (3 texts); Belden and Hudson, *Brown*, II, No. 176 (2 texts), Schinhan, IV (3 tunes); Fuson, *Ballads*, p. 58; *Bulletin of Tenn. Folklore Society*, 3(1937):95; Combs, *Folk-Songs du Midi*, p. 219 (3 listed); Henry, *Folk-Songs*, No. 46; Belden, *Ballads*, p. 224.

Sung by Jim in the Final Session of 1955, who said of it: "Here is the song about the old big ram. I used to hear my grandfather on my mother's side sing it. He'd come up there and set around and sing about the big ram. I'm going to try to sing part of it." This grandfather was Lewis Harris, who still spoke with an Irish accent.

11. Purty Polly
(Laws P 36B)

This story first appeared in England in 1750 as a garland or broadside titled "The Gosport Tragedy, or the Perjured Ship's Carpenter." It was composed by some ballad maker and seller, presumably using some actual happening. It had thirty-five quatrains.

The story, though long and drawn-out, is as follows: A ship's carpenter while on shore leave courts a young and beautiful mason's daughter. Though she pleads that she is too young and that her parents do not approve, she continues to listen to his vows—that he will go to heaven for her or will anchor his ship and stay with her. She soon finds herself with child and then when he is to sail pleads for an honorable wedding. He sets a time and trysting place and leads her to a new-made grave on which he has dug most of the night. She pleads now for a life of disgrace, but he stabs her and buries her there.

His ship sets sail and soon the steward sees the ghost of a maiden with an infant in her arms. It is an omen of murder and disaster. The captain calls the crew together and threatens hanging if the murderer does not confess. Willie confesses killing Mary, and he "Died raving distracted that same night."

Laws, *Native*, gives the title "The Cruel Ship's Carpenter" at P 36A and a synopsis similar to mine above. At B he shows the reworkings of the ballad into shorter quatrains and subtitles it "Pretty Polly." His 20 references show that it is known in New England, but it is more so in Appalachia and the Midwest. Selected listings are these: Creighton and Senior, *Traditional*, p. 203; Sharp and Karpeles, *English*, I, No. 49 (21 texts); Cox, *Folk-Songs*, No. 89 (3 texts); Belden and Hudson, *Brown*, II, No. 264 (5 texts), Schinhan, IV (tunes to C, E, E1); Morris, *Folksongs*, p.

341; Fuson, *Ballads*, p. 69; Henry, *Songs*, p. 53; Combs, *Folk-Songs du Midi*, p. 144 (earlier version without new-dug grave, etc.); *JAF*, 20 (1907):262, and 40(1937):276. It is No. 11 in my *Tales*; I have entered another text in my Kentucky manuscript, No. 42.

It was sung by Dave at the First Session in 1952. He said of it, "I learnt it from a boy who come back from World War I. I put it to the banjo myself; I never heared anybody pick it."

12. The Bachelor Boy
(Laws Q 6)

One of a number of taming-the-shrew combats, this one is called "The Holly Twig" in Virginia and North Carolina, although a holly switch is not used in any text that I have seen. It is of British origin, with about 4 texts in various collections, the earliest in *West Country Garlands* (c. 1760). There is a reference (which I have not seen) in *Journal of the Folk-Song Society*, 3(1901):315, but it is not in Halliwell's *Nursery Rhymes* (first edition of 1842, which I have checked) as given by Belden and Hudson. Laws, *American Balladry*, has 9 entries for his study.

In America a dozen texts have been reported, all from Appalachia and the South: Sharp and Karpeles, *English*, I, No. 53 (3 texts from Va.); Belden and Hudson, *Brown*, II, No. 184 (2 texts), Schinhan, IV (1 tune); Chappell, *Folk-Songs*, p. 77; Henry, *Folk-Songs*, No. 36; Hudson *Folksongs*, p. 174; Randolph, *Ozark*, III, No. 367. The present piece was published in my *Bought Dog*, following story No. 7.

Dave recorded this one in our First Session in 1952 and named it as one of his father's favorites. When I took the transcription back to the men later, we noticed a stanza missing (Thursday morning's activities). On my trip up to Tom's cabin (described in the Introduction) Tom took up the song without hesitation and sang of all the days of the week, but, alas, with no electricity I could only jot down the missing part and insert it later.

13. Rich and Rambling Boy
(Laws L 12)

This or a similar title prevails for this piece only occasionally, while five or six others are used, such as "In Newry Town," "Wild and Wicked Youth," and "The Irish Robber." Belden considers it of Irish provenience and possibly related to "The Unfortunate Rake." He gives many British references but only two from America.

Laws, *Native*, enters about 15 references, including broadsides, for his study, mostly from the South. Selected listings are these: Davis, *Folk-Songs*, p. 282 (listed); Belden and Hudson, *Brown*, II, No. 121 (1 text), Schinhan, IV (4 tunes to different texts); Cambiaire, *East Tennessee*, p. 43; Henry, *Folk-Songs*, No. 116; Fuson, *Ballads*, p. 63; Combs, *Folk-Songs du Midi*, p. 184, 212 (listed); Belden, *Ballads*, p. 136; Randolph, *Ozark*, II, No. 148 (2 texts). For the curious, the Kentucky novelist James Still uses a stanza in *River of Earth*, p. 143.

During my First Session in 1952, Dave recorded many pieces before we went to Jim's place for two more hours. Again I took the transcription back later and when Jim saw it he missed three stanzas and obligingly recorded his version—included here. Both men had heard the piece from their father, Tom, when they were very young.

14. Sweetheart in the Army
(Laws N 42. Pretty Fair Maid)

Broadsides with the theme of the broken token began to appear in England in the late eighteenth century. The hero in them is generally a sailor, who returns in disguise after three to seven years. In later American versions he is usually a soldier. Child admitted at least one with this theme into his collection (No. 105). Belden, *Ballads*, p. 148 (4 texts) lists many printings of it in Scotland, Ireland, Wales, and in six shires of England, as well as several in America.

It has been reported widely in America, from Canada to Texas. Laws, *Native*, lists about 40 references, including broadsides. A selected list of instances is as follows: Creighton, *Songs*, p. 56; Sharp and Karpeles, *English*, II, No. 98 (5 texts, "The Broken Token"); Belden and Hudson, *Brown*, II, No. 92 (1 printed of 11), Schinhan, IV (15 tunes); Henry, *Folk-Songs*, No. 59 (3 texts); Scarborough, *Song Catcher*, p. 264; Cox, *Folk-Songs*, No. 92 (2 printed of 5); *JAF*, 29(1916):201; Fuson, *Ballads*, p. 77. I have ten or so texts in my files, one of which is entered in my Kentucky manuscript.

The present piece was sung during the First Session in 1952 by Dave with banjo. He was unable to recall when he first heard it.

15. The Knoxville Girl
(Laws P 35. Wexford Girl)

Notes on this ballad are quite complex since it is of early British origin and has many titles conforming to the places of murder or to the murderer's title. Aside from the two titles given above it is also called "The Oxford Girl," "The Cruel Miller, or Miller's Apprentice," and "The Lexington Girl." Belden (*Ballads*, p. 133) has traced the earliest source to a piece in the Pepys collection of a murder in 1684, and another called "The Berkshire Tragedy" or "The Wittam Miller" to a date around 1700. He says that it is in tradition in Norfolk and Dorset. Cox (*Folk-Songs*, No. 90) cites an Edinburgh chapbook text of 1744 wherein the miller named John Mauge was hanged at Reading (Berkshire) in that year.

Laws, *Native*, treats broadside variation and recomposition in Chapter IV, and especially this cluster from page 104, with full texts. At P 35 he has listed about 40 references showing the ballad distribution from Canada to Texas. Selected instances are these: MacKenzie, *Ballads*, p. 119; Flanders and Brown, *Vermont*, p. 83; Sharp and Karpeles, *English*, I, No. 71 (5 texts); Belden and Hudson, *Brown*, II, No. 65 (13, not all printed); Schinhan, IV (7 tunes); Shearin and Combs, *Syllabus*, pp. 13, 28; Belden, *Ballads*, p. 133 (2 texts); Randolph, *Ozark*, II, No. 150 (8 texts). Although I have often heard it sung, it is rare in Kentucky collections.

When I visited Jim in 1954 at his new place on a creek called Craft Colley for the weekend Seventh Session, I found that his son Frank had settled nearby. After we got under way, Frank brought out a guitar and recorded several modern pieces, including this one. He had played with some boys in a band for a few years. He was unable to recall the source of this one and his other pieces.

16. Rovin' Gambler
(Laws H 4)

Evidence that a song about a roving journeyman began in Britain is given by Belden (*Ballads*, p. 374) by tracing it in the stall prints of the last century. He says it is probably of Irish origin. In the text given by Sandburg (*American*, p. 312) from Delany's *Songbook* a Gamboling Man finds himself cooled with a fan in the dwelling of a London girl.

In America the hero becomes a guerrilla, or a railroad man, a soldier boy, or a gambling man. With so much sea-change and wide variation, Laws (*Native*) places it among American ballads. He lists about 30 references mostly from the South and Southwest. Selected references are these: Henry, *Songs*, p. 98; Belden and Hudson, *Brown*, III, No. 49 (3 texts), Schinhan, V (1 tune); Gardner and Chickering, *Ballads*, No. 75; Randolph, *Ozark*, IV, No. 835 (3 texts); Owens, *Texas*, p. 183; Lomax and Lomax, *American*, p. 150. A version is in my Kentucky manuscript, No. 63.

The present version was sung by Jim with banjo at the Final Session in

1955. He said of it, "I'll sing one now called the 'Rovin Gambler,' the one my father winned the champion prize on at Hyden when they let him out of jail to join the contest."

17. The Wagoner Boy

This is a favorite folk lyric, found in abundance in Appalachia and sparsely elsewhere. It has almost enough narrative to be a ballad, except that feeling is predominant, especially in those texts borrowing from "Old Smoky" and "The False-Hearted Lover." A composite of the story may be constructed, as follows: A wagoner (Willy) is leaving Nancy's home in North Carolina (or on New River) for Georgia or to join the army. He says her parents don't like him because he is poor or is a drinker, and he does not want to marry her for her gold. Nancy bewails his going and tries to dissuade him because of night travel or bad weather. When he persists in going she says that she then will court whom she pleases or that she would go with him but Mama has treated her kindly. In a few versions she decides to throw her belongings on the wagon and elope with him.

The piece has been most often reported from North Carolina: Belden and Hudson, *Brown*, III, No. 250 (3 texts and 3 fragments), Schinhan, V (8 tunes), and they cite 8 other references. It has also been reported by Sharp and Karpeles, *English*, II, No. 117 (5 texts); Scarborough, *Song Catcher*, p. 272 (9 texts); Henry, *Folk-Songs*, No. 90 (2 texts); Cox, *Folk-Songs*, No. 146 (a version sung by a courting lad in about 1870); Davis, *Folk-Songs*, p. 83 (19 listed); Wyman and Brockway, *Lonesome*, p. 64; Fuson, *Ballads*, p. 119.

During 1955 I had the Eighth, Ninth, and Tenth Sessions with Jim, Dave, and Joe, including a week on the road. At this time Jim recalled pieces and secured more from his father than usual. He recalled the present piece, heard from his father, with some difficulty.

18. Wild Bill Jones
(Laws E 10)

Since the history and provenience of this crime of jealousy are not known, it would be conjecture to name a time and place for it. It has been collected more often in Kentucky than in any other state. Lomax in *Folk Songs* (No. 140) summarizes a similar incident in a Clay County, Kentucky, feud. It has been collected almost entirely in the South, with no date apparently before 1900.

It is absent from the New England collections, from Cox's West Virginia volumes, the Frank C. Brown (N.C.), and the Belden (Mo.) collections. Most of the references are as follows: Sharp and Karpeles, *English*, II, No. 99; Chappell, *Folk-Songs*, p. 193; Henry, *Folk-Songs*, No. 113 (2 texts); Hudson, *Mississippi*, p. 239; Randolph, *Ozark*, II, No. 151; Richardson, *American*, p. 36 (reprinted by Lomax, *Folk Songs*, No. 140); Combs, *Folk-Songs du Midi*, p. 209 (listed); McGill, *Folk Songs*, p. 25.

The piece was first sung in the First Session in 1952 by Dave with banjo. Jim gave his version later, adding stanzas two and five. I prefer Dave's rendition (with the two stanzas added) because he could look far off with half-shut eyes while blending his plaintive voice with the gentle frail of the banjo strings and the steady pat of his foot. His melancholy singing of the piece and the tragic narrative itself haunted me long afterward, and I found myself trying to sing it. Dave said of it, "I heared my daddy pick and sing it; it's the second or third tune I ever learnt."

19. Willow Garden
(Laws F 6. Rose Connoley)

Data to establish the history and provenience of this tragic murder ballad are lacking. Lomax, *Folk Songs*, p. 261, states flatly that it is a West Virginia piece, perhaps because of the early dates given by Cox (see below). Although it has some kinship with other murder pieces, especially "The Jealous Lover," "The Knoxville Girl," and "On the Banks of the Ohio," some of the details suggest a separate crime.

Laws, *Native*, gives about 8 references, all from three states—Kentucky, West Virginia, and North Carolina. A selection of references are these: Cox, *Folk-Songs*, No. 91 (2 texts: A collected in 1915, but popular about 1895; B collected in 1917); Shearin and Combs, *Syllabus*, p. 28 (compiled in 1911); Belden and Hudson, *Brown*, No. 67 (2 texts), Schinhan, IV (tunes to 2 other versions); *JAF*, 52(1939):24; 59(1946):461; Lomax and Lomax, *Folk Song: USA*, p. 302 (reprinted in *Folk Songs*, as above). A version is in my Kentucky manuscript, No. 55.

Sung by Jim in the Tenth Session of 1955, heard from his father. Later he looked over the transcription and added the second stanza.

20. Frankie and Albert
(Laws I 3)

The time, place, and people relating to this (supposed) Negro crime have not been established yet. An extended note by Lomax, *Folk Songs*, p. 557, states that the ballad may have been heard before Vicksburg in 1863, and another rumor places it along the Mississippi in 1888. Also, a blues singer popularized it in a St. Louis bawdy house in the 1890's. Lomax guesses that it evolved from several white and Negro songs in the Mississippi Valley from 1850 to 1914. He also summarizes a lawsuit by a woman against Republic Pictures after that company used the song in a film; the woman claimed she had killed Allen Britt in St. Louis in 1899. He quotes another woman, Frankie Baker, who sang the song to a collector in Omaha in 1908 and "swore that she had killed her man in Kansas City some years previously, and then had composed this ballad." Versions of the piece have been reported over most of the South and rarely elsewhere.

Laws, *Native*, lists about 20 references and summarizes the Allen Britt data. Selected reportings are these: Belden and Hudson, *Brown*, II, No. 251 (10 texts), Schinhan, IV (3 tunes); Henry, *Folk-Songs*, No. 122 (5 texts); *JAF*, 24(1911):366; Hudson, *Mississippi*, p. 189; White, *American*, p. 214; Belden, *Ballads*, p. 330 (1 composite text; he gives the Lomax data—and more); Randolph, *Ozark*, II, 127 (6 texts); Lomax and Lomax, *American*, p. 103.

The present ballad was sung by Dave at our First Session in 1952. He did not give a source, but a version with this title appeared on a phonograph record (which I have not seen) before 1920.

21. Those Brown Eyes

At the Seventh, or Craft Colley (Letcher County), Session in 1954 I recorded all weekend from Jim and his son Frank. The son used the guitar and recorded several songs, including this piece. He did not seem to know (or want to recall) the sources of this or other of his recordings.

22. Jack Was a Lonely Cowboy
(Laws B 24. Cowboy Jack)

Cowboy material seems out of place in the hills of Appalachia, but Western pieces were quite popular in the 1920's and 1930's, drifting in with singers, collectors, mail-order booklets, and of course on phonograph records. During the depression there was a mini-renaissance of folk activities in the mountains and all over the country.

Laws, *Native*, has only two printed references and a recording on this sentimental ballad: Lomax and Lomax, *Cowboy*, p. 230; *Colorado Folksong Bulletin*, 2(1963):27; L. C. Record 899 B1 (Tex.). I have seen no other reports of it.

It was sung with guitar by Frank at the Seventh Session in Letcher County in 1954.

23. The Orphant Girl

This sentimental protest song appeared as early as the 1902 edition of the *Sacred Harp* and was reprinted by Jackson in *Spiritual*, p. 48. These sources credit the tune to Eld. C. G. Keith. Sandburg collected a variant in Iowa and credited it to settlers from Kentucky and Tennessee, saying further that it goes back to a broadside in England and Scotland (*American*, pp. 316–319, 2 texts). It just might not go back to a broadside, except distantly and in the spirit of the ballad muse. Henry (*Folk-Songs*, No. 138, 4 texts) obtained a copy of the piece from Mrs. Helen Tufts Baile, Cambridge, Massachusetts, who received it from John Oliver, Blount County, Tennessee, on April 10, 1931. At the end of the ballad (No. 138C) John Oliver writes that the "Song Ballad" was written by his great-uncle Daniel Brownlow Lawson for M. J. Lawson, August 15, 1880. This may not settle the question of origin, but the aftermath becomes clearer. After the "Ballad" received a tune and was entered in the religious hymnal, we see how it has been carried over the South and the Midwest.

Selected references are these: Scarborough, *Song Catcher*, p. 364; Chappell, *Folk-Songs*, p. 196; Henry, *Folk-Songs*, No. 138 (3 texts); D (listed) is identical to Sandburg's B. I find it also the same as Henry's *Songs*, p. 124; Belden and Hudson, *Brown*, II, No. 148 (14 listed, A and J printed), Schinhan, IV (tunes to C, F, H); Brewster, *Ballads*, No. 63; Shearin and Combs, *Syllabus*, p. 32; Cambiaire, *East Tennessee*, p. 26; *JAF*, 46(1933): 49; Randolph, *Ozark*, IV, No. 725.

The present version was sung unaccompanied by Dave at the Eight Session in 1955. Since he did not know the source, we may assume that he had recently learned it from popular singing and phonograph recording.

24. Brother Green

This melodramatic last farewell of a Civil War Yankee soldier is found as expected mostly in the upper South and the Midwest. The time of the incident is known, but the hero and the author are not yet identified. Belden, *Ballads* (p. 377, 1 stanza) says that the contributor gave the composer as Rev. L. J. Simpson on the death of a brother killed at Fort Donelson in February 1862. Old-timers in the Ozarks insist that it was written by a federal officer named Sutton, wounded at the battle of Wilson's Creek (Randolph, *Ozark*, II, No. 211, 2 texts).

Selected references are these: Henry, *Folk-Songs*, No. 131; Belden and Hudson, *Brown*, III, No. 393 (A printed; B and C listed), Schinhan, V (tunes for A and C); Henry, *Songs*, p. 212; Eddy, *Ballads*, No. 111; Brewster, *Ballads*, No. 47; Fuson, *Ballads*, p. 193; Wyman and Brockway, *Lonesome*, p. 18; Combs, *Folk-Songs du Midi*, p. 221 (listed).

Sung by Dave without banjo at the Eighth Session in 1955. He did not know it very well and left out some stanzas. He had no comment except that he had learned it from his father.

25. James A. Garfield
(Laws E 11)

James A. Garfield was shot in the railroad depot of Washington, D.C., on July 2, 1881, by Charles Guiteau, a disappointed office seeker. This was a national tragedy, compounded by the fact that the president lingered until September before the end, and also by the fact that the murderer in his trial tried to plead insanity and was not executed until June 30, 1882. Ballads were needed, and an unknown redactor produced this one that spread pretty well over the United States.

Two prototypes of the ballad are now known. Belden and Hudson in their headnote to *Brown*, II, No. 249 (12 texts, A, C, D, G, H, L printed) give two stanzas of "Lament of James Rodgers, Who Was Executed November 12th, 1858, for the Murder of Mr. Swanson. By J. A. D. Air— Home Sweet Home—." In four stanzas, it begins, "Come all you tender Christians . . ." At about the same time Olive Woolley Burt, researching for her *American Murder Ballads* (see ballad on pp. 226–227), found a text in Utah on a similar event: "In the year 1861, J. R. Birchell of Ontario, Canada, killed F. S. Benwell in the swamps near Elenheim . . . Birchell was arrested, tried, convicted, and sentenced to die." It begins with the same words given above and with a chorus beginning: "My name is J. R. Birchell, that name I'll never deny." Either one or both of these models seem to have been used for making the present piece.

It is thinly but widely scattered over the South and West. Laws, *Native*, enters about 20 references and gives four other possible patterns for this one. Selected references are these: Chappell, *Folk-Songs*, p. 188; Belden and Hudson, *Brown*, II, No. 249 as above, Schinhan, IV (tunes to C and

G) ; Eddy, *Ballads*, No. 128; Stout, *Folklore*, p. 110; Sandburg, *American*, p. 146; Randolph, *Ozark*, II, No. 134 (5 texts); Owens, *Texas*, p. 118; Hudson, *Mississippi*, p. 238; Arnold, *Folksongs*, p. 113.

Sung by Jim during the Seventh Session. He said he had heard it from his father.

26. Ellen Smith
(Laws F 11)

This murder ballad was sung and recorded from the 1890's to 1950 before it was finally documented. Summarizing the data furnished by Ethel Richardson (used also by Laws) and Belden and Hudson, I give the story as follows:

In the early 1890's near Mount Airy, North Carolina, Peter DeGraff began courting Ellen Smith. Apparently only fooling, he told others that he loved the girl but would never make her his wife. Ellen was unexpectedly found shot to death, with a letter in her bosom in Peter's handwriting. He was traced to Roanoke, Virginia, and as far away as New Mexico, but was finally brought back for trial (or came back voluntarily).

Trial was held in August 1893 in Forsyth County, and the verdict was death for the crime. Upon appeal to the North Carolina Supreme Court the presiding judge reviewed the facts of his flight and return and the letter. Appeal was denied. DeGraff, in jail, called for a guitar and composed a ballad, a line of which voiced his surprise when he learned that Ellen had been killed. He was executed. Feeling ran so high for and against the hanging that the court declared it a misdemeanor to sing the ballad at gatherings. Other songs on the murder have come to light; a passage in one has Peter confessing that jealousy caused him to murder Ellen.

Laws, *Native*, has 7 references and a few recordings of the ballad, all except one or two from Appalachia. Some listings are these: Belden and Hudson, *Brown*, II, Nos. 305 and 306, Schinhan, IV (tunes to 305 A and E); Henry, *Folk-Songs*, No. 109 (fragment); Combs, *Folk-Songs du Midi*, p. 188; Fuson, *Ballads*, p. 132; Williams, *Ballads*, p. 139; Hudson, *Mississippi*, p. 193.

The present piece was sung by Jim with banjo at the Ninth Session in 1955. I took the transcription back a few weeks later, and Jim went over it again, adding stanzas two and three. He had heard it from his father who believed that the crime took place on the Big Sandy River.

27. Mines of Coal Creek
(Laws G 9)

There are only five texts of this mine disaster available to me. Data on the event are given by George Korson (*Coal*, pp. 275–277): Eighty-four men and boys, out of a total payroll of eighty-nine, died in the Cross Mountain mine explosion at Briceville, Tennessee, on December 9, 1911. He quotes a United Mine Workers district president, William Turnblazer, as saying: "This ballad was composed and sung by Thomas Evans who died a few years ago at Esserville, Virginia. The explosion was in the Cross Mountain mine at Coal Creek, Tennessee."

Although Korson's version at stanza 3, line 1, gives the number dead as 150 (and, thus, given by Laws in his paraphrase), the number above (84) is probably correct. Recognized variants of the Korson ballad have been reported from Breathitt County, Kentucky: Henry, *Songs*, p. 84, and *Kentucky Folklore Record*, 3(1957): 99 (in his note editor D. K. Wilgus cites a variant in J. T. Adams, *Death in the Dark*, p. 96). I have not seen it. But the present text and one from Knox County entered in my Kentucky ballad manuscript (close variants) are distinctly different in theme and composition.

This piece was sung by Dave with banjo at our First Session in 1952. He said of it: "That was made up about the mines. They was a boy got killed by a slatefall in the mines, and before he died he wrote these verses on a rock and left it in the mines where he died."

28. Wreck of Old Ninety-Seven
(Laws G 2)

"Old 97" is the ballad that went to court. It was made famous by the Victor Talking Machine Company in the 1920's by recording a version dangerously close to the original author's copy. This was in 1924, and by 1927 the plaintiff David Graves George of Gretan, Virginia, filed suit for royalties. A summary of the trial (in which George won) and especially the appeals-court proceedings along with copies of the disputed versions are given by Belden and Hudson, *Brown*, II, No. 217 (5 texts—no tunes printed!). The wreck itself occurred on September 27, 1903, near Danville, Virginia, with the loss of ten lives.

The ballad is not so widespread in the collections examined, perhaps because of the copyright controversy. Laws, *Native*, enters 8 texts and 4 recording references, all except two from Appalachia. Selected instances are these: Cox, *Traditional*, p. 118; Henry, *Songs*, p. 79; Richardson, *American*, p. 42; Williams, *Ballads*, p. 335; Spaeth, *Read 'Em*, p. 119.

The present version was recorded by Frank with guitar at our Seventh Session. He had learned it sometime earlier from friends.

29. When I Left the Blue Ridge Mountains

This is a sad and rueful lament, quite poignant to me because I have heard it sung as early as 1920 in eastern Kentucky. A lusty young neighbor used to come by our house, sit at the organ playing and singing, "I was bornd and raised in old Virginia . . ." It has several titles, and exchanges stanzas with "Man of Constant Sorrow," "Little Birdie," etc.

Selected references are these: Sharp and Karpeles, *English*, II, No. 167 (4 texts "In Old Virginny"); Davis, *Folk-Songs*, p. 59 (7 listed); Belden and Hudson, *Brown*, III, No. 279, V (no tune); Henry, *Songs*, p. 24; Ritchie, *Singing*, p. 134; a text titled "Dark Hollow Blues" is in my Kentucky manuscript, No. 104.

It was recorded by Jim at our Tenth Session in late 1955. He said of it, "I heared it years ago but I don't remember when I did hear it first."

30. John Hardy
(Laws I 2)

The biographical data on John Hardy, the Negro steel-driver, are substantial, believable, grim, and in contrast to the wispy, spirit-like myth of another steel-driver, John Henry. There is enough first-hand and remembered data about Hardy to reconstruct his life and death and to give him a habitation and a name. Paraphrasing Cox and others, I give these data:

A coal-black Negro from Virginia appeared before the contractor on the east, or Summers County, side of the mountain to be tunneled and asked the boss Mr. Langhorn for a job. He was a strong, muscular black, about twenty years old and weighed about 200 pounds. He was hired as a steel-driver—a hammer swinger driving a heavy steel flat-ended bit into the rock several feet for explosive charges. With crews of perhaps over a hundred men on each side of the mountain the tunnel was completed in two or three years.

John Hardy then drifted south and in the 1890's we learn of his employment with the Shawnee Coal Company in McDowell County (Welch is the county seat). Hardy brought his reputation with him, gathering along the way his prowess with the women (he was single) and for drinking and gambling. One payday night he entered into a poker game with a group of blacks, but for opening ceremonies he laid a pistol on the table and said to it, "Now I want you to lay here, and the first nigger that steals money from me I mean to kill him!" About midnight he began to lose and to get desperate. He accused a player of cheating him of twenty-five cents. The man denied the charge but handed him a quarter. Hardy said, "Don't you know I won't lie to my gun?" and shot the man dead.

Although a line in a version of the ballad says he was too nervy to run, he hid out for a few days until he was caught and lodged in the jail at Welch. He was tried, convicted, and sentenced to be hanged. Unrepentant but threatening to kill himself at first, he was persuaded to accept his fate; in the last weeks of waiting he became reconciled and was baptised in the Tug River. His end came by hanging on Friday, January 19, 1894.

It seems to me that here is a study for students of hero creating and myth-making. For out of this story of blood, sacrifice, and death arose phoenix-like a heroic and mythic man the folk called John Henry.

A selected number of references, mostly from Appalachia, are these: Cox, *Folk-Songs*, No. 35 (9 texts); Belden and Hudson, *Brown*, II, No. 244 (3 texts), Schinhan IV (3 tunes, one from a different singer); Sharp and Karpeles, *English*, II, No. 87; Chappell, *Folk-Songs*, p. 179; Randolph, *Ozark*, II, No. 163 (3 texts); Sandburg, *American*, p. 24.

The present version was sung by Dave without accompaniment at the Eighth Session in 1955. He said of it: "This is one I used to hear played and sung on the banjo. John was cheated out of twenty-five cents by another player in a poker game. He handed it back, but John said, 'I ain't gonna lie to my gun.'"

31. Floyd Frazier
(Laws F 19)

The only evidence Laws had for placing this ballad in tradition was a text in Combs, *Folk-Songs du Midi* (pp. 155–157), plus a recording from Kentucky titled "Ellen Flanary," and four from Virginia. When it was sung to me in 1952 by Dave, he said, "It happened over here in Letcher County on the Pine Mountain Road, and her body was hid behind a big log. The old rotten log is laying there yet. A girl made up this song and went around to the jailhouse and sung it to him. He said, 'Let me out of here and kill her and then I don't care what you do with me.'"

In due time I made my way to Letcher County and found a man, Mr. J. C. Day of the county clerk's office, who gave the following information:

"I was justice of the peace at the time of the hanging of Floyd Frazier in 1908, 1910, somewhere in there. It was the biggest crowd of people ever to come to Whitesburg, 'cause that was the only legal hanging in this county—a man was took out of jail and hung before that and a colored feller later.

"Ellen Flanary, a widder with five or six children, was out pickin' greens in the early spring. Floyd must have tried to rape her and then thought he had to kill her—he never confessed. He covered her up with rocks behind a log—I weighed them for the court—250 pounds, left just her feet sticking out. They took him horseback to Bell County for safe-keepin'. He broke jail and went to workin' down there—never even changed his name. First jury was hung, eleven for hanging him. Got a jury from Knott County and they sentenced him to hang. He got an appeal. Next jury was from Floyd County and *they* sentenced him to be hung."

I went with him to the court records and found entries for this case from 1908 to 1909. The last paragraph may suffice here, the order from the Floyd County jury verdict:

It is therefore ordered and adjudged by the court that the defendant, Floyd Frazier, be taken by the sheriff of Letcher County and on July 9, 1909, between sunrise and sunset on said day by said sheriff, be hanged by the neck until he is dead. *Commonwealth Order Book,* No. 7, p. 260, Letcher County Court.

When the clerk took me to the archives to pull down the books, he pointed to a file and said I might want to see the rope. There in the drawer lay a noose with a tag on it reading: "Used in the hanging of Floyd Frazier, 1910." This date is incorrect. The rope is gone now, reported missing from the drawer recently.

32. Hiram Hubbard
(Laws A 20)

The story of Hiram Hubbard dramatizes the bushwhacking and guerrilla tactics used to terrorize the Kentucky mountain people during the Civil War. The Union military forces demanded service from every able-bodied man, as did the Kentucky State Guard and the Home Guard. On the other side, the Rebel forces penetrated the mountain passes at Cumberland Gap, Pound Gap, and the breaks of the Big Sandy River. Demanding and seizing provisions and recruits, they drove the old men and boys into caves. The women had to hide their livestock in the woods and bury their food and other possessions.

To track down this story, I encouraged a young Union College student to visit and interview some families of Hubbards in Knox, Clay, and Bell counties where they had lived for a hundred years. After they told her about the "awful" times during the war between the Republicans and Democrats, they told her of the legend: a man suspected of deserting one of the sides was seized, tortured, and murdered on Goose Creek, Knox County.

This is indefinite evidence, but it may be the best we can do after these 110 years. My references (same as Laws') are these: Combs, *Folk-Songs du Midi*, pp. 171, 208 (listed); Ritchie, *A Garland*, p. 57. I can add that Ritchie reprinted the ballad in her *Folk Songs of the Southern Appalachians*, p. 57.

During our Ninth Session in 1955, Jim and Dave recorded for some time and then recalled one about Hiram Hubbard, but they felt that only their father, Tom, knew it all. We had him come off the hill from his cabin, and as usual he went through it easily, except that his voice was shaky and off-key. After we had made out the words, Jim sang it through for the record.

33. Kaiser and the Hindenberger

When Jim wanted to put on this lampoon at our Ninth Session in 1955, I asked him to give some background information. He said, "I composed this un while I was in France in the World War [I]. Made it up myself and sung it." "Was it sung very much—did it become popular that you know of?" "Yeah boy, it was sung a lot by the boys, and the Army newspaper printed it and it spread all through the Army."

Knowing that it was a composed piece I hesitated to include it, but the refrain line, "Them boys of the Uncle Sam," sounded familiar. I might have heard snatches of it after that war. Perhaps its appearance here will jog the memories of some of that Army.

34. Young Lady in the Bloom of Youth

The father, Tom, sang parts of this piece as early as my First Session in 1952, and said that it was the best song he knew. For the record Dave also sang it at that time without accompaniment and with plaintive feeling. The folk (and the folk in us all) appear to get a spiritual catharsis from ballads of simple pity and forboding. I have seen no other instances of it in collections examined.

35. O Those Tombs

No related pieces in the materials examined. It was sung by Jim in 1955; he learned it from his mother.

36. I Saw a Sight All in a Dream

Another favorite that Tom liked and recorded in the fall of 1955. Later Jim and Dave helped me with the text and tune.

37. The Twelve Apostles

The fullest notes available to me on this cumulative song are by Belden and Hudson, *Brown*, II, No. 50 (2 texts), Schinhan IV (2 tunes). They trace the adventures of it in Europe, Britain, Canada, and America. One of their sources suggests that the ultimate origin of this kind of chant may be in Sanskrit literature. Another explores it in most countries of Europe and arrives at a very early printing in a form of the Hebrew Passover chant that was printed in Prague in 1526.

In America it has been reported by a dozen collectors from Canada to the Ozarks. Selected references are these: Greenleaf, *Ballads*, p. 91; *JAF*, 4(1891):215; 30 (1917):335; 62(1949):382; Shearin and Combs, *Syllabus*, p. 34; Henry, *Folk-Songs*, No. 37; Sharp and Karpeles, *English*, II, No. 207 (5 texts); Randolph, *Ozark*, IV, No. 605.

Sung by Jim without accompaniment at the Ninth Session in 1955. He remarked about it, "This is a song I heared my mother sing when I was a kid. They's supposed to be two a-singing it, but I'll do it by myself."

38. Bright and Shining City

No close versions discovered. Sung by Jim in 1955.

39. Glory Land

No related texts discovered. Sung by Jim in 1955.

40. Father Took a Light

No related texts discovered. Sung by Dave in 1955. He said of it, "This is an old song I heared my mother sing a many a time."

41. Climbing up Zion's Hills

Some related versions may be mentioned: White, *American*, p. 86 (2 fragments, faintly suggesting this song); Jackson, *White*, p. 183; Belden and Hudson, *Brown*, III, No. 624 (5 texts, C suggestive of this one), Schinhan, V (tunes to A, B, E). Sung by Dave in 1955. He said, "This is an old song; I've heared my mother sing it plenty a times, back 40 years ago."

42. The Lifeboat Is Coming

A possible version, especially the chorus, is reported by Randolph, *Ozark*, IV, No. 629. He reports seeing it in an old shape-note hymnbook with the title page gone; another in *Sacred Jewels* (No. 39). Sung by Jim in 1955; learned from his mother.

43. Lord, I've Started for the Kingdom

The texts in Belden and Hudson, *Brown*, III, Nos. 345 and 349, have some relationship, especially in the choruses. Sung by Jim in 1955; heard since he was a kid.

44. I'm All Alone in This World

There is a distinct variant reported by Jackson, *Spiritual*, No. 219, collected in 1932 in Tennessee but learned by his informant in the 1880's in North Carolina. He also cites a Negro version of the tune in William F. Allen et al., *Slave Songs of the United States*, p. 18. Distantly related pieces are reported by Henry, *Folk-Songs*, No. 115; and Belden and Hudson, *Brown*, III, No. 31 (3 short texts), Schinhan, V (tune for B). Sung by Jim in 1955; heard from his parents.

45. O Sinner Man

There are several separate songs warning of Doomsday in this way. Not many, however, have come into collections examined. The A text in Sharp and Karpeles, *English*, No. 208, is a close version, but the verses of B are "Jacob's Ladder," with the chorus taking up "Went to the rocks," etc. In their notes they say that the singer of A said it was a holiness song. Version B was heard at a Negro service. A few other references are these: Odum and Johnson, *Negro*, p. 76; *JAF*, 26(1913):153; Belden and Hudson, *Brown*, III, No. 116 (no references cited), Schinhan, V (tune); Randolph, *Ozark*, IV, No. 651 (no references).

Sung by Dave without accompaniment at the Ninth Session in 1955; heard from his parents.

46. I Got a Hope in That Rock

This and the preceding item I recall learning at an old singing school
in eastern Kentucky in the 1920's. I am surprised that they have not appeared in more collections. Some references are these: White, *American*,
p. 89; Fuson, *Ballads*, p. 204 ("Hide Thou Me"; also lines from "Jacob's
Ladder" and "Rock of Ages") ; Belden and Hudson, *Brown*, III, No. 547
(A printed; B, 1 stanza, listed; lines from "Rock of Ages"). Sung by Jim
with banjo in 1955; heard often throughout his life.

47. Will the Circle Be Unbroken?

This piece was made quite popular on the radio a few decades ago. It
does not appear in the collections examined. It was sung by Jim in 1955;
heard long ago in church, he said.

48. Praise the Lord, I Saw the Light

Another that has often been on radio programs. It does not appear in
collections. Sung by Jim in 1955; heard often in church and on radio.

49. Kingdom a-Comin'

This song, by a known author, anticipates the jubilation of the Negro
upon being freed. According to Ewen (*Great Men*, p. 42), it was composed by Henry C. Work in 1862, written in Negro dialect. It was his
most popular song up to that time; his most famous piece was "Marching
through Georgia."

The only reference available is White, *American*, p. 170 (2 texts). It
was sung by Jim in 1955; heard from his grandfather Lewis Harris, who
brought it from North Carolina.

50. Yankee Song

Another song sympathetic to the South during the War. No other reference to it is available. It was sung by Jim in 1955. He said, "Another
little old song from my grandpa Harris. He'd get around with us children
and sing us funny songs. He talked thick-mouthed as an Arsh and it'd
tickle us. And we'd get at him every time he come around to sing these
old Yankee songs and about the big ram, one thing and another. This song
he must a-knowed from the Revolution War."

51. Cumberland Gap

The Cumberland Gap, one of the great passes in history, was the main gateway of westering movement after the American Revolution. Later, during the Civil War, it became the American Thermopylae (not reflected in this satirical song). Boone's old Wilderness Trail pass changed hands between Union and Confederate forces six times in the four-year struggle.

The song, not widespread, has been reported almost entirely from the Appalachian states. Some references are these: Combs, *Folk-Songs du Midi*, p. 228 (listed as "Big Stone Gap," next song below. Editor Wilgus's note, *Brown* II, should read *Brown* III); Fuson, *Ballads*, p. 176; *JAF*, 44 (1931):241; Scarborough, *Song Catcher*, p. 65; Belden and Hudson, *Brown*, III, No. 329, and Schinhan, V (1 tune); Randolph, *Ozark*, III, No. 498 (fragment).

Sung by Jim to Dave's banjo accompaniment during the First Session in 1952. The boys were busy entertaining the large crowd and didn't remark about this piece.

52. Big Stone Gap

Big Stone Gap is a break in Big Stone Mountain, a Virginia spur of Pine Mountain Ridge with its Pound Gap. Confederate forces clambered through both gaps into Kentucky and the North. Pound Gap changed hands only three times during the Civil War.

This song, therefore, is a redaction of "Cumberland Gap," with choruses borrowed from "Sugar Babe" and "Crawdad" (see these songs below). Sung by Jim in 1954.

53. Back in the Hills

This seems to be a recent redaction of a song on a more serious subject. I have a piece in my files that begins, "Back in the hills of old Roane County." A goodnight piece, it is the lament of a prisoner, presumably on death row, longing for his freedom and his sweetheart in the hills of Roane County, Tennessee.

Except for my 2 or 3 other variants, I have not seen any evidence of this song in other collections. It was sung by Jim at the Tenth Session in 1955. He had learned it earlier in his career and heard it recently on radio.

54. My Daddy Was a Gambler

Although this version stops short of the hanging, present in others listed below, a prisoner is singing his goodnight lament. Since other texts name Missouri and Fort Smith (Arkansas), the setting of the unspecified crime seems to be in the Southwest.

All references available are these: Pound, *American*, p. 130; Belden, *Ballads*, p. 472; Randolph, *Ozark*, II, No. 146 (2 texts); Sandburg, *American*, p. 216 (off-handedly suggests that this is the original of "Prisoner's Song"). Randolph's informant told him that this was part of a long ballad about a murderer hanged at Fort Smith, Arkansas, in the 1870's; the letter mentioned in his text was a decoy sent by the sheriff in order to make the capture. Belden suggests that this piece is distantly related to "The Roving Gambler."

The present piece was sung by Jim at the Seventh Session in 1954. He had heard it in his younger days from his father.

55. Icy Mountain

A plaintive lament like this one, with its going-away mood, makes a good piece for listening or for square dancing—most of Jim's repertory was used for this typical American dance.

The only reference available is in Belden and Hudson, *Brown*, III, No. 278 (2 texts, 4 and 2 stanzas), Schinhan, V (tunes for A and another one entitled "I Am Going over the Rocky Mountains"). It was sung by Jim at the Seventh Session in 1954. He said he had heard it in his younger days.

56. Moonshiner

The sentiment of the piece is a mixture of scorn for the law, pride for his making and drinking, and envy toward women. The mix-up is the result of floating stanzas in it from "The Wagoner Boy" and "Rye Whiskey."

Its provenience is largely confined to Appalachia. Some references are these: Sharp and Karpeles, *English*, II, No. 156 (1 variant stanza); *Southern Folklore Quarterly*, 2 (1938) :160; Combs, *Folk-Songs du Midi*, p. 189; Randolph, *Ozark*, I, No. 61 (4 texts); Lomax and Lomax, *American*, p. 170 (reprinted in *Folk Songs*, No. 134); Belden and Hudson, *Brown*, III, No. 290 (2 texts, "Troubled in Mine," related), Schinhan, V (tunes for A, A1, A2).

Sung by Dave at the First Session in 1952. He said of it, "I heared that from my father—he handed that one down. It's an old song that has been played and sung ever since I was big enough to recollect anything."

57. Short Life of Trouble

A song that has been sung a great deal in Appalachia, it suits the lyrical mood of our hollows and the deadpan beat of our banjos. Surprisingly, it is scarcely represented in the collections examined. Many of the references given here have only floating stanzas of this one.

Some are these: Henry, *Folk-Songs*, No. 70 (same title, and most stanzas close); Fuson, *Ballads*, p. 127 ("Pass the Drunkard By"; chorus and a few stanzas similar); Sandburg, *American*, pp. 30, 110 (poor-boy themes).

Sung by Jim at the First Session in 1952. He said it was one of his father's favorites.

58. Chilly Wind

Since this version leaves out the first stanzas about going down the road feeling bad and about the girls jilting him, the piece is a reworking of the older song "I'm Going Down This Road Feeling Bad." Botkin, *Treasury* (p. 876), states that the words of "Chilly Wind" were composed by Woody Guthrie.

Even the older song hardly appears in the collections, although I have heard it often in Kentucky. The only other references are these: Belden and Hudson, *Brown*, III, No. 441 (1 text, entitled "I'm Going Down ..."), Schinhan, V (1 tune); Davis, *Folk-Songs*, p. 279 (title listed).

Sung by Jim with banjo at the Ninth Session in 1955; handed down by his father.

59. Darlin' Cory

The true intent of this song is confusing. The borrowing of stanzas and the multiple titles don't help the theme. It deals, of course, with marital troubles, with Cora the dominant character.

Some of the references are these: Sharp and Karpeles, *English*, II, No. 152 (2 texts, "The Gambling Man"); Fuson, *Ballads*, p. 134; Combs, *Folk-Songs du Midi*, p. 220 (listed; Wilgus cites *The Doc Watson Family*, Folkways record FA 2366); Henry, *Songs*, p. 102; Lomax and Lomax, *Best Loved*, No. 87.

Sung by Dave at our First Session in 1952; heard from his father. Jim went over the transcription and added stanza 5.

60. Greenback Dollar

Another jilted-love lyric that has been put together from many floating stanzas and even adapted as a protest song. Lomax, *Folk Songs*, No. 153, gives the traditional text in his headnote, and the protest version by Jim Garland at p. 292 (titled, "I Don't Want Your Millions, Mister"). Other references are these: Sharp and Karpeles, *English*, II, No. 167 (4 texts, "In Old Virginny," some related stanzas); Randolph, *Ozark*, IV, No. 733 (4 texts, titled "Don't Forget Me Little Darling").

Sung by Frank at the Seventh Session in 1954. He had learned it several years earlier from another young man.

61. In the Pines

The song is again a composite of lovers' quarrels and jealousy. It has been sung in Appalachia much more than it appears in the collections. The references are these: Sharp and Karpeles, *English*, II, No. 203 ("Black Girl," 1 stanza); Belden and Hudson, *Brown*, III, No. 283 (2 and a fragment), Schinhan, V (tunes for C, C1, D). Sung by Jim with banjo at the Tenth Session in 1955; heard from his father.

62. Little Birdie

A song with many titles and forms, this is a deeply felt and aching lyric. It is not "Little Sparrow," and it is not "I Wish I Was Single Again." A possible prototype might begin with the one printed by Spaeth, *Read 'Em* (p. 26, from Ohio, titled "A Married Woman's Lament," dated before 1850). A text with this early title and with several lines parallel to the present one is in Randolph, *Ozark*, III, No. 366. Other references are these: Eddy, *Ballads*, No. 70; Belden and Hudson, *Brown*, III, No. 28 (3 texts), Schinhan, V (tunes to A and C); Sharp and Karpeles, *English*, II, No. 86 (5 texts, "The Single Girl"); Combs, *Folk-Songs du Midi*, p. 226 (3 listed); Lomax, *Folk Songs*, No. 84 ("Single Girl.").

Sung by Dave at the First Session in 1952, with Jim on the banjo. Later Jim scanned the transcription and added the first stanza. They had heard it from their father and from others in the region, and I believe it was on a phonograph record in the 1920's. A variant is in my Kentucky manuscript, No. 95.

63. My Trunk Is Packed

There are no parallels to this one with a known author. The Couch boys must not have sung it often. It was sung by Dave at the First Session in 1952. He said, "I learnt that song from J. D. That's my brother Jim. He made it up when he come back from the Army [World War I]."

64. Old Reuben

The piece is sometimes called "Reuben's Train" because the subject is a railroader who drinks and gets into trouble. In the text in Lomax, *Folk Songs*, No. 302, old Reuben has had to flee to Mexico. Lomax conjectures that Negroes rose to engineers during Reconstruction but afterwards, in the South, were hounded out of the region. Other references are these: Belden and Hudson, *Brown*, III, No. 236 (A and B), Schinhan, V (tunes to A, C, D); Lomax, *Folk Song: USA*, p. 254; a variant is entered in my Kentucky manuscript, No. 94.

It was sung by Dave at our First Session in 1952. He said of it, "This is the first song I ever learnt, the first tune I ever played on the banjo—when I was about eight, nine year old and couldn't reach the neck. Dad noted it for me and I picked it." Jim went over the transcription later and added stanzas 7, 8, and 10.

65. Good-Bye, My Lover

This again seems to be a medley of floating stanzas making up a farewell lament. This one is not the song that usually starts, "See the train goin' round the bend . . ." It is more nearly related to some "Liza Jane" forms. I am unable, however, to discover closely related texts in the literature examined. It was sung by Dave at our First Session in 1952. This one, he said, was about the second song he learned on the banjo—when he was nine.

66. Bald Eagle

This short piece of jealousy and murder has some affinity with yodeling and blues material, but it is not to be found in the literature examined. The one-stanza item in Sharp and Karpeles, *English*, No. 265 (titled "Old Bald Eagle") is related in text and tune but is not close. Sung by Jim at our Tenth Session in late 1955. He didn't know when he had heard it first.

67. Paper of Pins

This is a wit-combat love song in early English and Scottish tradition, dating from about 1850, usually titled "The Keys of Heaven." It has this title in Sharp and Karpeles, *English*, No. 92 (six texts), and their notes trace it to Halliwell and to Newell, *Games*, No. 5 (3 texts). Other references are these: Belden, *Ballads*, p. 507 (3 texts); Belden and Hudson, *Brown*, III, No. 1 (13 texts, only A printed in full), Schinhan, V (tunes for A, E, H) ; Fuson, *Ballads*, pp. 82, 152; Thomas, *Devil's*, p. 160. The nonsense refrain in the present text does not occur in any others examined.

Sung by Dave at our Ninth Session in 1955. He said it was one his mother liked to sing for them. After Dave had ended, Jim reminded him of the last significant stanza.

68. Soldier, Won't You Marry Me?

Another dialogue that had its beginning in England and Scotland with more varied results. The girl is too eager in this one and is duped. It has been found in America from Canada to the Ozarks. Some references are these: *JAF*, 33(1920):158; Cox, *Folk-Songs*, No. 159; Newell, *Games*, No. 30; Sharp and Karpeles, *English*, II, No. 90 (3 texts); Belden and Hudson, *Brown*, III, No. 7 (6 texts; A and B printed), Schinhan, V (tunes for C and D) ; Fuson, *Ballads*, p. 77; Randolph, *Ozark*, I, No. 65.

Sung by Dave at our Tenth Session in 1955. He had heard his mother sing it many times. Jim tried to accompany Dave on the banjo and sometimes would call out the next garment to buy at the store.

69. Down the Road

Not so familiar as most of the mild laments in Appalachia. It is possibly a prison-window lyric. No parallels discovered. Sung by Jim at our First Session in 1952; heard from his father.

70. Cindy

A familiar sounding piece that hangs together well, although it is made up of many floating stanzas (as is No. 80 below—"Shoo Fly"). Some selected references are these: White, *American*, p. 161; Fuson, *Ballads*, p. 172; Belden and Hudson, *Brown*, III, No. 404 (6 texts), Schinhan, V (tunes for A, D, G) ; Thomas, *Singin'*, p. 23 (adapted to celebrate the Big Sandy River); Randolph, *Ozark*, III, No. 564 (2 texts). A variant is in my Kentucky manuscript, No. 128.

Sung by Jim at our Seventh Session in 1954; heard from his father.

71. Black-Eyed Susie

Belden (*Ballads*, p. xii) does not print his copy of this song, because he says it has a known author, whom he gives as Gay. I take him to mean John Gay, who would have composed the piece or its prototype in the eighteenth century. But as we have it today, it is a gay jig and square dance number. It has not been found often in American tradition: Belden and Hudson, *Brown*, III, No. 311 (2 short texts, no tune); Thomas, *Singin'*, p. 61 (tune only); Lomax and Lomax, *American*, p. 286; Randolph, *Ozark*, III, No. 568 (2 short texts).

It was sung by Jim at our Seventh Session in 1954; heard from his father.

72. Blue-Eyed Girl

This is a bright and snappy square dance piece with some borrowing of stanzas. It is not so well known in Appalachia. The only references available are these: Sharp and Karpeles, *English*, II, No. 266 (4 texts); Belden and Hudson, *Brown*, III, No. 286 ("Fly Around My Blue-Eyed Girl"), Schinhan, V (tunes for A, A1, B); their No. 310 has related lines.

Sung by Jim with banjo at our Seventh Session in 1954; heard from his father.

73. Georgia Buck

A pleasant song of Negro wit and reflection, it has some currency in Southern tradition. Some references are these: *JAF*, 24(1911):363; 44 (1931):434 (from Negro singing in South Carolina); White, *American*, p. 337; Belden and Hudson, *Brown*, III, No. 500 (3 short texts), Schinhan, V (3 tunes); Sharp and Karpeles, *English*, No. 196 ("Barbara Buck"); Randolph, *Ozark*, III, No. 523 (5 texts and fragments, "Shoot the Buffalo").

Sung by Jim at our Tenth Session in 1955. He said of it, "Here's a little old funny tune my dad used to sing around for us boys. We thought it was awful funny."

74. Idy Red

A lively banjo piece without definite stanzas, it is used for square dances and hoedowns in Appalachia and the Ozarks. It is not so widespread in distribution as "Cindy" and "Shoo Fly." With the passing of Southern country parties and dances it has faded away, but it has been reported from Virginia to Texas.

Some references are these: Belden and Hudson, *Brown*, III, No. 448 (1 short text, "I Got a Girl"), Schinhan, V (1 tune); Combs, *Folk-Songs du Midi*, p. 231 (listed); Randolph, *Ozark*, III, No. 442; Lomax and Lomax, *American*, p. 110 (from Texas); a variant in my Kentucky manuscript, No. 127.

Sung by Jim with banjo at our Tenth Session in 1955. He said, "This is an old frolic tune—'Old Idy Red.' It's a fiddle tune and a banjer tune too. I've heared it all my life."

75. I'm a-Longin' for to Go This Road

Another dance piece, it is made up of two or three songs, such as "Cindy," and has some lines and stanzas related to "Massa Had a Yaller Gal." It does not appear in the materials I have examined.

Sung by Jim with banjo in our Tenth Session in 1955. He said of it, "This is one of pap's old tunes, and it used to be popular when I was a kid."

76. Sourwood Mountain

It is one of the more common dance pieces and contrary courting songs of Appalachia and the Ozarks. It has kept its title and refrain (alternating lines), but the stanzas have accumulated and wandered in and out of it from "Liza Jane," "The Girl I Left Behind," and so on.

Selected listings are these: Gainer, *West Virginia*, No. 42; Combs, *Folk-Songs du Midi*, p. 228 (3 listed); Richardson, *American*, p. 89; Henry, *Folk-Songs*, No. 145 (3 texts); Belden and Hudson, *Brown*, III, No. 251 (11 texts and fragments), Schinhan, V (7 tunes); Sharp and Karpeles, *English*, No. 116 (3 texts); Fuson, *Ballads*, p. 170; Sandburg, *American*, pp. 125, 320; Randolph, *Ozark*, III, No. 417 (5, including fragments).

Sung by Jim to Dave's accompaniment on the banjo at our First Session in 1952. They had heard it all their lives.

77. Yonder Comes My Love

This piece has some rhythmic kinship with "Cindy" and with some lines found in "Idy Red." It seems to be a reworking of these and maybe other songs by Negro singers.

Some possible parallels are these: Belden and Hudson, *Brown*, III, No. 83 ("Yonder Comes a Georgia Girl," 2 stanzas, no refrain, no tune); Sandburg, *American*, p. 313; White, *American*, p. 335.

It was sung by Jim with banjo at our Seventh Session in 1954; heard from his father.

78. Little Brown Jug

One of the most rollicking and careless drinking songs, it has been reported in Wiltshire, England, and pretty well over America. Belden gives some data (cited and added to by Randolph) that the words were composed by J. E. Winner in 1869, and the tune by R. A. Eastburn, possibly a pseudonym for Winner. It was popular in minstrel and vaudeville shows in the 1880's and 1890's. A few notes are contributed by Spaeth, *Read 'Em*, p. 52.

Some listings are these: Belden and Hudson, *Brown*, III, No. 33 (22 in collection, text of A, fragments of B–G), Schinhan, V (tune for A); Combs, *Folk-Songs du Midi*, p. 233 (listed); White, *American*, p. 213; Belden, *Ballads*, p. 261; Randolph, *Ozark*, III, No. 408; Lomax and Lomax, *American*, p. 176.

Sung by Jim with banjo at our Seventh Session in 1954. He had heard it all his life. After seeing my transcription he added the last two stanzas.

79. Sugar Hill

Although it is in the vein of jig and dance pieces, Belden and Hudson place this song in their minstrel and Negro section. It does not have a refrain in the one other text available to me: Belden and Hudson, *Brown*, III, No. 416 (1 text, titled "My Long Tail Blue," no tune). They cite it in Damon, *Series of Old American Songs*, and say that George Washington Dixon sang it as early as 1827 and claimed authorship; they cite also *Christy's Negro Songster* (New York, 1855), p. 149, with chorus.

It was sung by Jim at our Seventh Session in 1954. He said, "Heard from my father when I was a kid."

80. Shoo Fly

The piece has been in oral tradition in Kentucky, though other collections do not have it—at least not by this title. It borrows related stanzas and a related tune from "Massa Had a Yaller Gal." The only text I have seen (not close) is in Randolph, *Ozark*, II, No. 273. In his note he assigns it to the Civil War period and gives the author as Thomas B. Bishop. He also finds it in Spaeth, *Read 'Em* (1927), p. 63, but it is not in Spaeth's paperback edition of 1959; Botkin, *American Play-Party*, p. 304 (as a game).

Sung by Jim with banjo at our Tenth Session in 1955. He said, "This is the song 'Shoo Fly.' I heared pap sing it and it used to be a popular song. About ever'body that'd come around would want him to play the 'Shoo Fly.'"

81. Cripple Creek

It is usually surmised that the piece either originated or was made famous during the gold rush days at Cripple Creek, Colorado. Belden and Hudson say that Colorado is named in a Nebraska text but that Perrow cites as a possible place the mining district of Cripple Creek in Wythe County, Virginia. At any rate, most texts, featuring a rough, muddy, rocky creek, have been reported in Appalachia, the South, and the Midwest.

Selected references are these: Belden and Hudson, *Brown*, III, No. 299 (2 short texts), Schinhan, V (tunes for B, C); Sharp and Karpeles, *English*, II, No. 241 (2 short texts); Shearin and Combs, *Syllabus*, p. 39; *JAF*, 3(1890):48; 28(1915):180, 181; Lomax, *Folk Songs*, No. 118.

Sung by Jim with banjo at our Tenth Session in 1955. He said, "This is another banjer song. We used to run sets by it—old square dance sets."

82. Old Corn Whiskey

This hoedown and square dance piece is a medley of lines and stanzas, and the title is usually "Lulu." It seems to be an older Southern dance number, with adaptations in Appalachia and the West.

Selected references are these: White, *American*, p. 304; Belden and Hudson, *Brown*, III, No. 183, Schinhan, V (tune); *JAF*, 22(1909):248; 26(1913):127; Lomax, *Folk Songs*, No. 178 (from *Cowboy Songs*, p. 263; a line of knife play with a Bowie gives it the Western flavor).

Sung by Dave at our First Session in 1952; heard from his father.

83. Old Coon Dog

This lively piece has so many floating stanzas and different titles that I have been unable to find a close parallel. Some listings are these: Sharp and Karpeles, *English*, No. 225 (3 short texts, titled "The Squirrel"); Belden and Hudson, *Brown*, III, No. 97 (5 texts, titled "Uncle Joe Cut off His Big Toe," no tune), III, No. 161 (6 texts, titled "Possum Up a Simmon Tree"), Schinhan, V (tunes to B, E, G); Randolph, *Ozark*, II, No. 280.

Sung by Jim without banjo at our Tenth Session in 1955. He said, "This here is an old banjer tune. Pap used to play and sing about the old coon dog and horse."

84. Mule Skinner Blues

A piece with the same title is in Lomax, *Folk Songs*, No. 152, with this headnote: "*Blue Yodel 8,* Jimmy Rodgers. Copyright Southern Music Co., used by permission. An excellent recording by the Monroe Brothers is the source of this version." The tunes of the two versions are related, except that the present text has no yodel. Stanzas 1 and 2 are also similar, but the others vary considerably.

Sung by Jim with accompaniment by Frank on the guitar at our Seventh Session in 1954. Jim broke a string on his banjo and with reluctance attempted the high-pitched tune. He didn't say where he had learned it.

85. Chisholm Trail

An old Western cattle-trail song reported early by John Lomax, *Cowboy,* p. 58. It is reprinted in Lomax and Lomax, *American,* p. 376, 39 stanzas. Their note says, "There remain hundreds of unprintable stanzas." A few other references are these: Belden and Hudson, *Brown,* III, No. 217 (1 text of 29 stanzas, no tune); Pound, *American,* p. 167; Sandburg, *American,* p. 266.

It was sung by Jim at our Tenth Session in 1955; heard recently.

86. Groundhog

This humorous hunting song is found in all states touching southern Appalachia and apparently nowhere else except in the Ozarks, where southern mountain people migrated in the westering period of the early nineteenth century. There is no definite clue as to its age, except a note by Lomax (*Folk Songs,* p. 251): "The song has a swift pace and a ferocity which seems inappropriate to the chase of a small and innocent marmot like the groundhog or woodchuck." And he quotes a stanza from David Crockett's time about catching a bear because "They loved bar-meat cooked and fried."

Selected notes are these: Belden and Hudson, *Brown,* III, No. 221 (3 texts), Schinhan, V (tunes to B, B1, C, D, E); Cox, *Folk-Songs,* No. 176; Gainer, *West Virginia,* No. 41; Henry, *Songs,* p. 5; Shearin and Combs, *Syllabus,* p. 38; Wyman and Brockway, *Lonesome,* p. 30; Combs, *Folk-Songs du Midi,* p. 220 (2 texts combined). A variant is entered in my Kentucky manuscript, No. 135.

Sung by Dave to Jim's banjo accompaniment at our First Session in 1952. They had learned it from their father.

87. Arkansas Traveler

This is one of the older forms of the piece, with the wit-combat interspersed with music, but, instead of playing the first strain of the famous fiddle tune, the Couches sang an apt refrain. Although it goes back to 1840 and is still popular, it has not been reported extensively except in Appalachia and the Southwest.

Some references are these: Cox, *Folk-Songs*, No. 179 (longest set of exchanges available; he attributes it to Mose Case in 1864); Belden and Hudson, *Brown*, III, No. 330 (only one exchange, no tune); Combs, *Folk-Songs du Midi*, p. 231 (2 listed); Lomax and Lomax, *American*, p. 267; Randolph, *Ozark*, III, No. 346 (careful notes and a full text). Randolph says, "Both words and music are usually credited to Colonel Sandford C. Faulkner, a well-known Arkansas character who died near Little Rock in 1875." He further states that "Faulkner was on a political mission in the wilds of Pope County, Arkansas, in 1840, when he met the mountain fiddler who figures in the song." Faulkner seems to have entertained crowds all over the South by performing the piece, until he became known as the Arkansas Traveler.

The present version was performed by Jim with banjo at our Final Session in 1955. It was one of his father's favorites. Jim spoke the words, of course, and between each exchange he frailed lustily on the strings and sang the refrain.

88. Old Dan Tucker

A popular minstrel number over 125 years old, with a known author, Dan D. Emmett. The author has been treated recently by David Ewen, *Great Men*, p. 18. He says, "The official public debut of the Virginia Minstrels took place at the Bowry Amphitheatre on February 6, 1843, as part of a circus show. . . . The program that evening not only marked the official debut of the Virginia Minstrels, but also of Dan Emmett as a song composer, for it presented two Dan Emmett all-time favorites, 'De Boatman's Dance' and 'Old Dan Tucker.' "

It is familiar to both black and white singers, is in many collections, and has accumulated scores of verses. Some references are these: White, *American*, p. 446; Belden and Hudson, *Brown*, III, No. 82 (30-odd items in collection, stanzas from A to F), Schinhan, V (tune for B); Gainer, *West Virginia*, No. 46; Davis, *Folk-Songs*, p. 154 (listed); Randolph, *Ozark*, III, No. 346 (5 texts); *JAF*, 24(1911):309; 25(1912):272; 27(1914): 131; 28(1915):284; 32(1919):488; 33(1920):116; 40(1927):23, 96; 54(1941):164.

It was sung by Dave with Jim on the banjo at our First Session in 1952. It was often sung by their father and others.

89. Cold Frosty Morning

A not-so-well-known black and perhaps minstrel song with heavy dialect, the piece has appeared in print in only five or six collections. References are as follows: White, *American*, p. 382; Belden and Hudson, *Brown*, III, No. 474 (2 texts), Schinhan, V (tune for B); Randolph, *Ozark*, II, No. 283 (2 texts). He cites a text by Herbert Halpert from Meridian, Miss., in 1939 (in *Check-List . . . Archive of American Folk Song*, 1942, p. 59).

Sung by Jim with banjo at our Tenth Session in 1955. He said, "This is a song sung about the Negroes. We thought it was so funny, we'd have Pap to sing it over and over and over."

90. Did You Ever See the Devil, Uncle Joe?

Another piece appropriate for Negro minstrels, but I am unable to find any parallels, unless a short version of "Shortenin' Bread" in White, *American*, p. 193, is a stanza. It was sung by Jim with banjo at our Seventh Session in 1954; heard from his father.

91. Do Johnny Booger

This has obviously been a popular Negro minstrel piece because of its many titles and reworkings. Some references are these: White, *American*, p. 168; Sharp and Karpeles, *English*, II, No. 248 ("Run, Nigger, Run," 1 stanza, from Kentucky); Scarborough, *On the Trail*, p. 100; Belden and Hudson, *Brown*, III, No. 457 (7 texts in collection, A, B, C, D printed), Schinhan, V (tune for F); Randolph, *Ozark*, II, No. 268 (1 text and a fragment, titled "Mister Booger"). Randolph states that "The Mister Booger" refrain comes from the chorus of an antebellum Negro reel known as "Johnny Booker."

Sung by Dave to Jim's banjo accompaniment at our Tenth Session in 1955. They had learned it from their father.

92. Cock Robin

This is one of the oldest nursery rhymes in England. Exhaustive notes are given by Opie and Opie, *Oxford*, No. 110. The Opies say it originated with the intrigues attending the downfall of Robert Walpole's ministry

(1742), because the date of the rhyme's known recording is around 1744. But they further say that it has words and terms that could push it back to the fourteenth century. Furthermore, Lomax in his note to a text (*Folk Songs*, p. 168) says: "The roots of Cock Robin probably go back to Nordic myths about the ritual murder and the bringing of fire and the spring; for the robin or the wren was often sacrificed in European renewal-of-the-year ceremonies."

But the song has not often been collected in American tradition—only two references available to me: Sharp and Karpeles, *English*, II, No. 213 (4 texts); and Fuson, *Ballads*, p. 56.

Before closing these notes I should like to pay tribute to Mary Harris Couch, the mother of this large family, for passing on her large store of children's songs and nursery rhymes. With so many songs and stories for all occasions, apparently so beautifully and memorably passed on, she is as near to a Mother Goose as one may find in real life. This version was sung by Dave without accompaniment at our Tenth Session in 1955. He said, "This here's a song my mother used to sing to us children about little Cock Robin."

93. Tree in the Mountains

This piece combines the nursery song with the cumulative tale to make a rather enduring folksong. Sharp and Karpeles (*English*, II, No. 206, 3 texts) list about 10 references for the song in Britain. Other selected references are these: *JAF*, 8(1895):87; Newell, *Games*, p. 111; Belden and Hudson, *Brown*, III, No. 133 (1 text), Schinhan, V (tune); Fuson, *Ballads*, p. 87; Scarborough, *Song Catcher*, p. 359; Henry, *Folk-Songs*, No. 148; Randolph, *Ozark*, III, No. 459; Gardner and Chickering, *Ballads*, No. 200.

Sung by Dave with banjo at our First Session in 1952. He had heard it from his mother.

94. The Old Grey Mare

A song of domestic animal trouble, this one is not well known in tradition, with only a few reports and those from the South. Some references are these: Belden and Hudson, *Brown*, III, No. 175 (1 text), Schinhan, V (tune); Sharp and Karpeles, *English*, II, No. 223 (3 texts); *JAF*, 26(1913):123.

Sung by Dave at our First Session in 1952; heard from both his father and his mother.

95. The Fox and the Goose

This nursery song of the fox bringing home the goose is a British import. It is quite well distributed in England and maybe more so in America, especially in the South and Midwest.

Selected references are these: Opie and Opie, *Oxford*, No. 171 (from *G G's Garland*, 1810); Cox, *Folk-Songs*, No. 163; Sharp and Karpeles, *English*, II, No. 226 (2 texts, "The Old Black Duck"); White, *American*, p. 177; Belden and Hudson, *Brown*, III, No. 129 (5 texts, one listed), Schinhan, V (tune to A); Brewster, *Ballads*, No. 77; Fuson, *Ballads*, p. 181; Stout, *Iowa*, p. 43; Eddy, *Ballads*, No. 91; Randolph, *Ozark*, I, No. 103 (4 texts).

Sung by Dave with banjo at our First Session in 1952; heard from his mother.

96. The Fox Chase

This narrative of an exciting fox hunt, with a banjo furnishing the mood and the rhythm, is an important instance of the cante-fable form. I have heard versions orally but cannot locate any in collections. Buell Kazee recorded a form of it for Brunswick in the late 1920's—and taped it for me about ten years ago.

It was spoken and sung with banjo by Jim at our Tenth Session in 1955. He played a rhythmic background on the banjo to suit the chase, slow quarter notes at first, stepping up until he broke into sixteenths, and broad frailing with the yodeling and yelling. He said of it, "This is the old fox chase Paw used to sing around for us."

97. Froggy Went a-Courtin'

This fabulous combination of nursery rhyme, animal jingle, and perhaps satire is of ancient British origin, found through the Isles, Europe, and North America. Comprehensive notes have been compiled by Opie and Opie, *Oxford*, No. 175. They trace it to its first entry in the Stationer's Register in 1580. As for the song itself, they further report: "The earliest extant text is in Ravenscroft's *Melismata* (1611) where the tune 'The Marriage of the Frogge and the Mouse' is made up of 13 verses, beginning:

It was the Frogge in the well,
Humble-dum, humble-dum.

> And the merrie Mouse in the Mill
> Tweedle, tweedle, twino."

They call attention to the fact that "The Frogge's Courtship" and the nursery rhyme "The Frogge in the Well" were once one song. Sharp and Karpeles, *English*, II, give the songs separate numbers (No. 220 for "A Frog He Went A-Courting," 11 texts; and No. 221 for "The Frog in the Well," 4 texts), but they annotate them together.

A history of the song has been made by Kittredge, "Notes," *JAF* 35 (1922):394. Other selected references are these: Cox, *Folk-Songs*, No. 162 (4 texts, 4 fragments); Belden and Hudson, *Brown*, III, No. 120 (27 texts, several not printed; one titled "Kitchie Ki-Mi-O" was adapted to blackface minstrelsy a hundred years ago), Schinhan, V (tunes for 13 pieces, some not in III, making 37 items in the *Brown* collection); Wyman and Brockway, *Lonesome*, p. 22; Thomas, *Devil's*, p. 154; Combs, *Folk-Songs du Midi*, p. 218 (8 listed); Belden, *Ballads*, p. 494 (7 texts).

Sung by Jim with banjo at our Seventh Session in 1954. He had often heard his father sing it.

98. Funniest Is the Frog
(Lynchburg Town)

Folk art is mature and wise and generous when it can turn the peculiarities of the frog into humor and fun. The last two stanzas suggest an antebellum minstrel piece, usually called "Lynchburg Town." The music is actually the tune of "Lynchburg Town," starting with the refrain.

Some references are these: White, *American*, p. 178; Belden and Hudson, *Brown*, III, No. 415 (9 texts, not all printed), Schinhan, V (tunes for A, B, E, J); *JAF*, 22(1909):249; Lomax, *Folk Songs*, No. 270.

Sung by Jim with banjo during our Tenth Session in 1955. He said, "Now I'll give you 'Funniest Is the Frog,' my father's song. He used to play and sing it."

99. The Little Piggee

A nursery rhyme and children's song from Britain, it has many variations in titles. Selected references are these: Sharp and Karpeles, *English*, II, No. 235 (2 texts); Belden and Hudson, *Brown*, III, No. 130 (3 texts, C not printed), Schinhan, V (tune for B); Cox, *Folk-Songs*, No. 175 (2 texts, 2 titles: "Old Sam Fanny," and "Old Joe Finnley"); Ritchie, *Singing*, p. 227; Eddy, *Ballads*, No. 68.

Sung by Dave without banjo at our First Session in 1952. He had often heard it from his mother and occasionally from his father.

100. The Cat Played Fiddie on My Fee

Another nursery rhyme and children's song coming from the British Isles, often called "The Farmyard" or "The Barnyard Song." It is of course related to "Old MacDonald." Sharp and Karpeles, *English*, II, No. 218, cite it in Halliwell, *Nursery Rhymes*, p. 332, and in Chambers, *Popular Rhymes*, p. 190.

In America some selected references are these: Newell, *Games*, p. 115; Davis, *Folk-Songs*, p. 187 (listed); Richardson, *American*, p. 77; Belden and Hudson, *Brown*, III, No. 124 (6 texts, not all printed), Schinhan, V (tunes for B, C, F); Wyman and Brockway, *Lonesome*, p. 6; Scarborough, *On the Trail*, p. 196; Randolph, *Ozark*, III, No. 352 (4 texts, titled "I Bought Me a Rooster").

Sung by Dave without banjo at our First Session in 1952. He had heard his mother sing it a great many times.

3. Notes to the Folktales and Riddles

Notes continue to be compiled for folktale collections, and studies continue to be made of individual tales or clusters of related tales. The purposes of these labors are to chart the adventures of tales over the world, to determine their origins, routes of travel, and popularity, and to analyze their types. These labors also lighten the work of succeeding compilers and students. The most important of such indexes and compilations for annotating the present collection are as follows.

Antti Aarne and Stith Thompson's *Types of the Folktale*, second revision, is used for classifying each tale and for tracing its distribution over Europe, Asia, Africa, Spanish America, and Franco-American Canada and Louisiana. Stith Thompson's *The Folktale* traces folktale types and clusters "from Ireland to India." His *Motif-Index of Folk-Literature* traces particles and motifs of traditional material over most of the world, but especially over the regions covered by the *Types* index. The *Motif-Index* covers the material of Scotland, England, and Ireland, while two other compilations list Irish material in detail: Séan Ó Súilleabháin's *A Handbook of Irish Folklore* and R. Th. Christiansen and Ó Súilleabháin's *The Types of the Irish Folktale*. A comparative index of English and American material (important for the American student) is Ernest W. Baughman's *Type and Motif-Index of the Folktales of England and North America*. For Latin America I use T. L. Hansen's *The Types of the Folktale in Cuba, Puerto Rico, the Dominican Republic, and Spanish South America*.

Most collections in America have notes and parallel listings, compiled by the authors or by other scholars. Herbert Halpert has garnered notes in an article, "Folktales in Children's Books: Some Notes and Reviews," for Chase's *Jack Tales*, and for Vance Randolph's Ozarks series, *Who Blowed Up the Churchhouse, The Devil's Pretty Daughter, The Talking Turtle*. Baughman has done so for Randolph's *Sticks in The Knapsack*. Richard M. Dorson has prepared valuable notes for his collections: *Bloodstoppers, Negro Tales, Jonathan Draws the Long Bow*, etc. I have continued the accumulation in my *South from Hell-for-Sartin* and in my most recent volume *Old Greasybeard: Tales from the Cumberland Gap*. The *Journal of American Folklore* has been indexed by Tristram P. Coffin: *An Analytical Index to the Journal of American Folklore*. These and other collections will be referred to by half-title in the following notes.

101. Jack and the Beanstalk

Type 328, The Boy Steals the Giant's Treasure.

There are two versions of this tale: one to three boys or girls steal from the giant, and one boy climbs a beanstalk for the same purpose. Also "Jack the Giant-Killer" is included under the type number, although it depicts Jack on a heroic giant-killing expedition. Under Type 328, therefore, the tale has been most often reported in Finland 54, Norway 24, and Ireland 89. For England and North America Baughman gives the tale two forms: 328A, Jack the Giant-Killer, and 328B, Jack and the Beanstalk. Under the latter number he lists variants of the tale in England, New England, Pennsylvania, Virginia, North Carolina, Tennessee, Missouri, and Australia.

From compilations and collections later than Thompson's revision of *Types* (1961) and Baughman's *England and North America* (1964), or from areas outside Baughman's coverage, I can add the following: For all forms of Type 328 the Irish *Types* Index (1963) lists 114; Coffin finds 6 in *JAF*, beginning in 1891. In my *Old Greasybeard* (1969) I have compiled notes for 4 tales under 328: Nos. 17, 18 ("Jack and the Beanstalk"), 19, and 32.

Remarks: Jim Couch later told this story, with only one trip up the beanstalk; Dave's version had the usual three trips up. Both of these men told the tale with richer idiom and surer grasp than did the boy Bob Mc-Daniel (age 12). But Bob was the first to relate it (and open my eyes to the Couch treasure of lore) and the only one to give the interesting fourth trip up for the banjo. Likely he, or some other mountain boy, added this motif—most natural thing to do in the mountains.

102. The Two Gals

Type 480, The Spinning-Women by the Spring.

Study: Warren E. Roberts, *The Tale of the Kind and the Unkind Girls* . . . ; Th. Christiansen, "A Norwegian Fairytale in Ireland?" *Béaloideas*, 2 (1929) : 235ff.

The listings under the type number reveal this to be a very popular tale over Europe. Some listings are the following: Finnish 108, Estonian 130, Swedish 129, German 78, Russian 53. Irish *Types* lists 106. For England Baughman lists 7, and for North America the following states: Massachusetts, New York 2, Virginia, North Carolina 2, Texas, Louisiana, Kentucky 6, and California. Coffin finds two in *JAF* 8(1895):143, and 38 (1925):368.

Additions: Parsons, *Bahamas*, No. 14 (8 variants); Leonard Roberts, *Bought Dog*, No. 7 (from *Mountain Life and Work*, 28, no. 4, pp. 24–28) ; *Old Greasybeard*, Nos. 21 and 22.

Remarks: The version printed in *Bought Dog*, with the "long leather bag" verses, is a very close variant of this one. It was told by Bob's grandmother. Warren Roberts in his study brackets these under one distinctively English form and concludes that the form probably originated in Denmark. Another English form of this tale, "The Three Heads in the Well," was told by Dave (No. 30 below). Warren Roberts thinks that this form probably came to England from France. This story was told by Bob McDaniel in 1951 from the telling of Mandy or Jim Couch.

103. Johnny Conscience

Type 326, The Youth Who Wanted to Learn What Fear Is.

This tale of haunted houses and gallows trees takes two directions and serves two purposes. In one form the boy goes through frightful adventures, only to learn what fear is or how to shiver and shake when someone pours ice water or a bucket of fish on him in bed (326). In the other a ghost is laid by revealing its murderer and properly dividing its hidden treasure (326A*). Both forms are represented in the literature examined. Found throughout the world, some listings under the type numbers are these: Finnish 47, Lithuanian 37, Danish 124, French 55, German 134, Polish 53, Franco-American 38, Scottish 8; Spanish-American 10, West Indies Negro 6. The Irish *Types* has 616 for Type 326 and 537 for 326A*. For England and Scotland Baughman lists 3. For North America he lists stories from the following states: New York, North Carolina 2,

Kentucky (Roberts, *South*, 4—from a total of 13 in my dissertation *Eastern Kentucky*), Arkansas, and Indiana. Coffin lists 7 in *JAF*, beginning in 1911.

I can add Dorson, *Negro Tales*, p. 128; *Midwest Folklore*, 6 (Spring 1956) :13–14; *Old Greasybeard*, Nos. 7 (motifs only) and 16 (cumulative notes); No. 59 below.

Remarks: I have arranged the stories in this collection in the order in which I collected them from the Couches over a period of four years. I found Joe Couch (teller of No. 159) in Appalachia, Virginia, in the last-but-one session with them. With now some 25 versions of this Type 326 collected in eastern Kentucky, I am at a loss to explain why it has rarely been reported outside Appalachia and the Ozarks. This variant was told by Jim in 1951.

104. Little Black Hunchety Hunch

Types: 301A, Quest for a Vanished Princess; Type 1535, The Rich and the Poor Peasant, III, Magic Cow-Hide, and V, The Fatal Deception.

The present story is a composite of two rather long and complex types, made more difficult to study because Type 301 has three forms. Type 301 begins with the hero as the son of a bear or the result of other supernatural birth and growth (I), and ends with a crucial recognition, as by a token of identity (VI). Type 301B begins with the strong man and companions setting out on adventures (I) and, like 301A, has no recognition denouement.

This is one of the many hero stories in folk tradition. Its strong hero has so many elemental adventures with natural and animal antagonists that the tale is sometimes called "The Bear's Son," and some students find parallels with *Beowulf*. But the story probably originated in India, and from the Middle East it has spread over most of the world. Some lists may be given for 301A as follows: Finnish 85, Lithuanian 61, German 105, Hungarian 55, Greek 48, Turkish 38, Scotland 5, England 1. Irish *Types* lists 193. For all forms Coffin lists 32 in *JAF*, beginning in 1893.

For North America Baughman lists these states: Virginia, North Carolina, Texas Border (Spanish) 2, Missouri (Beowulf), Kentucky (Roberts, *South* 1, M. Campbell, *Tales* 2), and New Mexico (Spanish). I add *Old Greasybeard*, No. 11 (notes pp. 182–183 add one Scottish from MacKay, *More West Highland Tales II*, No. 62). For Hansen, *Types*, Puerto Rico, Thompson lists 1, but it should be 7.

Type 1535 is best known by (and has been aided in transmission by) Andersen's "Big Claus and Little Claus." But the present fragmentary version suggests oral transmission by the modified part III from a magic cow-hide to a fortune-telling crow. It has had wide distribution over the world, as some representative listings under the type number reveal: Finnish 172, Lithuanian 106, Estonian 57, French 92, Flemish 13, German 89, Serbo-croatian 25, India 49, Puerto Rico 22, West Indies (Negro) 20. Irish *Types* lists 495. Thompson lists 3 for Scotland; Baughman lists 1 for Scotland and 1 for England. Coffin lists 12 in *JAF*, beginning in 1891.

For North America Baughman lists the following states: Massachusetts, New York, North Carolina 3, Louisiana 2, Texas (Spanish) 2, Missouri, Kentucky (Roberts, *South* 2), California, Mexico (Jalisco). I add Parsons, *Bahamas*, No. 38 (3), Beckwith, *Jamaica*, No. 23 (part V). Note that part Va, Trickster escapes from sack, when it appears alone is given the separate Type 1737, The Parson in the Sack to Heaven. I also add *Old Greasybeard*, No. 40.

Remarks: Jim told this story without a pause between types. But when one looks at a types index, such as the Irish, one realizes that borrowing and combining among the folk is the rule. In telling Irishman jokes Jim actually said, "I never did like to tell just one little old short joke."

105. The Old Woman and Her Pig

Type 2030, The Old Woman and her Pig.

This Formula tale (subtype Cumulative) has 9 other forms (A–J) and 5 others of rarer distribution (2030A*–E*). It has been rather thinly re-ported over Europe, Britain, and America, but with good showing in Afri-ca, the West Indies, and Spanish America. Some listings are these: Sweden 22, Hungarian 17, Scottish 8, West Indies (Negro) 7. The Irish *Types*, under the number and related forms, lists 165. Coffin lists 8 and 2 related forms in *JAF*, beginning in 1914. Baughman has 2 for Scotland and 3 for England. For North America he has listed Rhode Island 3, Texas (1 and 2 mentioned in ms.), Missouri, and Kentucky (M. Campbell, *Tales*, pp. 202–205). I can add Parsons, *Bahamas*, No. 61, and Fauset, *Nova Scotia*, No. 15 (3 variants).

Remarks: Although the animal and cumulative tales are rare in Anglo-American tradition, they are still extant (I have 12 in *Old Greasybeard* and 4 in this collection). The still rarer old cante-fable form of the Middle Ages also lingers on in Appalachia (see "Arkansas Traveler" and "The Fox Chase" below). During my earlier visits with Jim and his brothers they mentioned with some pride and remembrance how their mother would sing a tale. Finally Jim recorded this one, singing the first phrase with some speed, but slowing on the second and holding the last word:

I can't get to my little boy tonight,
It's almost dark but the moon shines.

The singing is repeated after each cumulation. I have not seen another singing form of Type 2030 in the literature examined.

106. Jack and the Bull Strap

Type 511A, The Little Red Ox; cf. 511, One-Eye, Two-Eyes, Three-Eyes.

This tale was so submerged in more dominant types, such as 510, Cinderella, 511 and 530, Princess on the Glass Mountain, that it was not given a type number by Aarne and Thompson in the 1910 and 1928 editions of *Types*. Yet the story was a distinct type in Norse, English, and Irish stories. In the Dasent, *Norse*, No. 50, a girl rides away on a bull and by the end has some Cinderella episodes. In Jacobs, *More English*, No. 48, a girl likewise runs away on a magic bull, and succeeds with episodes from Types 530 and 425A. In a letter to me while I was studying material for *South*, Sean O'Sullivan reported some 50 versions of the story in the Irish archives. It continues to appear and is in need of a study for clarification.

Some listings under the number are these: Icelandic 9, Hungarian 23, India 8, Franco-American 18. Irish *Types* gives these numbers: 511 (148), 510A (302), 510B (46). Nothing in Thompson or Baughman for Scotland or England. In *South*, No. 20, I cite Jacobs, *More English*, Nos. 48 and 79. Coffin lists 510 (20) and 511 (2) in *JAF*. For North America Baughman lists these states: Virginia, Arkansas, and Kentucky (Roberts, *South*, No. 20); in the notes to No. 20, pp. 230–231, I list 5; also Parsons, *Bahamas*, No. 17, and Faust, *Nova Scotia*, pp. 41–43.

Remarks: The magic strap and the cornucopia are interesting marvelous motifs in expediting this story—and others. But the rescue of the princess (from drowning and from fire) with horses appears in other types: although too vague to assign a number here, a similar exploit occurs in Type 300, the Dragon-Slayer, in Type 530, and in others. Told by Jim in 1951.

107. The One-Eyed Giant

Types: 1137, The Ogre Blinded; 1881, The Man Carried Through the Air by Geese; 1889C, Fruit Tree (Oak) Grows from Head of Deer (back of horse) ; 1890A, Shot Splits Tree Limb; 1890D, Ramrod Shot plus series of lucky accidents; 1895, A Man Wading in Water Catches Many Fish in His Boots (Shirttail); 1900, How the Man Came out of a Tree Stump.

The tall tale may once have been a single exaggeration or lie told by the raconteur, but as early as Munchausen (or mankind) they have been strung together and told by the local windy. In America they cycle around our frontiersmen, such as Paul Bunyan, Mike Fink, David Crockett, Daniel Boone. I shall give only minimum type listings to suggest their breadth of distribution.

For 1137 are the following under the type number: Finnish 25, Lappish 17, French 11, Greek 9. Irish *Types* gives 113. None given by Thompson or Baughman for Scotland. I list 5: Campbell, *West Highlands*, Nos. 5 (reprinted by Hartland, *Tales*, and by Jacobs, *Celtic*, No. 5), 6, 7 (2 others summarized), and 80 (notes report a vast number of others and adds, "as the Gaelic versions invariably introduce a woman, I do not believe that the stories come from Homer"); D. MacInnes, *Folk and Hero Tales*, No. 7. Baughman reports 3 for England, none for North America. I add Roberts, *Greasybeard*, No. 31 (full notes).

For 1881 a few listings are Lithuanian 5, Flemish 2, German 3, Russian 5, Japanese. Irish *Types* has 37. None for England or Scotland. Coffin has 2 for *JAF*. For North America Baughman has about 15: Alberta (French), U.S., New England, New York, North Carolina 2, Tennessee, Texas 3, Kentucky (Roberts, *South*), Indiana 2, Missouri, Illinois. I add Chase, *Grandfather*, No. 20, Roberts, *Old Greasybeard*, No. 44.

For 1889C, under the number are German, India, Spanish-American Argentina 2. Irish *Types* lists 17. None for England or Scotland. For North America Baughman has Alberta, Ontario, U.S., New York (Indian) 1 and other 3, Pennsylvania 2, Virginia, North Carolina, Tennessee, Missouri, Kentucky (Roberts, *South*, No. 69a), Indiana 2, Wisconsin, Michigan 2. I add Roberts, *Old Greasybeard*, No. 45 (notes list 2 others: Kentucky, MacKay, *Tall Tales*; and New Jersey, Halpert, "Folktales and Legends," p. 356).

For 1890A, under the number, Franco-American 1. None for England or Scotland. Irish *Types* for 1890 as a whole lists 24. Coffin lists none in *JAF*. For North America Baughman lists Alberta, U.S., New York 4, South, North Carolina, Mississippi, Louisiana (Spanish), Texas 2, Arkansas 2, Missouri 3, Indiana 2, Ohio, Illinois, Wisconsin, West. I add Roberts, *Old Greasybeard*, No. 43.

For 1890D, none under the number for Europe, England, or Scotland.

None in *JAF*. For North America Baughman lists New York, Pennsylvania, Virginia, North Carolina, Tennessee, Mississippi, Texas, Missouri 2, Indiana 3.

For 1895 Thompson lists Finnish 6, Flemish 3, German 2, Russian 1. None for England or Scotland. None in Irish *Types* nor in *JAF*. For North America Baughman lists U.S., Vermont, New Jersey 2, Michigan. I add Chase, *Grandfather*, No. 20, and *Old Greasybeard*, No. 43.

For 1900, Thompson lists Estonian 3, Slovenian, Russian 18. None for England, Ireland, Scotland. Coffin lists 3 in *JAF*. For North America Baughman lists U.S., New York, North Carolina 2, Missouri 2, Kentucky (Roberts, *South* 2), Indiana, Illinois, Wisconsin, New Mexico. I add Chase, *Grandfather*, No. 20, and *Old Greasybeard*, No. 44. See version by Joe Couch, No. 161. This text by Jim was printed in *Mountain Life and Work*, 30 (Winter, 1954):14–17, and reprinted in Roberts, *Bought Dog*, No. 5. Dave Couch told a third version of the tale that has not been printed yet.

Remarks: Within a period of three years I was fortunate enough to collect four variants of Type 1137, the first and only ones found (to my knowledge) in the New World. After studying the Scottish collecting master J. F. Campbell and learning of his many finds in tradition, including one-eyed giants with wives, children, and so on, I felt that these had a chance of being in age-old tradition. But rereading the *Arabian Nights* gave me second thoughts. Regarding Campbell's note about wives, Sir Richard Burton remarks dryly, "We cannot accept Mistress Polyphemus" (VI, 27n). These Couch episodes of Polyphemus could have entered oral telling in England after the Galland French translation of 1704–1717. Told by Jim in 1951.

108. Polly, Nancy, and Muncimeg

Types: 327, The Children and the Ogre; 328, The Boy Steals the Giant's Treasure, I and II.

Many of these stories are proving hard to classify, even for the indexers, because of the number of children involved. In them one to three girls, a girl and a boy ("Hansel and Gretel" 327A, or Tom Thumb 327B), or one to three boys (usually under 328) set out to seek their fortunes and unwittingly stay all night with a giant. They escape to their homes by magic or other means, or to a king's house, where one or all three are sent back to retrieve valuable objects from the giant. This story (if I am not deceived) is a successful combination of the two types given.

Under Type 327 are selected listings: Finnish 137, Swedish 21, French 82, Serbocroatian 15, Franco-American 57, West Indies (Negro) 37. None for Scotland or England. Irish *Types* gives 116. Baughman (under 327B) gives one each for Ireland and Aberdeen.

For North America, Coffin lists 17 in *JAF*, beginning in 1891. Baughman lists these states: Indiana (327), and under 327B Virginia and South Carolina, Louisiana (Negro), Kentucky (Roberts, *South* 2), Tennessee (327C). I add Fauset, *Nova Scotia*, No. 18; Hansen, *Types*, 327(2), 327A(25), 327B(3), and 4 others.

Notes for Type 328 are given at 101 above.

Remarks: In *Old Greasybeard*, No. 17, three boys set out to seek their fortunes and have somewhat the same adventures with a giant and his old woman. Although I placed it under 328, it is a combination of the two types. Such clusters as these are due analyses for clarification. Told by Jim in 1952.

109. Daub It with Clay

Type 425A, The Monster (Animal) as Bridegroom (Cupid and Psyche).

A longer variant of the story is annotated at No. 158 below. Told by Jim in 1952.

110. Corpse in Pieces

Type 326, The Youth Who Went Forth to Learn What Fear Is. The full story is annotated at No. 103 above.

Motif H1411.1, Fear test: staying in haunted house where corpse drops piecemeal down chimney. No. 103 above does not contain this motif, but a longer tale has it (No. 159 below). Told by Jim in 1952.

111. The Devil's Big Toe

Type 366, The Man from the Gallows.

Although this is only a portion of the story used to frighten children, it is quite common in Appalachia and elsewhere. In the main story a man steals the heart or clothing of a man on the gallows and gives it to his wife. The ghost comes to claim its property and carries off the man.

Under the number are these listings: Danish 39, French 23, Dutch 14, German 33, Italian 5, Polish 9. None for Scotland or England. None in Irish *Types*. Baughman has 4 for England.

For North America, Coffin lists 3 in *JAF*, first in 1934. Baughman lists the following states: New York, New Jersey, West Virginia, North Carolina 2, Georgia, Texas, Arkansas, Missouri, Kentucky (Roberts, *South* 2, M. Campbell, *Tales*), California. I add a study by Halpert, *Hoosier Folklore Bulletin*, 1 (1942):11, and 2 (1942):69; Roberts, *Old Greasybeard*, Nos. 4 and 5 ("Tailipoe"). See also No. 133 below.

Remarks: Another version of the story titled "The Golden Arm" (*South*, No. 12a) was one of Mark Twain's chillers, printed in *How to Tell a Story and Other Essays*, pp. 7–15. This variant was told by Jim in 1952.

112. Animals and Robbers

Type 130, The Animals in Night Quarters.

The tale has three forms, depending on the nature of the flight and the denouement. Type 130C, Animals in Company of a Man, has been reported in America (Jacobs, *English*, pp. 25–26, and Chase, *Jack*, No. 4).

But the main type number has been found in abundance, especially in northern Europe where most collecting and indexing have been done. Representative listings are these: Swedish 46, Danish 46, French 45, German 49, Flemish 48, Russian 11; one each from Scotland and England. Coffin lists 8 in *JAF*, beginning in the first volume of 1888. Irish *Types* has 86.

For North America Baughman lists U.S., Massachusetts, Connecticut, Virginia, North Carolina, Louisiana (Negro), Texas, Kentucky (Roberts, *South*, No. 1; M. Campbell, *Tales*, p. 226), Illinois (Lithuanian), Ohio, Michigan. I add *Old Greasybeard*, No. 2.

Remarks: Most versions of this tale found in Anglo-America seem to be retellings of the German popular version by the Grimm Brothers, "The Bremen Town Musicians." Although it has appeared in our school readers, most oral tellings have some variation.

113. Nip, Kink, and Curly

Types: 1525R, The Robber Brothers; 1653B, The Brothers in the Tree.

Type 1525, The Master Thief, has 22 forms, from A to R, all having some variation in the number of robbers, disguises, tricks, and the like. The total listings under the number (1525R) are these: Finnish-Swedish 2, Swedish 10, Norwegian 22, Serbocroatian 1, Greek 1. Since the second revision of *Types* (1961) was too late for the Irish *Types* indexers, they index the following only: 1525 (610), 1525D (5), and 1525E (7). Out of this vast number there could be a variant of my story, but I have not seen it in the Irish literature examined. No other items are listed by Thompson or Baughman for Ireland, England, or North America. None in Hansen for Spanish America. The only other texts that I know of are in Randolph, *Devil's Pretty Daughter*, pp. 190–191 (+1653B), and Roberts, *Old Greasybeard*, No. 39 (+853, 1525A, and 1653B).

Type 1653 has six forms, most dealing with the robbers under or in a tree. Under 1653B are selected listings: Lithuanian 60, Czech 16, Russian 11, German 7, Serbocroatian 10. None for Ireland, unless some are under 1653A (327 listed). None in Coffin, unless under 1653 (12). None by Thompson or Baughman for Ireland, England, or North America. I add Parsons, *Bahamas*, Nos. 46 and 47; Beckwith, *Jamaica*, No. 109; Carrière, *Missouri*, No. 68; Chase, *Grandfather*, No. 16; Randolph and Roberts as above. Hansen combines 1653 and 1653B. For the latter are 4 variants. Musick, *Green Hills*, No. 65 (Type 1653).

Remarks: When I first collected 1525R from Jim in 1952 or 1953, my quest for tales began to soar and sing. It then had only one other listing in folk literature—the 1928 revision of *Types* in "Types not Included," Finnish-Swedish 1. Dave, trying to recall his variant of it, seemed to get no further than a title. He thought it was called, "Will, Tom, and Jack." Other variants may have been lost—or still may be found. One wonders how these few reached Appalachia and the Ozarks from northern Europe.

114. Arshman and the Watch

1319A, The Watch Mistaken for the Devil's Eye (Tick). It is knocked to pieces.

These short numskull and merry anecdotes are found in the merry tale and jest collections of the fifteenth and sixteenth centuries. The English were telling them on the Welsh and Cornishmen, later on the Scottish, and finally on the Irish. In America they are on the Irish (Pat and Mike). They must have been brought here in the eighteenth century by the English, Scottish, and Scotch-Irish, and kept warm until the Irish began to arrive in large numbers in the middle of the nineteenth century. Some folklorists think that the Irish brought them, but surely they didn't bring a tide of numskull and stupid jokes told on themselves.

Under the number are these listings: Estonian 6, Rumanian 2, Flemish 4, Hungarian 6. The Irish *Types* lists 22. None for Scotland or England. Coffin lists 3 in *JAF*, beginning in 1899. For North America Baughman lists these states: Virginia (Negro), South (Negro) 2, Kentucky (Roberts, *South*), 2, Indiana, Michigan.

Remarks: This one and the next five or six were told in 1952 by Jim, who said that when he got started he liked to take his characters through several adventures—"never did like to tell one short joke." Compare this string with No. 150, "Seven Days' Journey."

115. Frog or Moose?

Type 1551, The Wager That Sheep are Hogs.

Under the number are listed a few studies and collections: English 1, Dutch 1, German 4, Italian 1, India 4, Franco-American (Carrière, *Tales*, 1), Spanish- and Portuguese-American 2; none for Scotland. The Irish *Types* lists 8. Baughman lists one for England, none for North America; none in *JAF* or in Hansen.

116. Frogs and the Rum

Type 1322A*, Grunting Pig. Numskull thinks that grunting pig is calling his name (closer than 1322, Foreign Language Thought to Be Insults).

Under the number is Hungarian 2. None for England or Scotland. Irish *Types* has 1 (under 1322). None in Baughman. Cf. Parsons, *Sea Islands*, No. 56, and Fauset, *Nova Scotia*, No. 72.

117. The Mon a-Coming

No type number applicable; hence no parallels.

118. Picking Mulberries

Type 1317*, The Dungbeetle Mistaken for a Bee.

No exact type or motif number for this one about the Irishman picking up "spradlin' bugs" and eating them with mulberries. I have collected a numskull joke nearer this type: Irishman is afraid of hornets; when a yellow-jacket whines around him, he mistakes it and says, "You can change your color but you can't change your voice." It is in Roberts, *South*, No. 45.

Under the type number are these: Finnish 2, Estonian 4, Swedish 9, Danish 10, India 2. None reported for Ireland, Scotland, England. Baughman lists one for Kentucky (Roberts, *South*, No. 44). It is not in *JAF* or Hansen.

119. I've Got the Job

No type number applicable; no parallels.

120. Arshman and the Kraut

No type number applicable; no parallels.

121. Arshmen and the Gold Mine

Type 1250, Bringing Water from the Well (Moon from River). Motif, J2133.5, Men hang down in a chain until top man spits on his hands.

It is pretty well known in tradition. Some lists under the number are these: Swedish 19, French 16, Dutch 5, German 25, Greek 3, India 3. English 4; none for Scotland. Irish *Types* 17. Coffin lists 8 in *JAF*, beginning in 1899; Hansen 2. Baughman lists 4 for England; for North America he lists: Canada, New York, New Jersey, Virginia (Negro), North Carolina, South, Florida (Negro), Ohio, Kentucky (Roberts, *South*, No. 41a, +1287), Indiana.

122. Arshmen Counting

Type 1287, Numskulls Unable to Count Their own Number. Motif J2031.1, numskulls count themselves by sticking their noses in the sand.

I have almost always heard this one immediately following the preceding one—most natural for the men coming out of the river to count up before they go on. Another case of combining tales. It is rather extensively reported in Europe, as follows: Finnish 23, Swedish 52, Flemish 8, German 6, India 13, French 19. None for Scotland; 3 for England. Irish *Types* lists 66. Coffin lists 5 from *JAF*, beginning in 1899. Baughman has 5 for England; for North America: South, North Carolina, Kentucky (Roberts, *South*, No. 41a +250 as above). None in Hansen.

123. Arshmen Squirrel Hunting

Type 1227, One Woman to Catch the Squirrel; Other to Get the Cooking Pot. Motif J2661.3, One woman (man) to catch squirrel, other to get the cooking pot.

Some of the lists are these: Finnish 75, Estonian 7, Swedish 20, Norwegian 3, Slovenian 3; none for England or Scotland. None in Irish *Types*; none in *JAF*. Baughman has none for England; for North America: Missouri 1, Kentucky 2 (Roberts, *South*, Nos. 40 and 56—combined with 1319* (terrapin taken to be cowdung), 1336, 1228, 1321D*, 1242, 1881, 1882, 1337, 1338, 1889). My No. 56 was published in *Mountain Life and Work*, 27 (Autumn, 1951):38–41, and in *Bought Dog*, No. 4.

124. Arshmen and the Red Pepper

Motif K1043, Dupe induced to eat sharp stinging fruit. It is close to 1339B, Fool is unacquainted with Bananas. Throws away fruit, finds the rest bitter; it is found in England, Canada, and the U.S. Under the motif number Baughman lists Kentucky (Roberts, *South*, No. 42).

125. Arshmen and the Gun

Type 1228, Shooting the Gun. Motif J2131.4.1. Since this type is concerned with looking down the gun barrel, the present jest does not fit it. Type 1228A, Fools Shoot from Wooden Gun, is closer.

Under the type number are a few lists: Finnish 22, Finnish-Swedish 1, Estonian 7, Livonian 1, German 1, Lithuanian 2, Hungarian 2, Russian 3, Greek 1. None for Scotland or England. Irish *Types* has 1. None in Baughman or in *JAF*. It is in Roberts, *South*, No. 56, as listed in No. 123 above, and in Fauset, *Nova Scotia*, No. 43.

126. Arshman Splitting Rails

No type applicable; no parallels available.

127. Arshman Never Tard Nor Hungry

Type 1561, The Lazy Boy Eats Breakfast, Dinner, and Supper One after the Other without working. Motif W111.2.6.

This not-so-dumb jest has a moderate distribution over Europe. Some lists under the number are these: Finnish 8, Estonian 9, Lithuanian 6, Swedish 5, Dutch 3, Flemish 3, Slovenian 5, Russian 12. Irish *Types* lists 40; none for Scotland, 1 for England. Coffin lists 1 from *JAF*, 48(1935): 177. Baughman lists 1 for England; for North America: Kentucky (M. Campbell, *Tales*, pp. 165–167), Indiana 3, Wisconsin. None in Hansen. Told by Dave in 1952.

128. I Up the Chimley

Stories of witchcraft, having so many variations, were not given type numbers, but the episodes of magic and of supernatural powers are abundantly covered in the *Motif-Index*. D55.2.2, Devil (Witch) makes self small; D1076, Magic headwear; D1531.8, witch flies with aid of word charm.

This last action motif is studied by Baughman. He lists Wales, Isle of Skye, Shropshire, Kent; New York, Maryland 2, Virginia (Negro) 2, North Carolina 2, Tennessee.

For related versions of this story, I have one in *South*, No. 35, where I list 4 for England and 5 for America. I now add *Béaloideas*, 2 (1930) :380;

3 (1931):246, and 3(1932):425–426 (notes give 2 other versions); MacManus, *Wonder*, No. 1; Whitney, *Maryland*, No. 2750. Told by Jim in 1952.

129. Bridling the Witch

Another witchcraft tale that stays rather stable as a story. The major motifs are these: G241.2.1, Witch transforms man into horse and rides him; G211.1, Witch in form of horse; G211.1.2, Witch as horse shod with horseshoes.

Under G241.2.1, Baughman lists 9 for England; for North America these: Ontario, Maine 4, Massachusetts, New York, Pennsylvania 1, Pennsylvania German 1, Maryland (German), Virginia, North Carolina 2, Tennessee, Illinois, Kentucky (Roberts, *South*, No. 37; here I list one each for Scotland and England and 3 for America). Told by Jim in 1952.

130. To the End of the World

Type 480, The Spinning-Women by the Spring.

This story was studied and lists given under No. 102 above. I can add for this subform the following: *Béaloideas*, 1 (1928): 349–356 (combined with 425A—see No. 109 above); 2 (1929–1930): 110–111, 223–224; 3 (1931): 272–273 (summary and notes, p. 275, give 4 other parallels); Seumas MacManus titles a collection *Well o' the World's End* which contains this form; Randolph, *Devil's Pretty Daughter*, pp. 198–200.

Remarks: In my notes to *South*, No. 13, Type 403 should read Type 480: Warren Roberts in his study found 403 to be rare in English (but not in Irish) tradition, and that stories like my Nos. 102 and 130 are English forms of 480. I correct this error in the notes to *Old Greasybeard*, No. 21; also No. 22 where this type is combined with 403A and 510A. Curiously enough, Type 480 is not listed in Hansen, but versions are entered under 403, A, B, *D, Type *778, and others to perhaps 20 or more. Told by Dave in 1952.

131. Cat and Rat

Type 2034, The Mouse Regains its Tail. Formula tales were classified by Archer Taylor in *JAF*, 46 (1933): 77–88. The type has 5 forms, according to characters and objects involved. Motif Z41.4.

Under the number are these lists: studies by Taylor, Wesselski, Newell (*JAF*, 18[1905]:34 n. 1); parallels in Grimm, Nos. 107–108; Berber 2, Coffin 2, African (2034C) 23. Irish *Types* lists 18. Thompson has none

for England or Scotland. I give Jacobs, *English*, No. 20 (heard in Australia), and No. 34 (from Halliwell, *Nursery Rhymes*, p. 154); Clouston,
Popular Tales, I, 289–313. For Scotland, J. F. Campbell, *West Highlands*,
No. 8; Jacobs, *Celtic*, No. 10 (combining Campbell's No. 8 with an Irish
text). Irish *Types* lists *Béaloideas* 1 (1928): 62, and 10 (1940): 299. I
can add these: *Béaloideas* 4 (1933): 201–203 (notes cite 6 other parallels); 5 (1935): 87–91. For England Baughman gives 1; for North
America: Massachusetts, New England 2, Texas.

Remarks: Students of the folktale have noted the scarcity of animal tales
in the American white population. With those listed above, with 5 (including cumulative) in *Old Greasybeard*, this one and Nos. 132, 138, and
139 below, and with 2 in Musick, *Green Hills*, we are gathering many
such tales still told in America. Told by Dave in 1952.

132. The Fox and the Cat

Type 20, Animals Eat Each Other Up.

Under the number are these references: Study by Krohn, Bär (Wolf)
und Fuchs (JSFO, VI, 81ff.); Finnish 48, Estonian 3, Norwegian 1;
Franco-American 1, West Indies (Negro) 1. Irish *Types* lists 14. None for
Scotland or England. Coffin lists 1 in *JAF*, 34(1921):68. None in Baughman or in Hansen.

Remarks: Only one or two reports of it in North America. It was printed
in *Mountain Life and Work*, 29 (Autumn 1953): 21–23, and reprinted
in Roberts, *Bought Dog*, No. 11. Told by Dave in 1952.

133. Tailipoe

Type 366, The Man from the Gallows.

Several forms have developed out of this story used in frightening children, this type found mostly among blacks, and No. 111 above ("Big
Toe") among whites (12 in my dissertation, listed in *South*, No. 12).

For this Negro form I can add: B. A. Botkin, *A Treasury of American
Folklore*, pp. 679–680 (from *JAF*, 47 (1934):341–343); J. C. Harris,
Uncle Remus Returns, pp. 52–78; Parsons, *Bahamas*, No. 95; Roberts,
Greasybeard, Nos. 4 and 5 ("Tailipoe"). Told by Dave in 1952.

134. Fat Man, Fat Man

Type 2028, The Fat Troll (Wolf) Who Was Cut Open.

Under the number are these: Danish 13, Icelandic 1, French 1, Russian
18. None for Scotland or England. Irish *Types* gives 1. Not in *JAF*. For

England Baughman has none; for North America: Virginia 1, Kentucky (Roberts, *South*, 2). Halpert, "Folktales in Children's Books," p. 68, discusses the above Virginia tale by Chase, *Grandfather*, No. 7. I add *Greasybeard*, No. 8 (notes cite its reprint in *Midwest Folklore*, 6 [Summer 1956]: 83–85). Told by Virgil Couch in 1952.

135. Chew Tobaccer, Spit, Spit, Spit

Type 73, Blinding the Guard.

This rather eroded formula or cante-fable tale does not have enough narrative to place it for sure; however, it is typical of material from African and Negro sources. Under the number are these listings: Spanish 2, Slovenian 1, India 1, Franco-American 2; Spanish-American—Hansen 7, West Indies (Negro) 3, American Indian: Thompson, *European*, II, 440–441; African 10. None in Irish *Types*; none for Scotland, England, or North America in Thompson or Baughman. I add Parsons, *Sea Islands*, No. 15 (note 4, p. 28, gives several references); Roberts, *Greasybeard*, No. 10 (notes summarize the above material and the diffusion of animal tales). Told by Virgil Couch in 1952.

136. Couch Family Riddles

In his monumental classification Archer Taylor handles only that body of riddles dealing with comparisons. Those telling a story, including "Neck riddles" (those in which the teller's life is at stake), he leaves for another study. A few of the Couches' riddles are printed as fillers in Roberts, *Bought Dog*.

a. Answer: Boar and dog in a cornfield. Parsons, *Sea Islands*, p. 152, Nos. 3 and 4; Fauset, *Nova Scotia*, p. 151, No. 45 (5 variants); *Bought Dog*, No. 8.

b. Answer: Gray squirrel. *Bought Dog*, No. 9.

c. Answer: He nursed the king's wife's breast through a gold ring in the garden. Neck Riddle. Parsons, *Sea Islands*, p. 168, No. 106; Fauset, *Nova Scotia*, p. 169, No. 141.

d. Answer: My. Beckwith, *Jamaica*, p. 205, No. 205 (note gives English variant); *Bought Dog*, No. 10.

e. Answer: Twelve pairs of boots; man named Each took a pair. *Béaloides*, 4 (1934):342 (11 pears); Parsons, *Sea Islands*, p. 169, No. 108; Beckwith, *Jamaica*, p. 207, No. 214 (note gives English and Scottish versions); Fauset, *Nova Scotia*, p. 148, No. 33 (2 variants); Whitney, *Maryland*, No. 2680.

f. Answer: Woman had to make a riddle to free her lover, so she took her little dog named Love, killed it, and put pieces around, one under her chair, one in her right hand, one in a tree. Neck riddle. Parsons, *Sea Islands*, p. 157, No. 37; Fauset, *Nova Scotia*, p. 242, No. 4 (3 variants).

g. Answer: A deer. *Bought Dog*, No. 11.

h. Answer: Spinning wheel. *Béaloideas*, 3 (1932):414, No. 10; 145, No. 29; *Bought Dog*, No. 12.

i. Answer: A blackberry. Taylor, Nos. 1384 to 1393; Fauset, *Nova Scotia*, p. 157, No. 78.

j. Answer: Groundhog. Taylor, No. 546; *Bought Dog*, No. 13.

k. Answer: Five male hogs soused into the water.

l. Answer: Man named Bone eat a bone up a tree; reckon he was free. Fauset, *Nova Scotia*, p. 143, No. 3 (3 variants). Neck Riddle.

m. Answer: Wasper. Taylor, No. 338; *Bought Dog*, No. 2.

n. Answer: Agg (egg). Taylor, No. 739; Parsons, *Sea Islands*, p. 165, No. 74; Beckwith, *Jamaica*, p. 211, No. 230; Fauset, *Nova Scotia*, p. 163, No. 107 (3 variants).

o. Answer: Well. Taylor, No. 1325; Parsons, *Sea Islands*, p. 156, No. 28; Beckwith, *Jamaica*, p. 212, No. 231; Fauset, *Nova Scotia*, p. 156, No. 74 (2 variants).

p. Answer: Negro on brown horse with black kittle on his head. Taylor, No. 64; Campbell, *West Highlands*, II, 409, No. 2; Fauset, *Nova Scotia*, p. 159, No. 82 (2 variants).

q. Answer: Old woman a-milkin'. Taylor, No. 977; Beckwith, *Jamaica*, p. 202, No. 181 (note gives 3 earlier versions).

r. Answer: Cow. Taylor, No. 1476; *Béaloideas*, 4 (1933): 144; Campbell, *West Highlands*, II, 412, No. 11; Parsons, *Sea Islands*, p. 154, No. 15; Fauset, *Nova Scotia*, p. 155, No. 58 (2 variants).

s. Answer: Watch. Taylor, No. 1310; Parsons, *Sea Islands*, p. 163, No. 63; Fauset, *Nova Scotia*, p. 158, No. 73; Whitney, *Maryland*, No. 2687; *Bought Dog*, No. 4.

t. Answer: Walnut. Taylor, No. 1275.

u. Answer: Shoes. Taylor, No. 453; *Béaloideas*, 4 (1933):145.

v. Answer: Agg in a duck's belly. Taylor, No. 170; Fauset, *Nova Scotia*, p. 162, No. 96 (2 variants).

w. Answer: Horseshoe nail. Taylor, No. 188; *Béaloideas*, 4 (1933): 144.

x. Answer: Cow bell. Taylor, No. 247.

y. Answer: Jonah in the whale. Biblical. Beckwith, *Jamaica*, p. 213, No.

239 (note cites Scottish version). The Jamaican riddle is exact, lacking one line, although Jim asserted that he made this one up.

z. Answer: Index finger as long as the middle one. Parsons, *Sea Islands*, p. 160, No. 48.

aa. Answer: A blind mule.

bb. Answer: Peanut (in the hull). Taylor, Nos. 1579 to 1581.

cc. Answer: Abel. Biblical.

dd. Answer: Cain and Abel. Biblical.

ee. Answer: He was a serpent. Biblical.

ff. Answer: Churn. Taylor, No. 1445; Parsons, *Sea Islands*, p. 157, No. 34.

gg. Answer: Chimley. Taylor, No. 1437; Parsons, *Sea Islands*, p. 165, No. 73.

hh. Answer: The king guessed four but they was just one. Neck Riddle.

ii. Answer: It'll sink four, too.

jj. Answer: Andrew (and drew). Conundrum. Parsons, *Sea Islands*, p. 172, No. 144; Beckwith, *Jamaica*, p. 206, No. 206 (3 variants; notes give 3 English versions); Fauset, *Nova Scotia*, p. 148, No. 30 (3 variants).

kk. Answer: None if it was cement. Puzzle.

ll. Answer: No smoke from an electric train. Puzzle.

mm. Answer: Sawbriar. Taylor, No. 1295; Parsons, *Sea Islands*, p. 165, No. 72; *Bought Dog*, No. 1.

nn. Answer: Railroad. Taylor, No. 43.

oo. Answer: Wagon. Taylor, No. 316; Parsons, *Sea Islands*, p. 164, No. 67.

pp. Answer: Cards you card wool with. Taylor, No. 20.

qq. Answer: Newspaper. Taylor, No. 1498; Parsons, *Sea Islands*, p. 174, No. 174; Fauset, *Nova Scotia*, p. 156, No. 64.

rr. Answer: Black hen went in a black stump come back out and left a agg. Taylor, No. 867.

ss. Answer: Honey bees. Taylor, Nos. 887–904; *Béaloideas*, 4(1933): 145, No. 27; Parsons, *Sea Islands*, p. 163, No. 62; Fauset, *Nova Scotia*, p. 155, No. 55; *Bought Dog*, No. 7.

137. The Magic Sausage Mill

Type 565, The Magic Mill.

Antti Aarne made a study of Types 563, 564, and 565 (JSFO, 27 [1911]: 1–96) but was unable to decide whether they had spread from India over Europe, or vice versa. They are scattered over northern Europe and have been carried to the New World. Some listings for 565 are these: Finnish 52, Danish 26, German 15, Slovenian 5, Franco-American 3, West Indies (Negro) 2. The Irish *Types* lists 89. None for Scotland or England. None in Baughman for England or North America. None in *JAF* or in Hansen. Some notes may be found with the following references: Bolte and Polivka in their study of Grimm No. 103; Dasent, *Norse*, pp. 8–13; *Béaloideas*, 3 (1931): 59 (English summary; note p. 63 cites another Irish text).

Remarks: The story has been aided on its journey to America by print since it was (I believe) in our readers. Dave the teller stated that he had heard it from his wife's grandfather around 1900. Since this grandfather could not read, we can see how a tale is taken into the oral idiom and psychology of the mountain people. It was printed in *Mountain Life and Work*, 30 (Spring, 1954): 12–15, and reprinted in Roberts, *Bought Dog*, No. 3.

138. The Three Piggies

Type 124, Blowing the House In. Motif K714.2, Victim tricked into entering box.

The story is rather thinly scattered over western Europe, the British Isles, and the New World. Some listings under the number are these: Danish 3, French 47, Spanish 3, German 8, Hungarian 3, Turkish 3, Franco-American 11, West Indies (Negro) 3. None for Scotland, 1 for England. Irish *Types* 19; Coffin lists 11 in *JAF* beginning in 1901; Hansen (Cuba) 3. Baughman for England 1; for North America: New Hampshire, New York 2, New Jersey (Negro) 2, North Carolina 3, South Carolina (Negro, 1, other 1), Missouri. Halpert, "Folktales in Children's Books," p. 68. I can add *Greasybeard*, No. 1 (full notes, pp. 176–177). Told by Dave in 1952.

139. The Tar Baby

Type 175, The Tarbaby and the Rabbit. Motifs: K741, Capture by tarbaby; K581.2, Briar-patch punishment for rabbit.

The story has been reported in western Europe, India, and Japan, but it is more evident in Africa and South America. Under the number are these selected lists: Latvian 2, French 2, Spanish 9, India 11, Hansen 29, West Indies (Negro) 35, African 35, Philippines 2. None for Scotland or England. None in Irish *Types*. None in Baughman for England or North

America, but Coffin lists 55 in *JAF*, beginning in 1890. We know it from Harris, *Uncle Remus*, pp. 7–11.

Risking some overlapping, I can add: Parsons, *Bahamas*, Nos. 10 (3 variants), 11, and 12 (footnotes cite many parallels); Parsons, *Sea Islands*, Nos. 6, 7, 13, 14 (3 variants), and 15; Beckwith, *Jamaica*, Nos. 21 (3 variants) and 59 (many others in notes, pp. 244–245); Fauset, *Nova Scotia*, Nos. 22 and 24 (2 variants); Carrière, *Missouri*, Nos. 6 and 7 (both introduced by Type 15, Theft of Butter).

Remarks: To my knowledge this is the first report of the tar baby in Appalachia, although many stories in my collection suggest a Southern influence. Blacks, both free and slave, have lived well up on the rivers of eastern Kentucky. Told by Dave in 1952.

140. Granddaddy Bluebeard

This kind of legend may not be derived from Type 955, The Robber Bridegroom, although the type is found in Appalachia. Instead, this one is based on some horrifying incidents on our many frontiers when men drove their stock to the lowland markets or rafted goods and logs down to the mills. After receiving large sums of money and after trading, they would set out on horseback or even afoot for home with the money in a secret belt. Legends grew up of robberies where they would be lured to spend the night. Not many of these have been reported by collectors. See my three in *South*, No. 104a, b, c.

Type 1115, Attempted Murder with Hatchet, may be closer, since it is in wide circulation, although about the stupid ogre. Some lists under the number: Finnish 195, Swedish 33, Danish 47, German 23, African 10, Hansen 1. Irish *Types* lists 108. Thompson has 4 for England, none for Scotland. None in *JAF*. Baughman also has 4 for England; for North America: Louisiana (Negro) 1, Arkansas 1 (with 1088). Told by Dave in 1952.

141. My Mommy Killed Me

Type 720, My Mother Killed Me; My Father Ate Me.

This is "The Juniper Tree," No. 47 in the complete Grimm collection, studied by Bolte and Polivka (I, 412). Other references under the number are these: Finnish 26, Estonian 53, Danish 23, Scottish 2, English 3, French 62, Dutch 17, German 45, Franco-American 8, Hansen 4. Irish *Types* lists 5. Coffin lists 11 in *JAF*, beginning in 1917. Baughman for Scotland lists 1, for England 4; for North America: Pennsylvania (from Georgia

Negro), South (Negro), North Carolina (Negro) 3, South Carolina (Negro 1, other 2), Georgia (Negro), Louisiana (Negro), Texas, Missouri, Arkansas, Kentucky (Roberts, *South*, No. 27 1; M. Campbell, *Tales*, pp. 212–216, 1), Michigan, California (from Arkansas). I can add *Greasybeard*, No. 27 (notes and summary, pp. 195–196).

Remarks: The story is not to the liking of Appalachian tellers, and yet they are willing to continue it in tradition. Just as Dave cut this one short, so did Mr. Allen in recording the *Greasybeard* version. Told by Dave in 1952.

142. Rat or Mouse?

This one belongs in Type 1365, The Obstinate Wife. Of the forms from A to K, Type 1365G*, Rats or Mink, is closest. The only reference is French Canadian. No other version discovered. Told by Dave in 1952.

143. Sambo and Golder

Cf. Type 169H*, The Man in the Wolves' Den with the wolves' cubs. Another man mounts guard before the den. He snatches the tail of the she-wolf. The man in the den wonders at the darkness around him. The only reference under the number is Latvian 2. Irish *Types* lists 26.

A related one is Type 1229, If the Wolf's Tail Breaks. Under the number are these: Wesselski, *Hodscha Nasreddin*, I, 216, No. 48; Swedish 4; West Indies (Negro), Flowers, 585. No other references or parallels discovered. Told by Dave in 1952.

144. Groundsow Huntin'

Cf. Type 1930, Schlaraffenland. (Land of Cokaygne.) Land in which impossible things happen: doves fleece a wolf, roast fowls fly, etc. Motif, X950. It is found over northern Europe, Africa, and Spanish America. Irish *Types* lists 71. Baughman lists 2 for England; for North America: Kentucky (Chase, *Grandfather*, 137–139), Nevada, California. No others discovered.

A closer number is Type 1935, Topsy-Turvy Land. Land where all is opposite from the usual. Under both numbers Thompson lists Grimm, Nos. 158, 159. And under this number Wienert, FFC, 56, 44ff.; Russian: Afanasiev (*1931C) 8. I add Roberts, *South*, No. 78; *Greasybeard*, Nos. 49 and 50 (under Type 1931).

Remarks: In my notes (*South*, p. 266) I quote an informant as saying that he learned the piece from a phonograph record, and Chase, who finds his embedded in an old mummers' play. I also list Jacobs, *More English*, No. 51; in his notes (p. 245) he says that this material goes back to mummers' plays and to stories in Grimm. I have 6 or 8 variants of this tale in my files, and, since they are a mixture of the language and not the impossible happenings of Type 1930, they are perhaps 1935. *Greasybeard*, No. 50, I believe is correctly indexed. Told by Dave in 1952.

145. The Colored Preacher

Cf. Type 1186, With his Whole Heart. The judge carried off. This is Chaucer's tale of the Friar, who is cursed with such sincerity that the devil carries him off. Another type in the section on jokes about the parson is closer: Type 1745*, Parson Sees the Devil. The parson denies the existence of the devil (vilifies him). The bear-showman lets the bear climb up the pulpit. The parson thinks the bear is the devil. Listed are Livonian 1, Russian 1. I have seen no other variants of this joke. Told by Dave in 1952.

146. Big Frait and Little Frait

Type 1676A, Big 'Fraid and Little 'Fraid. Motif K1682.1.

It is related to (perhaps derived from) Type 1791, The Sexton Carries the Parson (see next tale).

Under the number (1676A) are these lists: Canada, England, U.S., American Negro (Michigan); Dorson, *Negro Folktales*, No. 151. Cf. Spanish-American: Hansen (**367, Puerto Rico) 1. None for Scotland. Irish *Types* lists 52. Baughman has for England: Wales 1; for North America: New Jersey 2, Pennsylvania (Negro), Virginia (Negro), North Carolina, South Carolina, Florida (Negro), Louisiana (Negro), Missouri, Indiana (from Pennsylvania 1, other 1), Illinois, Kentucky (Roberts, *South*, p. 134—should read 136, No. 60a; in the notes, p. 257, I assign type and motif numbers, which now should be corrected as above to agree with revisions of *Types* and *Motif-Index*. I can add Addy, *Household Tales*, No. 4; Campbell, *West Highlands*, II, 398, No. 5. Told by Dave in 1952.

147. Counting the Nuts

Type 1791, The Sexton Carries the Parson. Motifs: X143.1, X424.

This, one of the most omnipresent anecdotes in Appalachia, has two slightly different plots. (1) Boys carry their crippled father to the cemetery to prove to him that they have seen or heard something. When the evidence is unmistakable the boys throw their father down and flee. When they get home, there sits the father already rested from his run. (2) Boys are in the cemetery or near it counting and dividing their bag of nuts, corn, potatoes, saying, "I'll take this one and you take that one . . ." They are overheard by passers-by, who think God and the Devil are dividing up the souls. They flee.

Under the number are these selected listings: Finnish 131, Swedish 48, Scottish 6, English 4, German 34, French 12. Irish *Types* lists 248. Coffin lists 12 and 3 related in *JAF*. Baughman lists for England 4; for North America: Canada 3, New York, New Jersey, Maryland, Virginia 2, North Carolina 8, South Carolina, South, Texas, Mississippi, Missouri 2, Indiana 5, Kentucky 6, Illinois 2, Michigan. I add *Greasybeard*, No. 42. Told by Dave in 1952.

148. The Arshmen and the Cushaw

A numskull story, this one is related to Type 1319, Pumpkin Sold as an Ass's Egg. With 13 forms of the type, a cushaw thought to be a rattlesnake is not among them. Under the number (1319) it is reported from England to India. Coffin lists 8 in *JAF*, beginning in 1899; Hansen lists 2. Baughman cites Clouston, *Noodles*, for lists in England, Algeria, and India; for North America he lists Ontario, New Jersey, Virginia, North Carolina, South, Mississippi, Texas, Arkansas, Kentucky (Roberts, *South*, No. 46), Ohio, Indiana, Idaho, California. Told by Bige Couch in 1952.

149. The Holy Ghost

Cf. Type 1718*, God Can't Take a Joke. Finnish 37.

The meaning is almost the same in the present text. No other references for England, Ireland, or Scotland. None in Baughman or Hansen. I add related ones: Parsons, *Sea Islands*, No. 46; Fauset, *Nova Scotia*, No. 141 (3 variants). Told by Alvis Couch in 1952.

150. Seven Days' Journey

a. No type close. A World War I veteran and wit, Mr. Jake Johnson of my community, used to tell many adventures of his hobo trips; these two items I can remember especially.

b. No type close, but it is a variant of No. 40 in Fauset, *Nova Scotia*, on Pat and Mike.

c. No type close. See variants in MacManus, *Donegal Fairy Stories*, No. 4 (supperless guests play several tricks on the host, only one common to these).

d. No types close.

e. No types close.

f. No types close.

g. Type 1688A*, Jealous suitors. Two suitors go courting the same girl; maim each other's horses. Lithuanian (*1693) 5. Cf. Irish *Types*, No. 1688, The Unlucky Courtship; 12 listed. One in Roberts, *South*, No. 55 (where I list Dasent, *Norse*, No. 6); Dorson, *Jonathan*, pp. 91–93, from *Spirit of the Times*, 16 (1847):38.

Remarks: Both Jim and Dave called the set of jests "The Eleven Days' Journey," but they could not think of the others at this late-night session. The swapping or passing around of turns in this chain of tales and others between Jim, Dave, and sometimes one of the sons is in the fine tradition of storytelling. During Dave's turn he named one of his nephews in the group as his companion on the courting trip, the one who lost his pants to the cow. A–D told by Jim, and E–G told by Dave in 1952.

151. Seven Dead Indians

Type 956B, The Clever Maiden Alone at Home Kills the Robbers.

Under the number are these selected listings: Lithuanian 65, German 36, Italian 21, Czech 39, Russian 12, Greek 10, Turkish 18, Franco-American 12, West Indies (Negro) 2; none for England, 1 for Scotland. The Irish *Types* lists 140. Baughman lists none for England; for North America: New York 1. Coffin lists one in *JAF*, 50(1937):32.

Remarks: Indian legends continue to be told in Appalachia. There are several in my files; see *South*, Nos. 82, 83 (Jenny Wiley), 84, and No. 152 in this collection. Told by Dave in 1954.

152. Old Indian Binge

No type or motif number applicable. I had recorded a variant of this real Indian legend in the same county of Harlan before Dave told this one in 1954.

153. We Killed a Bear

No type or motif number close. I have heard this as a retort, as when someone brags, "We got the job done." "Yeau," another retorts, "we killed a bear, but papa shot it." Told by Dave in 1954.

154. The Hairy Woman

This is the fourth variant of a curious primitive legend I have collected in eastern Kentucky. There is no type close. A motif from Type 301, I, is B635.1, The Bear's Son. Human son of woman who marries a bear acquires bear characteristics. This form is reported in Spain and in Spanish America. Only Type 301A has been so far recovered in Appalachia. It is not likely that "The Hairy Woman" and the type were ever together.

One variant of this legend appeared in *South*, No. 79; this one and another appeared in *Western Folklore*, 16(January, 1957): 48–51. Told by Joe Couch in 1954.

155. All at One Shot

Types: 1890D, The Man Shoots Ram-Rod Full of Ducks; 1895, Man Wading in the Water Catches Many Fish in His Boots.

These types are annotated under No. 107 above. I add Fauset, *Nova Scotia*, No. 95 (both types); Randolph, *We Always Lie*, pp. 120–121 (both types). Told by Joe Couch in 1954.

156. Leaping Painter

No type or motif number close. There are more frightening stories on the panther than on any other mountain wild game, including the bear. There were wild cougars in Appalachia until the twentieth century. See Connolly, *Discovering*, pp. 184–186. Told by Joe Couch in 1954.

157. The Magic White Deer

Types: 303, The Twins or Blood-Brothers; 401, The Princess Transformed into a Deer.

Again we have a combination of two famous old tales, both pretty well distributed over the world. Under Number 303 are these studies: Ranke, *Die Zwei Brüder* (FCC, 114, 770 versions used); Bolte and Polivka, I, 528 (Grimm, Nos. 60, 85). Selected lists include the following: Finnish 139, Estonian 21, Lithuanian 47, Swedish 28, Norwegian 38, Spanish 4, Danish 67, Scottish 4, French 68, Flemish 15, German 101, Hungarian 47, Russian 41, India 8, Franco-American 15, Spanish-American—Hansen 12, Rael (U.S.) 3, West Indies (Negro) 14; American Indian: Thompson, *European*, II, 323ff. Irish *Types* lists 327; Coffin lists 10 in *JAF*, beginning in 1901. Baughman lists 2 for Scotland, Borders 1 (from Chambers); for North America: Missouri, Kentucky (Roberts, *South* 2; M. Campbell, *Tales* 1). I add MacManus, *Corners*, No. 8; Beckwith, *Jamaica*, Nos. 83 and 104; Fauset, *Nova Scotia*, No. 8.

For Type 401 are these listings: Bolte and Polivka, II, 218, 330f. (Grimm, Nos. 93 and 137); Danish 21, Scottish 2, Flemish 5, German 4, Italian 10, Hungarian 40, Russian 14, Franco-American 4; Spanish-American: Hansen none, Rael 1. The Irish *Types* lists 3, and Coffin lists one in *JAF*, 38 (1925): 349. Baughman has none for England, and for North America he lists one for Virginia or North Carolina (Chase, *Jack*, pp. 127–135; it is combined with 400); Arkansas (Randolph, *Turtle*, pp. 130–133).

Remarks: This is a substantial combination of the two stories. It was not so well told by Joe Couch (in 1954), but I was surprised—and elated—that it was in the family repertory at all. Jim, who was with me at Appalachia, Virginia, recognized it when Joe got started, but I did not try to obtain Jim's telling of it. I have collected a few episodes of Type 303, but this is my first version of 401.

158. In the Cat Hide

Type 425A, The Monster (Animal) as Bridegroom. Motif H1923.2.0.1, Task: carrying water in sieve, sieve filled with moss.

Under the number Thompson lists 4 important studies of this ancient tale. A selected list of his parallels are these: Bolte and Polivka (Grimm, No. 127), Estonian 16, Lithuanian 15, Danish 87, English 4, Spanish 1, German 65, Rumanian 29, Greek 71, Turkish 46, India 7, Hansen 13. The Irish *Types* places all 275 parallels under 425. Coffin lists 18 in *JAF* for all forms. Baughman lists Ireland, Wales, Scotland, Derby, Lincoln 3, London; and for North America: New England, New York, North Carolina, Arkansas, Kentucky (M. Campbell, *Tales*, 2; Roberts, *South*, 2). I add Fauset, *Nova Scotia*, No. 18; Musick, *Green Hills*, No. 36; Roberts, *Greasybeard*, No. 20. See No. 109 above.

Remarks: The motif above and the butterfly guide or the pursuit of a ball are introductions to Types 313, 327, and 328 in some American versions. Other motifs of 313 in this story are the key and the secret room (not dead victims revealed but stacks and stacks of greenbacks!). Told by Joe Couch in 1954.

159. The Hainted House

See notes above of the longer version No. 103. Told by Joe Couch in 1954.

160. The Orphant Boys

Motif K2150, Innocent made to appear guilty.
No parallels discovered. Told by Joe Couch in 1954.

161. Johnny Sore-Nabel

See No. 107 above for notes to Type 1137, The Ogre Blinded. Here is another episode from the Third Voyage of Sindbad the Seaman, the Valley of the Serpents (VI, 22–34). In the Arabian version Sindbad escapes the one serpent by tying himself within a log crate too large for the serpent to swallow. The third episode of the present story follows rather closely the "Old Man of the Sea" adventure in the Sixth Voyage (VI, 58–68). The evidence is clear that at least the present story is derived from the Arabian Nights, not necessarily from the prolix edition of Sir Richard Burton's *The Book of the Thousand Nights and a Night*. When it entered English tradition is challenging enough for further study. Told by Joe Couch in 1954.

4. Type Numbers of the Folktales

The following type numbers are arranged numerically according to the Aarne-Thompson *The Types of the Folktale* (second revision). Story numbers follow the type descriptions.

5. Short Genealogy of the Couches

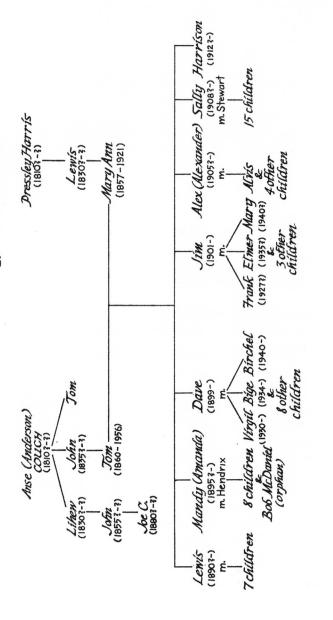

6. Bibliography

Aarne, Antti. "Die Zaubergaben," *JSFO*, 27(1911):1–96.

――――, and Stith Thompson. *The Types of the Folktale*. 2d rev. FFC, No. 184. Helsinki: Suomalainen Tiedeakatemia, Academia Scientiarum Fennica, 1961.

Adams, James T., comp. *Death in the Dark: A Collection of Factual Ballads of American Mining Disasters*. Big Laurel, Va.: Adams-Mullins Press, 1941.

Addy, Sidney Odall. *Household Tales with Other Traditional Remains Collected in the Counties of York, London, Derby, and Nottingham*. London: D. Nutt, 1895.

Allen, William F., et al. *Slave Songs of the United States*. New York, 1867.

Arnold, Byron. *Folksongs of Alabama*. University, Ala.: University of Alabama Press, 1950.

Baring-Gould, S. *A Book of Nursery Songs and Rhymes*. 2d ed. London: Methuen & Co., 1906.

Barry, Phillips, Fannie H. Eckstorm, and Mary W. Smyth. *British Ballads from Maine*. New Haven: Yale University Press, 1929.

――――. *Bulletin of the Folksong Society of the Northeast*. Cambridge, Mass.: The Powell Printing Co., 1930–1937; reprint edited by Samuel P. Bayard. BSS, vol. 11. Philadelphia: American Folklore Society, 1960.

Baughman, Ernest W. *Type and Motif-Index of the Folktales of England and North America*. Bloomington, Ind., and the Hague: Mouton, 1966.

Béaloideas. The Journal of the Folklore of Ireland Society. Dublin, 1928–.

Beckwith, Martha W. *Jamaica Anansi Stories.* MAFLS, vol. 17. New York: American Folklore Society, 1924.

Belden, H. M. *Ballads and Songs Collected by the Missouri Folklore Society.* Columbia: Mo.: University of Missouri, 1940, 1955.

Belden – Hudson – Schinhan. *See Frank C. Brown Collection.*

Bolte, Johannes, and George Polivka. *Anmerkungen zu den Kinder- und Hausmärchen der Brüder Grimm.* 5 vols. Leipzig, 1913–1932.

Botkin, Ben A. *American Play-Party Song.* Lincoln: University of Nebraska Press, 1937; Reprint ed., New York: Frederick Ungar, 1963.

———. *A Treasury of American Folklore.* New York: Crown Publishers, 1944.

Brewster, Paul G. *Ballads and Songs of Indiana.* Folklore Series, no. 1. Bloomington: Indiana University Press, 1940.

Bulletin of the Folksong Society of the North-east. Edited by Phillips Barry. Cambridge, Massachusetts: The Powell Publishing Co., 1930–1937; reprint edited by Samuel P. Bayard. BSS, vol. 11. Philadelphia: American Folklore Society, 1960.

Bulletin of the Tennessee Folklore Society. Murfeesboro, Tennessee, 1935–.

Burt, Olive Woolley. *American Murder Ballads.* London and New York: Oxford University Press, 1958; paper edition, New York: Citadel Press, 1964.

Burton, Sir Richard F. *The Book of the Thousand Nights and a Night.* 17 vols. London, 1885–1888. (Printed for the Burton Club for private subscribers only.)

Cambiaire, Celestin P. *East Tennessee and Western Virginia Mountain Ballads.* London: Mitre Press, 1934.

Campbell, J. F. *Popular Tales of the West Highlands.* New ed. 4 vols. Paisley and London: Alexander Gardner, 1890.

Campbell, Marie. *Tales from the Cloud Walking Country.* Bloomington: Indiana University Press, 1958.

Carrière, Joseph Médard. *Tales from the French Folklore of Missouri.* Evanston, Ill.: Northwestern University Press, 1937.

Chambers, Robert. *Popular Rhymes of Scotland.* New ed. London and Edinburgh: W. & R. Chambers, 1870.

Chappell, Lewis W. *Folk-Songs of Roanoke and the Albemarle.* Morgantown, W.Va: Ballad Press, 1939.

Chase, Richard. *Grandfather Tales.* Boston: Houghton Mifflin, 1948.

—————. *The Jack Tales.* With an appendix compiled by Herbert Halpert. Cambridge, Mass.: Houghton Mifflin, 1943.

Child, Francis James. *English and Scottish Popular Ballads.* Boston and New York: Houghton Mifflin, 1882–1898; reprint ed., New York: Dover, 1965.

Christiansen, R. Th. 'A Norwegian Fairytale in Ireland?" *Béaloideas,* 2 (1929):235–245.

Clemens, Samuel L. [Mark Twain]. *How to Tell a Story and Other Essays.* New York: Harper and Brothers, 1897.

Clouston, W. A. *The Book of Noodles.* London: A. C. Armstrong & Son, 1888.

—————. *Popular Tales and Fictions, Their Migrations and Transformations.* 2 vols. London: Scribner and Welford, 1887.

Coffin, Tristram P. *An Analytical Index to the Journal of American Folklore.* Philadelphia: American Folklore Society, 1958.

—————. *The British Traditional Ballad in North America.* Philadelphia: American Folklore Society, 1950; revised ed., 1963.

Colorado Folksong Bulletin. Boulder: University of Colorado, 1962–.

Combs, Josiah H. *Folk-Songs du Midi des Etats-Unis.* Paris: Les Presses Universitaires de France, 1925. Revised, translated, and enlarged edition by D. K. Wilgus. Austin, Texas: University of Texas Press, 1967.

—————. *Folk-Songs from the Kentucky Highlands.* New York: G. Schirmer, 1939.

Connolly, Tom. *Discovering the Appalachians.* Harrisburg, Pennsylvania: Stackpole, 1970.

Cox, John Harrington. *Folk-Songs of the South.* Cambridge: Harvard University Press, 1925; reprint ed., Detroit: Folklore Associates of Gale Research, 1963.

—————. *Traditional Ballads and Folksongs Mainly from West Virginia.* Edited by George Boswell. Philadelphia: American Folklore Society, 1964.

Creighton, Helen. *Songs and Ballads from Nova Scotia.* Toronto and Vancouver: J. M. Dent and Sons, 1932.

—————, and Doreen H. Senior. *Traditional Songs from Nova Scotia.* Toronto: Ryerson Press, 1950.

Curtin, Jeremiah. *Irish Folk-Tales Collected by Jeremiah Curtin.* Edited by Séamus Ó. Duilearga. Dublin and Cork, 1944.

Dasent, Sir George Webbe. *Popular Tales from the Norse.* New York: G. P. Putnam's Sons; Edinburgh: David Douglas, 1904.

Davis, Arthur Kyle. *Folk-Songs of Virginia. A Descriptive Index and a Classification.* Durham. N.C.: Duke University Press, 1949.

————. *More Traditional Ballads of Virginia.* Chapel Hill: University of North Carolina Press, 1960.

————. *Traditional Ballads of Virginia.* Cambridge: Harvard University Press, 1929; Reprint ed., Charlottesville: University of Virginia Press, 1970.

Delaney's Scotch Song Book. New York: William W. Delaney, 1910.

Dorson, Richard M. *Bloodstoppers and Bearwalkers. Folk Traditions of the Upper Peninsula.* Cambridge: Harvard University Press, 1952.

————. *Buying the Wind. Regional Folklore in the United States.* Chicago and London: University of Chicago Press, 1964.

————. *Jonathan Draws the Long Bow.* Cambridge: Harvard University Press, 1956.

————. *Negro Folktales in Michigan.* Cambridge: Harvard University Press, 1956.

Eddy, Mary O. *Ballads and Songs from Ohio.* New York: J. J. Augustin, 1939; Reprint ed., Detroit: Folklore Associates of Gale Research, 1964.

Ewen, David. *Great Men of American Popular Song.* Englewood Cliffs, N.J.: Prentice-Hall, 1970.

Fauset, Arthur Huff. *Folklore from Nova Scotia.* Philadelphia: American Folklore Society, 1931.

Flanders, Helen Hartness. *Ancient Ballads Traditionally Sung in New England.* Critical analyses by Tristram P. Coffin and music annotations by Bruno Nettl. 4 vols. Philadelphia: University of Pennsylvania Press, 1961–.

————, and George Brown. *Vermont Folk Songs and Ballads.* Brattleboro, Vt.: Stephen Daye Press, 1931.

Fowke, Edith Fulton. *Folk Songs of Canada.* Waterloo, Ontario: Waterloo Music Company, 1959.

Frank C. Brown Collection of North Carolina Folklore. Vols. 2 and 3 edited by Henry M. Belden and Arthur Palmer Hudson; vols. 4 and 5 edited by Jan P. Schinhan. Durham, N.C.: Duke University Press, 1952–1961.

Fuson, Henry Harvey. *Ballads of the Kentucky Highlands.* London: Mitre Press, 1931.

Gainer, Patrick W. et al., eds. *The West Virginia Centennial Book of One Hundred Songs: 1863–1963.* Morgantown and Charleston, W.Va.: Centennial Commission, 1963.

Gardner, Emelyn E., and Geraldine J. Chickering. *Ballads and Songs of Southern Michigan*. Ann Arbor: University of Michigan Press, 1939.

Greenleaf, Elizabeth B. *Ballads and Sea Songs of Newfoundland*. Cambridge: Harvard University Press, 1933.

Greig, Gavin. *Folk-Song of the Northeast*. Peterhead, Scotland: "Buchan Observer" Works, 1914.

Grimm, Jacob, and Wilhelm Grimm. *Grimm's Fairy Tales*. Translated by Margaret Hunt, revised by James Stern. New York: Pantheon Books, 1944.

Halliwell, James O. *The Nursery Rhymes of England*. London: T. Richards, 1842, 1886.

Halpert, Herbert. "Folktales and Legends from the New Jersey Pines." Ph.D. dissertation, Indiana University, 1947.

———. "Folktales in Children's Books: Some Notes and Reviews." *Midwest Folklore*, 2(1952):59–71.

Hansen, T. L. *The Types of the Folktale in Cuba, Puerto Rico, the Dominican Republic, and Spanish South America*. Berkeley and Los Angeles: University of California Press, 1957.

Harris, Joel Chandler. *Uncle Remus Returns*. Boston: Houghton Mifflin, 1918.

Hartland, Edwin Sidney. *English Fairy and Other Folktales*. London and New York: Walter Scott, 1890.

Haywood, Charles. *Bibliography of North American Folklore and Folk Song*. New York: Greenburg, 1951.

Henry, Mellinger E. *Folk-Songs from the Southern Highlands*. New York: J. J. Augustin, 1938.

———. *Songs Sung in the Southern Appalachians*. London: Mitre Press, 1933.

Hoosier Folklore Bulletin. Bloomington, Ind.: Hoosier Folklore Society, 1942–1946.

Hudson, Arthur Palmer. *Folksongs of Mississippi*. Chapel Hill: University of North Carolina Press, 1936.

Jackson, George Pullen. *Spiritual Folk-Songs of Early America*. New York: J. J. Augustin, 1937.

———. *White and Negro Spirituals*. New York: J. J. Augustin, 1944.

———. *White Spirituals in the Southern Uplands*. Chapel Hill: University of North Carolina Press, 1933.

Jacobs, Joseph. *Celtic Fairy Tales*. New York: David Nutt, 1892.

———. *English Fairy Tales*. New York: David Nutt, 1890.

————. *More English Fairy Tales*. New York: David Nutt, 1895.

Journal de la Société Finno-ougrienne. Helsingfors, 1886–.

Journal of American Folklore. Philadelphia and Austin, Texas: American Folklore Society, 1888–.

Journal of the Folk-Song Society. London: Folk-Song Society, 1899–1931.

Kentucky Folklore Record. Magazine of the Kentucky Folklore Society. Bowling Green, 1955–.

Kinlock, George Ritchie. *The Ballad Book*. London and Edinburgh, 1827.

Kittredge, George L. "Notes on 'The Frog's Courtship.' " *JAF*, 35(1922): 392–399.

Korson, George G. *Coal Dust on the Fiddle*. Philadelphia: University of Pennsylvania Press, 1943.

Laws, G. Malcolm, Jr. *American Balladry from British Broadsides*. BSS, vol. 8. Philadelphia: American Folklore Society, 1957.

————. *Native American Balladry. A Descriptive Study and A Bibliographical Syllabus*. BSS, vol. 1. Philadelphia: American Folklore Society, 1950; revised ed., 1964.

Lomax, Alan. *The Folk Songs of North America*. New York: Doubleday, 1960.

Lomax, John Avery, and Alan Lomax. *American Ballads and Folk Songs*. New York: Macmillan, 1934.

————. *Best Loved American Folk Songs*. New York: Macmillan, 1947.

————. *Cowboy Songs and Other Frontier Ballads*. New York: Sturgis and Walton Co., 1910; revised and enlarged ed., New York: Macmillan, 1938.

————. *Folk Song: U. S. A.* New York: Duell, Sloan and Pearce, 1947.

McGill, Josephine. *Folk Songs of the Kentucky Mountains*. New York: Boosey and Co., 1917.

MacInnes, D. *Folk and Hero Tales. Waifs and Strays of Celtic Tradition*. Argyllshire Series, no. 11. London: Macmillan, 1890.

MacKay, John G. *More West Highland Tales*. Vol. 2. London: Oliver and Boyd, 1960.

MacKay, Percy. *Tall Tales of the Kentucky Mountains*. New York: Macmillan, 1924, 1926.

MacKenzie, W. Roy. *Ballads and Sea-Songs from Nova Scotia*. Cambridge: Harvard University Press, 1928.

MacManus, Seamus. *In Chimney Corners: Merry Tales of Irish Folklore*. Garden City, N.Y.: Doubleday, Page & Co., 1912.

————. *Donegal Fairy Stories*. Eau Claire, Wisc.: E. M. Hale & Co., 1900.

―――. *Donegal Wonder Book.* Eau Claire, Wisc.: E. M. Hale & Co., 1926.

―――. *The Well o' the World's End.* New York: Macmillan, 1939.

Midwest Folklore. Bloomington: Indiana University Press, 1951–1962.

Moore, Ethel, and Chauncey O. Moore. *Ballads and Folksongs of the Southwest.* Norman: University of Oklahoma Press, 1964.

Morris, Alton C. *Folksongs of Florida.* Gainesville: University of Florida Press, 1950.

Mountain Life and Work. Publication of the Council of the Southern Mountains. Berea, Kentucky, 1924–.

Musick, Ruth Ann. *Green Hills of Magic: West Virginia Folktales from Europe.* Lexington: University Press of Kentucky, 1970.

Newell, W. W. *Games and Songs of American Children.* New York and London: Harper and Brothers, 1883, 1903; reprint ed., New York: Dover, 1963.

Niles, John Jacob. *The Ballad Book of John Jacob Niles.* Boston: Houghton Mifflin, 1960, 1961.

Odum, Howard W., and Guy B. Johnson. *The Negro and His Songs.* Chapel Hill: University of North Carolina Press, 1925.

―――. *Negro Workaday Songs.* Chapel Hill: University of North Carolina Press, 1926.

Opie, Peter, and Iona Opie. *The Oxford Book of Nursery Rhymes.* Oxford: Oxford University Press, 1951.

Ó Súilleabháin, Séan. *Handbook of Irish Folklore.* Dublin: Folklore of Ireland Society, 1942; reprint ed., Detroit: Folklore Associates of Gale Research, 1963.

Ó Súilleabháin, Séan, and R. Th. Christiansen. *The Types of the Irish Folktale.* FFC, no. 188. Helsinki: Suomalainen Tiedeakatemia, Academia Scientiarum Fennica, 1963.

Parsons, Elsie Clews. *Folk-Lore of the Sea Islands, South Carolina.* MAFLS, vol. 16. New York: American Folklore Society, 1918.

―――. *The Folk-Tales of Andros Islands, Bahamas.* MAFLS, vol. 13. New York: American Folklore Society, 1918.

Pound, Louise. *American Ballads and Songs.* New York: Charles Scribner's and Sons, 1922.

Ralston, W. R. S. *Russian Folk-Tales.* London: Smith, Elder & Co., 1873.

Randolph, Vance. *The Devil's Pretty Daughter and Other Ozark Folk Tales.* With notes by Herbert Halpert. New York: Columbia University Press, 1955.

————. *Ozark Folksongs*. 4 vols. Columbia, Mo.: State Historical Society of Missouri, 1946–1950.

————. *Sticks in the Knapsack and Other Ozark Folk Tales*. With notes by Ernest Baughman. New York: Columbia University Press, 1958.

————. *The Talking Turtle and Other Ozark Folk Tales*. With notes by Herbert Halpert. New York: Columbia University Press, 1957.

————. *We Always Lie to Strangers: Tall Tales from the Ozarks*. New York: Columbia University Press, 1951.

————. *Who Blowed Up the Church House? and Other Ozark Folktales*. With notes by Herbert Halpert. New York: Columbia University Press, 1952.

Ranke, Kurt. *Die Zwei Brüder: Eine Studie zur vergleiechenden Märchenforschung*. FFC, no. 114, Helsinki, 1934.

Richardson, Ethel Parks. *American Mountain Songs*. New York: Greensburg, 1927; reprint, 1955.

Ritchie, Jean. *Folk Songs of the Southern Appalachians*. New York: Oak Publications, 1965.

————. *A Garland of Mountain Songs from the Ritchie Family of Viper, Kentucky*. New York: Broadcast Music, Inc., 1953.

————. *The Singing Family of the Cumberlands*. New York: Oxford University Press, 1955; reprint ed., New York: Oak Publications, 1964.

Roberts, Leonard W. "Eastern Kentucky Folk-Tales: A Collection and A Study." Ph.D. dissertation, University of Kentucky, 1954.

————. *I Bought Me A Dog: Eleven Authentic Folktales from the Southern Mountains*. Berea, Ky.: Council of the Southern Mountains, 1954; reprint, Pikeville, Ky.: Appalachian Studies Center, 1972.

————. *Old Greasybeard: Tales from the Cumberland Gap*. Detroit: Folklore Associates of Gale Research, 1969.

————. *Nippy and the Yankee Doodle: Folk Tales of the Southern Mountains*. Berea, Ky.: Council of the Southern Mountains, 1958.

————. *South from Hell-fer-Sartin: Kentucky Mountain Folktales*. Lexington: University Press of Kentucky, 1955; reprint ed., Berea, Ky.: Council of the Southern Mountains, 1964, and Pikeville, Ky.: Appalachian Studies Center, 1972.

————. *Tales and Songs of the Couch Family*. Microcard ed., Series A., No. 30, UK 59–18. Lexington: University Press of Kentucky, 1958; reprint ed., West Salem, Wisc.: Microfilms, Inc., 1969.

————. *Up Cutshin and Down Greasy: Folkways of a Kentucky Mountain Family*. Lexington: University Press of Kentucky, 1959.

Roberts, Warren E. *The Tale of the Kind and the Unkind Girls: AA–Th 480 and Related Tales.* Supplement Series of *Fabula: Zeitschrift für Erzählforschung* (Reihe B: Untersuchungen, Heft I, Berlin, 1958).

Sacred Jewels. Edited by R. E. Winsett. Dayton, Tenn., 1939.

Sandburg, Carl. *The American Songbag.* New York: Harcourt, Brace, & World, 1927; reprint, 1955.

Scarborough, Dorothy. *On the Trail of Negro Folk-Songs.* Cambridge: Harvard University Press, 1925.

———. *A Song Catcher in Southern Mountains.* New York: Columbia University Press, 1937.

Sharp, Cecil, and Maud Karpeles. *English Folk Songs from the Southern Appalachians.* 2 vols. London: Oxford University Press, 1932; reprint, 1952, 1960.

Shearin, Hubert C., and Josiah Combs. *A Syllabus of Kentucky Folk-Songs.* Transylvania Studies in English, 2. Lexington, Ky.: Transylvania Printing Co., 1911.

Smith, Reed. *South Carolina Ballads.* Cambridge: Harvard University Press, 1928.

Southern Folklore Quarterly. Gainesville: University of Florida, for the Southeastern Folklore Society, 1937–.

Spaeth, Sigmund. *Read 'Em and Weep: The Songs You Forgot to Remember.* New York: Arco Publishing Co., 1959.

Spirit of the Times. Edited by William T. Porter. New York, 1831–1861.

Still, James. *River of Earth.* New York: Viking Press, 1940.

Stout, Earl J. *Folklore from Iowa.* MAFLS, vol. 29. New York: American Folklore Society, 1936.

Taylor, Archer. *English Riddles from Oral Tradition.* Los Angeles and Berkeley: University of California Press, 1951.

Thomas, Jean. *Ballad Makin' in the Mountains of Kentucky.* New York: Henry Holt and Co., 1939; reprint ed., New York: Oak Publications, 1964.

———. *Devil's Ditties: Being Stories of the Kentucky Mountain People and the Songs They Sing.* Chicago: W. Wilbur Hatfield, 1931.

———, and Joseph A. Leeder. *The Singin' Gatherin'.* New York: Silver Burdett Co., 1939.

Thompson, Stith. *European Tales Among the North American Indians.* Colorado College Publications, no. 2. Colorado Springs: Colorado College Press, 1919.

———. *The Folktale.* New York: Dryden Press, 1946.

————. *Motif-Index of Folk-Literature.* 6 vols. Bloomington: Indiana University Press, 1932–1936; revised ed., 1955–1958.

Wesselski, Albert. *Der Hodscha Nasreddin.* 2 vols. Weimar, 1911.

Western Folklore. Berkeley and Los Angeles: University of California Press, 1942–.

White, Newman I. *American Negro Folk-Songs.* Cambridge: Harvard University Press, 1928.

Whitney, Annie, and Caroline C. Bullock. *Folk-Lore from Maryland.* MAFLS, vol. 17. New York: American Folklore Society, 1925.

Wienert, W. *Die Typen der griechisch-römischen Fabel.* FFC, no. 56. Helsinki, 1925.

Williams, Alfred. *Folk-Songs of the Upper Thames.* London: London Mercury, 1923.

Williams, Cratis D. *Ballads and Songs.* Microcard ed., Series A, No. 15. Lexington: University Press of Kentucky, 1937; reprint ed., West Salem, Wisc.: Microfilms, Inc., 1969.

Wyman, Loraine, and Howard Brockway. *Lonesome Tunes: Folk Songs from the Kentucky Mountains.* New York: Boosey & Co., 1916.

————. *Twenty Kentucky Mountain Songs.* Boston: Oliver Ditson Co., 1920.

7. Index of Titles and First Lines of Folksongs and Riddles

Riddle, song, and tale titles are in italics.